T0181983

Communications
in Computer and Information Science   2101

Rationale

The CCIS series is devoted to the publication of proceedings of computer science conferences. Its aim is to efficiently disseminate original research results in informatics in printed and electronic form. While the focus is on publication of peer-reviewed full papers presenting mature work, inclusion of reviewed short papers reporting on work in progress is welcome, too. Besides globally relevant meetings with internationally representative program committees guaranteeing a strict peer-reviewing and paper selection process, conferences run by societies or of high regional or national relevance are also considered for publication.

Topics

The topical scope of CCIS spans the entire spectrum of informatics ranging from foundational topics in the theory of computing to information and communications science and technology and a broad variety of interdisciplinary application fields.

Information for Volume Editors and Authors

Publication in CCIS is free of charge. No royalties are paid, however, we offer registered conference participants temporary free access to the online version of the conference proceedings on SpringerLink (http://link.springer.com) by means of an http referrer from the conference website and/or a number of complimentary printed copies, as specified in the official acceptance email of the event.

CCIS proceedings can be published in time for distribution at conferences or as post-proceedings, and delivered in the form of printed books and/or electronically as USBs and/or e-content licenses for accessing proceedings at SpringerLink. Furthermore, CCIS proceedings are included in the CCIS electronic book series hosted in the SpringerLink digital library at http://link.springer.com/bookseries/7899. Conferences publishing in CCIS are allowed to use Online Conference Service (OCS) for managing the whole proceedings lifecycle (from submission and reviewing to preparing for publication) free of charge.

Publication process

The language of publication is exclusively English. Authors publishing in CCIS have to sign the Springer CCIS copyright transfer form, however, they are free to use their material published in CCIS for substantially changed, more elaborate subsequent publications elsewhere. For the preparation of the camera-ready papers/files, authors have to strictly adhere to the Springer CCIS Authors' Instructions and are strongly encouraged to use the CCIS LaTeX style files or templates.

Abstracting/Indexing

CCIS is abstracted/indexed in DBLP, Google Scholar, EI-Compendex, Mathematical Reviews, SCImago, Scopus. CCIS volumes are also submitted for the inclusion in ISI Proceedings.

How to start

To start the evaluation of your proposal for inclusion in the CCIS series, please send an e-mail to ccis@springer.com.

Khalid S. Soliman

Editor

Artificial intelligence and Machine Learning

41st IBIMA International Conference, IBIMA-AI 2023
Granada, Spain, June 26–27, 2023
Revised Selected Papers

 Springer

Editor
Khalid S. Soliman
International Business Information Management
Association
Norristown, PA, USA

ISSN 1865-0929   ISSN 1865-0937 (electronic)
Communications in Computer and Information Science
ISBN 978-3-031-62842-9   ISBN 978-3-031-62843-6 (eBook)
https://doi.org/10.1007/978-3-031-62843-6

This Springer imprint is published by the registered company Springer Nature Switzerland AG
The registered company address is: Gewerbestrasse 11, 6330 Cham, Switzerland

If disposing of this product, please recycle the paper.

Preface

This volume of CCIS contains the revised papers (post-proceedings) of IBIMA-AI 2023, the 41st IBIMA International Conference on Artificial Intelligence and Computer Science, 26–27 June 2023, Granada, Spain. It showcases a diverse array of research papers spanning various disciplines within the realm of Artificial Intelligence, Machine Learning, Information Systems, Communications Technologies, Software Engineering, and Security and Privacy. This collection comprises 30 full and 8 short papers out of 58 papers in total submitted to the conference, where each paper was sent to 3 reviewers in a triple-blind review process and was revised according to review comments. This collection serves as a testament to the relentless pursuit of knowledge and innovation in our ever-evolving technological landscape.

In the section on Artificial Intelligence and Machine Learning, papers cover a wide range of applications, from sustainable spatial development and speech denoising to reinforcement learning in algorithmic trading and the integration of Internet of Things (IoTs) with Wireless Sensor Networks (WSNs). The exploration of AI and geodata for local community sensitization, neural network compression, and the enhancement of voice user interfaces underscores the significance of AI and ML in addressing real-world challenges and improving user experiences.

In the section on Information Systems and Communications Technologies, researchers delve into topics such as security management for Vehicular Ad Hoc Networks (VANETs), exploration of recommendation systems techniques in finance, and implementation of common-use electric equipment in railway environments. These endeavors aim to enhance the efficiency, reliability, and security of communication networks and technological infrastructures.

Meanwhile, in the section on Software Engineering, scholars explore methodologies, architectures, and tools aimed at improving the quality, performance, and maintainability of software systems. From the architecture of mobile applications to the use of random methods in test case generation, researchers strive to streamline development processes and deliver robust software solutions.

Finally, Security and Privacy concerns have become paramount in an era characterized by omnipresent connectivity and digitalization. The papers included in this section address diverse and current security threats and privacy challenges, ranging from ransomware attacks and watermarking schemes to differential privacy models and crowd dynamics modeling.

The research presented in this proceedings book attests to the vitality of the academic community and its unwavering dedication to advancing knowledge and driving technological progress. We extend our sincere appreciation to all authors for their invaluable contributions, as well as to the reviewers whose diligence and expertise ensured the quality and rigor of the submissions.

We hope that this collection will inspire further research, collaboration, and innovation in the fields of Artificial Intelligence, Machine Learning, Information Systems, Communications Technologies, Software Engineering, Security, and Privacy. May the insights gathered from these papers pave the way for future advances and findings, ultimately enriching our collective understanding and shaping a brighter, more technologically empowered future.

April 2024   Khalid S. Soliman

Organization

General Chair of the Conference

Khalid S. Soliman   International Business Information Management
Association, USA

Program Committee

Khalid S. Soliman	International Business Information Management Association, USA
Marta Biegańska	Poznań University of Economics and Business, Poland
Houssemeddine Derbel	University of Nevada, USA
Grażyna Kowalewska	Uniwersytet Warmińsko-Mazurski w Olsztynie, Poland
Monika Hadaś-Dyduch	University of Economics in Katowice, Poland
Piotr Michał Borkowski	University of Szczecin, Poland
Tadeusz A. Grzeszczyk	Warsaw University of Technology, Poland
Agnieszka Piasecka-Robak	University of Lower Silesia, Poland
Jarosław Pawłowski	Nicolaus Copernicus University in Toruń, Poland
Cristian Bucur	Petroleum-Gas University of Ploieşti, Romania
Imad Saleh	University of Paris 8, France
Błażej Nowak	Poznan University of Technology, Poland
Paweł Kaczmarek	Military University of Technology, Poland
Tarik Beldjilali	Moncton University, Canada
Zijjiang Yang	York University, Canada
Daniel Tomiuk	University of Québec in Montréal, Canada
Teuku Aulia Geumpana	University of Newcastle, Australia
Gabriel Jekateryńczuk	Military University of Technology, Poland
Josef Dvořák	University of West Bohemia, Czechia
Piotr Kosiuczenko	Military University of Technology, Poland
Alena Buchalcevova	Prague University of Economics and Business, Czech Republic
Meseret Yihun Amare	University of Pardubice, Czech Republic
Artur Arciuch	Military University of Technology, Poland
Grzegorz Dydkowski	University of Economics in Katowice, Poland
Michał Glet	Military University of Technology, Poland

Octavian Dospinescu	Alexandru Ioan Cuza University, Romania
Grzegorz Popek	Wroclaw University of Science and Technology, Poland
Petr Doucek	Prague University of Economics and Business, Czech Republic
Agnieszka Stanimir	Wroclaw University of Economics and Business, Poland
Josef Botlík	Silesian University in Opava, Czechia
Livia Sangeorzan	Transilvania University of Brașov, Romania
Bartłomiej Terebiński	War Studies University, Poland

Contents

Artificial Intelligence and Machine Learning

Integration of Internet of Things (IoTs) with Wireless Sensor Networks
(WSNs) for a Transformative Secure Community Mindset Applied Deep
Learning Models and Natural Language Processing Techniques 3
    Pascal Muam Mah, Iwona Skalna, Tomasz Pełech-Pilichowski,
    Gilly Njoh Amuzang, Micheal Blake Somaah Itoe, and Ning Frida Tah

Semi-automated Classification of Non-functional Arabic User
Requirements Using NLP Tools 20
    Eman Awad, Nabil Arman, and Faisal Khamayseh

K-Nearest Neighbor in Assessing Trends of Cameroonians Most Attractive
Communal and Cultural Diversity Cities in Poland Based on Natural
Language Processing and Artificial Intelligence 30
    Pascal Muam Mah, Gilly Njoh Amuzang, Micheal Blake Somaah Itoe,
    and Ning Frida Tah

Artificial Intelligence and Geodata for Local Community Sensibilization
to Sustainable Spatial Development 43
    Jozef Hernik, Hans Joachim Linke, Karol Krol, Tomasz Salata,
    Anita Kukulska-Koziel, and Katarzyna Cegielska

Wave-U-Net Speech Denoising 52
    Tomasz Walczyna and Zbigniew Piotrowski

Neural Network Compression 58
    Marta Bistroń and Zbigniew Piotrowski

Expanding the Capabilities of Voice User Interface for Math Formula
Editor Through Interactive Commands 62
    Agnieszka Bier and Zdzislaw Sroczynski

Reinforcement Learning in Algorithmic Trading: An Overview 71
    Przemysław Czuba

Proposal of a System for Prototyping and Validation of Drug Efficacy
and Safety Evaluation Methods 78
    Dawid Bugajewski

Leading Trends in AI: A Literature Review 86
    Zbigniew Piotrowski, Karolina Blaszczuk, and Emilia Gabrielczyk

Improvement of the Objects Sorting Process Using Machine Learning
on the Example of a Created Prototype 93
    Kamil Węgrzyn

Information Systems and Communications Technologies

Security Management for Vehicular Ad Hoc Networks by Software
Defined Network Paradigm 107
    Lamaa Sellami, Rejab Hajlaoui, Bechir Alaya, and Sami Mahfoudhi

Implementation of Common-Use Electric Equipment in the Railway
Environment with Respect to Electromagnetic Compatibility 119
    Leszek Kachel, Artur Dłużniewski, and Łukasz John

Exploring the Potential of OLSR Steganography for Confidential
Communication 131
    Gabriel Jekateryńczuk and Zbigniew Piotrowski

Recommendation Systems Techniques in Finance's Perspective:
A Conceptual Research 135
    Manal Alghieth

PC-Based Electronic Testbed for Comprehensive Security Evaluation
of IoT Devices 143
    Marek Michalski

Analysis of Time Reaction During Different Approaches to Command
Handling in NetFPGA Hardware 151
    Marek Michalski

The Adoption of Spatial Information Technology in Precision Agriculture 159
    Paolo Fetahu and Mukesh Srivastava

Identifying Critical Success Factors (CSF) for Cyber Supply Chain Risk
Management (CSCRM): A Qualitative Study Using Agency Theory 173
    Ryan Firth and Mukesh Srivastava

VLSM Techniques for Optimizing Real IPv4 Networks 187
    Marek Michalski

Review and Criteria for Selecting Open-Source Tools for Managing
Wireless Local Networks 195
Piotr Augustyniak, Jakub Skóra, and Piotr Zwierzykowski

Laboratory Studies of Infrared Radiation Transmission of Camouflage Net
Materials Used on the Battlefield 210
Krzysztof Szajewski, Paweł Kalinowski, Anna Szajewska,
and Paweł Szczepaniak

Theoretical and Practical Aspects of the Evil Twin Attack. The Attacker's
Perspective and Defense Methodology 224
Piotr Augustyniak, Olgierd Rogowicz, and Piotr Zwierzykowski

UAVs Communication Redundancy Checking Graph Algorithm 237
Stanisław Skrzypecki

Computer-Aided Design of Electric Drives with FEA Software 250
Michał Manka, Grzegorz Karpiel, and Daniel Prusak

Software Engineering

ABAP Unit Testing Performance and Quality Analysis in SAP HANA 267
Marek Gałązka and Jerzy Szymański

The Use of Random Methods in the Process of Generating a Set of Test
Cases 280
Kazimierz Worwa

The Architecture of the Mobile Application for Android with the Use
of the MVVM Pattern and the HILT, Livedata, Room, Retrofit and Kotlin
Coroutines Libraries 296
Paweł Kaczmarek and Zbigniew Piotrowski

Common Problems in Application Development 308
Filip Majerik and Monika Borkovcova

System for Preparing and Executing Math Exams Online – A Case Study 318
Dawid Bugajewski and Monika Bugajewska

Security and Privacy

Watermarking Scheme for Physical Documents 333
Michał Glet, Kamil Kaczyński, and Paweł Zielski

Extended Differential Privacy Model: Additional Performance
and Security Considerations 338
    Olga Dziegielewska and Boleslaw Szafranski

Hiding Data in Printed Documents 349
    Michał Glet, Kamil Kaczyński, and Paweł Zielski

Computer Modeling of Evacuation Patterns Comparison and Crowd
Dynamics: A Use of NetLogo 356
    Livia D. Iancu, Paul A. Dragoi, and Camelia Delcea

Concurrent Programs, Finalizers and Cleaners in Java - Security Problems 368
    Jerzy Krawiec, Piotr Gorny, and Maciej Kiedrowicz

Examining Telework Adoption Through Cybersecurity and Industry 5.0 379
    Arturo Bedon, Francisco A. Pujol, and Tamai Ramirez

Damages Caused by Ransomware and Selected Preventive
Countermeasures 389
    Lukas Vaclavik

Ransomware Attack on the QNAP Device: A Case Study 402
    Jakub Bajera and Michał Glet

Author Index 407

Artificial Intelligence and Machine Learning

Integration of Internet of Things (IoTs) with Wireless Sensor Networks (WSNs) for a Transformative Secure Community Mindset Applied Deep Learning Models and Natural Language Processing Techniques

Pascal Muam Mah[1]([✉]), Iwona Skalna[1], Tomasz Pełech-Pilichowski[1],
Gilly Njoh Amuzang[2], Micheal Blake Somaah Itoe[2], and Ning Frida Tah[2]

[1] AGH University of Science and Technology, Krakow, Poland
{mah,skalna,tomek}@agh.edu.pl
[2] Silesian University of Technology, Gliwice, Poland

Abstract. The amalgamation bond between human-to-machine communications (H2M) with the Internet of Things (IoTs) technology has played a major role in easing the burden on conventional living methods in most developed communities. Wireless sensor networks (WSNs) integrated with the Internet of Things (IoTs) are paving the way to society 5.0 of a shared community sphere with the people, environment and economic growth. The study propose a neural language processing-deep learning model (scoring model) for data security and information encoding as part of the fight to ensure security for communications and data sharing. Recently, machine-machine (M2M) has dominated human-machine (H2M) coexistence. The global economy has survived and flourished in Industry 4.0 without compromising on our community standards, environment, and economic growth. The little share approach in Industry 4.0 is now manifesting in global climate change impacts. The study uses a community mindset transformation appraisal (CMTA) concept and applied deep learning knowledge and natural language processing data. Wireless sensor networks (WSNs) nodes are used as edges of redistributed data and sensor nodes. A formulated data flow is applied to deep learning model summation of data flow (DLMSDF) concept. Formulated data is applied to the input, hidden layers, and output layers to demonstrate a possible method to monitor data flow. Based on information on deep learning models summation of data flow (DLMSDF), a grade of 30 bits were recorded as input data equal to output and a score of 4.58 and 4.0909 for Class B and Class A respectively. This is as per the behavioral influence of the Internet of things and wireless sensor networks on data security for community mindset. We concluded that the Integration of IoTs with WSNs can secure a perfect transformative community mindset free of security threats, corruption, racism, poverty, dominant attitudes, and lack of information.

Keywords: wireless sensor networks · internet of things · deep learning · natural language processing · transformative secure community mindset

K. S. Soliman (Ed.): IBIMA-AI 2023, CCIS 2101, pp. 3–19, 2024.
https://doi.org/10.1007/978-3-031-62843-6_1

1   Introduction

Wireless sensor networks have achieved a considerable boost in community development due to their flexibility in solving problems in different domains [3–5]. Reliable data collection techniques, whose aim is to ensure that sensed data are received successfully by a sink [1]]. Wireless sensor networks have the potential to change our lives in many different ways. In recent years WSNs have been successfully applied in various application domains which uphold transformative community mindset awareness to most things we do unknowingly that affect and retard growth. WSNs are network systems developed for sensing and monitoring vital signs of the environment and area by using distributed and connected sensor nodes [2]. The changes within communities require a boost in the network of devices that can gather information and then communicate it through any wireless systems to the community leaders. Wireless sensor networks have surveillance and Monitoring capacity to secure and detect threats in areas like environmental temperature, humidity, air pressure, and noise level of the surrounding. In modern communities, typical wireless sensor network technologies are network protocols, network topology control, data fusion, data management, QoS assurance, time synchronization, and location information.

2   Literature Review

Thanks to the Internet of Things (IoTs) that improve time-to-school via an e-learning platform, time-to-market via e-shopping, time-to-hospitals via e-healthcare services, and many others. The Internet of Things allows connectivity with everything desirable for human consumption giving sensors small gateways the ability to dynamically and remotely change run-time behavior without codes [6–8]. The tremendous change in technology has engaged in a wide variety of ways in transforming mindsets for better communication within communities. The integration of the Internet of Things with wireless sensor networks can enhance a cyber security-free community [9–11]. The security landscape continues to evolve which increases cyber security challenges. The Internet of Things security is the technology segment that focuses on safeguarding connected devices and networks. When integrated with wireless sensor networks, it will securely capture information and send it to central administration for proper attention. Deep learning is a branch of artificial intelligence that contains input layers, hidden layers, and output that is trained using machine learning algorithms to understand humans and function like the human brain in the form of neurons. Deep learning has many models of supervised, unsupervised, and reinforcement learning that allows human-related data acquisition for decision-making [12, 13].

Wireless Sensor Networks (WSNs) have a wide range of applications and scenarios in computer vision that range from simple detection to robotic visualization [14, 15]. Open-source training platforms like Pytorch, SpaCy, Tensor Flow, Bert, Python, Jupyter Notebooks, anaconda, and Numpy train deep learning models to build models faster, validate, and accurately. Deep learning models are trained using machine learning algorithms helps to increase security in wireless networks, and reduce congestion problems.

3 Wireless Sensor Networks can be Classified into

- Static and Mobile WSN.
- Deterministic and Nondeterministic WSN.
- Single Base Station and Multi Base Station WSN.
- Static Base Station and Mobile Base Station WSN

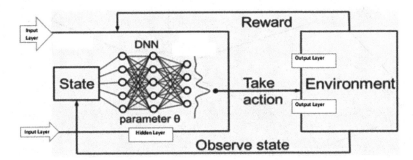

Fig. 1. External input to the internal output

Figure 1 represents data circulation within system software for the internet of things and wireless sensor networks. From input to the state of standards of an application or community standards to deep neural networks into a pre-examination of observed state. Action can be taken to limit or expand the network within system administrators before sending to the external environment or community.

The hidden layers that self-multiply or allocated to data during training is a set of roles provided to secure information. The same manner in providing a set of rules to govern data for miners is possible to set the same roles to monitor this data from being stolen. The only challenge with machine learning is that training a system to handle data for the sake of preparation or analysis is time-consuming, costly, and difficult. Figure 1 is an example of how to predetermine the inflow of data or network and how to manage it till final users and keep track of it.

4 Wireless Sensor Networks and the Internet of Things with Radio Frequency Identifiers

To achieve a higher level of security, the study proposes an integrated system that allows the Internet of Things to monitor and secure weak nodes of wireless sensor networks. RFID can help to detect location by collecting information from the GPS. RFID can work with just short distance signals but can effectively share concise and precise information on time and cheaply. Wireless sensor networks and the Internet of Things can communicate faster with RFID and build stronger nodes for wireless sensor networks.

Figure 2 briefly explains the flow of data between wireless sensor networks and the Internet of Things. There is an energy supply unit that receives energy from a generator.

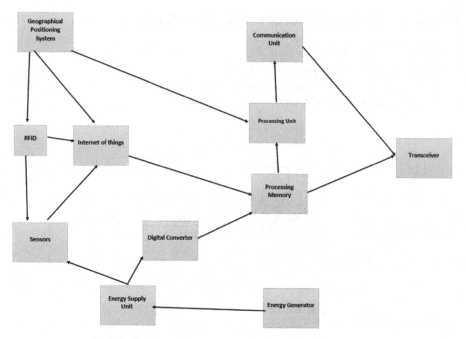

Fig. 2. Internal lower input to internal higher input.

Sensors receive power from the energy supply unit and send it to the system servers to power connectivity with objects and devices (Internet of Things). The processing memory sends the data from the system to the processing unit and then to the communication unit. The final destination is the transceiver which distributes to community users with a keen attention and desire to enhance security of users through devices-objects connectivity with the help of Internet of Things. Sensors are network systems that are controlled by servers and other devices to achieve a desirable outcome. If integrated with the Internet of Things which can connect with almost everything, it is possibly easier to identify security breaches based on location tracking and device uses. Deep learning can work in a very smart system to document the number of output layers or data receivers or community users of the internet. Once the output number or users changes, there is an indication of the data breach if the changes are not equivalent to same responses from the input. GPS is a satellite signal that helps navigate and can perfectly work well with a 5G network to provide more access to our daily connectivity's with either items or related user's objects and also provide more capacity for the Internet of Things to connect with other devices. NB: The bases of this approach lays with faster connectivity as it concerns humans whom are very difficult to manage. When there is fast internet there is fast connectivity over short and long distances. As it stand at the moment only satellite internet (5G) can provide this fast internet connectivity. The approach assume that internet of things is just a technology that enable connectivity with devices and object with the use of internet. When involved with 5G network, the level of connectivity improves.

For instance, communication amongst students in a student community are frequently based on academic disciplines. It is easier to identified non-academic communication using visual audio and text automated systems. There are systems such as ChatGPT that can detect and segment information. With the artificial intelligence systems like ChatGPT, it is possible to track down intruders in any community especial in student zone who are not students or academicians based on their communication content.

5 Deep Learning Innovative Expectations on Community Security

The role of digital technologies has been as a main solution to carter and manage the challenges that come with an economic and community shift to cloud systems. Deep learning is an added option and powerful adoption [16]. Data security is the heart of human dignity and a priority for business growth [17]. Machine learning has addressed a lot of issues beginning with data classification, prediction, forecasting, decision-making, and the fight against climate change. Presently, security is one of the major concerns for the business world, administrators, and even computer wizards. The following steps are set by this study as forceps areas needed for machine learning. The study called this area of concern as the objective of effectively managing the challenges the world faces with security issues.

The First Objective is the Need for a Blended Behavioral Mindset Change Toward Technological Innovation. The management and collection of valuable physiological needs and data is a great way to change our thinking, feeling, and respect for each other privacy. This has to start with new laws governing the usage and sharing of data. The new shift in digitalization is like a surprise to the world and new education is needed to enable us to understand and monitor our surroundings with iMotions. There is a need for a holistic technology that cohabitates with humans and the existing digital space. Machine learning is one of the technologies that have this approach to cohabitating digital space but little training has been provided to the general public. Even with open access, remote areas still fall below requirement due to a lack of internet access to benefit from open libraries like Jupiter, anaconda, tensor flow, and many others. The World-leading behavioral analysis software for human behavior research should emphasize the need for all to know, have access and talk with a specialist.

The Second Object is the Need for Modernized Socio-technical Drivers that Will Accelerate a Balance Transition. One of the effective ways to mitigate the impact of data and Security breaches is to enable a far-reaching transformation of electricity, internet, open access, and limited privatization of network systems and autonomous systems. The amalgamation towards a sustainable system that is fully free or with fewer bridges is that which people don't go underground to have access to their needs. A sustainable socio-technological mindset is possible to achieve by focusing efforts to change our attitude towards security issues by examining the reactions of the past. The government should be fully engaged in the fight against security and community mindset. Security issues should not be limited by industrial policies, cultural norms, and political motivations.

The Last Objective is the Need for Digital Technologies that Provide Access to Information, Challenges, and Impact on the Globe. The world needs to respond better and faster to divided systems, data scarcity, and breaches to achieve global health, and market-free systems with intelligent automation. Optimizing relationship management with intelligent servers, services, systems, and applications is what the world needs to timely respond to the growing security shift. Digital factory solutions should engage together with consultancy and local users. The reason is that digital solutions and community consultancy are both ICT tools that are collaborating to better share human needs and their impact on humans. Access to information and communication technology differ considerably across the globe with heavy impact. Many efforts made to close this digital divide and if successful, a better harmonize approach to fight security breaches can be achieve.

6 Results

In this section, we provide details on how text or speech content can be classified into different parts of the speech based on data obtained via NLP means that help in decision-making. Data clustering here helps health practitioners to make proper decisions. This section represents the stages of documenting the inflow of data and outflow to determine if there is a breach or not. This section provides brief statistics that can be the program to allow algorithms to perfectly monitor network flow and strange communication.

7 Solution on Language Structure

7.1 Determination of Behavior Oriented Drive and Influential Function Of IoTs-WSNs on content Extraction

Figure 3 as per (Figs. 7 and 8), provide data classified into different groups Class A and Class B. The group mark with red are made up of metric range substitute and metrics range for a single individual called Class B and that with green is called Class A which constitute of metrics range substitute and metrics range. To obtain influence rate, metric range substitute is divided by sum of metric range then multiple by behavior score. *Class A MR = 11 and MR^S=9 while Class B:::)) MR = 12 and MR^S=11.*

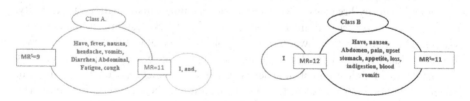

Fig. 3. Metrics range substitute and metrics range

SOLUTION CLASS A

BIF=Behavior oriented drive and influential function of internet of thoughts on *content extraction*

Class A MR =11 and MR^S=9

F=push factors of

D=Dependent parameters

MR=Metrics Range

MR^S= *Metrics Range Substitute*

BS=Behavior Score (Also human five sense organs)

KBS=key benefits score

$$Eq = \int(D) \, \frac{MR^S}{\Sigma MR} \times BS$$

====)))) $\int(D) = \frac{9}{11} \times 5$
====))) $\underline{\int(D) = 4.0909}$

SOLUTION CLASS B

BIF=Behavior oriented drive and influential function of internet of thoughts on *content extraction*

Class B MR =12 and MR^S=11

F=push factors of

D=Dependent parameters

MR=Metrics Range

MR^S= *Metrics Range Substitute*

BS=Behavior Score (Also human five sense organs)

KBS=key benefits score

$$Eq = \int(D) \, \frac{MR^S}{\Sigma MR} \times BS$$

====)))) $\int(D) =$
$\frac{11}{12} \times 5$

====))) $\underline{\int(D) = 4.58}$

The statistics above detailed how the level of situation for both class of data. The class with higher amount require attention than class with lower score value. From the statistics we can say that the influence score is grade "Very Good" as per classification is achieve by both class but Class B is better than Class A with behavior score of 4.58 and 4.0909 respectively.

Solution on Deep learning distribution of data

HLP=Hidden layer pattern Value

HL=Hidden Layers

IL^S= *Input Layers*

OL=Output Layer

$$Eq = \int(OL) \, \frac{IL^S}{HL} \times HLPV$$

====)))) $\int(OL) = \frac{30}{6} \times 5$
====))) $\underline{\int(OL) = 30}$

From the solution, we can see that input equal to output. With the above system, it is possible to achieve a stable data flow with the integration of the internet of things and wireless sensor networks.

NB: To calculate hidden layer pattern value, you must know the required output determine to supply. Once you know the exact output required to supply a given data set, you calculate the hidden layer pattern value by dividing the total number of an input layer by the total output. This is to allow the possibility to monitor data usage amongst users in a community.

8 Applied Method

This section represents a step taken to explain the approach author used to develop the study. The following are subtitles: community transformative secure mindset, deep learning neural network for transformative community secure mindset, internet of things and wireless sensor networks integration architecture, stages to secure transformative community mindset communications using deep learning and natural language processing, and Communication secure transformative community with deep learning and natural language processing.

9 Community Setup and Deep Learning Layers

The way system administrations are being arranged in the physical environment is similar to system software setups. All algorithms are built to manage data generated by humans and the same way we produce this data is the same way computer administrators use to build and develop programs to manage the data.

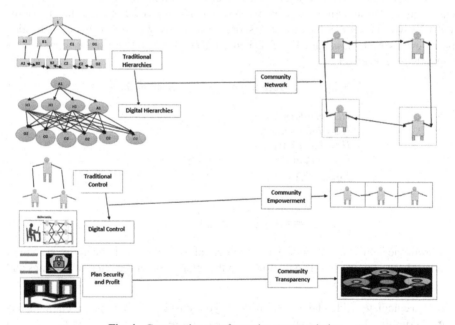

Fig. 4. Community transformative secure mindset

Figure 4 represents the community's transformative secure mindset. Figure 4 represents three (3) stages which are traditional hierarchies to digital hierarchies, traditional control to digital control, and plan security and profit. These three (3) stages represent a move from a difficult system to a liberal system where there are networks of people, systems, information, transparency, freedom, and community empowerment.

How a community system administration is built determines the pattern of relationship between community dwellers. Security challenges in every community start with system management. A good community is built on a network system that allows and cohabitates togetherness, sharing, care for oneness, and collaboration. A community free from political divides, cultural divides, religious divides, marketing divides, and other social divides is a community free from a security breach. Figure 4 represents a system network that will build a community mindset free from security breaches. From system setup with similar deep learning algorithms to collaborative networking, and community empowerment to community transparency full of business opportunities.

10   Network Security Distribution and Deep Learning Standards

In a secure community, network distribution can take a similar format that will hinder hackers from taking advantage, These deep learning approach is an example of a standard distribution of network that will allow easy access to monitor unauthorized users. The system allows the software to document the amount of input and output.

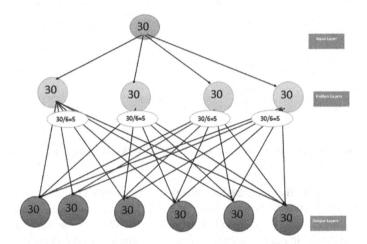

Fig. 5. Deep learning neural network for transformative community secure mindset.

Figure 5 represents a deep neural network that can be integrated to achieve a community transformative secure mindset. In the deep learning self-explain Fig. 5, a single input with standard value is distributed amongst hidden layers. The aim is to achieve a fixed input and output and a possible faster approach to detect a break in the flow of data. In Fig. 5, one (1) input distribute data to four (4) hidden layer and this data end up in six (6) output layers.

Figure 5 explains a system where output is predetermined by understanding the number of expected users. This allows the deep learning algorithm to monitor the flow of data effectively and securely. With a single input and a known output center, it is possible to monitor breaches as the hidden layers enable the system administrator to monitor shortage and excess direction.

11 Integration Architecture Internet of Things and Wireless Sensor Networks

This section shows how the Internet of things can be distributed alongside wireless sensor networks to monitor and identify devices, systems, areas, and locations where security challenges are predominant or occur and how often. It is possible to build a device with the modern application and install it with all devices to track down hackers, or simply install an optimizer of the internet of Things to identify and track down people who exceed community norms.

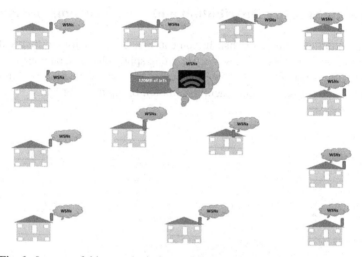

Fig. 6. Internet of things and wireless sensor networks integration architecture

Figure 6 represents the integrated architecture of the Internet of Things and wireless sensor networks. Figure 6 shows a community of 13 houses with a well-developed sensor of the Internet of Things installed on each home. This Internet of Things sensor help identified the quality and quantity of the network and supply data to wireless sensor networks. Internet of Things overseas if the level of internet supply from the main control unit is stable or stolen or broken or not. The 13 homes in this imaginable community are registered in the main supplier center. Any additional user is identified by the Internet of Things and information is sent to the control unit for follow-up or tracking down.

Figure 6 represents a community with an Internet of thing software server that automatically switches off the Internet and sends signals to a wireless sensor network about a system breach. This is a system that can work for a community with similar laws, and respect for each other, has a community networking system, community empowerment system, and community transparency desire mindset.

For instance, communication amongst students in a student community are frequently based on academic discipline. It is easier to identified non-academic communication using visual audio and text automated systems. There are systems such as ChatGPT that can detect and segment information. With the artificial intelligence systems like

ChatGPT, it is possible to track down intruders in any community especial in student zone who are not students or academicians based on their communication content.

Internet of things technology can be used to automatically switch off internet connection once a non-academic text or audio content is detected in each community especially in a purely academic setting. Since internet of things connect with devices and objects. The sensors network system will be able to act in similar way like alert systems that sends signal to the internet of things technology to respond with an adequate action. Some countries already uses systems of this nature especial at airports to detect fetching text or facial view of suspected persons.

12 Natural Language Processing and Deep Learning for a Community Security Mindset

The language of a people is an ideal identity that cannot be cheated or easily broken without being fully integrated into it. One of the ways to track outsiders is a constant request for digital translation. The following paragraphs explain how natural language can be determined using a parts of speech to extract content.

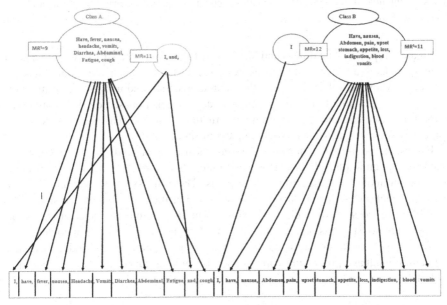

Fig. 7. Stages to secure transformative community mindset communications using deep learning and natural language processing

Figure 7 represents the stages required to secure transformative community mindset communications using deep learning and natural language processing. In a community with every device and user identified, it is possible to track unidentified habitats. The study uses parts of speech as what identifies a community and certain culture to suggest a deep learning model that follows standard parts of speech.

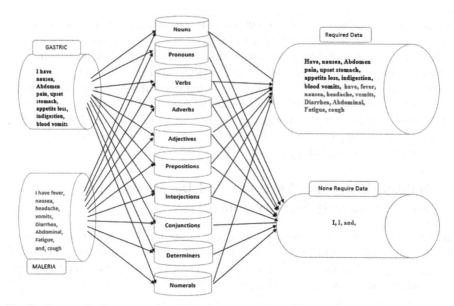

Fig. 8. Communication secure transformative community with deep learning and natural language processing

Figure 8 represents laydowns and how parts of speech can be structured into a deep learning model to achieve content awareness. This system can help community leaders track down known dwellers based on their communication and uses of the community language. It is possible to identify unknown native speakers based on their communication tone, ascends, and proper grammar structure of words. This study uses this to suggest a deep learning system based on parts of speech.

For instance, communication amongst students in a student community are frequently based on academic discipline. It is easier to identified non-academic communication using visual audio and text automated systems. There are systems such as ChatGPT that can detect and segment information. With the artificial intelligence systems like ChatGPT, it is possible to track down intruders in any community especial in student zone who are not students or academicians based on their communication content.

To achieve a communication-secure transformative community with deep learning and natural language processing parts of speech can be grouped into two levels as per Table 1.

Table 1. Metrics range and metrics range substitute

Metrics Range	Nouns	Adjectives	Adverbs	Verbs	Prepositions	Pronouns	Conjunctions	Interjections	Determiners	Numerals
Metrics Range Substitute	Nouns	Adjectives	Adverbs	Verbs	Prepositions	Interjections	Numerals			

Table 1 above represents elements of the part of speech that the study uses to evaluate the influence of technology application with a deep learning model using natural language processing that can help a secure community. The classification is following the English language standard.

13 Discussion of Application of Community Secure Mindset

This section discussed possible areas of securing information, method, and how business enterprises use the internet of Things, wireless sensor networks, RFID, deep learning, and natural language processing to manage and circulate goods and services.

14 Community Secure Mindset for Logistic Services

A community secure mindset is a system that allows working together, empowering for global success and advancing maximum transparency. This system of community mindset can also be achieved within a logistics enterprise. Logistics inventory tracking systems are one of the most important information distribution between suppliers and customers. In recent years, Confidence was built and trust was restored between customers and suppliers when timeliness existed within short notice. With the coming of modern technology, confidence has shifted from Just being timely updates but transparency throughout the supply chain. With the Inventory tracking systems, logistics managers have been seriously assisted throughout delivery services with the help of RFID, wireless sensor networks, and the Internet of Things. The Internet of Things connects customers' devices, and home and wireless sensor network nodes with RFID to maintain maximum security. Logistics managers nowadays use the Internet of Things, RFID, and wireless sensor networks to plan for the following.

- Stock distribution
- Re-stocking of warehouse
- Predictive analytics systems.
- Location management tools.
- Drone-based delivery.
- Automated vehicles.

Figure 9 represents some of the aspects of logistic systems and services manage properly and secured using wireless sensor networks, the Internet of Things, RFID, deep learning, and the Internet of Things. The following paragraphs provide details on the services.

Stock Distribution. Thanks to the advancement in technology that distribution can take place at any time be it manpower-wise or autonomous systems. Wireless sensor networks have been able to navigate through communities, capture locations and share with system administrators. Knowing the area before embarking on delivery has been one of the most important aspects of wireless sensor networks for logistics managers. The Internet of Things has tremendously boosted security within logistics services. The Internet of Things is capable of identifying security threats and pretexting wireless network nodes [18]. The RFID helps navigate throughout the process by locating and directing the movement of the distribution from supplies to consumers.

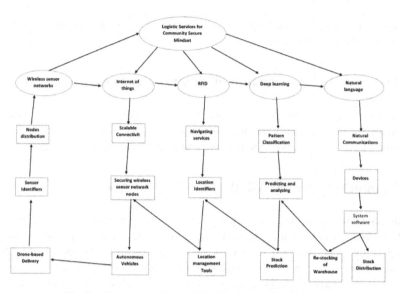

Fig. 9. Community Secure Mindset for Logistic Services

Re-stocking. RFID is several logistics devices that help register stocks in advanced systems incorporated with the Internet of Things to track the warehouse and the shop supply chain. The wireless sensor networks collect information from warehouses and send them to management units.

Predictive analytics systems. The level of predetermining of future sales, security threats, and increased supplies has relatively improved in the few past years. Thanks to the tracking systems. RFID, wireless sensor networks, and the Internet of Things are radicalizing the supply chain with advanced methods of monitoring and evaluation systems [19]. This has made it quite easier to track and predict outcomes in a very simple way.

Location management tools. Thanks to modern technology. Nowadays, RFID systems help navigate through the warehouse, sea, communities, and globally. Suppliers take it very easy to identify customers' locations.

Drone-based Delivery. Most logistics managers use drones to monitor the warehouse and production systems. The challenges of underemployment and the need for hiring an expert to run some underground monitoring are over. Risky monitoring and distribution services are handled by drones.

Automated Vehicles. Logistics services are handled by mostly automated vehicles, trains, and plains nowadays. With the emergence of self-driverless cars, it is possible to remotely access and deliver goods to customers [20]. Drones are already running most of these services.

15 Communication Security with Digitalized Method (Scoring Model)

This a neural language processing system of securing communication and information using a deep learning model approach. This is a systematic approach developed by the study to secure communication between the author and the intended receiver. This model can secure communication in several ways using code. With the proposed method as a model, a piece of information can be coded in two-layer method, three-layer method and many more base on communication between the producers and users.

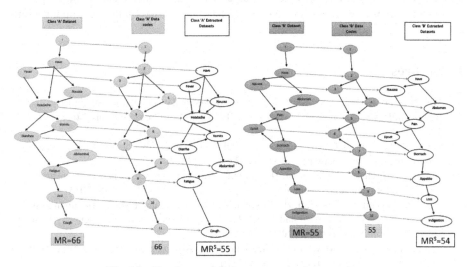

Fig. 10. (Scoring model) for communication security.

Figure 10 represents a piece of data coded with the reference total of each stage. Any modification difference from that of intended producers will not be accepted by the end users. This model of information securing can code a language or communication and share only codes. Once the intended receiver has the software, he or she can interpret the data and even if the data is breached or modified, it cannot be interpreted because the real data remain between the producers and intended receiver and can be modified with prior notice between the two parties.

16 Conclusion

This study is concerned with the application of wireless sensor networks (WSNs) technology with the Internet of Things (IoTs) to large-scale environmental monitoring communicative transformation to shape people's minds on their wrongs through monitoring systems. Based on formulated information for deep learning models summation of data flow (DLMSDF), a grade of 30 bits was recorded as input data equal to output. We concluded that the Integration of IoTs with WSNs can secure a perfect transformative community mindset free of security threats, corruption, racism, poverty, dominant attitudes, and lack of information. We designed an integrated framework that takes into consideration both the operational, and application-specific needs of a well-defined community. We explain WSNs and IoTs using deep learning to secure communication, run language checks for non-nature speakers, and present a deep learning model approach to secure stable WSNs using IoTs for community use.

For instance, communication amongst students in a student community are frequently based on academic discipline. It is easier to identified non-academic communication using visual audio and text automated systems. There are AI systems such as ChatGPT that can detect and segment information based on content. With the artificial intelligence systems like ChatGPT, it is possible to track down intruders in any community especial in student zone whom are not students or academicians based on their communication content.

References

1. Wei, X., Guo, H., Wang, X., Wang, X., Qiu, M.: Reliable data collection techniques in underwater wireless sensor networks: a survey. IEEE Commun. Surv. Tutorials **24**(1), 404–431 (2021)
2. Khalaf, O.I., Romero, C.A.T., Hassan, S., Iqbal, M.T.: Mitigating hotspot issues in heterogeneous wireless sensor networks. J. Sens. **2022**, 1–14 (2022)
3. Rawat, P., Singh, K.D., Chaouchi, H., Bonnin, J.M.: Wireless sensor networks: a survey on recent developments and potential synergies. J. Supercomput. **68**(1), 1–48 (2014)
4. Raza, M., Aslam, N., Le-Minh, H., Hussain, S., Cao, Y., Khan, N.M.: A critical analysis of research potential, challenges, and future directives in industrial wireless sensor networks. IEEE Commun. Surv. Tutorials **20**(1), 39–95 (2017)
5. Islam, M.M., Hassan, M.M., Lee, G.W., Huh, E.N.: A survey on virtualization of wireless sensor networks. Sensors **12**(2), 2175–2207 (2012)
6. Albreem, M.A., Sheikh, A.M., Alsharif, M.H., Jusoh, M., Yasin, M.N.M.: Green Internet of Things (GIoT): applications, practices, awareness, and challenges. IEEE Access **9**, 38833–38858 (2021)
7. Sadeeq, M.A., Zeebaree, S.: Energy management for internet of things via distributed systems. J. Appl. Sci. Technol. Trends **2**(02), 59–71 (2021)
8. Vermesan, O. (ed.).: Next Generation Internet of Things–Distributed Intelligence at the Edge and Human-Machine Interactions. CRC Press (2022)
9. Gardašević, G., Katzis, K., Bajić, D., Berbakov, L.: Emerging wireless sensor networks and Internet of Things technologies—Foundations of smart healthcare. Sensors **20**(13), 3619 (2020)
10. Farash, M.S., Turkanović, M., Kumari, S., Hölbl, M.: An efficient user authentication and key agreement scheme for heterogeneous wireless sensor network tailored for the Internet of Things environment. Ad Hoc Netw. **36**, 152–176 (2016)
11. Gubbi, J., Buyya, R., Marusic, S., Palaniswami, M.: Internet of Things (IoT): A vision, architectural elements, and future directions. Futur. Gener. Comput. Syst. **29**(7), 1645–1660 (2013)
12. Angelopoulos, A., et al.: Tackling faults in the industry 4.0 era—a survey of machine-learning solutions and key aspects. Sensors **20**(1), 109 (2019). https://doi.org/10.3390/s20010109
13. Ali, E.S., et al.: Machine learning technologies for secure vehicular communication in internet of vehicles: recent advances and applications. Secur. Commun. Netw. **2021**, 1–23 (2021). https://doi.org/10.1155/2021/8868355

14. Abraham, A., Falcon, R., & Koeppen, M. (eds.).: Computational Intelligence in Wireless Sensor Networks: Recent Advances and Future Challenges (2017)
15. Corke, P., Wark, T., Jurdak, R., Hu, W., Valencia, P., Moore, D.: Environmental wireless sensor networks. Proc. IEEE **98**(11), 1903–1917 (2010)
16. Schmitt, M.A.: Deep Learning in Business Analytics: A Clash of Expectations and Reality. arXiv preprint arXiv:2205.09337 (2022)
17. Mittal, A., Hooda, R., Sofat, S.: Lung field segmentation in chest radiographs: a historical review, current status, and expectations from deep learning. IET Image Proc. **11**(11), 937–952 (2017)
18. Hu, F., Xie, D., Shen, S.: On the application of the internet of things in the field of medical and health care. In: 2013 IEEE international conference on green computing and communications and IEEE Internet of Things and IEEE cyber, physical and social computing, pp. 2053–2058. IEEE (2013)
19. Li, H., Hua, J., Li, J., Li, G.: Stock forecasting model FS-LSTM based on the 5G Internet of things. Wireless Commun. Mob. Comput. **2020**, 1–7 (2020). https://doi.org/10.1155/2020/7681209
20. Ding, Y., Jin, M., Li, S., Feng, D.: Smart logistics based on the internet of things technology: an overview. Int. J. Log. Res. Appl. **24**(4), 323–345 (2021)

Semi-automated Classification of Non-functional Arabic User Requirements Using NLP Tools

Eman Awad[✉], Nabil Arman, and Faisal Khamayseh

Department of Computer Science and IT, Palestine Polytechnic University, Hebron, Palestine
196003@ppu.edu.ps, {narman,faisal}@ppu.edu

Abstract. Requirements Engineering is the first phase in software development life cycle and it also plays one of the most important and critical roles. The Requirements document mainly contains both Functional Requirements (FR) and Non-Functional Requirements (NFR). NFR specifies the quality attributes of the system including security, reliability, performance, maintainability, scalability, and usability. NFR defines the properties that a software product must have in order to meet the business needs of its users and represent additional constraints on the quality and properties of the software system. When developing a system, the developer has to prioritise the NFR from the user requirements document. Categorising these requirements requires specialised skills, experience, and domain knowledge. This process is a difficult and time-consuming task for developers. It is worthwhile to implement an automated or semi-automated classification of NFR from requirements documents. This procedure reduces the manual work, time, and mental effort associated with identifying specific NFR from a large number of requirements. This research paper gives a brief description of the NFR and its categories then it summarises the relevant previous work regarding NFR classification. The most previous studies that worked on the classification of NFR used machine learning algorithms to build an automated classification. This process needs a large amount of data to handle the learning phase, that is, hard to apply on non-functional user requirements written in languages other than English such as Arabic.

Keywords: Requirements Engineering · Functional Requirements · Non-Functional Requirements · Machine Learning · Classification techniques

1 Introduction

Requirements are considered as one of the most important entities in software development. It plays an important role in the success or the failure of the project. Requirement Engineering is crucial in the development of software processes. Requirements Analysis is a part of requirement engineering which helps in determining the expectations of the user related to the newly or modified product. [1] proposed that Requirement analysis is a lengthy process which determines whether these stated requirements are complete or incomplete. User requirements are categorised into Functional Requirements (FR) and Non-Functional Requirements (NFR). FR specify a particular function to be provided

© The Author(s), under exclusive license to Springer Nature Switzerland AG 2024
K. S. Soliman (Ed.): IBIMA-AI 2023, CCIS 2101, pp. 20–29, 2024.
https://doi.org/10.1007/978-3-031-62843-6_2

by the developed software. It deals with input and output behaviour of the system. NFR are described as the quality attributes of the system. These requirements are also called quality requirements. Determining the NFR is one of the most difficult steps during software development. These requirements describe how the system should operate in a certain environment. It covers a variety of quality attributes that include performance, reliability, security, operability, usability of the system. Figure 1 shows the different attributes of NFR categories along with their attributes:

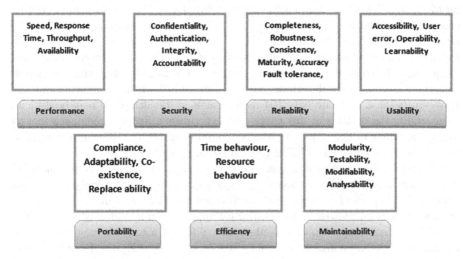

Fig. 1. Main Categories of Non-functional Requirements and their Attributes

There are several techniques applied in the extraction process of NFR. The previous studies showed that most of the techniques used in the extraction process of NFR are supervised. However, the supervised learning approach is labour-intensive and has much overhead to train the model. If the training data are not available, then the domain experts will prepare training data manually. [2] stated that the analyst reads the requirement document and classifies NFR manually. In case of a large dataset, extra effort is required to train the data and to get acceptable results. Furthermore, these systems are effective for small systems while facing challenges on a large scale or when the system is not well structured. The principal drawback of applying supervised methods to NFR detection is related to the amount of pre-categorized requirements needed to reach good levels of precision in the classification process.

This study performed a literature review on previous research attempts studying the different techniques and methods used to extract, identify and classify non-functional requirements. The rest of the paper is organised as follows: Sect. 2 presents the relevant literature and related studies. Section 3 presents summary and discussion. Finally, Sect. 4 highlights our conclusion and future work.

2   Literature Review

In this section, a review of the research studies worked on automatic identification, classification and analysis of non-functional requirements is performed.

[3], proposed an experiment that categorised NFR into several categories including availability, security, usability, loo and feel, legal and licensing, maintainability, operability, performance, scalability, fault tolerance, portability from the requirements document for an IoT-oriented healthcare system. Logistic Regression (LR), Support Vector Machine (SVM), Multinomial Naive Bayes (MNB), K-Nearest Neighbour (KNN), ensemble, Random Forest (RF), and hybrid KNN rule-based machine learning (ML) algorithms are the used machine learning techniques that are taken into consideration for categorization while Bag of Words (BoW) and Term Frequency-Inverse Document Frequency (TF-IDF) are used for feature extraction. For categorization purposes, a new dataset is also created which includes requirements for IoT-oriented healthcare systems. However, because there are only 104 requirements in this dataset, it may be difficult to generalise the findings of this study. The experiment's findings concluded that an average accuracy of 85.7% may be attained by utilising TF-IDF for feature extraction and a hybrid KNN-rule based ML algorithm for the classification.

[4] proposed a programmed approach to distinguish and classify Non-Functional Requirements (NFR) utilising semantic and syntactic investigation by applying machine learning (ML) approaches on unconstrained documents. The author utilised a dataset of open necessities archives (unadulterated) that comprises 79 unconstrained requirements reports in several shapes. In their method, four different natural language processing techniques, including statistical and state-of-the-art semantic analysis offered by Google word2vec and bidirectional encoder representations from transformers models were used to extract features from the requirement phrases. The obtained accuracy was up to 87% using statistical factorization and up to 92% utilising word embedding semantic approaches. Additionally, the accuracy was increased by 2.4% when numerous models trained on various features were combined compared to the top individual classifier. To classify the prerequisite sentences, authors utilised four distinctive ML approaches including Naive Base (NB), Back Vector Machines (SVM), Calculated Relapse (LR), and Convolutional Neural Network (CNN). The proposed strategy can easily classify NFR into five categories: reliability, performance, security, availability, and usability, that had been identified by IEEE-Std 830–1993 as being the most frequently taken into account NFR in the majority of domains and software projects.

[5], employed a semi-supervised machine learning approach where training datasets are not required. However, the Wikipedia data dump that used to train their model can be somewhat supervised. Initially, the Non-functional requirements (NFR) is extracted from the Software Requirements Specification(SRS) document using the well-known indicator terms from the literature. Semantic similarity is measured using the model trained on Wikipedia data for NFR extraction. The Words to vector (Word2Vec) model training process is then laid out. The Python Natural Language Processing (NLP) library is used to extract the requirement statements from the SRS document and perform pre-processing before calculating semantic similarity. To improve the extraction's efficiency, they applied the pre-processing, Part Of Speech (POS) tagging and augmentation of

words. The categories of NFR detected in this study are: (legal, look and feel, maintainability, operational, performance, scalability, security, usability, fault tolerance and portability). The proposed method is examined in this work using the tera-PROMISE and CCHIT datasets. They also looked into how pre-processing affected how well NFR extraction worked. They first used the method with conventional pre-processing and gathered the data in the form of precision-recall. Then, word augmentation and POS tagging pre-processing were used as the applied approach. As a result, NFR extraction performance was gradually improved. The final product performed better than other used methods overall. The average precision, recall and F-measure values for the CCHIT dataset were calculated as 55%, 85%, and 64%, respectively. The average precision, recall and F-measure values for the PROMISE dataset were calculated as 75%, 59%, and 64%, respectively.

[6], proposed an empirical research, that four feature selection methods and seven machine learning algorithms were used to automatically categorise NFR into eleven categories including: (availability, legal, look and feel, maintainability, operational, performance, scalability, security, usability, fault tolerance, and portability) in order to identify the optimal combination. Precision, recall, F1-score, and accuracy of the classification results using all possible combinations of approaches and algorithms were all measured statistically during the study. The procedure compared Bag of Words (BoW) and Term Frequency-Inverse Document (TF-IDF) feature extraction methods with Naive Bayes (NB), K-Nearest Neighbours (KNN), Support Vector Machines (SVM), Stochastic Gradient Descent SVM (SGD SVM) and Decision Trees (D-tree) machine learning algorithms. The BoW, TF-IDF (character level), TF-IDF (word level), and N-gram feature extraction methods were used to evaluate each algorithm's performance in classifying software needs. This system used text encoding techniques after pre-processing the text data to remove any unnecessary text. The NB, KNN, SVM, and D-tree algorithms were trained and tested on the encoded data. The Support Vector Machines (SVM), Stochastic Gradient Descent SVM (SGD SVM) classifier were found to produce the best results, with precision, recall, F1-score, and accuracy reported as 0.66, 0.61, 0.61, and 0.76 respectively. A higher average score was also shown by the TF-IDF (character level) feature extraction technique compared by the competition.

[7] used the user-reviews of the well-known App platforms, Apple App Store, Google Play, and Windows Phone Store, which have over 4 million apps for their classification. These reviews are considered very important for developers as they help them in the maintenance and evolution for the software. The authors classified these reviews into four categories of NFR as reliability, usability, portability, and performance. They combined four classification strategies: Bag of Words (Bow), Term Frequency-Inverse Document (TF-IDF), chi-square (CHI2), and AUR-Bow which were proposed in their work, with three machine learning algorithms including Naive Bayes, J48, and Bagging to classify user reviews. The authors conducted tests to compare the F-measures of the classification results. They found that the combination of AUR-Bow with Bagging accomplished the finest result, mainly a precision of 71.4%, a recall of 72.3%, and an F-measure of 71.8% among all the combinations. Finally, they concluded that user-reviews used in their study were better classified using the Bagging algorithm with Naïve Bayes and J48.

[8], employed a multi-step unsupervised methodology for the purpose of finding and classifying the Non-Functional Requirements (NFR) into security, performance, accessibility, accuracy, portability, safety, legal, privacy, reliability, availability, and interoperability categories. The earliest methods for classifying and identifying NFR employed manually classified data to train the model. However, large training data sets are not always accessible, making it difficult to achieve high accuracy. To support NFR traceability, a method was utilised to extract natural language content from source code. Software requirements were taken into consideration while using word semantic similarity algorithms. To create the requirements-word clusters that make the most sense, cluster configuration was used. To determine the clustering configurations that produce the most cohesive groups of functional requirement words, a thorough, systematic investigation of several word semantic similarity approaches and clustering algorithms were performed. The idea of semantic coherence of generated word clusters was captured by a semantically aware cluster quality function. To conduct our investigation, three software systems from various application fields were chosen. The findings demonstrated that average linkage (AL), a hierarchical clustering technique, was superior to partitioning algorithms at producing thematic groups of Functional Requirements (FR) terms (k-medoids). Their suggested method demonstrated a moderate level of complexity that enabled it to scale on larger systems without encountering problems with time and space constraints. Their suggested method was unsupervised, thus it worked with the least amount of modification with no need of any data set.

[9], proposed an automated approach for the detection of Non-Functional Requirements (NFR) using the Fuzzy Similarity Based K-nearest Neighbour (FSKNN) which is a classification algorithm based on requirement sentences. Semantic variables and semantic relatedness measures were not taken into account in the FSKNN algorithm. Different non-functional requirements from text documents were categorised by their proposed system. The system analysed training data by labelling it, classifying it, and measuring the semantic similarity between various classes and phrases. The training data labelling is faster when done automatically than when done manually. The semantic relatedness of the terms was determined using the Hirst & S-Onge (HSO) approach. The approach examines the semantic relationships between each class and the processed phrase. The results demonstrated that the accuracy was increased by 43.7% with the addition of semantic parameters compared to the fuzzy similarity-based K-nearest neighbour algorithm's accuracy of 41.4%.

[10], proposed a classification system for Non-Functional Requirements (NFR) for Information Systems (IS). There are numerous proposed classification schemes for NFR, but none of them describe the needs for IS, web-based systems or real-time systems. The classification of NFR was proposed as a tree-like structure. Similar NFR were found for both real systems and web-based systems in this classification method. The software requirements specification document must include the NFR that are part of the classification scheme for IS. For information systems, reliability and availability are two crucial NFR. The classification scheme further divided the dependability requirement into accuracy, maturity, and completeness. This paper depends on the similarity of the NFR to identify the different categories. Accuracy and confidentiality are considered two non-functional requirements that are common to both real-time systems and information

systems. Interoperability and privacy are two NFR that are common to both web-based systems and information systems. Security, performance, and usability requirements are also common to both real-time systems and web-based systems.

3 Summary and Discussion

Many researchers have worked on the classification of NFR. They used different approaches and proposed automated classification methods depending on machine learning algorithms which need several datasets to train the model they used. Other researchers have proposed semi-automated classification techniques in cases where few datasets were available. The following table summarises the main differences between the previous attempts discussed in the literature review above (Table 1):

Table 1. Comparison of NFR Extraction and Classification Techniques

Proposed	Main Aims	Technique for NFR extraction	Dataset Used	Output NFR classes
Khurshid, Imtiaz, Boulila, Khan, Abbasi, Javed, Jalil (2022)	Automated Classification of NFR From IoT Oriented Healthcare Requirement Document	For classification ML algorithm: LR, SVM, MNB, KNN, RF, KNN rule-based For Feature Extraction: BoW and TF-IDF	New dataset is created which includes requirements for IoT-oriented healthcare systems	availability, security, usability, look and feel, legal and licensing, maintainability, operability, performance, scalability, fault tolerance, portability
Shreda and Hanani (2021)	Automated Classification of NFR utilising semantic and syntactic investigation	ML approaches: NB, SVM, LR, CNN NLP techniques: Random and Word embedding vectorization methods	The author utilised a dataset of open necessities archives (unadulterated) that comprises 79 unconstrained requirements reports	reliability, performance, security, availability, and usability
Younas et al. (2020)	Semi-automated Classification of NFR from Wikipedia data dump	Semi-supervised machine learning approach	Wikipedia data dump that used to train their model The tera-PROMISE and CCHIT datasets are used for testing	legal, look and feel, maintainability, operational, performance, scalability, security, usability, fault tolerance and portability

(continued)

Table 1. (*continued*)

Proposed	Main Aims	Technique for NFR extraction	Dataset Used	Output NFR classes
Rahman and Siddik (2019)	Automated classification of NFR for finding out the best pair of ML and feature selection	ML algorithm: MNB, GNB, BNB, KNN, SVM, SGD SVM, and DTree. Feature selection techniques: BoW and TF-IDF	Not specified	availability, legal, look and feel, maintainability, operational, performance, scalability, security, usability, fault tolerance, and portability
Liang (2017)	Automated classification of NFR from augmented App user reviews	ML algorithm: Naive Bayes, J48, and Bagging Four classification strategies: Bow, TF-IDF, CHI2, and AUR-Bow (which proposed in their work)	the user-reviews of the well-known App platforms, Apple App Store, Google Play, and Windows Phone Store	reliability, usability, portability, and performance
Williams, G (2016)	Unsupervised methodology for finding and classifying the NFR	Systematic analysis of a series of word similarity methods and clustering techniques, then used word semantic similarity algorithms	Unsupervised method so no dataset needed	security, performance, accessibility, accuracy, portability, safety, legal, privacy, reliability, availability, and interoperability
Rochimah and Yuhana (2015)	Automated NFRs extraction through semantic factors	Fuzzy similarity based k-nearest neighbour algorithm (FSKNN)	1.Itrust 2.CCHIT 3.World Vista US veteran health care health care 4.Online Project Marking System SRS	Performance and accessibility
Gazi and Sadiq (2015)	Classification of NFRs from Information systems	A tree-like structure of the proposed classification scheme is given	Information system	Availability, performance, security, usability, privacy, access control, accuracy, reliability

The following table summarize the main advantages and disadvantages of the previous work (Table 2):

Table 2. Advantages and Disadvantages of the proposed

Proposed	Advantages	Disadvantages
Khurshid, Imtiaz, Boulila, Khan, Abbasi, Javed, Jalil (2022)	-Achieved accuracy of 85.7% -Used seven ML algorithms -Classify the NFR into eleven categories	The small size of the tested dataset
Shreda and Hanani (2021)	-Achieved accuracy between 84% and 87% using statistical vectorization method - Achieved 88% to 92% using word embedding semantic methods	Only five categories of NFR were considered
Younas et al. (2020)	-Achieved average precision recall and F-measure values: 75%, 59%, and 64%, respectively -Classify the NFR into ten categories	Only one ML algorithm was used
Rahman and Siddik (2019)	- Achieved best results using SGD SVM classifier where precision, recall, F1-score, and accuracy reported as 0.66, 0.61, 0.61, and 0.76 respectively	It should consider other significant machine learning feature extraction techniques such as Chi Squared, and classification algorithms such as bagging, boosting
Liang (2017)	-Achieves the highest F-measure of 71.8%, with a precision of 71.4% and a recall of 72.3% respectively	Only four categories of NFR were considered
Williams, G (2016)	-Classify the NFR into eleven categories -Unsupervised, thus it can work with the least amount of modification and not need any data set	Should use more different types of word semantic similarity methods and clustering techniques, to get more word clusters
Rochimah and Yuhana (2015)	Improve accuracy and reduce error rate and hamming loss	Additional search for semantic relatedness reduce recall
Gazi and Sadiq (2015)	Extracting NFRs in IS through classification scheme	Classification not include quality attribute

4 Conclusion and Future Work

Manual classification of NFR is hard and time consuming. Accordingly, there is a significant need to classify them automatically or semi-automatically in order to save time and effort of the software developers. Consequently, we conducted an analysis of various automatic and semi-automatic NFR extraction methods from the software requirement documents. The goal of this study is to minimise the time and expense involved in finding NFRs for a software project. The analyst can recognize various NFRs with the aid of automatic NFR extraction which makes manual identification less effortful. Although most of the previous studies focused on English language, there are several studies that handled NLP on Arabic language. Arabic language is more ambiguous than other languages due to its morphological, syntactic and semantic characteristics. Accordingly, [11] said that a proper NLP tool will be used to tokenize, diacritic, morphological disambiguation, POS tagging and lemmatize the requirements. This process converts the non-functional Arabic user requirements which are written in an unstructured form into requirements written in standard Arabic requirements. Our next research effort will be building a set of heuristics for classifying Arabic language requirements by using different NLP tools to analyse the Arabic dataset. The proposed method will be implemented using python programming language.

References

1. Singh, P., Singh, D., Sharma, A.: Rule-based system for automated classification of non-functional requirements from requirement specifications. In: International Conference on Advances in Computing, Communications and Informatics (ICACCI), pp. 620–626 (2016). https://doi.org/10.1109/ICACCI.2016.7732115
2. Sommerville, Software engineering, 9th Edition. ISBN10, 137035152, p.18 (2011)
3. Khurshid, S.I., Boulila, W., Khan, Z., Abbasi, A., Javed, A., Jalil, Z.: Classification of non-functional requirements from IoT oriented healthcare requirement document. Front. Public Health. 18(10), 860536 (2022). https://doi.org/10.3389/fpubh.2022.860536. PMID: 35372217; PMCID: PMC8974737
4. QA Shreda AA Hanani 2024 Identifying non-functional requirements from unconstrained documents using natural language processing and machine learning approaches IEEE Access https://doi.org/10.1109/ACCESS.2021.3052921
5. M Younas DNA Jawawi I Ghani 2020 Extraction of non-functional requirement using semantic similarity distance Neural Comput. Appl. 32 7383 7397
6. Haque, M.A., Abdur Rahman, M., Siddik, M.S.: Non-functional requirements classification with feature extraction and machine learning: an empirical study. In: 1st International Conference on Advances in Science, Engineering and Robotics Technology (ICASERT), pp. 1–5 (2019). https://doi.org/10.1109/ICASERT.2019.8934499
7. Lu, M., Liang, P.: Automatic classification of non-functional requirements from augmented app user reviews. In: EASE'17: Proceedings of the 21st International Conference on Evaluation and Assessment in Software Engineering (2017)
8. A Mahmoud G Williams 2016 Detecting, classifying, and tracing non-functional software requirements Requirements Eng. 21 357 381
9. DA Ramadhani S Rochimah UL Yuhana 2015 Classification of non-functional requirements using semantic-FSKNN based ISO/IEC 9126 TELKOMNIKA (Telecommun. Comput. Electron. Control) 13 4 1456 1465

10. Y Gazi MS Umar M Sadiq 2015 Classification of NFRs for information systems Int. J. Comput. Appl. 115 22 19 22
11. Alami, N., Arman, N., Khamayseh, F.: A semi-automated approach for generating sequence diagrams from Arabic user requirements using a natural language processing tool. In: 2017 8th International Conference on Information Technology (ICIT) (2017)

K-Nearest Neighbor in Assessing Trends of Cameroonians Most Attractive Communal and Cultural Diversity Cities in Poland Based on Natural Language Processing and Artificial Intelligence

Pascal Muam Mah[1(✉)], Gilly Njoh Amuzang[2], Micheal Blake Somaah Itoe[2], and Ning Frida Tah[1,2]

[1] AGH University of Science and Technology, Krakow, Poland
mahpascal01@gmail.com
[2] Silesian University of Technology, Gliwice, Poland

Abstract. Introduction: Time and distance are the most essential factors in life. The time spent on content reveals the NLP structure and distance between key content words reveals KNN algorithm representation. One of the most widely used classification algorithms in machine learning is the K-nearest neighbor (KNN). In recent years, the trend of migration has increased tremendously as compared to a decade ago.

Aims: Aim to evaluate the impact of migration in recent years using KNN to understand the most essential time-distance factors promoting such adventures. Also, revealed how time (NLP) and distance (KNN) necessitated Cameroonians' zeal for Poland and city choice.

Problem: Time on data content (NLP) and distance on data content (KNN) is causing millions of pieces of information to go unnoticed. Also, a lot of cacophony has been in the air about Cameroonians scrambling in the Polish embassy for Polish visas, and in Polish borders that sends a mixed signal to social media, western world about the Cameroon government.

Material and method: This study uses natural language processing to capture key comments, survey distance between key content and assess how artificial intelligence automates content to the understanding of Cameroonians to identify the most attractive communal and cultural diversity cities in Poland. The study uses questionnaires with the help of some embodiment factors that explain migration trends of most Cameroonian to Poland and choice of cities. The study uses a TF-IDF and bag of words model to identify K value for K-nearest neighbor approach and a concise NLP classified key content.

Results: Based on K-nearest neighbor analysis TF-IDF and bag of words model, where results were classified into most attractive, and least attractive. Warsaw city is the most attractive communal and cultural diversity city in Poland while Gdańsk is the least. A total of 17 questionnaires reveal that Warsaw is the most attractive communal and cultural diversity city in Poland with about 49% respondents and Gdansk is the least attractive with about 2% respondents.

Conclusion: Warsaw is the K-nearest city closest to Cameroonians most attractive communal and cultural diversity city. Based on K-nearest neighbor analysis,

K. S. Soliman (Ed.): IBIMA-AI 2023, CCIS 2101, pp. 30–42, 2024.
https://doi.org/10.1007/978-3-031-62843-6_3

the study concluded that the fabulous and exotic facilities, services, amenities, education system, job opportunities and affordable life are amongst the reasons for the migration trends and choice of cities.

Keywords: K-nearest neighbor · natural language processing · artificial intelligence · data classification · migration

1 Introduction

K-nearest neighbor is supervised learning that deals with regression problems and classification challenges [1, 3]. K-nearest neighbor algorithm used machine learning technique to predict group attributes of data instances [2]. Text classification has been widely achieved using K-nearest neighbor algorithms. K-nearest neighbor has become a more popular algorithm in text classification [7]. The art of classifying data or a text content to enable and ensure understanding is a natural language processing approach that aims at fulfilling the K-nearest neighbor algorithm that holds the most essential information.

The KNN and NLP fulfill the process of monitoring and classifying public opinion based on different aspects of communication such as understanding, reporting, informing, investigating, revealing, forecasting and predicting.

Artificial intelligence helps in automating all the processes and steps that require human efforts [5]. The process of monitoring public opinion in order to reduce the time required to understand inside and outside of data content has been achieved recently with automated AI applications. Thus AI narrows down the distance between actual receivers of data content and time required. Most applications of natural language processing use artificial intelligence to automate classified information. Fertile conducting of more complex activities that require a greater vision require artificial intelligence [4]. Text classification, and clustering uses application of natural language processing to capture and redistribute public opinions in a proper network approach and in a well-organized structure. Natural language processing in the field has presented one of the best approaches and applications of public opinion with the help of keywords.

Time on data content (NLP) and distance on data content (KNN) is causing millions of pieces of information to go unnoticed. That is why this study uses the Cameroonian migration trends to explain the situation that is not fully supported by data but by human emotions. There's a need to tackle the causes to allow ample time to solve this issue than throwing accusations on individual actions. Cameron has been notorious for corrupt practices and bad governance. In recent years, since 2016 till date there's a lot going on in Cameroon but this has not been attempted to resolve by the international community. This study decided to attempt to evaluate the impact of migration in recent years using KNN to allow the public global community and the media to understand the most essential time-distance factors promoting migration trends of Cameroonians. This study can be applied to other countries.

Natural language processing has established a lot of opportunities to automate human activities through software with a number of automated process steps using machine learning and artificial intelligence. Digital transformation is the major area that has established the opportunity for different applications to automate human activities through software [6]. The K-nearest neighbor algorithm is one of the most used machine learning techniques that automate human activities through spoken, written and documentary

2   Study Validation Technique and Methodological Approach

The process flow of the study follows application of model experimental validation. The model validation and verification stages in this study are summarized in Fig. 1 below.

In this section, the experimental validation uses deep learning models and natural language processing. Deep learning focuses on the K-nearest neighbor algorithm and natural language processing focuses on frequency inverse document frequency (TF-IDF) and bag of words (BOW) Model.

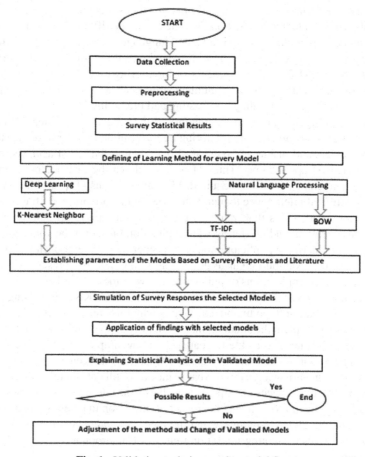

Fig. 1. Validation technique and material flow

Figure 1 represent preprocessed and tested by statistical validation methods, and it is divided into sample technique and testing sets validation using the K-nearest neighbor algorithm and bag of words model of natural language processing. The sample survey responses were used to learn to achieve the bag of words model algorithm.

2.1 Literature Review

This section contain definition of key terms, and different between K-nearest neighbor and natural language processing.

2.2 Definition of Key Terms

K-nearest neighbor: This is a supervised simple machine learning algorithm used to solve classification and regression problems [8]. K-nearest neighbor is one of the common classification methods, which function on the basis of the use of distance measures [9].

Natural Language Processing: This is a branch of artificial intelligence that deals with the design and implementation of algorithm systems able to interact through human language [10]. Natural language processing creates unique opportunities that systematically document users' details from digitized free-text [11]. Natural language processing is the task of converting unstructured human language [12].

Artificial Intelligence: This is the science and engineering of making intelligent [13]. Artificial intelligence is the study of how to build or program computers to enable them to do what minds can do [14].

The K-nearest neighbors algorithm is a non-parametric supervised learning method first introduced by Evelyn Fix and Joseph Hodges in 1951 [15, 16]. The components that affect the importance of words in a document called Term Frequency factor and Inverse Document Frequency (IDF) factors [17, 18]. Term frequency of words in a document (TF) is weight that depends on the distribution of said document words. The importance of words in s document are understood based on their frequency. When talking about inverse document frequency, each word in the document and its weight depend on the distribution frequency [19, 20]. There are different ways to compute independence words especially particular words class. The chi-square statistic is a score that can be used to determine the features of document with the highest values.

Natural language processing provides approaches that are used to achieve data normalization and data dimensionality reduction [21, 22]. The birth of modern digital services improved the classification effect thanks to natural language processing. This study uses K-nearest neighbors to analyze the closest factors leading migration trends of Cameroonians to Poland and their most attractive communal and cultural diversity cities. Amongst eight factors that determine the nearest desire for travel to Poland and the most attractive communal and cultural diversity cities, there exist the most attractive factor. The study uses the "K" in K-nearest neighbor (KNN) to be the push factor trends or parameter that determines the closest neighbor to include in the alternative process for the most attractive communal and cultural diversity cities and migration motivation. The study uses the following cities (Warsaw, Krakow, Silesian, Wroclaw, Poznan, Gdansk, Lodz, and Lublin) as data points with the help of eighteen alternative push factors of parameters that forces Cameroonian to focus on the closest factor "K" kNN. Amongst seventeen factors there exist only one or few closest desires "K".

2.3 Differences Between K-nearest Neighbor and Natural Language Processing

The main distinction between natural language processing when performing content classification and clustering with the K-nearest neighbor algorithm is time and distance.

Natural language processing engages in various processes to reduce the time we require to understand a long line of content or document while the K-nearest neighbor algorithm represents the distance between datasets that belong to the same layers of document content.

Natural language processing required a Preprocessing approach to enable and ensure feature extraction while the K-nearest neighbor algorithm represents distance between datasets with features to ensure a proper choice.

Natural language processing required preprocessing and introduction of datasets that K-nearest neighbors require adjusting the parameters to achieve a classifier. K-nearest neighbor (KNN) provides a more helpful method of data classification that helps us understand the likelihood that something is going to happen or has happened or is close to happening.

On the other hand, natural language processing breaks down the steps, stages and present data of what has happened or will happen or data of what is close to happen.

3 Applied Method

This section contain methodological analysis on data preprocessing, construction of word vector structure with TF-IDF, analysis of Bag of Words with survey responses, Weight Strategy, and TF-IDF Application Calculation Process of data Classification in the following paragraphs provide details on how the study was carried out.

3.1 Data Preprocessing

Data were collected from 40 respondents in seventeen (17) categorical survey questions, for a choice of eight (8) attractive cities. The cities were Warsaw, Krakow, Silesian, Wroclaw, Poznan, Gdansk, łódź and Lublin. The respondent indicated a random identity (respond sheet) answer sheet that includes cities as class of dataset like Warsaw, Krakow, Silesian, Wroclaw, Poznan, Gdansk, łódź, and Lublin. 40 respondents were identified randomly distributed as per survey as training data, including Warsaw 418, Krakow 181, Silesian 65, Poznan 55, Wroclaw 33, Gdansk 18, łódź 38, and Lublin 44,

Respondents are registered in the study survey as a list, and total response data are considered as a list. Based on the survey responses, a segmentation method was applied based on bag of words model. This study segments the city names as word counts that appear in each question for use in training and test sets.

3.2 Construction of Word Vector Structure with TF-IDF

TF-IDF means term frequency-inverse document frequency. TF-IDF is a statistical method that measures and evaluates how relevant a word is to a document in a collection of documents. This section deals with structured representation of survey responses.

Here we constructed a Word Vector Structured representation of text categorization that mainly counts the frequency of words in the survey response.

The study uses eighteen questions classified into eight cities to examine the most and least attractive communal and cultural diversity city.

This was done by multiplying the metrics on how many times a word (city name) appears for each question in the survey responses, and the inverse response frequency of all the total words (city names) across the set survey datasets. TF-IDF has many uses. The most significant is its ability in automating text analysis which is very useful for scoring words in machine learning algorithms for Natural Language Processing (NLP).

3.3 Analysis of Bag of Words with Survey Responses

Bag of Words (BoW) is a process that simply counts the frequency of words in a document. The vector for a document, unlike the study survey, has the frequency of each word as indicated by studies in the corpus for documents. The key difference between bag of words and TF-IDF is that the bag of words does not incorporate any sort of inverse document frequency (IDF) but it is only a frequency count (TF).

3.4 Weight Strategy

TF-IDF indicates that the word frequency reverses the frequency of the document. This study uses TF-IDF with the intended stress that Word frequency should not reduce the frequency of documents but instead make the documents with highest frequency words are more visible. The sole aim is to stress the importance of the survey responses. TF-IDF assumed that a word or phrase that appears in a high frequency in a document rarely appears in other documents and when this happens, it is considered suitable for Classification.

3.5 TF-IDF Application

Determining the importance of a word is to a document is useful in many ways.

Information Retrieval. TF-IDF invention was for document search and is also used to deliver results of survey, search queries and keyword automation. TF-IDF gives frequently appear words a higher score. Most search engines use TF-IDF scores in its algorithm. The study uses TF-IDF to obtain results for the study based on the strict survey responses.

Keyword Extraction. TF-IDF is very useful for keywords extraction from text. The study sees this very close to the questionnaires used in this study. The questionnaires were tailored to the basic and concise needs of Cameroonians in Poland to understand their most favorite attractive communal and cultural diversity city. The site uses search engine to identify the most desired attention for foreigners and a survey questionnaire was built. The highest scoring words in the survey responses indicated the most relevant needs of Cameroonians and therefore was considered keywords for that survey.

3.6   The Classifier

K-nearest neighbor algorithm calculates that most of the k nearest neighbors in a dataset or document belong to a certain category, and the sample also belongs to this category. The algorithm in this study involves a simple main objective of distance measurement. The k-value selection is based on a bag of words (BOW) model. The experiment of K value selection is performed using a bag of words model and the optimal k value is selected from the eight (8) categories of datasets set in this study for the most city and respond from survey determine the k value (Fig. 2).

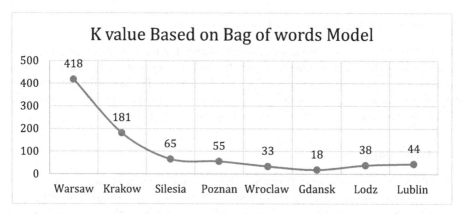

Fig. 2. K value based on bags of words

The seventeen (17) survey questionnaires generate data by a simple cross-validation method of eight (8) categorized selected cities. The test set is validated by using the datasets obtained as the training set interfere with by a sample selection of frequently appeared words using bag of words model.

The results show that the effect is the best appearance or frequency based on bag of words model is 418. K = 418. Warsaw was the most frequency amongst all the eight categories set in this study for seventeen (17) sample questionnaires.

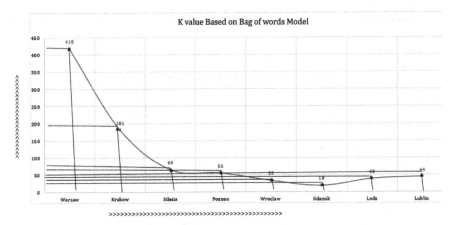

Fig. 3. Frequency and dimensionality law of BAW model

Figure 3 represents BAW model assumption that the higher the frequency of words the lower the dimensionality. Based on the study, Warsaw contain the highest frequency and represents the K value in the study.

Accuracy validation technique $= \frac{TP+TN}{TP+TN+FP+FN}$

Warsaw = TP, Gdansk = TN, Krakow = FP, and Wroclaw = FN

True Positive = TP, True Negative = TN, False Positive = FP, and False Negative = FN

$\frac{450+18}{450+18+181+33} = 0.68\%$

$= 68\%$

4   Results

This study uses sample questions to determine the most attractive communal and cultural diversity city in Poland. The sample questionnaires we shared only amongst Cameroonians. The sample questions were share in the WhatsApp group for Cameroonians in Poland. The following statistics were collected. The study score words with the chi square function and sorted the words frequency using the bag-of-words model is clearly better than the filtered mode [23]. Survey questions and respondents are possible with the application of bag of words model and chi square [24]. Empirical analyses are based on chi square, especially non-filtering findings like the survey applied in this study.

4.1   Formula of Chi Square

$$X^2 = \sum \cdot \frac{(Oi - Ei)^2}{Ei}$$

$x^2 = Chi\ Square$

$Oi = Observed\ value$

$Ei = Expected\ value$

The statistics were evaluated based on chi square observation from sample questionnaires to statistical presentation.

Table 1. Survey Based on Bags of word (BOW)

No	Surey Questions	Warsaw	Krakow	Silesia	Poznan	Wroclaw	Gdansk	Lodz	Lublin	Total Responses per question
1	The Most Learning Institutions City	28	10	3	3	2	2	2	2	52
2	The Most Beautiful City	26	12	4	2	2	1	3	2	52
3	The Most Learning Facilities City	25	11	3	3	0	0	1	2	45
4	The Most Foreign Learning Courses City	26	10	3	4	1	0	3	4	51
5	The Most Polish Language Learning Centers	27	13	0	4	0	1	4	2	51
6	The Most Attractive Jobs Opportunities	29	11	5	4	3	1	2	2	57
7	The Most City with Foreign Recipes	28	13	2	5	4	1	4	1	58
8	The Most City with Foreign Access to Housing	22	13	7	4	4	0	4	2	56
9	The Most Foreign Accessories City	26	15	5	4	2	1	0	4	57
10	The Most City with Foreign Organizational Units	30	11	4	4	2	1	0	3	55

(*continued*)

Table 1. (*continued*)

No	Surey Questions	Warsaw	Krakow	Silesia	Poznan	Wroclaw	Gdansk	Lodz	Lublin	Total Responses per question
11	The Most Foreign Shops City	26	9	9	4	4	1	2	3	58
13	The Most Secure City	25	6	5	5	1	1	3	4	50
14	The Most Inhabitant City with Cameroonians	23	10	6	3	5	2	6	3	58
15	The Most Fastest City with Legalization of stay	22	16	4	4	1	2	1	5	55
16	The Most Expensive City	28	10	4	2	0	2	2	2	50
17	The Most Welcoming City	27	11	1	0	2	2	1	3	47
	Grand Total	418	181	65	55	33	18	38	44	852

Table 1 was made up of seventeen (17) questions. The target of the questionnaires was to determine the most attractive communal and cultural diversity city in Poland for Cameroonians. In the survey, eight (8) cities were targeted.

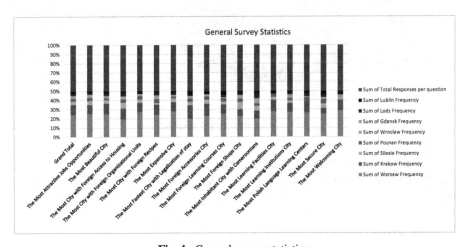

Fig. 4. General survey statistics.

Figure 4 represent the type of seventeen (17) questions, number of response for each question. Each question was to evaluate and examine the most attractive communal and cultural diversity cities.

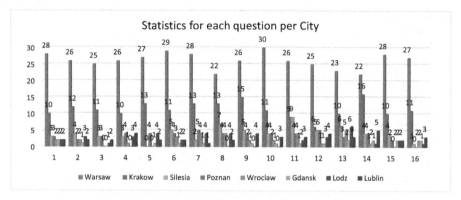

Fig. 5. Statistics per city

Figure 5 represents the eight cities and the amount of respondents to each. From Fig. 5, Warsaw is the highest city with a positive response. The least city was Gdańsk with about 18 respondents.

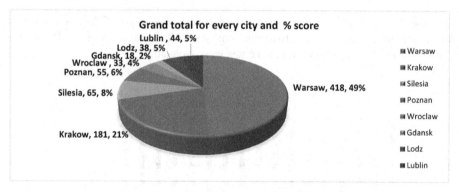

Fig. 6. Percentage score per respondents

Figure 6 represents eight cities with Warsaw with 49%, Krakow with 21%, Silesia with 8%, Poznan with 6%, Wroclaw with 4%, Gdansk with 2%, łódź with 5% and Lublin with 5%.

5 Conclusion

In this study, we investigate the most attractive communal and cultural diversity cities in Poland for Cameroonians with the used of sample questionnaires. Results indicated Warsaw as the most attractive communal and cultural diversity city in Poland. The study findings were validated using deep learning with K-nearest neighbor algorithm structure analysis and natural language processing validated model of bag of words and frequency-inverse document frequency (TF-IDF). The study confirm the following:

I. The accuracy of bag-of-words can be achieve by simple procedure and lay down rules.
II. The performance of classifier of a set data for any task can be achieve depending on the technicality of the dataset and intended purposed.
III. The application of higher thresholds for chi-square model can enhances feature dimension without necessarily optimization

6 Declaration of Material Used

All data underlying the results are available as part of the article and no additional source data are required or reserved somewhere respond from survey determine the k value.

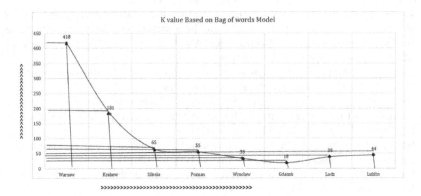

Declaration Conflict of Interest. We certify that we have no affiliations with or involvement in any organization or entity with any financial interest or non-financial interest in the subject matter or materials discussed in this manuscript. We have no financial or proprietary interests in any material discussed in this article.

References

1. Sen, P.C., Hajra, M., Ghosh, M.: Supervised classification algorithms in machine learning: a survey and review. In: Mandal, J.K., Bhattacharya, D. (eds.) Emerging technology in modelling and graphics. AISC, vol. 937, pp. 99–111. Springer, Singapore (2020). https://doi.org/10.1007/978-981-13-7403-6_11
2. Soofi, A.A., Awan, A.: Classification techniques in machine learning: applications and issues. J. Basic Appl. Sci. **13**, 459–465 (2017)
3. Hackeling, G.: Mastering Machine Learning with scikit-learn. Packt Publishing Ltd. (2017)
4. Jarrahi, M.H.: In the age of the smart artificial intelligence: AI's dual capacities for automating and informing work. Bus. Inf. Rev. **36**(4), 178–187 (2019)

5. Romao, M., Costa, J., Costa, C.J.: Robotic process automation: a case study in the banking industry. In 2019 14th Iberian Conference on information systems and technologies (CISTI), pp. 1–6. IEEE (2019)
6. Schmitz, M., Dietze, C., Czarnecki, C.: Enabling digital transformation through robotic process automation at Deutsche Telekom. In: Urbach, N., Röglinger, M. (eds.) Digitalization cases. MP, pp. 15–33. Springer, Cham (2019). https://doi.org/10.1007/978-3-319-95273-4_2
7. Trstenjak, B., Mikac, S., Donko, D.: KNN with TF-IDF based framework for text categorization. Procedia Eng. **69**, 1356–1364 (2014)
8. Mahesh, B.: Machine learning algorithms-a review. Int. J. Sci. Res. (IJSR) **9**, 381–386 (2020)
9. Modaresi, F., Araghinejad, S.: A comparative assessment of support vector machines, probabilistic neural networks, and K-nearest neighbor algorithms for water quality classification. Water Resour. Manage **28**(12), 4095–4111 (2014)
10. Lauriola, I., Lavelli, A., Aiolli, F.: An introduction to deep learning in natural language processing: Models, techniques, and tools. Neurocomputing **470**, 443–456 (2022)
11. Rouillard, C.J., Nasser, M.A., Hu, H., Roblin, D.W.: Evaluation of a natural language processing approach to identify social determinants of health in electronic health records in a diverse community cohort. Med. Care **60**(3), 248–255 (2022)
12. Voytovich, L., Greenberg, C.: Natural language processing: Practical applications in medicine and investigation of contextual autocomplete. In: Staartjes, V.E., Regli, L., Serra, C. (eds.) Machine Learning in Clinical Neuroscience. ANS, vol. 134, pp. 207–214. Springer, Cham (2022). https://doi.org/10.1007/978-3-030-85292-4_24
13. Hamet, P., Tremblay, J.: Artificial intelligence in medicine. Metabolism **69**, S36–S40 (2017)
14. Boden, M.A. (ed.): Artificial intelligence. Elsevier (1996)
15. He, C., Ding, C. H., Chen, S., Luo, B.: Intelligent machine learning system for predicting customer Churn. In 2021 IEEE 33rd International Conference on Tools with Artificial Intelligence (ICTAI), pp. 522–527. IEEE (2021)
16. Hu, X., Wang, J., Wang, L., Yu, K.: K-nearest neighbor estimation of functional nonparametric regression model under NA samples. Axioms **11**(3), 102 (2022)
17. Robertson, S.: Understanding inverse document frequency: on theoretical arguments for IDF. J. Documentation **60**(5), 503–520 (2004)
18. Polettini, N.: The vector space model in information retrieval-term weighting problem. Entropy **34**, 1–9 (2004)
19. Rathi, R.N., Mustafi, A.: The importance of Term Weighting in semantic understanding of text: a review of techniques. Multimed. Tools Appl. **82**, 9761–9783 (2022)
20. Ozyegen, O., Kabe, D., Cevik, M.: Word-level text highlighting of medical texts for telehealth services. Artif. Intell. Med. **127**, 102284 (2022)
21. Nistor, A., Zadobrischi, E.: The influence of fake news on social media: analysis and verification of web content during the COVID-19 pandemic by advanced machine learning methods and natural language processing. Sustainability **14**(17), 10466 (2022)
22. Kaczmarek, I., Iwaniak, A., Świetlicka, A., Piwowarczyk, M., Nadolny, A.: A: machine learning approach for integration of spatial development plans based on natural language processing. Sustain. Cities Soc. **76**, 103479 (2022)
23. Fouzia Sayeedunnissa, S., Hussain, A.R., Hameed, M.A.: Supervised opinion mining of social network data using a bag-of-words approach on the cloud. In: Bansal, J.C., Singh, P., Deep, K., Pant, M., Nagar, A. (eds.) Proceedings of Seventh International Conference on Bio-Inspired Computing: Theories and Applications (BIC-TA 2012): Volume 2, pp. 299–309. Springer India, India (2013). https://doi.org/10.1007/978-81-322-1041-2_26
24. Obasa, A.I., Salim, N., Khan, A.: Hybridization of bag-of-words and forum metadata for web forum question post detection. Indian J. Sci. Technol. **8**(32), 1–12 (2016)

Artificial Intelligence and Geodata for Local Community Sensibilization to Sustainable Spatial Development

Jozef Hernik[1] , Hans Joachim Linke[2] , Karol Krol[1(✉)] , Tomasz Salata[1] ,
Anita Kukulska-Koziel[1] , and Katarzyna Cegielska[1]

[1] Department of Land Management and Landscape Architecture, University of Agriculture in
Krakow, Faculty of Environmental Engineering and Land Surveying, Aleja Mickiewicza 21,
31-120 Krakow, Poland
{jozef.hernik,karol.krol,tomasz.salata,anita.kukulska-koziel,
katarzyna.cegielska}@urk.edu.pl
[2] Institute of Geodesy, Technische Universität Darmstadt, Franziska-Braun-Straße 7, 64287
Darmstadt, Germany
linke@geod.tu-darmstadt.de

Abstract. Ongoing urbanisation processes call for immediate monitoring of land-use changes combined with sustainable spatial management. Advances in technology result in a tendency towards digital monitoring. What is more, digitalisation is provided for in legal regulations on spatial planning. There is, however, a research gap regarding methodological and practical aspects of the role of new technologies and geodata in the process. The problem captured the attention of researchers and practitioners from an international and interdisciplinary GeoSen team. The project's objective is to devise an IT system to identify land-use and land-cover changes with dedicated tools and computing algorithms. GeoSen uses remote-sensing data processed with artificial intelligence algorithms. Its macroscale research is intended to identify trends and changes in land management and landscape, while the microscale segment tests the IT system. Final algorithms will be published as an interactive online platform that will stimulate the activity of participants in spatial planning, leading to effective and sustainable use of space and its resources.

Keywords: GreenTech · WebGIS · AI algorithms · smart villages · public participation

1 Introduction

Urban and rural land faces numerous developmental challenges in many countries. The literature mentions land use as the primary aspect of the environment and its role in development (especially sustainable development), environmental and economic transformations [6], strong urbanisation trends of various kinds [10, 21], or agricultural abandonment [3]. Land as a resource dwindles due to urbanisation processes. The resource is finite [4], which calls for in-depth analysis [14]. Therefore, the postulate of rational land management, treating it as a good of high economic, environmental, and social value, is completely valid. The complex and multifaceted process of intensive urbanisation progresses dynamically, often chaotically and indiscriminately (Simon, 2008), causing adverse land-use and land-cover changes [2, 15]. Urbanisation has grown to become commonplace, resulting in multiple ramifications [16]. Prevention of these ramifications should be one of the priorities of regional and spatial policy. It is because the consequences of intensive urbanisation – like the development of environmentally valuable areas, deforestation, defragmentation and/or degradation of landscape, increased air, soil, and water pollution, reduced agricultural land, and higher social and infrastructural costs – are so vast that they affect the economy, society, environment, and spatial governance. Therefore, it seems to be vital to identify factors that determine these phenomena and the spatial distribution of any trends. Decision-makers need guidelines, strategies, and analytical solutions to transform all European Union (EU) states into modern, resource-efficient, and economically-competitive countries to successfully face these adverse phenomena. The European Commission promotes this approach in its European Green Deal, which urges every EU member state to take action to improve the efficiency of resources by transforming into 'the clean circular economy', preventing degradation of biodiversity (or sometimes its complete loss) and reducing pollution.

One of the issues evident todays is the unreasonable and excessive conversion of land into buildable areas. Regardless, neither residents nor grassroots or environmental organizations have adequate tools to be heard and make meaningful statements on ungrounded and excessive conversions into buildable land. This approach is indirectly linked to participatory planning, where good practices of public responsibility and participation are employed. The goal of participatory planning is for well-informed and job-oriented public to exhibit acceptance and support for jointly chosen planning solutions with their socioeconomic, cultural, and environmental consequences [12]. Participatory planning guarantees the right to object or consent so that problems of sustainable spatial management are resolved together and local community leaders are engaged. Moreover, the reasoning behind it is that people affected by a decision should have a say in the matter. Therefore, participatory planning is a space for mediation where planning and regional policies converge and spatial planning and spatial management priorities are combined. These collisions yield sustainable socioeconomic development that respects cultural heritage [8]. The concept involves stimulation of the society and a broad, multilevel, and multicultural social dialogue, which may help develop better spatial solutions that are more acceptable to the public, leading to better use of space. This approach balances the needs of local communities and economic stakeholders with the protection and conservation of cultural assets and the natural environment. It stems from the integration of engineering, technical, and urban planning efforts with public consultations and environmental mediation.

Participation of local communities in urban planning activities is possible also thanks to WebGIS. It is referred to as a new paradigm for implementing a modern GIS spatial information system updated from spatial databases and online services. This technology provides broad and public access to spatial data for all users of the map portal [17]. The notion is consistent with the broader concept of international spatial information infrastructure. In light of Directive 2007/2/EC of the European Parliament and of the Council of 14 March 2007 establishing an Infrastructure for Spatial Information in the European Community (INSPIRE), we propose to create a European spatial information infrastructure and streamline access to spatial data. The directive has been transposed into the national Polish law with the Act of 4 March 2010 on the infrastructure for spatial information. Spatial data were not legally required to be used in urban planning – zoning plans included – before 2020. Moreover, there were no standards that would offer principles for creating digital spatial databases used in spatial planning and management. This resulted in non-uniform documentation with semantic inconsistencies. In light of the INSPIRE directive, the statutory objectives were, thus, difficult or even impossible to achieve [9]. Regulations in place from 31 October 2020 oblige authorities responsible for spatial planning and management to prepare digital planning data. The same applies to documents published before that date. Detailed guidelines can be found in the Regulation of the Minister of Development, Labour, and Technology of 26 October 2020 on spatial datasets and metadata for spatial management. This led to the need for the digitalisation of zoning plans. They also had to be published in a digital form on websites and as geoportals.

Considering the complexity of the problems at hand, we wish to emphasize the need for a search for new content and technology solutions to support spatial planning in Poland and globally. The right input that may be useful in this case is remote-sensing and satellite data collected and processed with GIS tools. GIS tools streamline the analytical process and can handle comprehensive, multi-dimensional spatial analyses. What is more, the last decade saw great advances in satellite remote sensing, artificial intelligence, and machine learning applications [5]. Note here that the search for new research directions and methods to better understand phenomena and processes in the space around us is considered critical and a priority in light of strong urbanisation trends leading to significant landscape transformations [19]. It is important also due to legal provisions, which are unable to completely protect environmentally valuable land against development [7]. The key capability needed in this regard is to be able to identify, and particularly, model structural and functional patterns that occur in space and the environment [11]. Therefore, we found a research gap that needs to be addressed: how new technologies and spatial data can be used in spatial planning. The objective of this paper is to present to the international research community the characteristics of the international research project Artificial Intelligence and Geodata for Sensibilisation of Local Communities for Sustainable Spatial Development, GeoSen.

The remainder of the paper is structured as follows: Sect. 2 describes the general characteristics of the GeoSen research project, including its conceptual and geographic areas of interest. Section 3 presents the methodology, focusing on guidelines for the design of artificial intelligence (AI) algorithms for detecting land-cover changes and spatial relationships based on urban and landscape characteristics. Section 4 ventures into the anticipated results of the analytical and project effort. The paper ends with a discussion and a summary where the potential uses of the tools are considered.

2 General Characteristic of GeoSen

GeoSen's objective is to devise an IT system to identify land-use and land-cover changes with dedicated tools and computing algorithms. The research input will be remote-sensing data at various resolutions processed with AI techniques. Eventually, the algorithms will be published as an interactive platform (web application) for visualising and verifying the results of analyses. It will stimulate the activity of participants in spatial planning, leading to effective and sustainable use of space and its resources. To this end, we will complete in-depth analyses of changes in land management, landscape, and settlement-network structure of the study areas. The macroscale research will identify the main trends and changes in land management and landscape in the study areas.

The macroscale study area covers three voivodeships in southern Poland (Małopolskie, Świętokrzyskie, and Śląskie) and two lands of a similar area in Germany (Hesse and Rhineland-Palatinate) shown in Fig. 1.

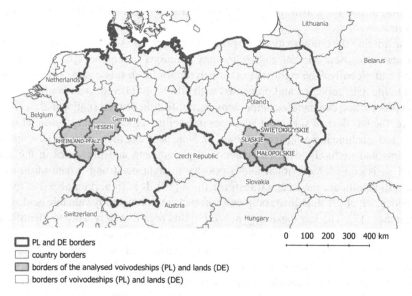

Fig. 1. Study area of GeoSen. Source: own study.

The research area in Poland was selected intentionally considering such differences in spatial management as different settlement-network and land-use structures or significantly variable landscapes and topographies. The microscale study area will cover selected Polish and German model municipalities, where land-use changes are dynamic amidst an environmentally and culturally valuable landscape.

The theme of artificial intelligence and geodata for local community sensibilisation to sustainable spatial development is part of the sustainable urban planning framework. The application of artificial intelligence and geodata in GeoSen is aimed at supporting modern spatial planning at the local level (municipalities) and regional level with artificial intelligence. The artificial intelligence systems to be used in the project are combined with remote-sensing technology (satellite imagery) for continuing recording, pattern recognition, and tracking of structural changes and land-cover and land-use changes. They also identify urban-rural relationships reflected in spatial data. The technology can manage large datasets and continuously and automatically monitor land use and land cover changes.

The planned project is also consistent with 'smart use of data' because it uses GIS spatial information systems to acquire and analyse data. The GIS tools will be used for data monitoring and management, which is crucial considering the priority of sustainable spatial management. Moreover, GeoSen will aid rational spatial management, which furthers the paradigm of sustainable rural and urban development and smart villages. The project will also contribute to the implementation of the European Commission's Green Deal postulates.

3 Research Methodology

The objective is to analyse data for the selected study areas on the macroscale to identify repeating patterns in the representative areas of the project partners – including sets of trends and tendencies in land-use and land-cover changes – to convert identifiable dependencies into a package of quantifiable analytical assumptions that can be programmed as a series of algorithms reflecting urban and landscape processes (Fig. 2).

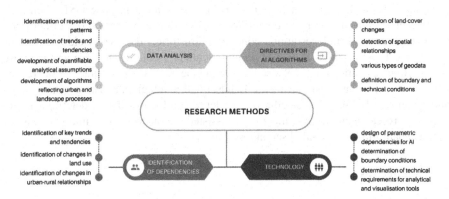

Fig. 2. Research methods and basic assumptions of GeoSen. Source: own study.

The analytical effort is expected to yield guidelines for designing AI algorithms that will detect land-cover changes and spatial relationships based on urban and landscape characteristics from various types of input data (satellite, radar, optical, high-, medium-, low-resolution, and aerial high-resolution) and define boundary and technical conditions regarding the usability of data and tools for developing analytical systems.

The analytical part will involve such items as the identification of key trends and tendencies in land-use changes and urban-rural relationships. Other planned tasks include 1) designing parametric dependencies as the foundation for the AI algorithms, 2) determining boundary conditions, that is the minimum resolution of remote-sensing data, required to identify spatial changes, and 3) designing a conceptual diagram with technical requirements for analytical and visualisation tools.

They should yield tools for analysis and visualisation as the working foundation for rural and urban development processes. The tool will be a fully functional WebGIS platform, where the results of AI analyses can be displayed. It will identify changes in land use and cover from satellite and aerial images at the microscale and macroscale. Launch of the WebGIS platform on the GEOM server and user testing.

4 Forecast Results

The value of AI-backed assessment of planning data and databases for spatial planning will grow in the future because it will facilitate managing a large amount of data and information automatically. The automation of analytical processes will help precisely define land use variability and identify trends and directions of development. With such visual tools for interactive space forming as WebGIS, residents will be able to take an active part in planning processes. It will help them visualise their conceptions and ideas regarding problems discussed by the community.

Use of radar (Sentinel-1) and visual (Sentinel-2) data offering higher terrain (10/20 m) and temporal (up to 3 days) resolutions will facilitate more precise determination of boundaries and land use directions. The application of the SuperResolution technology developed by project partners will improve both the quality and quantity of information from Landsat (from 30 m to 4 m of ground sample distance, GSD), Sentinel-2 (10 m and 20 m to 2.5 m), or Planet Scope (3.7 m to 1.5 m of GSD). Furthermore, the incorporation of high-resolution commercial historical data will yield correlations concerning Landsat and – at a later point – Sentinel-2 data in land use and land-use trends. High-resolution data will also help define the quality and accuracy of the results of work with free and easily available Landsat and Sentinel data. The auxiliary aerial photographs and commercial satellite data under test protocols will help determine future necessary research and development in AI-assisted remote sensing to improve feasible future capabilities for spatial observations.

5 Discussion

Strong anthropogenic activity is considered to be the main cause of adverse spatial and environmental transformations, which lead to socioeconomic and cultural changes according to the literature [13]. It is said to be the dominant factor in changes in the Earth's surface. Authors also emphasize the strong link between suburbanisation and urbanisation pressure [1] characterised by an intensification of the conversion of agricultural production land into developed land, mainly residential. Consequently, continuing acquisition of data on landscape changes becomes crucial to ensure ongoing monitoring of land use [3].

In Poland, land earmarking is regulated in local zoning plans. But being optional, local zoning plans have been enacted in a little over 30% of the country in 2020. The remaining areas are developed according to zoning approvals. These instruments lack long-term perspective and are often subjective. For this reason, the Polish spatial planning system is believed to be chaotic, problematic, a source of spatial chaos, and failing to ensure spatial governance according to literature and strategic government documents [20].

The project will result in an IT solution (system) that will use historical and modern remote-sensing data to determine land-use and land-cover changes. It will be the basis for identifying current development trends and forecasting future ones. The IT system will further engage local communities and other stakeholders in learning about historical changes, tracking current trends, and identifying ongoing changes in land use. Local communities will not be merely passive observers. Special tools available through the web service will empower them to make individual suggestions in an interactive interface (participatory planning). This way, they will flag important objects, such as historical sites, valuable natural assets, or spatial needs of the community.

The following short-term effects are expected: 1) an analysis of changes in land cover and land use in the study area using aerial and satellite data and artificial intelligence; 2) sensibilisation of participants in spatial planning processes to the possibility of continuous monitoring of changes in land use and land cover using remote-sensing data; 3) application of the tools in geomarketing analyses to identify growth areas, improve sale efficiency, and reorganise sale regions.

The following long-term effects are expected: 1) an increase in public participation and awareness of local communities regarding spatial planning; 2) making up-to-date data on land-use and land-cover changes available for study work and then planning documents as needed by spatial planning experts; 3) broader collaboration among businesses and research institutions in the field of AI in spatial management; 4) contribution to urban and rural sustainable development through spatial planning processes that employ the tools for analysis and visualisation of land-use and land-cover changes devised under the project.

6 Conclusions

The IT solution (system) for generating, processing, analysing, and visualising land-use and land-cover changes from remote-sensing data will enrich the toolbox of the participating organisations. Furthermore, it can be used by public administration (especially local governments), urban planners and architects, and research institutions for informed land management both today and in a long-term perspective. This, in turn, implements the rural sustainable development paradigm of 'smart villages', and the European Green Deal.

The project's results will help its partners create a practical guide for the tools to promote and commercialise the results. The guide will contain examples of how the system can be used (analyses, algorithms) to aid decision-making and planning. The knowledge capital gained under the project can be put to work in future innovative research projects and endeavours. It will contribute to expanding and improving common experiences and skill sets, which might be valuable in future research-programme applications.

The final product of the project will be an interactive platform (web application) for visualising and verifying the effects of algorithms with a responsive user interface and a remote sensing–data algorithm to support rural and urban sustainable development.

The products will aid spatial planning on the local and regional levels. Note that the microscale analysis is crucial. Sustainable rural development and smart villages are decided and managed on the municipal level. In addition, international partners will contribute a broader outlook on the matters and methods for handling the issues in other countries.

The planned future application of the IT solution (system) may contribute to 1) the identification of the land-use, land-cover, and any structural changes thereof following Earth observations (remote sensing, satellite imagery) using artificial intelligence; 2) the improvement of the awareness of local decision-makers and population regarding the practical implementation of sustainable development and the European Green Deal through visualisation of historical data and current changes; 3) the initiation of an effort to further the sustainable development of rural areas, smart villages, and the European Green Deal, including promotion of balanced urban-rural relationships.

The interactive and responsive 'system' will fetch spatial data that can then be subject to public consultations. This may yield multiple alternative planning solutions for decision-makers to select a socially acceptable one. Moreover, the project will improve the availability of spatial information and its impact range. It will also create the opportunity to educate local communities regarding the environmental consequences of irrational zoning of buildable land. This can help shape environmentally-responsible attitudes and a greater public acceptance for environmentally-friendly solutions in line with the spirit of the green deal. It would be a meaningful and tangible contribution to improved awareness of sustainable spatial development.

Acknowledgment. The research was carried out as part of the scientific project entitled: Artificial intelligence and geodata for sensibilisation of local communities for sustainable spatial development GeoSen (WPN/4/65/GEOSEN/2022) co-financed by The National Centre for Research and Development in Poland from the 4th German – Polish call for bilateral R&D cooperation in the field of digitization of the economy. Website: https://geosen.urk.edu.pl (accessed on 27 April 2023).

References

1. Cegielska, K., Kukulska-Kozieł, A., Salata, T., Piotrowski, P., Szylar, M.: Shannon entropy as a peri-urban landscape metric: concentration of anthropogenic land cover element. J. Spatial Sci. **64**(3), 469–489 (2019). https://doi.org/10.1080/14498596.2018.1482803
2. Cegielska, K., et al.: Land use and land cover changes in post-socialist countries: some observations from Hungary and Poland. Land Use Policy **78**, 1–18 (2018). https://doi.org/10.1016/j.landusepol.2018.06.017
3. Czesak, B., Różycka-Czas, R., Salata, T., Dixon-Gough, R., Hernik, J.: Determining the intangible: detecting land abandonment at local scale. Remote Sens. **13**(6), 1166 (2021). https://doi.org/10.3390/rs13061166
4. Kong, F., Yin, H., Nakagoshi, N., James, P.: Simulating urban growth processes incorporating a potential model with spatial metrics. Ecol. Ind. **20**, 82–91 (2012). https://doi.org/10.1016/j.ecolind.2012.02.003
5. Gawronek, P., Noszczyk, T.: Does more mean better? Remote-sensing data for monitoring sustainable redevelopment of a historical granary in Mydlniki, Kraków. Herit. Sci. **11**(1), 1–17 (2023). https://doi.org/10.1186/s40494-023-00864-0

6. Helfenstein, J., et al.: Farmer surveys in Europe suggest that specialized, intensive farms were more likely to perceive negative impacts from COVID-19. Agron. Sustain. Dev. **42**(5), 84 (2022). https://doi.org/10.1007/s13593-022-00820-5

7. Hernik, J., Gawroński, K., Dixon-Gough, R.: Social and economic conflicts between cultural landscapes and rural communities in the English and Polish systems. Land Use Policy **30**(1), 800–813 (2013). https://doi.org/10.1016/j.landusepol.2012.06.006

8. Knapik, W., Król, K.: Inclusion of vanishing cultural heritage in a sustainable rural development strategy–prospects, opportunities, recommendations. Sustainability **15**(4), 3656 (2023). https://doi.org/10.3390/su15043656

9. Król, K.: Current trends in the usage of the digital version of the local master plan (eMPZP), as illustrated with the example of Tomice municipality. Geomatics, Landmanag. Landscape **3**, 23–33 (2018)

10. Kudas, D., Wnęk, A., Tátošová, L.: Land use mix in functional urban areas of selected central European countries from 2006 to 2012. Int. J. Environ. Res. Public Health **19**(22), 15233 (2022). https://doi.org/10.3390/ijerph192215233

11. Kukulska-Kozieł, A.: Buildable land overzoning. Have new planning regulations in Poland resolved the issue? Land Use Policy **124**, 106440 (2023). https://doi.org/10.1016/j.landusepol.2022.106440

12. Legacy, C.: Is there a crisis of participatory planning? Plan. Theory **16**(4), 425–442 (2017)

13. Noszczyk, T., Cegielska, K., Rogatka, K., Starczewski, T.: Exploring green areas in Polish cities in context of anthropogenic land use changes. Anthropocene Rev. **10**(3), 710–731 (2022). https://doi.org/10.1177/20530196221112137

14. Noszczyk, T., Rutkowska, A., Hernik, J.: Determining changes in land use structure in Małopolska using statistical methods. Pol. J. Env. Stud. **26**(1), 211–220 (2017). https://doi.org/10.15244/pjoes/64913

15. Różycka-Czas, R., Czesak, B., Cegielska, K.: Towards evaluation of environmental spatial order of natural valuable landscapes in suburban areas: evidence from Poland. Sustainability **11**(23), 6555 (2019). https://doi.org/10.3390/su11236555

16. Różycka-Czas, R., Czesak, B., Staszel, A.: Which polish cities sprawl the most. Land **10**(12), 1291 (2021). https://doi.org/10.3390/land10121291

17. Salter, J.D., Campbell, C., Journeay, M., Sheppard, S.R.J.: The digital workshop: exploring the use of interactive and immersive visualisation tools in participatory planning. J. Env. Manag. **90**(6), 2090–2101 (2009)

18. Simon, D.: Urban Environments: Issues on the Peri-Urban Fringe. Annu. Rev. Environ. Resour. **33**(1), 167–185 (2008)

19. Starczewski, T., Rogatka, K., Kukulska-Kozieł, A., Noszczyk, T., Cegielska, K.: Urban green resilience: experience from post-industrial cities in Poland. Geoscience Front. **14**(4), 101560 (2023). https://doi.org/10.1016/j.gsf.2023.101560

20. Stelmach-Fita, B.: European land use spatial data sources and their role in integrated planning: opportunities and challenges for Poland. Land **10**(11), 1138 (2021). https://doi.org/10.3390/land10111138

21. Wnęk, A., Kudas, D., Stych, P.: National level land-use changes in functional urban areas in Poland, Slovakia, and Czechia. Land **10**(1), 39 (2021). https://doi.org/10.3390/land10010039

Wave-U-Net Speech Denoising

Tomasz Walczyna[(✉)] and Zbigniew Piotrowski

Military University of Technology, Warsaw, Poland
{tomasz.walczyna,zbigniew.piotrowski}@wat.edu.pl

Abstract. The paper will present a method for de-noising human speech using Wave-U-Net, specifically the Demucs v3 model - an algorithm for separating sounds made by instruments in music tracks. This version of the model is characterized by the use of not only a wave but also a spectrogram. It is a hybrid method. Since the previous Demucs version has already been used in de-noising scenarios, a comparative analysis of the two ways was carried out in the reference. In addition, the effect of the cost function on the learning process, and the final result, was examined. The model was trained on white noise and noise from potential backgrounds occurring in everyday life. When trained on the same data, the newer algorithm provides better results in a shorter training time.

Keywords: Speech Denoising · Artificial Intelligence · Deep Learning

1 Introduction

Speech de-noising is a long-known problem. Given a noisy input signal, we filter out unwanted noise without degrading the signal of interest. One can imagine someone talking during a video conference and music playing in the background. The speech-denoising system removes background noise to improve the speech signal in this situation. In addition to many other use cases, this application is essential for video and audio conferencing, where noise can significantly reduce speech intelligibility.

Classic solutions for speech denoising typically use generative modeling. The idea is to use statistical methods, such as Gaussian mixtures, to build a model of the noise of interest. Then, we can use it to recover the source (clean) audio from the input noise signal. However, developing neural networks shows that deep learning often outperforms such solutions when extensive data sets are available.

In a real-world environment, speech signals are inevitably disturbed by ambient noise, transmission media, and electrical noise inside communication devices. This interference significantly degrades the performance of the speech processing system and affects speech quality. Speech de-noising aims to restore clear speech from noise-polluted signals, crucial for applications such as automatic speech recognition (ASR) and hearing aids. Many classical denoising and speech enhancement methods based on the statistical difference between speech and noise characteristics have been proposed, such as spectrum subtraction [3], Wiener filtering [13], the subarray method [7], nonnegative matrix factorization (NMF) [18], and minimum mean square error (MMSE) [8]. A

K. S. Soliman (Ed.): IBIMA-AI 2023, CCIS 2101, pp. 52–57, 2024.
https://doi.org/10.1007/978-3-031-62843-6_5

shortcoming of conventional methods is that their effectiveness significantly decreases in non-stationary, noisy environments (chirping birds, traffic, etc.). Wiener filter, among others, requires two separate audio signals to take full advantage of its benefits. In many situations, having a two-microphone system is practical, but in more general cases, the ability to process noise from a single stream would be beneficial. With classical methods, there can also be noticeable speech distortion in the audio in cases where the spectral properties of the background noise overlap with those of the speech. The subtraction nature of the filter can remove parts of speech that sound similar to background noise. With the development of deep learning, many of these problems have been solved. Deep learning methods attempt to model the nonlinear relationship between mixture and pure speech signals without knowledge of the noise statistics. With the use of a learning set, respectively, it is possible to train the model in such a way that it filters out the noise in a particular case.

Although the work mainly oscillates around Demucs architecture [6], it is also worth mentioning the current state of the art using deep neural networks in solving the problem. The deep learning approach is mainly based on many training datasets. Deep neural networks contain many non-linear hidden layers, showing great potential for capturing complex relationships between noise and clean utterances. Many papers have compared trained models for de-noising or speech separation [2, 9, 17]. For removing noise from images, a common way is to use classical auto-encoders or U-Net-type architectures [12]. The same applies to audio - these are the most common solutions [11]. However, due to the temporal nature of sound, algorithm developers also implement models based on recursion, using sample sequentiality or attentional mechanisms [17]. Many algorithms [5, 6, 16] combine these solutions and make further, different improvements. In addition to working on the sound, some solutions use other information specific to the chosen problem [1]. The Demucs v3 model [4] was chosen for the primary analysis of the application to the de-noising process because of its construction that includes both U-net and LSTM architectures and attentional mechanisms that are often used in the process. In addition to the model's basic structure, there are other aspects, such as the nature of the processed signal. In the case of sound, these are most often wavelets or spectrograms. The Demucs model analyzed in version three is distinguished by its hybrid nature, enhancing performance [4].

2 Proposed Solution

Analyzed Hybrid Demucs extends the original architecture with multi-domain analysis and prediction capabilities. The model consists of a time branch, a spectral branch, and shared layers. The temporal branch processes an input waveform like a standard Demucs. The hybrid architecture is shown in the figure below (Fig. 1).

The proposed solution is a modification of HDemucs applied to a different problem than the original one. The differences are: the training datasets are different, and an additional dataset for noise has been introduced; the training procedure for the problem has been changed; different types of cost functions have been tested.

The changes made to the model are minor. Within the configuration of such parameters as the number of initially hidden channels, among others, the previous version of

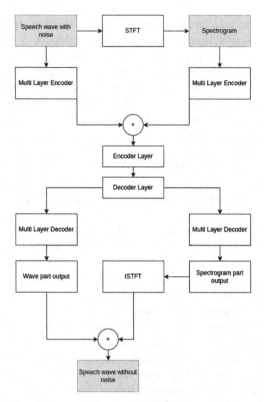

Fig. 1. Demucs hybrid architecture. The time, STFT, and spectral encoder process the input waveform. The two representations are summed when their dimensions overlap. The decoder is built symmetrically. The output spectrogram goes through the ISTFT and is summed with the waveform outputs, giving the final model output.

Denoiser [5] was suggested, and the same parameters were used in the solution. In addition, as the source task posed to HDemucs [4] was sound separation, the model expected several outputs. In the solution, the goal is only noise removal, so the dimensionality of the output was reduced to 1 - sound without noise.

The task was to de-noise speech - in the first part, comparing the initial stage of training for different models and cost functions using such datasets as:

- LibriSpeech ASR [10] corpus as a source of clean speech of various speakers; in total, about 500 h of recordings were used
- MUSAN [14] - dataset containing various types of sound recordings representing possible background, noise

In order to create a dataset containing noise recordings, recordings taken from the above datasets were combined during training. The noise on the utterances was applied with arbitrary power and offset, so the model received a completely different sound sample as input each time. In addition, 10% of the dataset contained samples containing white noise instead of those obtained from the MUSAN dataset. The sound was sampled at 16000 Hz, and the length of the segment on which the model was trained was 2 s.

The training procedure for analyzing different model configurations took about 25,000 iterations, i.e., six epochs. The Adam optimizer with an initial learning step of $4e^{(-4)}$ was used as part of the training. In addition, a scheduler was used that reduced the learning rate every 7,000 iterations by half. The input was given samples in batches equal to 32. Every 500 iterations, validations were performed on the test samples. As part of the training progress tracking, and was used with a configured Sweeper to track and compare different types of cost functions and models. As part of the cost functions comparing the model output with the clean audio extracted from the LibriSpeech dataset, they used:

- Manhattan Distance - L1
- Multi-resolution STFT [19] implemented in the aura loss [15] module. This cost function compares spectrograms for a different number of bins in a window. This cost function uses three sizes - 512, 1024, and 2048.
- Random-resolution STFT implemented in the aura loss module This cost function, compared to its predecessor, is characterized by random variation in the number of bins in the window for each iteration. As in the predecessor, three quantities were used, but they range here from 16 to 16384 (with a multiplication step of the number 2 - 16, 32, 64....).

3   Results

In order to compare the training process, the graphs obtained when training the two models for three different cost functions are shown below (Figs. 2 and 3).

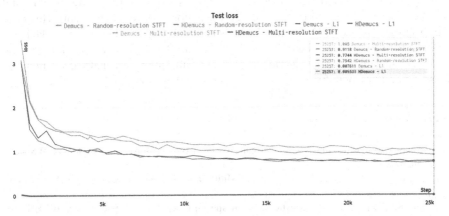

Fig. 2. Test data cost function for both models and three different cost functions

As can be seen in the accompanying graphs, HDemucs achieve a lower cost function value and thus provides better results in de-noising.

The chosen cost function also has a significant impact on the training process. Despite using the Multi-resolution STFT cost function in the source project (the previous version

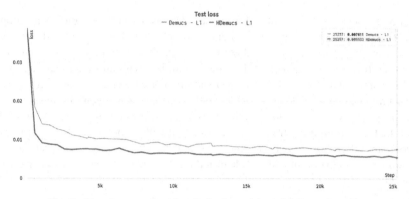

Fig. 3. Test data cost function for both models and L1 cost function

of Demucs), this function, in this case, gives worse results. This is dictated by the fact that when the L1 function is used, there is no specific crunching in the resulting audio tracks due to the loss of phase information in the STFT. This situation occurs only when the model is trained long enough or more straightforwardly. However, in the case of shorter or more complex training data, a model trained on the L1 metric performs worse in removing the noise. The Random-resolution STFT cost function achieves similar results to Multi-resolution STFT.

4   Conclusions

The above work shows the more significant potential of the new version of Demucs in denoising speech compared to its predecessor. The choice of the cost function used is vital if the evaluated values are in different representations (wave/spectrogram). However, the spectrogram-based cost function is characterized by faster achievement of the noise removal goal with concomitant speech degradation. The wave-based cost function, on the other hand, quickly converges to a clear sound path. However, it inefficiently removes noise. Combining both functions is a good solution that works well in practice.

References

1. Triantafyllos, A., Chung, J.S., Zisserman, A.: The Conversation: Deep Audio-Visual Speech Enhancement' (2018)
2. Arian, A., Kehtarnavaz, N.: A Review of Multi-Objective Deep Learning Speech Denoising Methods (2020)
3. Boll, S.: Suppression of Acoustic Noise in Speech Using Spectral Subtraction. IEEE Trans. Acoustics, Speech, and Signal Processing **27**(2), 113–20. https://doi.org/10.1109/TASSP. 1979.1163209 (1979)
4. Défossez, A.: Hybrid Spectrogram and Waveform Source Separation (2022)
5. Defossez, A., Synnaeve, G., Adi, Y.: Real Time Speech Enhancement in the Waveform Domain (2020)
6. Défossez, A., Nicolas U., Bottou, L., Bach, F.: Music Source Separation in the Waveform Domain (2021)

7. Ephraim, Y., Van Trees, H.L.: A Signal subspace approach for speech enhancement. IEEE International Conference on Acoustics Speech and Signal Processing, vol. 2, pp. 355–58 (1993). https://doi.org/10.1109/ICASSP.1993.319311

8. Loizou, P.C.: Speech Enhancement: Theory and Practice, Second Edition, 2nd edn. CRC Press, Boca Raton (2013)

9. Michelsanti, D., et al.: An overview of deep-learning-based audio-visual speech enhancement and separation. IEEE/ACM Transactions on Audio, Speech, and Language Processing **29**, 1368–96 (2021). https://doi.org/10.1109/TASLP.2021.3066303

10. Vassil, P., Chen, G., Povey, D., Khudanpur, S.: Librispeech: An ASR Corpus Based on Public Domain Audio Books. In: 2015 IEEE International Conference on Acoustics, Speech and Signal Processing (ICASSP), pp. 5206–10 (2015)

11. Ashutosh, P., Wang, D.: TCNN: temporal convolutional neural network for real-time speech enhancement in the time domain. In: ICASSP 2019 - 2019 IEEE International Conference on Acoustics, Speech and Signal Processing (ICASSP), pp. 6875–79 (2019)

12. Olaf, R., Fischer, Ph., Brox, Th.: U-Net: Convolutional Networks for Biomedical Image Segmentation. In: Navab, N., Hornegger, J., Wells, W.M., Frangi, A.F. (eds.) Medical Image Computing and Computer-Assisted Intervention – MICCAI 2015, Lecture Notes in Computer Science, pp. 234–41. Springer International Publishing, Cham (2015)

13. Pascal, S., Filho, J.: Speech enhancement based on a priori signal to noise estimation **2**, 629–32 (1996)

14. Snyder, D., Chen, G., Povey, D.: MUSAN: A Music, Speech, and Noise Corpus (2015)

15. Steinmetz, C.J., Pons, J.P.S., Serrà, J.: Automatic Multitrack Mixing with a Differentiable Mixing Console of Neural Audio Effects (2020)

16. Tan, K., Wang, D.: A Convolutional Recurrent Neural Network for Real-Time Speech Enhancement (2018)

17. Kai, W., He, B., Zhu, W.P.: TSTNN: two-stage transformer based neural network for speech enhancement in the time domain. In: ICASSP 2021 - 2021 IEEE International Conference on Acoustics, Speech and Signal Processing (ICASSP), pp. 7098–7102 (2021). https://doi.org/10.1109/ICASSP39728.2021.9413740

18. Wilson, K.W., Raj, B., Smaragdis, P., Divakaran, A.: Speech Denoising Using Nonnegative Matrix Factorization with Priors. In: 2008 IEEE International Conference on Acoustics, Speech and Signal Processing, pp. 4029–32. ICASSP (2008). https://doi.org/10.1109/ICASSP.2008.4518538

19. Ryuichi, Y., Song, E., Kim, J.M.: Parallel Wavegan: a fast waveform generation model based on generative adversarial networks with multi-resolution spectrogram. In: ICASSP 2020 - 2020 IEEE International Conference on Acoustics, Speech and Signal Processing (ICASSP), pp. 6199–6203 (2020)

Neural Network Compression

Marta Bistroń[(✉)] and Zbigniew Piotrowski

Military University of Technology, Gen. Sylwestra Kaliskiego 2, 00-902 Warsaw, Poland
{marta.bistron,zbigniew.piotrowski}@wat.edu.pl

Abstract. The paper presents the problem of neural network compression, focusing mainly on deep neural networks (DNNs). The negative effects of overparameterisation of models and basic compression techniques used in practice are discussed. For each method, several current implementations described in the literature are presented, describing their operating principles and achieved effects at given model compression ratios.

Keywords: neural networks · neural network compression · decomposition · pruning · quantization

1 Introduction

Neural network compression is the process of reducing the size of a network without significantly impairing its performance, which was achieved during training. With the increasingly widespread access to high-end computing machines equipped with GPUs or TPUs, as well as easier access to massive data sets, developing highly efficient and performant neural network algorithms has become increasingly easier [1]. It often happens that models are overparameterized at the design stage to achieve high accuracy, resulting in high memory consumption [2], and thus also high energy consumption, which has a harmful impact on the environment. The recently popular ChatGPT tool, developed by OpenAI, is characterised by extremely high performance and accuracy of responses, but due to its approximately 1,000 times larger model size than typical language models, the training time is estimated to be around 355 years of computational time, assuming that the model was trained on a standard neural network chip or GPU [3].

In addition to ecological issues, the implementation of a very complex neural algorithm on end devices with limited memory resources and battery life is also a challenge, as in the case of mobile devices. The development of smartphones, laptops, and other mobile devices has also contributed to the development of artificial intelligence-based applications, particularly dedicated to mobile devices - Mobile Deep Learning Applications (MDLAs) [4].

Due to the increasing number of parameters and the complexity of neural models, neural network compression has become an important branch in the development of machine learning models. There are many techniques that can be applied to reduce the size of the network without affecting its efficiency, including quantisation, low-dimensional representation learning, reducing of insignificant connections and layers,

K. S. Soliman (Ed.): IBIMA-AI 2023, CCIS 2101, pp. 58–61, 2024.
https://doi.org/10.1007/978-3-031-62843-6_6

compression of weight matrices, as well as pruning and scaling. The ultimate result of the performed operations is not only the reduction of the network size and necessary memory resources, but also the improvement of performance, defined by shortening the time of network training and evaluation.

In the further part of the article, selected neural network compression techniques and examples of their applications described in the literature are presented.

2 Methods of Neural Network Compression

Any method of reducing the size of a neural network model that allows for a decrease in resource requirements and overall improvement in model performance is called neural network compression. Depending on the specific model, different methods or combinations of methods may be necessary. Below are described the most popular compression methods.

2.1 Quantisation

Quantization involves replacing the values of the neural network weights with quantized values belonging to a discrete interval. In practice, the conversion of weights that are real numbers to fixed-point 8-bit numbers is used. Quantisation significantly reduces memory and computation requirements, with only a slight loss of model accuracy.

In [5], the authors proposed a compression method that utilizes weight quantization and lossless source coding. Vector quantisation was used to compensate for the main problems associated with entropy-constrained scalar quantisation (ECSQ). To develop the best vector quantiser, the authors used a modified Linde-Buzo-Gray (LBG) algorithm. Combining the developed random quantization method with lossless source coding allowed for the compression of AlexNet [6], MobileNet [7], and ShuffleNet [8] architectures with a compression ratio of about 10.

Quantisation-aware training is an additional support for the quantisation method, which allows for the application of weight quantisation techniques without loss of accuracy because quantisation occurs during the model training stage. The accuracy loss that occurs during conventional training and subsequent quantisation is compensated for by quantisation-aware training. During this method, the model simulates the transition to a lower precision level, while during the backward propagation step, the correct level of weight accuracy is maintained, resulting in quantisation error that is optimised through the appropriate selection of parameters during the training procedure.

2.1.1 Pruning

Pruning involves removing nodes from a neural network that do not significantly impact the final results of the model's operation. In this way, the number of network parameters is reduced, allowing for a decrease in memory resource requirements and the number of required computations. In the review article [9], the authors distinguish several basic methods that allow for obtaining a compressed model.

Depending on the structure, non-structural pruning can create an extensive (sparse) neural network, which, despite fewer parameters, may be a difficult architecture to learn due to its incompatibility with modern libraries and hardware. The second approach is structural pruning, in which entire neurons, filters, or channels are removed within groups, which facilitates the use of hardware and software for optimizing computations [10].

Node reduction is achieved through the evaluation of the absolute values of model parameters. Methods comparing results locally, such as within a layer, or globally by comparing parameter values in independent parts of the model architecture are distinguished. Pruning can apply to all weights at once within one step, iteratively in several steps, or dynamically described by a more complex function.

In the publication [11], the authors compared the performance of two pruning methods for a fully connected network (FCN) and a convolutional neural network (CNN). Two approaches were used: magnitude-based pruning and random pruning. The basic element of the analysis is the iterative demonstration that the difference between the pruned and target weight matrices, as well as the difference between the results for a given layer in the pruned and target networks, is small. The paper presents a general theoretical analysis that can also be applied to other neural network models.

2.1.2 Matrix Decomposition

The idea of the method is to decompose the weight matrix of a neural network into several smaller matrices, which allows for reducing memory requirements and computational complexity. There are many known methods of matrix decomposition, with one of the most popular being SVD - Singular Value Decomposition. The method is based on factorising the matrix into three matrices according to the formula:

$$A = UWV^T,$$

where:
U - the matrix of orthonormal eigenvectors of AA^T;
V^T - the transpose of the matrix containing orthonormal eigenvectors of A^TA;
W - the diagonal matrix of singular values, which are the square roots of the eigenvalues of A^TA.

In [12], the authors present a compression method based on SVD decomposition, but omitting the fine-tuning step, which is necessary in the classical approach to improve the initial compression results. The authors modified the way of approximating values by applying an approach less sensitive to outliers. The method was tested for several natural language processing networks: BERT, DistilBERT, RoBERT and XLNet. For all models, the proposed method allowed for higher accuracy at the same compression rate compared to conventional SVD.

Another approach is tensor decomposition. This is any scheme for representing a data tensor as a sequence of elementary operations defined for other, usually simpler tensors. Commonly used schemes are tensor rank decomposition, higher-order SVD, Tucker decomposition, or hierarchical Tucker decomposition.

In their work [13], the authors used selected tensor decomposition methods to compress a deep neural network model. They used the ADMM (alternating direction method of multipliers) optimisation technique that solves convex optimisation problems by dividing the tensor into smaller parts. According to the approach, the entire DNN model is trained in the original structure, but gradually acquires the desired low tensor rank characteristic. Then, decomposition and fine-tuning to high accuracy are performed. The authors verified the effects of the method on various classification models for the CIFAR dataset. At compression rates of 2.3 and 2.4, an improvement in accuracy of several percentage points compared to the original models was achieved.

3 Summary

The compression of neural networks is currently a significant research problem. Huge models with billions of parameters are suboptimal both economically and environmentally - due to the carbon footprint generated during training. The need to solve this problem results in the emergence of further variants of compression methods using various optimization algorithms discussed in the article.

References

1. Marinó, G.C., Petrini, A., Malchiodi, D., Frasca, M.: Deep neural networks compression: a comparative survey and choice recommendations. Neurocomputing **520**, 152–170 (2023)
2. Allen-Zhu, Z., Li, Y., Liang Y.: Learning and generalization in overparameterized neural networks, going beyond two layers. Advances in Neural Information Processing Systems, 32 (2019)
3. Martineau, K.: Shrinking deep learning's carbon footprint. MIT Quest for Intelligence (2020). [Online], [Retrieved March 24, 2023], https://news.mit.edu/2020/shrinking-deep-learning-carbon-footprint-0807
4. Wang, Y., et al.: A survey on deploying mobile deep learning applications: a systemic and technical perspective. Digital Commun. Netw. **8**(1), 1–17 (2022)
5. Choi, Y., El-Khamy, M., Lee, J.: Universal deep neural network compression. IEEE J. Select. Topi. Sign. Proce. **14**(4), 715–726 (2020)
6. Krizhevsky, A., Sutskever, I., Hinton, G.E.: ImageNet classification with deep convolutional neural networks. Proc. Adv. Neural Inf. Process. Syst., pp. 1097–1105 (2012)
7. Howard, A.G., Zhu, M., Chen, B., et al.: MobileNets: Efficient convolutional neural networks for mobile vision applications. International Journal of Intelligence Science **11**(1) (2017)
8. Zhang, X., Zhou, X., Lin, M., Sun, J.: ShuffleNet: An extremely efficient convolutional neural network for mobile devices. Proc. IEEE Conf. Comput. Vision Pattern Recognit., pp. 6848–6856 (2018)
9. Blalock, D., Ortiz, J.J.G., Frankle, J., Guttag, J.: What is the state of neural network pruning? Proceedings of Machine Learning and Systems (2020)
10. Li, H., Kadav, A., Durdanovic, I., Samet, H., Graf, H.P.: Pruning filters for efficient convnets, arXiv preprint arXiv:1608.08710 (2016)
11. Qijan, X., Klabjan, D.: A probablilistic approach to neural network pruning. Proceedings of the 38 th International Conference on Machine Learning (2021)
12. Tukan, M., Maalouf, A., Weksler, M., Feldman, D.: No Fine-Tuning, No Cry: Robust SVD for Compressing Deep Networks. Sensors **21**(5599) (2021)
13. Yin, M., Sui, Y., Liao, S., Yuan, B.: Towards Efficient Tensor Decomposition-Based DNN Model Compression with Optimization Framework. Computer Vision and Pattern Recognition Conference CVPR'2021 (2021)

Expanding the Capabilities of Voice User Interface for Math Formula Editor Through Interactive Commands

Agnieszka Bier[✉] and Zdzislaw Sroczynski

Faculty of Applied Mathematics, Silesian University of Technology, Gliwice, Poland
{agnieszka.bier,zdzislaw.sroczynski}@polsl.pl

Abstract. In this paper we present the concept and implementation of the voice-controlled editing tool of complex mathematical notation. In our previous works ([2, 3]), we introduced the basic system, which enables both dictation and reading of mathematical expressions in nearly natural language. This work describes an enhancement of the basic solution, that allows for editing existing formulas using voice commands. The main challenge in this task is to navigate properly across the expression to get the desired accuracy on corrections, insertions and deletions of particular symbols. We address this problem by extending the basic command set with commands referring to the graphical visualization of the edited expression and combining them with the programmed internal structure of particular expression components.

Keywords: voice user interface (VUI) · verbalization · interactive command · and parsing mathematical notation

1 Introduction

The dynamic increase in the computational power of computer hardware observed in recent years has made speech recognition and generation available on regular office computers (laptops or desktops) as well as popular mobile devices. Natural speech synthesis has already reached a quality that makes distinguishing the result from a human narrator's recording difficult. Simultaneously, speech recognition can be carried out with accuracy allowing for effective dictation of the text. As a consequence, more and more attempts to implement voice-based user interfaces instead of standard input/output devices such as a monitor, keyboard, mouse, or touchscreen are taken within various application areas. Human-computer interaction (HCI) solutions using natural voice can be found in self-service store checkouts, cars, smart speakers, or popular mobile devices. In most cases, they rely on an appropriate command dictionary. The output information is presented in graphic, verbal, or mixed form depending on the context. Designed in this way, the interaction guarantees a user experience (UX) similar to an interpersonal conversation, significantly reducing the need for training and familiarization with computer systems' operation principles. This is particularly evident in solutions that support physically or visually impaired persons, for whom alternative methods of communication with a computer system are often the only acceptable solution.

© The Author(s), under exclusive license to Springer Nature Switzerland AG 2024
K. S. Soliman (Ed.): IBIMA-AI 2023, CCIS 2101, pp. 62–70, 2024.
https://doi.org/10.1007/978-3-031-62843-6_7

Voice user interfaces (VUIs) are becoming increasingly popular due to the advancements in speech recognition technology and the growing demand for a more intuitive and natural way of interacting with computers. Synthetic speech is used to read messages, commands, and longer texts, creating the illusion of communication with a live speaker. In recent years, there has been widespread use of voice bots for marketing purposes, including sales automation, promotion of offers, as well as servicing and navigation in automatic customer service centers (call centers), voicemail, or banking transaction systems. The voice interface is also an important component of automatic translators, which can both translate spoken text in real-time and synthesize the correct pronunciation of translated fragments simultaneously into multiple languages. Voice messages are also essential to interactive self-service Point of Sale (POS) terminals, such as self-checkout machines. They guide the customer through the process of registering products in the cart, payment, and resolving any issues that arise.

In turn, human-machine communication through a voice interface, i.e. dictating commands, text messages, or control messages, has become a common and convenient solution, especially in situations and on devices that, by their nature, make it difficult to enter text easily using a keyboard. Examples include control messages for in-car devices in modern cars or intelligent multimedia devices – TVs, speakers and cell phones [12]. Communication is often two-way: it is possible to dictate an e-mail or SMS message as well as to have it read synthetically by the device. These solutions are also used to support disabled persons, including those with visual or hearing impairments or upper limb disabilities [9]. Commonly used systems include Siri and Cortana, as well as accessibility options and screen readers: "VoiceOver" in the Apple iOS system, "Talkback" in the Google Android system McTear and Callejas [13], "Dictation and device control" in the Windows system, as well as audio description and/or transcription of graphic and video files embedded on websites.

In this paper, we present a particular example of the design and application of a voice user interfaces for editing mathematical content. The developed tool can be used as an educational assistance and enables effective human-computer communication using natural speech.

2 Design of the Voice User Interface for Mathematical Content

Implementing a voice interface between a user and a computer system should enable effective and precise human-computer communication. This is particularly important for systems operating on complex data structures, such as long mathematical expressions. The typical approach to editing and processing such data leverages document description languages similar to programming languages (LaTeX, MathML), or mouse-controlled visual editors, or solutions that operate on images (e.g., generated on a touch screen or graphics tablet) and their automatic analysis, followed by conversion into a structured form. Verbalization, i.e., the conversion of structural notation into natural spoken form, as well as the ability to dictate an expression with automatic interpretation and conversion into a structured form, are two essential elements that allow for the design of a complete voice interface for editing mathematical expressions. Such an interface is crucial in e-learning solutions for visually and physically impaired people [1] and as a tool for visualizing mathematical formulas in other contexts.

In this paper we focus on the parsing component of the whole math editing pipeline, i.e. transforming the captured verbal form of the expression into its symbolic representation and vice versa. For a comprehensive review of speech recognition approaches for mathematical expressions we refer the reader to [8, 10, 11, 14–16].

The semantics of mathematical notation is determined not only by the meaning of individual symbols and special characters (e.g., sums, roots, integrals) but also by their mutual graphical arrangement (e.g., limit over n vs limit of n) and the context or subject area (e.g., vector vs. point vs. matrix). The above characteristics make it challenging to automate the reading and writing of mathematical notation based on a set of voice commands [7]. In natural language, the same mathematical formula can be read in many equivalent ways. For example, the fraction 1/n can be read as "1 divided by n", "1 over n", "1 in the numerator and n in the denominator" or "one nth". Therefore, in the process of verbalizing mathematical notation, it is essential to establish a set of rules and strictly adhere to them when orally introducing or reading formulas.

Our "Formula Editor" allows for visual editing, dictation, searching, and verbalization of saved mathematical expressions [3]. In the described tool (see Fig. 1), verbalization rules were designed and implemented for basic types of mathematical notation, such as roots, fractions, sums, products, limits, etc. Each rule consists of a basic command (a keyword, e.g. "fraction") and supporting commands that aim to reflect the graphical arrangement and interdependence between symbols within a given rule (e.g., "in the numerator", "in the denominator"). In many cases, to obtain unambiguous notation, it is also necessary to indicate the end of the expression to which the given command applies (e.g. "end of the fraction").

The result of dictating a mathematical formula is transmitted to the editor using a mobile assistant application, which receives the sound stream from the input device and transcribes the words into text format. The main processing step for the input text is implemented in the Editor in the form of the above mentioned rules. Each rule is defined as:

```
natural_language_phrase~internal_format_EQED
```

where ~ (tilde) is a separator, the left side is the command content, and the right side is the command notation in the EQED format, an internal format of the "Formula Editor" consisting of a set of LaTeX macro definitions.

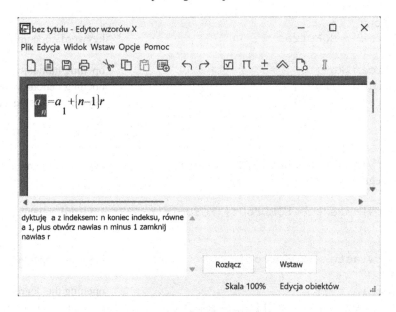

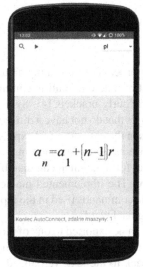

Fig. 1. Graphic user interface of the "Formula Editor" environment supporting the editing of mathematical expressions using a voice interface (MS Windows application on the left, mobile assistant application on the right).

Below we provide some examples of rule definition notations for fractions and roots in Polish:

Fraction:

`ułamek~ \EQEDfrac`	keyword opening the fraction
`w liczniku~{`	opening numerator
`w mianowniku~}{`	opening denominator
`koniec ułamka~}`	keyword closing the fraction

Root:

`pierwiastek stopnia~\EQEDroot{`	keyword opening the root of degree
`pierwiastek z~\EQEDroot{\EQEDplain{}}{`	keyword opening the root of
`pierwiastek~\EQEDroot{`	keyword opening the root of
`stopnia z~}{`	opening the degree
`pod pierwiastkiem~}{`	opening the argument
`koniec pierwiastka~}`	keyword closing the root

These rules illustrate the process of translating natural language speech into a structural notation based on a set of macro definition commands consistent with the syntax of LaTeX, with arguments in curly brackets [4]. Symbols #, @, and $ have also been introduced to handle subscripts that do not have a direct terminating command or require merging with other elements in the case of nested expressions (similarly to parentheses).

The rules described above allow the dictated mathematical expression to be saved in the editor's EQED internal format, which can then be automatically converted to the output symbolic/visual form. The implemented mathematical notation translator also verifies the correctness of the commands used in the input stream and makes corrections to the keywords by scanning backward.

The processed formula can be exported to one of the standard mathematical notation formats (LaTeX, MathML) or displayed in visual form. It is also possible to convert an EQED-format expression back to the text, verbalized and ready to be read. Similarly, the possibility of dictating a mathematical expression to a system that provides its translation into natural language allows for searching among verbalized formulas from the repository based on partial information. Verbalization increases the quality of the search, which can be implemented with the help of standard algorithms used for approximate text comparison. A search module based on such assumptions and the results of a sample query is described [2]. Moreover, this approach can lead to effective solutions for plagiarism detection, which were elaborated on ([5, 6]).

In this way, the "Formula Editor" can be used as an educational aid for the automatic processing of digital sources containing mathematical notation - textbooks, collections of exercises, lecture materials, etc.

3 Interactive Editing Commands

To enable interactive editing, correction, and reuse of mathematical formula fragments, additional commands have been embedded in the mobile assistant application. This solves the problem of entering longer sequences of symbols or subexpressions, which can be a challenge even for an experienced operator. The user also does not have to remember the complete structure of a complex mathematical expression, thanks to the preview generated in real-time on the mobile terminal screen. The cursor is also visualized in the preview, providing orientation in the formula editing process.

The introduced commands, which have been tested in the Polish language version, can be divided into the following categories:

1. local: those that only change the content of the buffer in the mobile assistant application: delete word, delete all (used primarily for corrections, when voice recognition at mobile device gives a wrong suggestion for given word),
2. global: those that affect the content of the edited mathematical expression: undo, redo, a new formula, insert (predicted fragment of the formula from the buffer to the editor), clear (selected fragment of the formula in the editor), show (refresh the preview of the formula from the editor on the mobile device screen - automatically triggered for most other actions) ,
3. navigation: those that affect the cursor position: left, right, up, down, into (e.g. entering under the square root).

The trigger word in Polish has been chosen as "wykonaj" ("execute"), due to its suitable length and low probability of error or accidental use. The entire scheme of voice commands is encoded in appropriately prepared configuration files, both for the mobile application and the main formula editor. Therefore, any corrections, extensions, or introductions of further language versions are convenient and efficient.

In Table 1 we demonstrate the usage of introduced navigation and editing commands on a few examples (actually tested in the Polish language) and the effect of its application to a given initial formula.

The introduction of additional commands in the mobile assistant application brings significant advantages over dictating a long mathematical expression at once. By using these commands, users can easily edit, correct, and reuse specific parts of the equation without the need to remember the entire structure. This saves time and minimizes errors, especially when dealing with long sequences of symbols and sub-expressions. Additionally, users can benefit from the real-time preview generated on the mobile terminal screen, allowing them to visualize and adjust the mathematical expression as they go.

Moreover, the new commands not only allow for easy correction and manipulation of the equation but also provide users with precise control over the cursor's position, enabling them to move left, right, up, down, or center, as needed. This feature, combined with the visual preview, makes it easier for users to orient themselves in the editing process and ensures that the final expression is accurate and complete. Furthermore, the trigger word "execute" simplifies the entire process by minimizing the likelihood of errors or accidental use, and the entire voice command system is easily configurable and expandable, supporting additional languages and enhancements as needed.

Table 1. Examples of commands and their effect on edited mathematical expressions.

Initial expression (with the current position of the cursor visualized)	Commands	Result
$y=2x+5$	execute clear	$y=2+5$
$y=2+5$	execute new formula	
$\dfrac{x}{y}+\dfrac{1}{2}$	execute up, execute clear, execute up, 3, execute insert	$\dfrac{3}{y}+\dfrac{1}{2}$
$1-\sqrt{5}$	execute right, execute right, execute into, execute clear, execute into, 7, execute insert	$1-\sqrt{7}$

4 Summary

The dynamic development of voice user interfaces observed in recent years, as well as their increasingly widespread use in everyday devices, opens up new possibilities for building educational tools and supporting people with physical, visual, or hearing disabilities. This paper explains the difficulties and challenges in interpreting verbal mathematical notation and its automatic processing. In this context, we describe the design assumptions and implementation of the original tool "Formula Editor" for dictating and listening to mathematical expressions and propose an extension that allows for voice-controlled corrections of entered mathematical content. The application allows users to enter, play back and correct mathematical notation using intuitive voice commands, making it a supplement to existing e-learning systems that support formulae written in mathematical notation. An important area requiring such tools is the education of people with disabilities, particularly in the field of mathematical and engineering sciences, where the symbolic notation is the basis for information representation. The development of e-learning technologies and the popularization of remote forms of education in recent years also require the search for solutions aimed at optimizing human-machine communication methods resembling interpersonal interactions. Voice interfaces appear to be a key element in this sort of communication.

References

1. Attanayake, D., Denholm-Price, J., Hunter, G., Pfluegel, E., Wigmore, A.: Speech interfaces for mathematics: opportunities and limitations for visually impaired learners. In: IMA International Conference on Barriers and Enablers to Learning Maths: Enhancing Learning and Teaching for All Learners, pp. 1–8 (2015)
2. Bier, A., Sroczyński, Z.: Towards semantic search for mathematical notation. Federated Conference on Computer Science and Information Systems (FedCSIS) **2018**, 465–469 (2018)
3. Bier, A., Sroczyński, Z.: Rule based intelligent system verbalizing mathematical notation. Multimedia Tools and Applications **78**(19), 28 089–28 110 (2019)
4. Bier, A., Sroczyński, Z.: Rule-based intelligent system for dictating mathematical notation in Polish. In: Mauri, J.M. (ed.), ACHI: The Thirteenth International Conference on Advances in Computer-Human Interactions, pp. 352–356. Valencia, Spain (2020). 21–25 November 2020, ISBN 978-1-61208-761-0
5. Bier, A., Sroczyński, Z.: Reliability assessment of the automatic plagiarism detection system for various editing patterns in documents containing complex mathematical notation. J. Phys: Conf. Ser. **1828**(1), 012109 (2021)
6. Bier, A., Sroczyński, Z.: Comparison of complex mathematical notation and applications for searching and plagiarism detection. In: Soliman Khalid, S. (ed.) Proceedings of the 40th International Business Information Management Association Computer Science Conference (IBIMA), 23–24 November 2022, pp. 189–194. Sevilla, Spain (2022). Theory and practice in modern computing: vision 2025 during global crisis, Proceedings of the International Business Information Management Association Conference, 2022, International Business Information Management Association, ISBN 979-8-9867719-1-5
7. Cuartero-Olivera, J., Hunter, G., Perez-Navarro, A.: Reading and writing mathematical notation in e-learning environments. eLearn Center Research Paper Series 4, 11–20 (2012)
8. Erikkson, Y., Westling B.: Design of Interfaces for People with Blindness. Designing the Complete Learning Environment for Braille Users Studying Mathematics. ACHI 2021: The Fourteenth International Conference on Advances in Computer-Human Interactions, pp. 16–21 (2021)
9. Jaskulska, A., et al.: Exploration of Voice User Interfaces for Older Adults — A Pilot Study to Address Progressive Vision Loss, Conference on Multimedia, Interaction, Design and Innovation, pp. 159–168. Springer, Cham (2020)
10. Junior, A., Mendes, L., Da Silva, S.: Math2Text: Software para geração e conversão de equações matemáticas em texto - limitações e possibilidades de inclusão, pp. 99–115. RISTI (2020)
11. Kherdekar, V., Naik, S.: Speech recognition system approaches, techniques and tools for mathematical expressions: a review. Int. J. Sci. Technol. Res. **8**(08), 1225–1263 (2019)
12. Kowalski, J., et al.: Older adults and voice interaction: A pilot study with Google Home. In: Extended Abstracts of the 2019 CHI Conference on human factors in computing systems, pp. 1–6 (2019)
13. McTear, M.F., Callejas, Z.: Voice application development for Android. Packt Publishing Ltd. (2013)
14. Mejía, P., Martini, L., Grijalva, F., Larco, J., Rodriguez, J.: A Survey on Mathematical Software Tools for Visually Impaired Persons: A Practical Perspective, pp. 66929–66947. IEEE Access (2021)
15. Shokat, S., Riaz, R., Rizvi, S.S., Abbasi, A.M., Abbasi, A.A., Kwon, S.J.: Deep learning scheme for character prediction with position-free touch screen-based Braille input method. Hum. Cent. Comput. Inf. Sci. **10**, 41 (2020)

16. Soares, B., Francisco, C., Medeiros, E., Medeiros, S., Medeiros, R.: Propostas de ensino de mathematics para deficientes visuais: revisao sistematica exploratoria da lietratura. HOLOS **8**, 1–37 (2020)

Reinforcement Learning in Algorithmic Trading: An Overview

Przemysław Czuba[✉]

Faculty of Cybernetics, Institute of Computer and Information Systems, Military University of Technology, Kaliskiego Str. 2, 00-908 Warsaw, Poland
przemyslaw.czuba@wat.edu.pl

Abstract. This article provides a overview of the application of reinforcement learning in algorithmic trading. Reinforcement learning is a type of machine learning that involves an agent making a series of decisions and receiving rewards or punishments based on the outcomes. In algorithmic trading, reinforcement learning has been used to optimize trading strategies, improve portfolio management, and enhance market prediction. The article discusses various reinforcement learning algorithms and approaches from state of the art research and their applications in financial markets. The article also highlights the challenges and limitations of using reinforcement learning in algorithmic trading and suggests potential future directions for research in this field.

Keywords: Deep learning · Deep reinforcement learning · Quantitative trading · Algorithmic trading

1 Introduction

In recent years, the intellectual pursuit surrounding artificial intelligence (AI) has seen a meteoric surge, resulting in an extensive and growing body of research that is consistently refreshed with annual scholarly contributions. This phenomenon can be substantially attributed to the astounding success of deep learning (DL) techniques, which hinge upon the architecture of deep neural networks (DNN) - conceptual structures borrowed directly from our understanding of the neural architecture of the human brain. These methodologies have advanced to the frontiers of diverse applications, including but not limited to speech recognition, image classification, and natural language processing.

In an intriguing confluence, a sister discipline of deep learning, known as deep reinforcement learning (DRL), has also been basking in the academic spotlight, earning recognition and intrigue within the research community. DRL is essentially an intricate tapestry of techniques, singularly concerned with how an intelligent agent learns through sequential interactions within an uncharted environment, ultimately aiming to optimize cumulative rewards. These techniques harness the power of DL to abstract and generalize information obtained from these interactions. A multitude of recent victories in applying DRL further underscores its competence in solving convoluted, sequential decision-making problems.

K. S. Soliman (Ed.): IBIMA-AI 2023, CCIS 2101, pp. 71–77, 2024.
https://doi.org/10.1007/978-3-031-62843-6_8

In parallel, we can explore the realm of algorithmic trading (AT), a field that has seen extensive utilization across diverse financial assets such as stocks, cryptocurrencies, and foreign exchanges. This modality of trading involves constant buying and selling of a given asset to garner profits, where time is neatly divided into discrete units. Traders begin with a predetermined amount of capital and at each discrete time unit, or 't', they can choose to buy, hold, or sell a variable amount of shares, effectively altering their positions. The ultimate objective is to augment the final net value when the trading period concludes.

Algorithmic trading can be realized through either rule-based systems or machine learning (ML) centric paradigms. Rule-based systems incorporate preordained rules, crafted by human experts, which the algorithm follows to trade in the financial markets. These can be based on conventional trading methodologies, mathematical models, or bespoke strategies. In contrast, ML-based algorithmic trading employs machine learning algorithms that are trained on historical data to participate in the financial markets without direct human intervention.

Moreover, it must be noted that ML-based algorithmic trading poses a substantial advantage over its rule-based counterpart. Specifically, 1) ML algorithms are capable of extracting patterns, discerning relationships, and assimilating knowledge from the past data without the necessity for guidelines or strategies set by domain experts, and 2) the potential of ML in algorithmic trading approaches lies in the discovery of profitable insights that may remain elusive to human traders.

In this paper, I aim to compare different research studies that have looked at using deep reinforcement learning for algorithmic trading. By putting these studies side by side, we can get a better understanding of the methods are used and how well these methods work.

2   Related Work

Millea, A. work [9] discusses the use of hierarchy in problem-solving and model-based RL for predicting the trading environment. It also delves into defining and analyzing multiple risk measures that can act as reward-shaping mechanisms for the agent. The survey emphasizes the significance of state representations in financial markets for the effectiveness and efficiency of DRL agents. The specific focus of the survey is on the cryptocurrency market.

Felizardo, L et al. [6] on the other hand is one of the most recent surveys available. Researchers identifies state-of-the-art methods and highlight the integration of RL concepts with trading problems. The authors suggest promising approaches for future research and emphasize the potential of combining RL with other machine learning techniques. They note the increasing adoption of modern RL approaches and advancements in areas like natural language processing and forecasting methods.

The following paper, analysis is strictly limited to contributions subsequent to the year 2020. I chosen most recent and most cited works only (more than 10 citations). Empirical findings, garnered from a comprehensive analysis of Scopus data, illustrate an escalating interest in this field of study. Prior to this point, the average number of papers published annually wavered around the forty mark. However, recent years have witnessed a marked uptick in academic curiosity and prolific writing on the subject, underscoring the growing relevance and dynamism of this research area.

2.1 Algorithmic Trading as RL Problem

Formulating financial trading as a Reinforcement Learning (RL) allows an RL agent continuously interacts with an non-stationary environment - the financial market in this case - striving to evolve towards an optimal strategy. The process can be encapsulated as a Markov Decision Process (MDP), represented by a quintuplet (S, A, P, R, γ).

Here, S is an ensemble of states $\{s_1, s_2,..., s_m\}$, A represents the range of feasible actions $\{a_1, a_2,..., a_n\}$ accessible at each state, P is a probability matrix enabling the shift of environment from state s_t to s_{t+1} influenced by the chosen action at time t. R denotes the set of rewards contingent on each state's action, and γ is the discount factor ranging between [0, 1], employed to balance immediate rewards with long-term gains.

During the course of an RL problem, the agent, at each instant t, executes an action a_t from A in a state s_t from S and subsequently receives a reward r_t from R. Following this, the environmental state transitions from s_t to s_{t+1}, guided by the transition probabilities P. The agent's prime objective is to maximize a cumulative reward G_t, which is the sum of discounted rewards.

The formulation of RL challenges is of paramount importance - even the most effective algorithms can fall short in delivering desirable outcomes without the right models.

2.2 MDP Model for Stock Trading

To apply RL to Algorithmic trading problem we need to model it as a Markov Decision Process (MDP) as follows [13]:

- State s: a vector that includes stock prices, the stock shares, the remaining balance and any other information which should be available to the agent,
- Action a: a vector of actions over stocks. The allowed actions on each stock include **selling**, **buying**, or **holding**, which result in decreasing, increasing, and no change of the stock shares, respectively.
- Reward r: the direct reward of taking action a at state s and arriving at the new state s'.
- Policy $\pi(s)$: the trading strategy at state s, which is the probability distribution of actions at state s.
- Q-value $Q_\pi(s, a)$: the expected reward of taking action a at state s following policy π.

2.3 Performance Measurements

Most widely used performance metrics for AT models are [1]:

- **Sharp ratio**: (SR_t) at time t is calculated as the average return earned above the risk-free return, for the same time interval, per the volatility of the earned return,

- **Profit and Loss** (PnL): is calculated by subtracting the cost or purchase price of the asset from the sale price or current market value of the asset, taking into account any transaction costs, fees, or other expenses associated with the trade,
- **Accumulated Wealth Rate** (AWR): it is defined as the sum of all profits and losses occurring during the test trading period T divided by the available cash at the start of the trading,
- **Average Profit Return** (APR): it is defined as the average of the annual return rate, calculated as the average of the accumulated wealth rate gained during each year in the test period,
- **Average Sharp Ratio** (ASR): it is defined as the average of the annual sharp ratio during the test trading period T,
- **Average Maximum Draw Down** (AMDD): the Maximum Draw Down (MDD) is defined as the maximum loss from a peak to a trough in the value of the trading portfolio during time interval T, while AMDD is the average of the annual MDD during the test trading period,
- **Average Calmar Ratio** (ACR): the Calmar Ratio (CR) is defined as the average profit return during some interval divided by the MDD during this interval, while ACR is the average of the annual Calmar Ratio (CR) during the test trading period T,
- **Sortino ratio** (SOR_t): evaluates an investment's risk-adjusted returns, focusing specifically on the downside risk. It measures the excess return of an investment above a specified target or risk-free rate, divided by the downside deviation of returns.

3 Methods

In an effort to establish a more uniform analysis and to bridge the existing gaps in research comparisons, this study will evaluate the selected papers based on a set of pre-defined criteria. These include:

- **Algorithm**: The type of RL algorithm utilized and its specific characteristics will be evaluated.
- **Reward calculation**: The method employed to compute the rewards, and its subsequent influence on the RL agent's learning process, will be scrutinized.
- **Input data**: The nature and quality of data used as input to the algorithm will be examined.
- **Multi-agent**: The applicability of the method to multi-agent environments, as well as its adaptability to the competitive nature of trading, will be examined.
- **Timeframe**: The timeframe of trading, be it high-frequency or long-term, and the adaptability of the method to various timeframes, will be evaluated.
- **Indicators**: The financial indicators utilized in the study, including price, volume, and other technical or fundamental indicators, will be considered.

By adhering to these comprehensive criteria, the aim is to provide a more balanced and thorough comparison across different studies in the domain of algorithmic trading with reinforcement learning.

- **Results**: The reported outcomes of each study will be scrutinized, considering not only their positive results but also their limitations and challenges.

Table 1. Comparison of research studies in the literature of RL based Algorithmic Trading

Ref	Algorithm	Reward calculation	Input data	Multi-agent/ Ensemble	Timeframe	Results
[10]	Hierarchical DQN	Profit/loss from a position	OHLCV EUR/USD	Yes	Multi-timeframe	Avg. cumulative return 56.4%
[1]	A2C+DBN + LSTM	Sharpe ratio	OHLCV Indexes	No	Daily	Avg Sharpe ratio 0.525
[8]	RDPG+GRU	Diff. Sharpe ratio	OHLC Indexes	No	1 Minute	Sharpe ratio 0.842
[11]	DQN	Daily Returns	OHLCV Stocks	No	Daily	Sharpe ratio 1.484
[4]	DDPG+LSTM	Protfolio value change	OHLC Stocks	No	Daily	Cumulative 311% Return
[13]	PPO+A2C+DDPG	Protfolio value change	Close, Stocks	Yes	Daily	Sharpe ratio 1.3
[12]	PPO+Distill	Profit/loss from a position	OHLC, Forex	No	1 Hour	Mean 40% PnL
[2]	Q-learning	Rate of Return	OHLC Indexes	No	Daily	ROI 60.36
[5]	DQN/DDQN/DDDQN	Profit after action	OHLCV Stocks	No	Daily	Avg. profit 38.39%
[7]	CNN+LSTM + DDQN	Profit rate + Sharpe ratio	OHLCV Stocks	NO	Daily	Sharpe ratio 0.97

Table 1 summarizes most recent approaches to the problem. It's clear that there's a lot of variation in how approaches are designed. Each method uses different types of data, data sizes, and measurement methods, which makes it hard to compare them directly. One important aspect that affects how these methods work is the way rewards are calculated. The type and structure of the rewards can greatly change the performance and decision-making of the trading algorithms. However, there's one area that hasn't been studied enough: multiagent approaches. These could offer interesting and more complex learning possibilities, but so far, they haven't received much attention in research on RL-based algorithmic trading.

Adding to the diversity and potential gaps in the field, it's also notable that not many approaches currently utilize financial indicators in their reinforcement learning models for algorithmic trading. Indicators like moving averages, RSI, and Bollinger Bands, which are commonly used in traditional trading strategies, are often overlooked in these machine learning methodologies. This could be an area for potential exploration and development in future research, given the historical success and widespread use of these indicators in manual trading strategies.

4 Technologies

Python is widely regarded as the preferred programming language for reinforcement learning (RL) algorithms implementation due to several key factors. First and foremost, Python's simplicity and readability make it accessible to both beginners and experts in the field. Its extensive libraries, such as *TensorFlow*, *PyTorch*, and *NumPy*, provide powerful tools for implementing complex RL algorithms and efficiently handling large-scale data processing. RL frameworks like *OpenAI Gym* and *RLlib* contribute to its popularity among researchers and practitioners.

RLlib [14] is a state-of-the-art reinforcement learning library designed to facilitate research and development in the field of artificial intelligence. It offers a comprehensive suite of tools and algorithms for training and evaluating reinforcement learning agents across various domains and applications.

OpenAI Gym [15] stands out as the premier choice for reinforcement learning environments due to its remarkable features and contributions to the field. It offers a diverse range of pre-built environments, allowing researchers to experiment with various tasks and scenarios across domains. Two contemporary tools, *gym-anytrading* [16] and *gym-mtsim* [17], have come to the forefront in facilitating RL in trading applications. *Gym-anytrading*, an OpenAI gym environment, offers a versatile framework for designing and testing RL agents in trading scenarios, supporting both single and multi-asset environments. Its flexibility in dealing with custom financial indicators and rewards systems makes it an invaluable tool for financial modelers. On the other hand, *gym-mtsim*, another OpenAI gym extension, provides a MetaTrader trading simulator, allowing for the development and evaluation of algorithmic trading strategies in a most popular trading environment. The fusion of such technologies in the hands of skilled practitioners is accelerating the progression of algorithmic trading, opening up new dimensions in financial market predictions and strategic implementations.

5   Conclusion

This paper dives into the world of algorithmic trading boosted by reinforcement learning. Right now, there's a noticeable lack of a standard method for comparing different trading approaches. Plus, many studies only use a small selection of possible performance measures, which could limit our understanding and the wider use of these methods.

Most of the research so far mainly focuses on situations with only one agent. This approach doesn't really take into account the dynamic and sometimes competitive nature of actual trading environments. There's also not a lot of research on trading with shorter timeframes or using multiple timeframes.

Still, despite these hurdles, the field of algorithmic trading using reinforcement learning is an interesting area for further research. This field, with its constantly changing environment, is a challenging but exciting direction for future studies. As researchers continue to investigate and make sense of these challenges, we can expect to see important advances that will greatly influence the future of financial markets and trading technology.

References

1. AbdelKawy, R., Abdelmoez, W.M., Shoukry, A.: A synchronous deep reinforcement learning model for automated multi-stock trading. Prog. Artif. Intell. **10**, 83–97 (2021). https://doi.org/10.1007/s13748-020-00225-z
2. Aloud, M.E., Alkhamees, N.: Intelligent algorithmic trading strategy using reinforcement learning and directional change. IEEE Access **9**, 114659–114671 (2021). https://doi.org/10.1109/ACCESS.2021.3105259
3. An, B., Sun, S., Wang, R.: Deep reinforcement learning for quantitative trading: challenges and opportunities. IEEE Intell. Syst. **37**, 23–26 (2022). https://doi.org/10.1109/MIS.2022.3165994
4. Conegundes, L., Pereira, A.C.M.: Beating the stock market with a deep reinforcement learning day trading system. In: 2020 International Joint Conference on Neural Networks (IJCNN). Presented at the 2020 International Joint Conference on Neural Networks (IJCNN), pp. 1–8. IEEE, Glasgow, United Kingdom (2020). https://doi.org/10.1109/IJCNN48605.2020.9206938

5. Dang, Q.-V.: Reinforcement learning in stock trading. In: Le Thi, H.A., Le, H.M., Pham Dinh, T., Nguyen, N.T. (eds.) Advanced Computational Methods for Knowledge Engineering, Advances in Intelligent Systems and Computing, pp. 311–322. Springer International Publishing, Cham (2020). https://doi.org/10.1007/978-3-030-38364-0_28

6. Felizardo, L.K., Paiva, F.C.L., Costa, A.H.R., Del-Moral-Hernandez, E.: Reinforcement Learning Applied to Trading Systems: A Survey (2022). https://doi.org/10.48550/ARXIV. 2212.06064

7. Li, Y., Liu, P., Wang, Z.: Stock Trading Strategies Based on Deep Reinforcement Learning. Scientific Programming 2022, 1–15 (2022). https://doi.org/10.1155/2022/4698656

8. Liu, Y., Liu, Q., Zhao, H., Pan, Z., Liu, C.: Adaptive quantitative trading: an imitative deep reinforcement learning approach. AAAI **34**, 2128–2135 (2020). https://doi.org/10.1609/aaai. v34i02.5587

9. Millea, A.: Deep reinforcement learning for trading—a critical survey. Data **6**, 119 (2021). https://doi.org/10.3390/data6110119

10. Shavandi, A., Khedmati, M.: A multi-agent deep reinforcement learning framework for algorithmic trading in financial markets. Expert Systems with Applications **208**, 118124 (2022). https://doi.org/10.1016/j.eswa.2022.118124

11. Théate, T., Ernst, D.: An application of deep reinforcement learning to algorithmic trading. Expert Systems with Applications **173**, 114632 (2021). https://doi.org/10.1016/j.eswa.2021. 114632

12. Tsantekidis, A., Passalis, N., Tefas, A.: Diversity-driven knowledge distillation for financial trading using deep reinforcement learning. Neural Networks **140**, 193–202 (2021). https:// doi.org/10.1016/j.neunet.2021.02.026

13. Yang, H., Liu, X.-Y., Zhong, S., Walid, A.: Deep reinforcement learning for automated stock trading: an ensemble strategy. In: Proceedings of the First ACM International Conference on AI in Finance. Presented at the ICAIF '20: ACM International Conference on AI in Finance, pp. 1–8. ACM, New York New York (2020). https://doi.org/10.1145/3383455.3422540

14. Ray-project: RLlib [Software] (2022). Retrieved from https://github.com/ray-project/ray. Accessed 19 May 2023

15. OpenAI: OpenAI Gym [Software] (2022). Retrieved from https://gym.openai.com/. Accessed 19 May 2023

16. AminHP: gym-anytrading [GitHub Repository] (2022). Retrieved from https://github.com/ AminHP/gym-anytrading. Accessed 19 May 2023

17. AminHP: gym-mtsim [GitHub Repository] (2022). Retrieved from https://github.com/Ami nHP/gym-mtsim. Accessed 19 May 2023

Proposal of a System for Prototyping and Validation of Drug Efficacy and Safety Evaluation Methods

Dawid Bugajewski[✉]

Cybernetics Faculty, Military University of Technology, Warsaw, Poland
dawid.bugajewski@wat.edu.pl

Abstract. COVID-19 pandemic showed how fast new drugs can be introduced and the need for reliable drug efficacy and safety evaluation methods. Lack of past data that could be used for evaluation and validation of such methods limits possibility to work on them before real data is available. Using a common electronic health record data type as well as possibility to generate synthetic data could allow early validations and end to end testing of such methods. To address these limitations, a system was proposed system that allows for end-to-end patient population generation, data transformation and method evaluation. The system utilizes existing and well-known patient generation framework Synthea, as well as OMOP CDM data model along with patient level prediction framework. Existing solutions were extended for the purposes of the system including possibility of modelling adverse drug reactions in Synthea and orchestrated for seamless execution. Proposed system allows for prototyping and validating drug efficacy and safety methods using existing state-of-the art tooling as well as providing a holistic approach to method evaluation and testing.

Keywords: eHealth systems · pharmacovigilance · drug safety · drug effiacy

1 Introduction

Common usage of Electronic Health Records (EHR) allowed for rapid development of intelligent healthcare in recent years, including disease diagnosis and treatment recommendations [1], automated adverse drug signals detection [2] or applications of deep learning for medical reasoning [3, 4]. Over the years several EHR data standards emerged including SNOMED-CT [5], HL7 [6], FHIR [7] or OMOP CDM [8]. Standardized health records further allow for exchange of reasoning models and reduce time needed to create new ones. This is further amplified by availability of big both real and synthetic electronic health records like MIMIC III [9–11] or Synthea [12] and adverse drug effects databases like EudraVigilance [13] or Faers [14]. Data can be also obtained from clinical trial research data aggregators like Vivli. As one of the potential data sources a telemonitoring system was considered that could help augment reasoning with real-time data [15].

K. S. Soliman (Ed.): IBIMA-AI 2023, CCIS 2101, pp. 78–85, 2024.
https://doi.org/10.1007/978-3-031-62843-6_9

This paper was divided into three sections. First section describes data sources that were considered as well as used models and subsystems. Second section describes general system architecture as well as important improvements to existing systems. Third section describes first results obtained while using the system initial implementation. In the end obtained results were summarized and future work directions have been described.

2 Data Sources and Models

With the goal of creating a system for a seamless prototyping and validation of the drug efficacy and safety evaluation commonly available data sources and ways to interact with them had to be identified. Some of considered elements of the systems as well as the ones selected as part of the system include modelling of patient life space, publicly available data sources as well as adverse drug effects data sources.

2.1 Patient Space Model

Initially it was planned to direct research towards more classical mathematical model and describing the problem as a decision model similar to the one proposed in [16] and formulated as follows:

- Patient $x \in X$, where X is set of patients.
- Health parameter $p_i(x, t)$,
- Parameters value set $S_i = [s_i^{min}, s_i^{max}]$,
- Patient life space $S = S_1 S_2 \ldots S_n$,

Then for such patient which is represented as a set of points in a life space following parameters can be defined that would describe ideal point for health as well as how far is patient state from given disease. Those parameters were illustrated for simplified two-dimensional space on Fig. 1.

- Perfect health $Q(x) = (q_1(x), q_2(x), \ldots, q_n(x))$,
- Health indicator $||Q(x) - P(x)||$,
- Disease pattern $D(x) = (d_1(x), d_2(x), \ldots, d_n(x))$,
- Disease indicator $||D(x) - P(x)||$

Having the following drug efficacy and safety can be described as change of distance from ideal health and the disease in the space for individual patient as well as for the population by:

- Patient safety: Change of distance from ideal health $\Delta Q(x, t_k) = ||Q(x) - P(x, t_k)|| - ||Q(x) - P(x, t_o)||$,
- Population safety: Average change of distance from ideal health $\Delta Q(X, t_k) = \frac{\sum_{x \in X} \Delta Q(x, t_k)}{|X|}$, |,
- Patient efficacy: Change of distance from disease $\Delta D(x, t_k) = ||D(x) - P(x, t_k)|| - ||D(x) - P(x, t_o)||$,
- Patient safety: Average change of distance from ideal health $\Delta D(X, t_k) = \frac{\sum_{x \in X} \Delta D(x, t_k)}{|X|}$, |

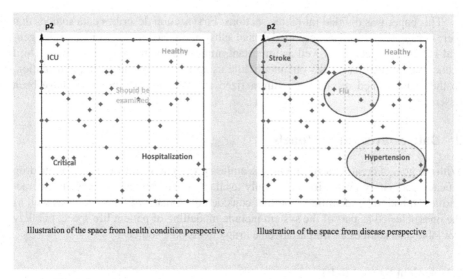

Illustration of the space from health condition perspective   Illustration of the space from disease perspective

Fig. 1. Illustration of the health space from condition and disease perspective.

While being considered this approach was not further evaluated due to difficulty of obtaining data in proper format as well as the definitions of perfect health and disease patterns for patients.

2.1.1   Publicly Available Data Sets

Among considered data sets were ones available publicly like MIMIC III or Synthea synthetic data as well as clinical data sets available on demand on Vilvi. There is a significant number of research papers about using MIMIC III for evaluation of drug recommendation systems, however MIMIC III encounters as an ICU lack history that could be useful for assessing drug efficacy and safety. Due to long process of getting access to clinical data set in the end only synthetic data generated with Synthea was selected for further research.

2.1.2 Real Data Set from Long Term Care and Telemonitoring

As a part of work on telemonitoring system described in previous work [15] real data sets from long term care was obtained with a possibility of enriching the data with real time parameters gathered from the telemonitoring system. Unfortunately, in the end the group of patients that was part of the pilot monitoring group didn't have data in obtained EHR data set. The data set was useful for creating and evaluating system against a real-life data however it wasn't provided in any of the common data sets but in internal EHR system structure which required transformation of the data to common format. Data set contained 4432 long term patients that were patients in facilities in Warsaw.

2.1.3 Idea of a Method for Drug Safety and Efficacy Evaluation

General idea behind a method for drug safety and efficacy that was to be evaluated with the proposed system has been shown on Fig. 2.

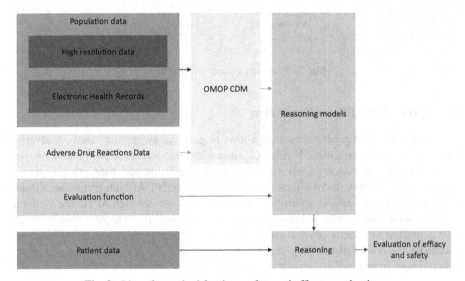

Fig. 2. Idea of a method for drug safety and efficacy evaluation.

3 System Architecture

The system consists of three major elements: Synthea generator with adverse drug effect modelling and medication diversification [17], converter from Synthea format to OMOP CDM [18] and Patient Level Prediction [19] package as well as a custom orchestrator web application to easily prototype and validate methods. System architecture is presented on Fig. 3.

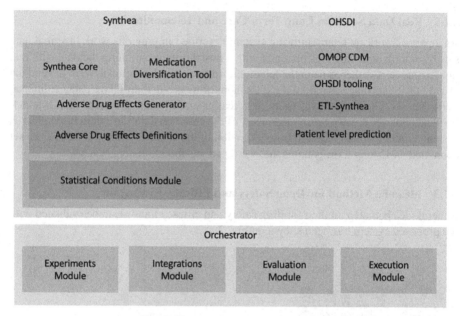

Fig. 3. Proposed system architecture.

3.1 Adverse Drug Effects Generation

Adverse drug effects generator module allows to generate symptoms based on adverse drug reactions generated using FAERS data and administered drugs. The module allows also for manual provision of adverse drug effects definition and supports generating them using probability distributions as well as through REST API integration with third party generators. In such cases current state of patient is sent through API in the Synthea format. Along with the possibility of generation of adverse effects there is possibility of easy definition of generic adverse effects that doesn't have to be connected to the drug but can be based on statistics for given disease to generate a background signal and allow to better tune in and evaluate reasoning methods.

3.2 Pipeline Orchestration

The pipeline orchestration is done by a custom Orchestrator which is a docker container containing all of prerequisites as well as web dashboard to manage experiments, integrations and their evaluation and execution. More detailed architecture of the orchestrator was presented on Fig. 4.

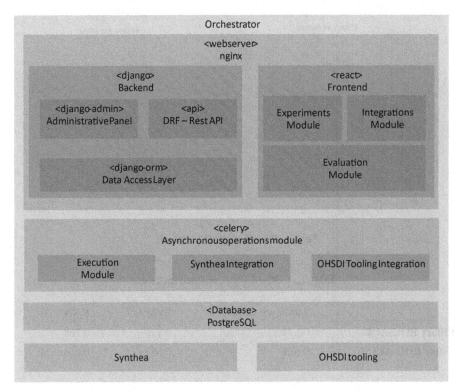

Fig. 4. Architecture of orchestrator.

4 Testing with Proposed Method

For testing purposes using the earlier introduced reasoning method idea a following method parameters were proposed:

1. Drug – COVID-19 vaccine,
2. Security evaluation function: will the patient have any of following symptoms or events? Death – 0, heart inflammation – 0.5, thrombosis – 0.5, none of those – 1,
3. Efficacy evaluation function: will the patient be admitted to hospital or die of COVID-19? Yes – 0, No – 1,
4. Dataset – 1,000,000 records, 70% training data, 15% test data, 15% validation data.

As classification methods the following were selected linear regression, KNN and SVM. Results with those methods are shown as a ROC curve on Fig. 5 and AUC values were presented in Table 1.

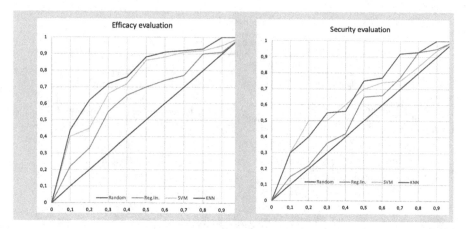

Fig. 5. ROC of evaluated methods.

Table 1. ROC-AUC of evaluated methods.

	Linear regression	SVM	KNN
Effiacy ROC-AUC	0,627	0,725	0,768
Safety ROC-AUC	0,561	0,637	0,668

5 Conclusions

Proposed system allows for prototyping and validating drug efficacy and safety methods using existing state-of-the art tooling as well as providing a holistic approach to method evaluation and testing. Possibility of executing tests end to end with a little supervision should positively affect development of new methods. In the end none of considered real data sources was not selected for the purposes of the system because of the insufficient observation timelines, complicated representation of data or data misalignment. Thanks to providing a containerized execution environment the solution can be easily deployed anywhere without a need for extensive configuration. Prepared adverse effects module further enhances the Synthea framework possibility to generate highly impactful synthetic data. Further work related to the system might relate to extensive testing of the implemented adverse drug effects and the orchestrator and publishing them on Github as well as performing extensive studies of existing methods using the proposed system.

References

1. Ali, Z., et al.: Deep learning for medication recommendation: a systematic survey. Data Intell. **5**(2), 303–354 (2022). https://doi.org/10.1162/dint_a_00197
2. Bate, A., et al.: A Bayesian neural network method for adverse drug reaction signal generation. Eur. J. Clin. Pharmacol. **54**(4), 315–321 (1998). https://doi.org/10.1007/s002280050466

3. Miotto, R., Wang, F., Wang, S., Jiang, X., Dudley, J.T.: Deep learning for healthcare: review, opportunities and challenges. Brief. Bioinform. **19**(6), 1236–1246 (2018). https://doi.org/10. 1093/bib/bbx044

4. Miotto, R., Li, L., Kidd, B.A., Dudley, J.T.: Deep patient: an unsupervised representation to predict the future of patients from the electronic health records. Sci. Rep. **6**(1), Art. no. 1 (2016). https://doi.org/10.1038/srep26094

5. Donnelly, K.: SNOMED-CT: The advanced terminology and coding system for eHealth. Stud. Health Technol. Inform. **121**, 279–290 (2006)

6. Dolin, R.H., et al.: The HL7 clinical document architecture. J. Am. Med. Inform. Assoc. **8**(6), 552–569 (2001). https://doi.org/10.1136/jamia.2001.0080552

7. Bender, D., Sartipi, K.: HL7 FHIR: an agile and restful approach to healthcare information exchange. In: Proceedings of the 26th IEEE International Symposium on Computer-Based Medical Systems, pp. 326–331. IEEE, Porto, Portugal (2013). https://doi.org/10.1109/CBMS. 2013.6627810

8. Voss, E.A., et al.: Feasibility and utility of applications of the common data model to multiple, disparate observational health databases. J. Am. Med. Inform. Assoc. **22**(3), 553–564 (2015). https://doi.org/10.1093/jamia/ocu023

9. Goldberger, A.L., et al.: PhysioBank, PhysioToolkit, and PhysioNet: Components of a New Research Resource for Complex Physiologic Signals. Circulation **101**(23), (2000). https:// doi.org/10.1161/01.CIR.101.23.e215

10. Alistair, J., Tom, P., Roger, M.: MIMIC-III Clinical Database. PhysioNet. (2015). https://doi. org/10.13026/C2XW26

11. Johnson, A.E.W., et al.: MIMIC-III, a freely accessible critical care database. Sci. Data **3**(1), Art. no. 1 (May 2016). https://doi.org/10.1038/sdata.2016.35

12. Walonoski, J., et al.: Synthea: an approach, method, and software mechanism for generating synthetic patients and the synthetic electronic health care record. J. Am. Med. Inform. Assoc. **25**(3), 230–238 (2018). https://doi.org/10.1093/jamia/ocx079

13. Postigo, R., et al.: EudraVigilance medicines safety database: publicly accessible data for research and public health protection. Drug Saf. **41**(7), 665–675 (2018). https://doi.org/10. 1007/s40264-018-0647-1

14. C. for D. E. and Research: FDA Adverse Event Reporting System (FAERS) Public Dashboard. FDA (2021). Available: https://www.fda.gov/drugs/questions-and-answers-fdasadverse-event-reporting-system-faers/fda-adverse-event-reporting-system-faers-public-dashboard. Accessed: 10 June 2023. [Online]

15. Bugajewski, D.: Telemonitoring System for Home Care During COVID-19 Pandemic – a Case Study, pp. 12776–12782

16. Ameljańczyk, A., Ameljańczyk, T.: System monitorowania bezpieczeństwa zdrowotnego państwa i jego zagrożeń. Rocz. Kol. Anal. Ekon. Szk. Gł. Handlowa **25**, 9–20 (2012)

17. Medication Diversification Project: CodeRx. https://coderx.io/projects/medication-diversification. Accessed 10 June 2023

18. OHDSI/ETL-Synthea: Conversion from Synthea CSV to OMOP CDM. https://github.com/ OHDSI/ETL-Synthea. Accessed 10 June 2023

19. Reps, J.M., et al.: Design and implementation of a standardized framework to generate and evaluate patient-level prediction models using observational healthcare data. J. Am. Med. Inform. Assoc. **25**(8), 969–975 (2018). https://doi.org/10.1093/jamia/ocy032

Leading Trends in AI: A Literature Review

Zbigniew Piotrowski, Karolina Blaszczuk$^{(\boxtimes)}$, and Emilia Gabrielczyk

Military University of Technology, Warsaw, Poland
zbigniew.piotrowski@wat.edu.pl, blaszczuk.karolina@wp.pl

Abstract. This article is a literature review of leading trends in artificial intelligence (AI), with a particular focus on Large Language Models. It is difficult to find anything about news in the literature. The Authors have attempted to provide the newest information and definitions, introducing the reader to how they work and how they can be used. The article focuses on a review of available information on the latest technological developments, i.e. self-supervised algorithm. Furthermore, the following article acts as a compendium of knowledge about large language models, data compression in language models, LlamaIndex, self-supervised nodes or neural network poisoning attacks. The authors conducted a thorough analysis of recent developments and advances related to AI topics. They read the newest publications, conference papers, journals and reputable websites to extract and identify key trends. They have attempted to answer the question "What are the potential implications of emerging technologies?". The answer is simple - cyber attacks. Unfortunately, cyber attacks on neural networks, specifically poisoning attacks, are already occurring. Cyber security professionals have quite a task. AI are intelligent machines capable of mimicking humans, and when infected they can be dangerous. GANs are the vaccine here. AI is a fast-growing field of science that has been increasingly successful recently. Autocorrect on the phone, personalised search according to our expectations or ChatGPT is the work of AI, and this is only a substitute for its possibilities. Undoubtedly, the increasing use of AI is making our lives easier, but it also poses new risks.

Keywords: AI · SOM · GAN · LLM · LLaMA · Deepfake · Poisoning Attacks · Data Compression

1 Fundamentals of Artificial Intelligence

Artificial intelligence is a term defined by John McCarthy in 1955 as "the science and engineering of making intelligent machines". [1]. Artificial Intelligence is made up of basic subsets. The first subset is machine learning (ML). ML are the algorithms that create models [2].These are based on experience and data [3]. Deep machine learning refers to the use of extensive neural networks, which name derives from the neurons in the human brain. They are the prototype of these [4]. Like neurons, they constantly work (compute) real-world representations [3]. An important element in the development of AI is the correct choice of algorithm depending on the needs. ML can be divided into three main groups - supervised learning, unsupervised learning and reinforcement learning.

K. S. Soliman (Ed.): IBIMA-AI 2023, CCIS 2101, pp. 86–92, 2024.
https://doi.org/10.1007/978-3-031-62843-6_10

Supervised learning is an approach in which algorithms are based on input data [5]. Unsupervised learning algorithms analyse unlabelled input data, seraching for patterns in it [6]. There is also a hybrid method called semi-supervised learning, which combines the methods described above. As opposed to the previous methods, reinforcement learning has no input data, but an environment. In a trial-and-error environment, just like a human, the algorithm collects data automatically and learns to make optimised decisions [7].

2 Self-supervised Algorithm

A method of teaching that has been used recently is a method based on self-monitoring. Self-supervised involves defining a pretextual task (using unlabelled data). In order to solve it, the model learns their representations [8]. It can then use them to solve other tasks, i.e. natural language processing NLP or image recognition. Data2Vec is the first high-performance published self-supervised learning algorithm [9]. In this method, five basic operation steps can be distinguished [10]:

1. An encoder extracts a function from the masked input data, which is the output of the individual transform/linear layers.
2. An encoder endpoint management assistant (teacher) extracts features from unmasked inputs.
3 Unifications can be applied to the teacher outputs.
4. Encoder outputs are regressed by the projection block.
5. Losses are calculated based on the teacher-encoder outputs.

Compared to traditional methods, it is more advanced while offering much more possibilities.

3 Large Language Model

Large Language Model (LLM) is a digitised language model consisting of artificial neural networks with huge amounts of data, which are trained using self-supervised or semi-supervised learning [11]. Recent developments have been through the use of transformer architecture [12] with enhancements i.e. Transformer XL [13] and training based on masked language model (MLM) [14], as well as permutation language modelling (PLM) [15] [16]. Large Language Model Meta AI (LLaMA) is an LLM that, based on word-input data, predicts the next word based on recursive test generation. For this purpose, Meta has used the 20 most commonly used languages taking into account the Latin and Cyrillic alphabets [17]. Another example of an LLM is the GPT-4 (on which ChatGPT is based) based on Transformer-style model [18] and trained to predict the token in a document, based on publicly available data e.g. from websites [19]. It uses learning with reinforcement, which consists of information extracted from the user.

4 Data Compression

The increasing use of LLMs has forced adjustment to devices with small working memory. Traditional quantisation methods reduce the number of bits per model parameter, leading to a loss of accuracy. A new quantisation technique called Sparse-Quantised Representation (SpQR) is currently being implemented. It allows almost lossless compression. The principle of operation is based on the isolation of outliers [20] thus eliminating the influence of abnormal weightson the correct quantisation. Abnormal weights are stored at a higher precision, while the rest of the weights are compressed to 3–4 bits [20]. The following table summarises the number of average bits per parameter for 30B LLaMA model [21] (Table 1):

Table 1: Presentation of the data compression capabilities of average bits per parameter for 30B LLaMA model

Quantization technique	Average bits
SpQR	3.89
RTN	4
GPTQ	4

RTN – Round-to-nearest.
GPTQ - Generative Pre-trained Transformer models.

5 Llm Indexes

The LlamaIndex (GPT Index) is a 'data framework' that allows the LLM [22] to be extended with external data through various types of indexes [23]:

- Index list,
- Vector base index,
- Index tree,
- Keyword table index.

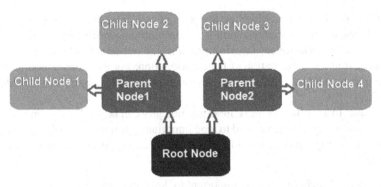

Fig. 1. Source (Own) Diagram of the index tree [23]

For example, an Index Tree (Fig. 1) from a set of nodes forms a hierarchical tree whose root is the source. It then expands it to include parent nodes (the trunk), which in turn include further child nodes (leaves). The query selects a subordinate node with a parent node. The number of nodes depends on the subordinate branching factor [23].

6 Self-Supervised Nodes (Som)

Self-supervised nodes is a technique that introduces an element of self-organisation into neural networks. They are nodes or neurons that have the capacity to adapt and learn from available data. The essence of self-supervised nodes is the ability to self-organise, i.e. create an internal structure or organisation based on unstructured input data. This process is inspired by the functioning of the human brain, which has the ability to self-supervise and adapt in a changing environment [24]. Self-supervised nodes operate through two main mechanisms: competitive learning and associative learning. Competitive learning involves competition between nodes for input resources. Each node has internal weights corresponding to certain patterns. When the input is presented, nodes with patterns close to them become active. Other nodes are suppressed or modify their weights, to better match the training data. Associative learning is the ability of nodes to form associations. Based on input data, a node can learn representations of certain combinations. The correlations detected allow for better analysis of future tasks. The ability to adapt to a changing environment or input data makes it useful, when the full fructure of the datais not known or the data is unstructured. Neural networks with self-supervised nodes can be more flexible and able to deal with a wide variety of situations, which is important in areas such as data processing, image analysis or pattern recognition [24].

7 Poisoning Attacks

Poisoning attacks in neural networks refer to situations in which input data are intentionally modified to introduce noise or false information [25]. One example of an attack in neural networks is the overlaying of a spectrum from another image onto the original image, resulting in a modified image. Contaminating images by overlaying a spectrum from another image is also a military threat. Here are some possible examples:

- Attacks on video systems: Modified images can pose a threat to vision systems such as surveillance systems, facial recognition or automotive security systems. By distorting images, attackers can introduce false information or avoid detection by security systems.
- Disinformation and propagation of false information: For example, a modified image that can appear authentic can be used to manipulate public opinion or create false narratives.
- Military use: In a military context, modified imagery can be used as a form of disinformation or camouflage. It can be used to hide important information from reconnaissance systems or to disrupt an enemy's ability to analyse images effectively, in order to make tactical decisions.

In the face of such threats, it is important to develop resilience techniques in neural networks to detect and defend against distorted data. Examples of approaches include the use of methods for verification and authentication of data, analysis of input data integrity, the use of anomaly detection techniques or the use of advanced generative models to verify data authenticity [25]. Using advanced generative models, such as GANs (Generative Adversarial Networks), neural networks can be trained to identify anomalies in the images, helping to detect forgeries.

8 Gans – Generative Adversarial Networks

GANs are a type of machine learning models that consist of two main components: a generator and a discriminator. GANs were introduced by Ian Goodfellow and his team in 2014 [26]. The generator in a GAN network has to generate new data, such as images, sounds or text, based on some probability distribution. For example, in the case of image generation, the generator creates images that are supposed to resemble images from the training set, but which do not actually exist in reality. The generator receives a vector of random numbers as input and tries to transform it into data of a suitable format [26]. The discriminator, on the other hand, has the task of distinguishing the real data from the data generated by the generator. In the case of image generation, the discriminator receives an image as input and tries to assess whether it is true (coming from the training set) or false (generated by the generator). The discriminator is trained in such a way that its ability to discriminate between true and false data is as high as possible [26]. The process of training the GAN consists of an iterative game between the generator, and the discriminator. The generator tries to generate more and more realistic data to fool the discriminator, while the discriminator tries to get better and better at distinguishing real data from false ones. As training progresses, both models get better and better at their tasks, until they reach a state of equilibrium where the generator generates high-quality, near-authentic data [27]. The creation of deepfakes through GANs is one of the main applications of these networks and has made a great impression on the field of robotics.

9 Deepfake

Deepfake is a technique in which generative countermeasure networks are used to create realistic manipulations of multimedia such as images, video, sound or text [28]. In the field of robotics, deepfakes have gained popularity due to their use in creating realistic human-robot interactions. For example, virtual agents - computer programmes - can use deepfakes to generate realistic speech or facial expressions, which contributes to more natural interactions with users, thereby evoking a potential threat. This allows the agent to present different emotions and react to situations in a more human-like manner. Examples of popular virtual agents include Siri from Apple, Alexa from Amazon or Google Assistant. One example of the use of deepfakes in robotics is a project by a research team from Stanford University. The researchers used deepfakes to generate realistic recordings of facial expressions on robotic commands [29]. As a result, the robots were able to better understand and respond to users' emotions and intentions, which improved the quality of human-robot interaction.However, it is important to highlight that deepfakes also have the potential for unethical and harmful use, e.g. by creating false information or manipulating the human image. It is therefore important to use these technologies in responsible manner and an informed understanding of their potential social impact.

10 Summary

Researchers and engineers are constantly developing AI, improving its effectiveness, efficiency and safety. AI applications include medicine, finance, transport, industry and education, and its potential to automate and create new solutions is enormous. However, the development of artificial intelligence can have serious social implications, relating to privacy, ethics and responsibility. It is therefore important to discuss, research and regulate to ensure safety.

Funding. This research was funded by the Military University of Technology, Faculty of Electronics,grant number UGB 22 864 on "Watermark embedding and extraction methods as well as aggregation and spectral analysis methods using neural networks".

References

1. Rich, E., Knight, K.: Artificial Intelligence, 2nd Edition, p. 3
2. Machine Learning. Tom Mitchell, McGraw Hill (1997)
3. https://hai.stanford.edu/sites/default/files/2020-09/AI-Definitions-HAI.pdf [20.06.2023r.]
4. Hopfield, J.J.: Neural networks and physical systems with emergent collective computational abilities. Proc. Natl. Acad. Sci. USA **79**, 2554–2558 (1982). Biophysics
5. Krzysztof, S.: Uczenie maszynowe z użyciem Scikit-Learn i TensorFlow, wyd. II, aktualizacja do modułu TensorFlow 2. Helion, Gliwice (2020)
6. Emre, Celebi, M.: Kemal Aydin Unsupervised Learning Algorithms (2016)
7. Introduction to RL and Deep Q Networks, TensorFlow
8. S4L: Self-Supervised Semi-Supervised Learning, Xiaohua Zhai, Avital Oliver, Alexander Kolesnikov, Lucas Beyer, Google Research, Brain-Team, online: https://openaccess.thecvf.com/content_ICCV_2019/papers/Zhai_S4L_Self-Supervised_Semi-Supervised_Learning_ICCV_2019_paper.pdf [20.06.2023r.]
9. Alexei, B., et al.: data2vec: A General Framework for Self-supervised Learning in Speech. Vision and Language, arXiv:2202.03555v3 [cs.LG] 25 Oct 2022, online: https://arxiv.org/pdf/2202.03555.pdf [20.06.2023r.]
10. https://github.com/arxyzan/data2vec-pytorch

11. Goled, S.: Online: "Self-Supervised Learning Vs Semi-Supervised Learning: How They Differ". Analytics India Magazine (2021). [20.06.2023r.]
12. Vaswani, A., et al.: Attention is all you need. In: Advances in neural information processing systems, pp. 5998–6008 (2017)
13. Devlin, J., Ming-Wei, C., Kenton, L., Kristina, T.: Bert: Pre-training of deep bidirectional transformers for language understanding (2018). arXiv preprint arXiv:1810.04805
14. Yang, Z., et al.: Xlnet: Generalized autoregressive pretraining for language understanding. In: Advances in neural information processing systems, pp. 5753–5763 (2019)
15. Pedro, C.H., Jason, A., Cynthia, B., Catherine, H., Matthew, H.: Combining pre-trained language models and structured knowledge, arXiv:2101.12294v2 [cs.CL] 5 Feb 2021, online: https://arxiv.org/pdf/2101.12294.pdf [21.06.2023r.]
16. https://ai.facebook.com/blog/large-language-model-llama-meta-ai/ [21.06.2023r.]
17. Vaswani, A., et al.: Attention is all you need. NeurIPS (2017)
18. OpenAI: GPT-4 Technical Report, arXiv:2303.08774v3 [cs.CL] 27 Mar 2023, online: https://arxiv.org/pdf/2303.08774.pdf [21.06.2023r.]
19. Dai, Z., et al.: Transformer-xl: Attentive language models beyond a fixed-length context (2019). arXiv preprint arXiv:1901.02860
20. Dettmers, T., et al.: SpQR: A Sparse-Quantized Representation for Near-Lossless LLM Weight Compression, arXiv:2306.03078v1 [cs.CL] 5 Jun 2023, online: https://arxiv.org/pdf/2306.03078.pdf [21.06.2023r.]
21. Touvron, H., et al.: Meta AI, LLaMA: Open and Efficient Foundation Language Models, arXiv:2302.13971v1 [cs.CL] 27 Feb 2023, online: https://arxiv.org/pdf/2302.13971.pdf
22. [https://pypi.org/project/llama-index/ [21.06.2023r.]
23. LlamaIndex 🦙0.6.30 (gpt-index.readthedocs.io) [21.06.2023r]
24. Samoorganizujące się mapy. Ostatnio dowiedziałem się o SOMach podczas ... I Abhinav Ralhan I Średni (medium.com) [21.06.2023r.]
25. Yang, C., Wu, Q., Li, H., Chen, Y.: Generative Poisoning Attack Method Against Neural Networks. online: 1703.01340.pdf (arxiv.org) [21.06.2023r.]
26. Pouget-Abadie, J., et al.: Generative Adversarial Nets Ian J. Goodfellow. online: 1406.2661.pdf (arxiv.org) [21.06.2023r.]
27. GAN Lab: Graj z generatywnymi sieciami przeciwstawnymi w przeglądarce! (polo-club.github.io) [21.06.2023r.]
28. Ilona Dąbrowska, D.: Nowy wymiar internetowej manipulacji, Zarządzanie Mediami. Tom 8(2), 89–10 (2020). https://doi.org/10.4467/23540214ZM.20.024.11803
29. www.ejournals.eu/ZM
30. Wykorzystanie sztucznej inteligencji do wykrywania pozornie doskonałych filmów typu deepfake (stanford.edu) [21.06.2023r.]

Improvement of the Objects Sorting Process Using Machine Learning on the Example of a Created Prototype

Kamil Węgrzyn[✉]

Cracow University of Economics, Cracow, Poland
s211242@student.uek.krakow.pl, kamilwegrzyn@gmail.com

Abstract. Various industries such as waste management, food production, automotive, and aerospace industries require precise sorting and categorization of products and waste. This is particularly important in the era of Industry 4.0, where automation and robotics in manufacturing processes are crucial. Machine Learning is an important tool in this process, enabling machines to improve their performance based on past experiences. Products, semi-finished goods, and waste can be differentiated based on color, weight, density, consistency, shape, dimensions, and chemical composition. There are advanced but costly methods for distinguishing products with different dimensions and shapes using sensors, scanners, cameras, or sets of sieves that allow only desired products to pass through. On the other hand, products with uniform shape and/or dimensions, as well as unique products (e.g., PET bottles in different colors), are recommended to be optically sorted based on the desired color. Currently available solutions are effective but too expensive for smaller facilities that want to automate their production or processing processes. The author has developed a prototype sorting device that, with further refinement, can be easily and inexpensively implemented in various industrial sectors. The device uses a photo-optical object detection mechanism, which compares the objects with basic color patterns programmed based on user color interpretation. The uniqueness of the device lies in its utilization of Machine Learning by comparing the color of the sorted sample with the reference shade obtained from an online database. The prototype project has demonstrated that current technologies enable the easy implementation of a complex automatic sorting process based on machine learning and scalable electronic infrastructure without incurring significant costs. The development of this device would find applications in many industrial sectors, both in sorting and collecting objects. It would be particularly useful in industries where traditional vacuum sorting is not feasible due to the risk of product damage.

Keywords: PET sorting · waste sorting · objects sorting · objects collecting · industry · prototype device

K. S. Soliman (Ed.): IBIMA-AI 2023, CCIS 2101, pp. 93–104, 2024.
https://doi.org/10.1007/978-3-031-62843-6_11

1 Introduction

The industry, ranging from waste management and food production to the automotive and aerospace sectors, requires the collection, sequencing, categorization, or arrangement of products, parts, and various categories of waste into appropriate sorting containers. Sorting elements are particularly important in the era of automated production lines, which should function autonomously or with minimal assistance from individuals overseeing the processing and/or manufacturing processes [1].

The fourth industrial revolution (Industry 4.0), which enters the industry and is characterized by advanced automation and robotization of manufacturing processes, serves as a strong motivator for innovators in the comprehensive management of the logistics chain. The concept of Industry 4.0 does not aim to eliminate humans from the manufacturing process but rather to support their work and optimize their existing job positions to increase production efficiency (https://www.sciencedirect.com/science/article/abs/pii/S0959652619347390 accessed on 06/10/2023).

One of the key tools implemented with Industry 4.0 is Machine Learning, which is an area of artificial intelligence dedicated to algorithms that improve themselves through experience. Within Machine Learning, implemented algorithms construct.

a mathematical model based on provided data, which serves as the training set (https://www.ibm.com/topics/machine-learning accessed on 06/10/2023).

This allows for forecasting, decision-making, and decision-taking without being explicitly developed by a programmer. Implementing Machine Learning enables increased efficiency, performance, reliability, and cost reduction compared to the use of conventional algorithmic software (Zhou and Liu, 2021).

The author of the article focuses on the sorting process, which is crucial for every industry sector.

Products, semi-finished goods, or waste can be differentiated based on various categories, including:

- color,
- specific mass,
- density,
- consistency,
- shape,
- dimensions,
- chemical composition.

In the case of products that differ in dimensions or shape, advanced sensors, scanners, cameras, or even sets of sieves can be used to distinguish them, allowing only products with desired shapes and/or dimensions to pass through.

For products with uniform shapes and/or dimensions, or for products where each unit is unique (such as crushed multi-colored PET bottles), optical differentiation of the product, for example, by detecting the desired color, should be employed.

There are many commercial solutions available on the market that offer detection for production lines based on sets of sensors and cameras, including high-quality cameras and X-ray scanners [6].

An example of such a solution is PET bottle sorters. Multi-colored PET bottles move along a sorting conveyor. When passing through the scanner, the appropriate color of the bottle is identified using advanced sensors and color detectors. After passing through the scanner, the bottles move under vacuum blowers, which, depending on the bottle category, either suction them to the desired level or allow them to continue sorting on the conveyor belt (Weber and Weber, 2010).

Figure 1 depicts an example of the discussed solution.

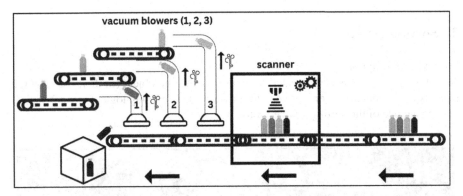

Fig. 1. Industrial sorter. Source: own development.

The presented solution, despite being effective and characterized by high throughput of the production line and 100% accuracy, is inaccessible to most smaller facilities that are starting to automate their manufacturing processes.

Therefore, the author of the paper has built a prototype of a sorting device that, with further refinement, can be successfully adapted with low cost to many industry sectors.

2   The Genesis of the Work and Prototype Description

Existing market solutions, despite their accuracy, are characterized by unaffordable prices, which discourages many companies from seeking opportunities to adopt automation in their manufacturing processes.

As part of the research on the possibilities of constructing a simple sorting device, a prototype device was created for sorting items marked with specially prepared labels. In the case of this project, the labels were color-coded and recognized.

by a detector mounted on the moving part of the device (the head).

The sorting device operates based on optical detection of the examined items. The uniqueness of the solution lies in the application of Machine Learning, which is achieved by comparing the color of the sorted sample with a reference shade obtained from an online database [1].

Machine Learning is implemented using a Machine Learning Control Device (MLCD) pilot, which is solely used to program the base colors based on the user's interpretation of color through the MLCD.

When the sorting device reads the RGB color of a labeled item, it compares the color with the base shade (value obtained from the database) and then decides which container the label should be placed into.

Additionally, a web application was created as an administrative panel for the operator of the prototype sorting device. With the help of the application, the operator can check the parameters read from peripheral sensors (RGB color read from the photo-optical sensor, data from IR gates, and limit switches) and modify the configuration of the executive elements (change the state of stepper motors, electromagnets) [15].

3   Sorting Device

Prototype Description:
A prototype device has been created to identify a specific object (in this case, colored tags) using an optical sensor that operates based on self-learning logic. Figure 2 depicts the appearance of the sorting device prototype.

Fig. 2. Sorting device prototype. Source: own development

The device consists of the following elements:

- conveyor belt, along which the colored tags to be sorted are transported,
- head, mounted on a linear guide,
- linear guide, an element on which the head moves. The guide is attached to a belt connected to a stepper motor.
- photo-optical sensor, identifying the type of colored tag,
- IR gates, serving as stops to determine the position of the head on the linear guide,
- limit switches, serving as safety devices for the head moving along the linear guide,
- sorting tray, containers where the colored tags are deposited,
- control unit, consisting of:
- ESP32 DevKitC ESP-WROOM-32U microcontroller by Espressif, which handles communication with the online database,

- Arduino Mega 2560 Rev3 - A000067 microcontroller, responsible for controlling the stepper motors, reading data from IR gates, reading parameters from the photo-optical sensor, and reading signals from the limit switches [4],
- PCB boards, serving as expansion modules for Arduino Mega,
- monostable buttons,
- stepper motor drivers.

The components of the head, conveyor belt, mounting of the linear guide, and other smaller structural elements were.

3D printed. The printing was conducted using Creality printers. [2].

Figure 3 presents the elements produced using 3D printing technology.

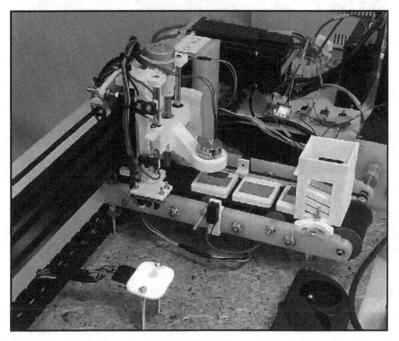

Fig. 3. Elements of the prototype made using 3D printing technology. Source: own development.

The sorting process:

1. Homecoming

   When the device is connected to a power source, the main head with the electro-magnet returns to the home position. The head stops when it reaches the limit switch. These zero points serve as reference positions for the containers where the sorted colored tags will be placed.

2. Collection and identification

   There are two monostable buttons located on the control center housing. Figure 4 shows the placement of the buttons on the control center housing.

Figure 4. Placement of monostable buttons on the control center housing. Source: author's own work.

Fig. 4. Control unit of the sorting device. Source: own development.

Table 1 defines the implementation of functionalities using the specified button on the device's housing.

Table 1. List of functionalities implemented by monostable buttons. Source: own development

Button	Functionality implemented
Green color	Start the sorting sequence
Black color	Reset the device

a. Tag Retrieval

By pressing the green button, the user initiates the sorting sequence. At this point, the electromagnet attached to the worm gear mechanism lowers itself to the lower end position. Once the end position is reached, the electromagnet is activated to retrieve the colored tag from the conveyor belt. After 3 seconds, the electromagnet returns to the upper position on the head.

b. Tag Identification

The tag, along with the electromagnet, moves along the linear guide to the first stop, which is the photo-optical sensor. When the IR gate is detected, the head stops, and the electromagnet with the tag is lowered to the lower end position.

Then, for a duration of 5 seconds, the tag is illuminated by LED lights and identified by the photo-optical sensor. The sensor collects RGB color data of the object and transmits it to the central controller.

Figure 5 depicts the process of tag identification.

Fig. 5. Tag scanning by the photo-optical sensor of the sorting device. Source: own development.

The RGB value scanned by the photo-optical sensor of the sorting device is compared with the RGB values.

of patterns scanned by MLCD and stored in an online database. The device compares both values and assigns the scanned sample to the pattern that best correlates with it in terms of RGB color deviation.

3. Sorting

The tag is moved to the appropriate bin. The position markers are defined using IR gates - as the head passes a specific gate, it memorizes its identifier in a sequence, allowing it to identify the corresponding bin.

The identified tags are placed in the respective bins based on their color. For example, a tag with a red marker will be placed in the red bin.

In the case of an unrecognized tag color or when a tag does not have a colored marker, it will be transported to the last black bin, where unrecognized tags are collected.

4   Items Subject to Sorting

The elements subjected to sorting, used in the prototype device, are metal objects covered with colored labels. These elements are also referred to as "tags" in the article.

The tags are carried by an electromagnet mounted on the head, which is in turn attached to a linear guide.

Figure 6 illustrates the appearance of colorful magnetic tags.

Fig. 6. Colorful magnetic tags. Source: Own development.

Learning Device - The Machine Learning Color Device (MLCD)

The Machine Learning Color Device (MLCD) is an auxiliary device for the color tag sorter. Its purpose is to facilitate the color learning process and transmit color definitions to the sorting machine, which conducts the actual sorting process of the color tags. The appearance of the MLCD pilot is illustrated in Fig. 7.

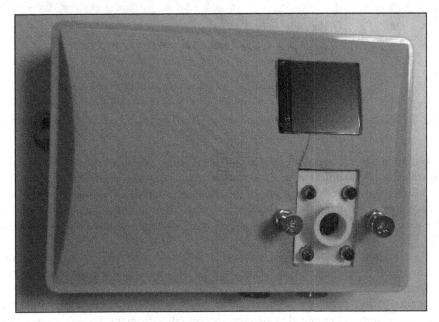

Fig. 7. Machine Learning Color Device. Source: own development.

MLCD is a portable device that operates on autonomous power from a Li-ion 18650 battery. To recharge it, you need to connect the device to a 5V power source, such as a power adapter, USB port on a laptop, or power bank.

MLCD is equipped with the following components:

- ESP32 DevKitC ESP-WROOM-32U microcontroller by Espressif,
- photo-optical sensor,
- IPS display based on the ST7789 driver,
- monostable buttons,
- battery power source.

The electronic components are mounted on printed circuit boards (PCBs) made of insulating material. The connections between soldering points (pads, drill points) are established by routing signal and/or current paths of varying widths [3].

To perform measurements, MLCD needs to be calibrated, which can be done during device startup.

Figure 8 illustrates the location of the main power switch on the MLCD housing.

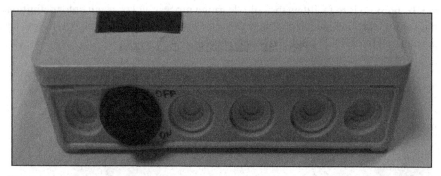

Fig. 8. Location of the main power switch on the MLCD device. Source: own development.

Calibration involves placing the tag with the side that does not have a colored marking, which is used to differentiate the elements, against the MLCD. The user performing the calibration presses the black side of the tag against the MLCD at a height indicated by two screws protruding from the device's casing. The calibration process takes 10 s, after which the IoT device connects to a predefined Wi-Fi network with internet access [17].

Once a secure connection to the internet is established, the device is ready to perform measurements on test tags, which will be used for later machine learning purposes [16].

Machine learning is possible after the calibration process of the photo-optical sensor is completed. To "teach" the color, a colored tag is held in front of the photo-optical sensor at a distance determined by two screws protruding from the device's casing. The color measurement process takes 10 s. After the designated measurement time, the color value read by the sensor is displayed on the built-in screen in the form of RGB values. At this point, the user decides which color the displayed color value is closest to. Table 2 indicates the functionality of the monostable buttons mounted on the MLCD device casing [5].

Table 2. Functionality of Monostable Buttons in the MLCD Device. Source: own development.

Button	Realized functionality
Green color	changes in the standard color for the read sample (red, blue, green),
Black color	acceptance of the selection and transfer of the correlation: baseline sample and read measurement to the online database

Figure 9 depicts the placement of buttons on the enclosure.

Fig. 9. Functional monostable buttons in the MLCD device. Source: own development.

After the color learning process is completed, MLCD attempts to establish a connection with a WebSocket - a communication protocol on the server that enables bidirectional data exchange through a single TCP connection [8].

The data transmission process concludes upon confirmation or rejection of the communication establishment. The user receives information on the screen.

Table 3 presents the content of displayed messages depending on the connection status (Bradshaw, Chodorow, and Brazil, 2020).

Table 3. Content of displayed messages depending on the connection status.

Communication and data transfer status	Displayed message
The success of communication and data transfer	WS TAK
Failure of communication and data transfer	WS NIE

Source: own development

The submitted patterns serve as a reference base for the sorting sequence performed by the sorting device. The process of comparing the reference data with the sample data is presented in the section dedicated to the sorting device.

5   Conclusions

The prototype of the sorting device successfully performs its tasks according to the adopted assumptions - it identifies the sampled items from the conveyor belt and correctly places them in the respective bins.

Manual tests conducted on June 15, 2023, demonstrated a 100% effectiveness of the device for two hundred continuous trials. The device correctly placed tags with red, blue, and green markers into their corresponding-colored bins. Tags without a colored marker were correctly placed in the black bin.

The development of the device would find applications in various industries, not only for sorting but also for object collection purposes. The device would be particularly suitable for industries where vacuum sorting cannot be applied due to the risk of damaging fragile products upon impact.

The prototype construction project has proven that, in the current technological conditions, implementing a complex process such as automatic object sorting based on machine learning and a scalable electronic infrastructure is easily achievable and does not require massive investments.

References

1. Cichosz, P.: Systemy uczące się. Warszawa: WNT (2000)
2. Forquignon, F.: 3D printing with Simplify3D. Independently Published, New York (2018)
3. Hadam, P.: Projektowanie systemów mikroprocesorowych. Warszawa: BTC (2004)
4. Hoffman, J.: Zostań mistrzem Arduino. Projekty dla początkujących i zaawansowanych. Warszawa: Helion (2019)
5. Horowitz, P., Hill, W.: Sztuka elektroniki 1. Sulejówek: Wydawnictwo Komunikacji i Łączności Sp. z o.o. (2022)
6. Horowitz, P., Hill, W.: Sztuka elektroniki 2. Sulejówek: Wydawnictwo Komunikacji i Łączności Sp. z o.o. (2022)
7. https://www.ibm.com/topics/machine-learning. Accessed on 06 Oct 2023
8. https://websockets.spec.whatwg.org/. Accessed on 06 Oct 2023
9. https://www.recycling-magazine.com/wp-content/uploads/2020/06/Autosort-5-LowRes.jpg. Accessed on 06 Oct 2023
10. ISO 27001: International Organization for Standardization. Information technology - Security techniques - Information security management systems - Requirements (2021)
11. ISO 9001: International Organization for Standardization. Quality management systems – Requirements (2015)
12. ISO 27001/IEC 62443: International Organization for Standardization & International Electrotechnical Commission. Information technology - Security techniques - Network and system security - Part 1: Terminology, concepts, and models (2018)
13. IEC 61499: International Electrotechnical Commission. Function blocks for industrial process measurement and control systems (2015)
14. IEEE 802.11: Institute of Electrical and Electronics Engineers. IEEE Standard for Information technology - Telecommunications and information exchange between systems - Local and metropolitan area networks - Specific requirements - Part 11: Wireless LAN Medium Access Control (MAC) and Physical Layer (PHY) Specifications (2016)
15. Jabraeil Jamali, M.A. et al.: Towards the Internet of Things. Cham: Springer Nature Switzerland AG (2020)
16. Niederliński, A.: Mikroprocesory mikrokomputery mikrosystemy. Warszawa: Wydawnictwa Szkolne i Pedagogiczne (1987)
17. Rusek, A.: Podstawy Elektroniki część 2. Warszawa: Wydawnictwo Szkolne i Pedagogiczne (1986)
18. Weber, R.H., Weber, R.: Internet of Things. Springer-Verlag, Berlin (2010)

Information Systems
and Communications Technologies

Security Management for Vehicular Ad Hoc Networks by Software Defined Network Paradigm

Lamaa Sellami[1], Rejab Hajlaoui[2], Bechir Alaya[2(✉)], and Sami Mahfoudhi[3]

[1] CONPRI Laboratory, University of Gabes, Zrig Eddakhlania, Tunisia
[2] Hatem Bettaher Laboratory (IResCoMath), Gabes University, Zrig Eddakhlania, Tunisia
alabechir@yahoo.fr
[3] Department of Management Information Systems and Production Management, College of Business and Economics, Qassim University, 6633, Buraidah 51452, Saudi Arabia
s.mahfoudhi@qu.edu.sa

Abstract. Considering the importance of direct communications between vehicles and between vehicles/infrastructure in a vehicular environment, the proposal of a new architectural approach taking advantage of the advantages of both communications is, therefore, a very important topic to discuss. In this perspective, we are developing a vehicular network using several access technologies and based on the SDN (Software Defined Network), to provide flexibility in their control and management. This flexibility is a necessity to efficiently manage available network resources and provide communication services tailored to Intelligent Transportation System (ITS) service requirements. Also, a good security and confidentiality management system are necessary to ensure the protection of vehicular networks. In this article, we also provide a scheme that prevents and informs attacks by managing the requirements of security management systems. The simulation results showed the effectiveness of the proposed schemes in terms of message loss rate, packet delivery rate, and delay reduction.

Keywords: Software Defined Network (SDN) · Vehicular Networks · Intelligent Transport System (ITS) · Privacy and Security

1 Introduction

The concept of a vehicular network opens up to various types of communications to meet the needs of the wide variety of new applications envisaged within the framework of the Intelligent Transportation System (ITS). In another parallel axis, network topologies have evolved and given birth to the SDN (Software Defined Network) architecture that is famous for the separation between the data plane and the control plane. We can present SDN as the first network architecture that provides an intelligent transformation from materialization to the software world as well as the hallmark of virtualization.

There has been a lot of research that has tried to apply SDN to VANET, with the objectives of quality of service (QoS), mobility, security, etc. It is therefore within this framework that this work falls, the contributions of which aim to develop the concept of VANET defined by SDNET Software (Software Defined Network to VANET). The goal of our work is to design a light solution (in terms of cryptographic operations execution time) to secure the SDN network in a VANET environment [1].

The first step is to specify a hybrid SDN-VANET architecture capable of meeting the challenges described above. This architecture is completed by an SDN controller placement solution for VANET network security against possible threats. We provide a dynamic approach capable of adjusting the optimal placement of controllers based on changes in network topology due to fluctuations in road traffic. In addition to the VANET network control service, we also offer a topology estimation service based on machine learning techniques to provide network control functions with a potential vision of the future state of the network, and therefore open them up to proactive and intelligent control of the network.

Vehicular networks have been designed to bring many advantages, such as the reduction of accidents, the comfort of drivers and passengers, the ease of payment for certain services such as parking, gasoline, games, and online network, audio and video downloads, etc. [2]. These applications involve the exchange of messages such as emergency messages, warnings of accidents that have occurred, road conditions at specific times, and driver assistance information. All these exchanges involving data and message content can influence the behavior of conductors and thus modify the topology of the network. This, therefore, implies a risk of danger of attack by malicious users who can alter the messages exchanged on the network [3]. It is therefore essential but difficult to design an effective system that preserves the security and confidentiality of information exchanged between vehicles on VANET networks. To address security and performance issues, we are introducing a secure and intelligent detection scheme with strong privacy preservation, allowing a VANET user to securely receive and share messages.

The rest of the paper is organized as follows: Sect. 2 highlights the patterns of Software Defined Network (SDN) adoptions and localizations in VANETs, as well as the protection and security mechanisms of VANETs in the literature. In Sect. 3, we introduce our first scheme, in which we first present the SDN paradigm by describing the key principles and design choices that guided the development of our architecture. Section 4 describes our privacy and security scheme applied to the VANET environment. Section 5 evaluates the solutions based on the analysis of the simulation results. Finally, Sect. 6 concludes the paper and recommends many guidelines for future analyses.

1.1 Related Work

The SDN adoption paradigm for VANET networks is primarily aimed at separating the control plane from the data plane in the VANET environment.

With this in mind, the authors of [4] proposed an ad hoc communication control between vehicles (V2V) and communications between vehicles and RSU (V2I) based on SDN. The SDN controller represents a single point of failure (SPOF). Our approach evokes the advantage of being able to dynamically reserve resources for a demanding security-type service.

In [5], SDN centrally calculates the optimal routing paths. The performance of the proposed approaches has surpassed the other approaches. The authors of [6] proposed

SDN-based network architecture for geo-diffusion in VANET networks. Truong et al. [7] explored the use of Fog Computing in an SDN-VANET architecture. Their proposal called FSDN integrates Fog computing to support constraining services in terms of latency as well as those based on location.

The authors of [8] proposed an approach based on distributed controllers. Their goals were to solve collision problems in very dense environments. The proposed approach implements a data plan composed of single network technology.

Heller et al. [9] initially investigated the effect of SDN controller location on network performance. The authors agreed that better localization of the SDN controller significantly reduces average latency. Researchers have studied the optimization of latency between nodes and SDN controllers [10], based on a modification of the K-means method. Also, the authors of [11] proposed an approach based on a linear formulation to analyze the trade-off between load balancing and latency.

Likewise, the authors of [12] have proposed to employ the Bargaining Game to find a compromise between three factors, namely, the latency between the switches and the controllers, the latency between the controllers, and load balancing between controllers.

Recently, the SDN paradigm has been extended to other types of networks other than VANET networks [14], such as IoT networks [13], WSN networks, cellular networks, etc.

A distributed approach is presented by Zaidi et al. [15] to detect Sybil attacks and the dissemination of false information from malicious vehicles. Each vehicle uses the Greenshields model [16] which describes the relationships between speed, density, and the flow of vehicles per hour on a road.

Rabah [17], working on Cryptosystems implementing security by elliptic curve algorithms, gave scientific suggestions to improve public-key cryptosystems.

Yuh-Min Tseng [18], worked on different Digital Signature schemes by not using any hash or message redundancy. The reason for this study was to save from Forgery Attacks that were proposed by Chang and Chang while working on digital signatures.

1.2 Dynamic Approach to Placing Controllers in the SDN Context

In this section, we first present the SDN paradigm by describing the key principles and design choices that guided the development of this architecture, and we analyze the various opportunities of the proposed architecture.

2 SDN Paradigm in the VANET Environment

In a VANET network, each network device is made up of a data plane and a control plane. The primary purpose of the data plane is the routing of data, while the control plane is responsible for all network control decisions, such as deciding from which interface data is routed.

With conventional networks, the same device comprises the control plane and the data plane. Each plane makes its own decisions independently. However, the SDN paradigm recommends the separation of the control plane and the data plane. This is because network control functions are outsourced from network equipment and arranged in software components on dedicated external equipment called SDN controllers.

This paradigm was proposed to introduce more flexibility and simplicity in the management and control of the network. In our architecture, the SDN controller is the central element. It communicates with the various nodes of the VANET network through a South-Bound Interface (SBI) protocol. While the North-Bound Interface (NBI) protocol expresses the need for the SDN controller.

The SDN controller provides an abstraction of the underlying network to network applications and services and is responsible for setting the various network policies. The data plane is made up of routing nodes often referred to as PFE for Packet Forwarding Element.

3 General Description of the Proposed Architecture

As the main basis, we integrate the SDN paradigm in our hybrid vehicle network service protection architecture. To improve the control of the VANET network and facilitate its management in addition to the advantages of hybridization, we still use the advantages of the SDN paradigm. Therefore, we can develop efficient VANET network protection algorithms which will be based on knowledge of the environment of the vehicle nodes, the global state of the communication networks (Multi-RAT), and finally the capacity for dynamic control of the networks. These different data can come from road authorities, VANET operators, etc. Our architectural goal is to separate the control plane from the data plane through intelligent integration of the SDN paradigm (see Fig. 1). Several policies are implemented by SDN controllers, maintaining the intelligence of the VANET network.

As shown in Fig. 1, the red and blue dotted lines distinguish the control paths and the data paths respectively. According to the instructions provided by the SDN controllers, the nodes of the data plane ensure the routing of the data. We can design three conceptual principles of our architecture, which are detailed in the following subsections.

1) Heterogeneous data plane (Multi-RAT) in the proposed architecture

We can notice by Fig. 1, that the data plane consists of components programmable via SDN, such as RSUs, vehicle nodes, and finally base stations. This choice is motivated by the vision of hybridizing DSRC and cellular technologies to take advantage of their advantages and to couple their capacities to effectively support ITS services. We consider that vehicles are equipped with two or more network interfaces. For example, one interface to access the RSU network (DSRC) and another to access the cellular network (LTE / 5G).

However, vehicle nodes are considered programmable via SDN, by default. The latest studies have shown the motivation of the SDN paradigm and that centrally computed routing is more efficient than distributed computed routing. According to the observed results of SDN controllers applied on VANET networks, it is clear that the vision offered by SDN can lead to an interesting reduction in the risk of collisions by controlling the transmission parameters. We assume that the interface posed in our architecture also allows performing the choice of wireless channels, power control, and routing.

The difference between data plane nodes lies in the features supported by each node and their specific characteristics. From the perspective of the SDN controller, the nodes are transparently controlled according to a unified model.

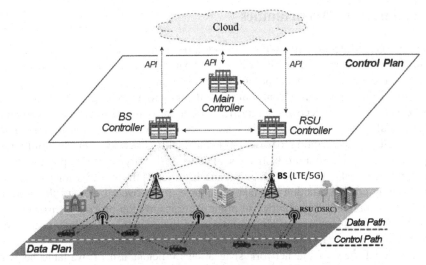

Fig. 1. Global vision of the proposed architecture.

3.1 Data-Driven Control

For more efficient network VANET control, SDN controllers can use data from external actors (such as route managers, VANET operators, etc.). This data is used to derive a potential view of the network status and to enrich the network overview.

The data exchange between system actors, the control plane, and the data plane represent the vehicle nodes for a detailed design of VANET services. To enrich the global vision built by SDN controllers, data plane data can be combined with external data.

This service can leverage information about the potential trajectory of MPP (Most Probable Path) vehicles to derive potential network attachment points for a given vehicle, which will help estimate potential network load. These data can be provided by ITS service providers, part of their services which is based on the vehicle's potential trajectory.

We cite the example of the eHorizon driving assistance service [19], which provides vehicles based on their MPP with condition road information. On the other hand, the potential network condition estimation service can take advantage of additional input weather data to accurately predict signal and network quality for nodes in a given area.

The network selection function can take advantage of this potential network vision to effectively guide vehicles in choosing which communications network to use. This decision will be based not only on the current condition of the two networks but also on their potential condition. However, ITS service providers can design services based on potential network quality data. For example, the route recommendation service can take advantage of this data to recommend routes for vehicles that provide a better network service quality. This property requires collaboration between the various systems actors for the data exchange.

4 Architecture Opportunities

The proposed architecture offers many opportunities in network control terms. They are mainly inherited from the properties of the SDN paradigm coupled with the advantages of vehicular communication technologies hybridization.

Network programmability contributes significantly to improving network quality of service management. Indeed, fine-grained programming of the network makes it possible to dynamically allocate resources at the scale of a flow. In addition, it offers the possibility of reconfiguring and adapting to variations in the quality of service. This flexibility fully responds to dynamic variations in this type of network. This dynamic of topology caused mainly by the mobility of vehicles requires an adaptation of the transmission parameters. The topology control function can take advantage of the overall view of the network to quickly reconfigure the topology to minimize transmission problems (interference, collision, etc.). Algorithms providing joint control involving both topology control and QoS management can be designed to ensure optimal performance.

The global view of the network state allows efficient use of available network resources, which many algorithms can take advantage of.

4.1 Security and Confidentiality Scheme

We present, in this section, a confidentiality and security scheme applied to the ITS environment. This scheme is based on five steps that are presented as follows.

4.2 Key and Certificate Sent by SDN

We assume that there is a Trusted Authority (TA) to initialize the whole system. We adopt AODV (Ad hoc On-Demand Distance Vector Routing)[20], as the routing protocol selected by SDN. We have {MesDem, MesRes, MesNot} in the format of the message "RREQ route request"[21], the three control messages which are initialized by SDN. The system will be initialized by SDN b performing the following steps.

1- The security parameters begin to initialize with the SDN by executing $R.Init(1^\delta)$. Knowing that R represents all of the RSUs which receive an optimum of the replica messages. $R.Init(1^\delta)$ allows for generating a bilinear environment $(t, \mathbb{G}_1, \mathbb{G}_2, \}_1, \}_2, i, \mathcal{F})$ where (δ, k) are the security parameters, $\mathbb{G}_1, \mathbb{G}_2$ two groups of order t, $\}_1$ is the generator of $\mathbb{G}_1$, and $\}_2$ is the generator of $\mathbb{G}_2$. The SDN selects s and s' in $\mathbb{Z}_t^*$ and calculates $x = \}_1^s \in \mathbb{G}_1$ and $y = \}_2^{s'} \in \mathbb{G}_2$. SDN then chooses a secure symmetric encryption algorithm $Enc(.)$, and a random number $k \in \mathbb{Z}_t^*$ selected as a master key. Next, it chooses two secure cryptographic hash functions Ω_1, Ω_2, such as $\to \mathbb{G}_1$, as $\Omega_2 : \{0,1\}^* \times \mathbb{G}_2 \to \{0,1\}^k$.

2- Depending on confidentiality requirements, SDN selects $\Delta\varepsilon$ and decides the certificate validity at $\Delta\varepsilon$.

3- SDN keeps the master key k as secret, and shares the system parameters in VANET$(t, \mathbb{G}_1, \mathbb{G}_2, \}_1, \}_2, i, \mathcal{F}, \Omega_1, \Omega_2, Enc(.), \Delta\varepsilon)$.

Suppose that we have a new vehicle node wishing to communicate with other nodes, for an RSU R_i in the cluster Cl_j, the SDN sends the certificate $Cert_{v_i}$, and the private key PK_{v_i} as follows:

1- SDN calculates $LID_{v_i} = Enc(ID_{v_i})$ which represents the login identity of the vehicle node with the master key k.
2- Then SDN defines the secret key $PK_{v_i} = \Omega_1(LID_{v_i})$, the public key $GK_{v_i} = s\}_1$, and an arbitrary number $\in \mathbb{Z}_t^*$.
3- Using the signature generation algorithm [22], SDN generates the signature χ_{v_i}.
4- Finally and safely SDN generates $LID_{v_i}, PK_{v_i}, and\, Cert_{v_i}$. SDN keeps track of the mapping between $Cert_{v_i}$ and the veritable ID_{v_i}.

Using the function $R.Monit(\chi_{v_i}, \}_1, GK_{v_i})$, the vehicle node v_i can verify the certificate $Cert_{v_i}$. We can discover then that our scheme can necessarily guarantee optimum confidentiality of the identity of the user of VANET by using this key distribution method.

A. The Certificate Update in the Proposed Scheme

A restoration policy has been implemented in our proposed scheme. Such, SDN can offer several certificates for each vehicle node. However, these certificates should not be used immediately after they arrive from SDN in the VANET network. Note again that only the certificates issued by RSU R_i belonging to the Cl_j study clusters are valid. As already presented in [23], we adopt in our scheme the technology of proxy re-signature cryptography. This technology is based on requesting the re-signing key from all nodes of Cl_j (N_j) and then deciding whether the certificates issued by the SDN and those issued by itself are the same or not. Suppose we have a real-time cT_k, then to obtain the re-signature keys corresponding to R_i, the vehicle node v_i can use the Scert signature certificates. We then present an algorithm that details the updated certificate.

ALGORITHM 1: CERTIFICATE UPDATE ALGORITHM

1. Select of $Cert_{v_i}, GK_{v_i}, \mathcal{G}_1$
2. if ($Cert_{v_i}$ is valid) Then
3. Calculate: C, D, S Such   a: $hms' \cdot GK_{v_i}$; $D \cdot \mathcal{G}_1$; $S = Enc_C(T_k\ concat\ Cert_{v_i,k})$
4. else (Reject)
5. if (S is valid during the gap time $T_{k+1} \cdots T_{k+N_j}$) Then
6. Calculate the re − signature key $RK_{v_i,k}$)
7. else (Reject)
8. if ($RK_{v_i,k}$ is valid) Then
9. Accept $RK_{v_i,k}$
10. else (Reject)

4.3 Verification and Signature

The vehicle node v_i uses the signature algorithm SigAlg, to sign the three messages {MyDem, MyRes, MyNot}. Also note SigAlg r epresents:

R.Sign$\left(K, PK_{v_i}, \text{MesDem}\right)$ Concat $h_{v_i, \text{MesDem}}$ where $K = \Omega_2(TP \cdot Cert_{R_j, v_i})$ represents the temporary key and TP is the time stamp, $Cert_{v_i}$ is the certificate of v_i issued by the SDN, and PK_{v_i} is the private key of v_i.

The other vehicle nodes wait for the receipt of the MesDem from v_i, then they begin to check if $Cert_{R_j, v_i}$ is valid. Then the vehicle nodes check if R.Check(MesDem, $h_{v_i, \text{MesRes}}$, K) is true to accept the message m_i.

We can define the detection time for $TimeDet_{v_i}$ attacks from v_i based on the following conditions: the time it takes to send the message MesDem, the real environment of VANET, and the transmission power and bandwidth of the VANET network, as follows:

$$TimeDet_{v_i} = \text{TN}_{MesDem} - \frac{OT}{LS} \quad (1)$$

Such that: LS is the light speed, TN_{MesDem} is the send time of the message $MesDem$, and OT represents the optimum transmission. To optimize the number of erroneous decisions $TimeDet_{v_i}$ must be carefully calculated. We can conclude that this is probably an attack if and only if $TimeDet_{v_i} < 0$.

5   Experimental Results

To study and evaluate the proposed architecture for vehicle networks programmable via SDN, the simulation environment must combine (in the majority of cases) both: (*i*) support for SDN programmable networks, (*ii*) a wireless communication medium, and (*iii*) a vehicular mobility medium.

To meet these simulation needs, we choose the use of MiniNet-WiFi [24]. We opt for a VANET network under SDN control, which consists of four RSU entities, each with a coverage of 600 m. We detail the characteristics of our network traffic in Table 1.

Table 1. Simulation parameters

Parameters	Setting
Simulation area (Phase 1)	500 m × 500 m
Simulation area (Phase 2)	2 km × 2 km
Paquet Size	1500 bytes
Traffic type	UDP
Vehicle speed	0–50 km/h
PHY/MAC Layer	IEEE 802.11p
Buffer size	41 Mbytes
Measuring interval	1 s
Bandwith	10 Mbytes/s

Figures 2 and 3 show the communication performance results between the car1 and car2 vehicle nodes with and without application of control, and with and without the presence of our security and privacy scheme (SPS). They show respectively the Round Trip Time (RTT) and the Packet Delivery Ratio (PDR).

We can conclude that the performance of the network deteriorates when the vehicle node car1 is attached to the entity RSU1 and the latter is overloaded. The Packet Delivery Ratio decreases by 30% and the Round Trip Time decreases from 111 ms to 449 ms.

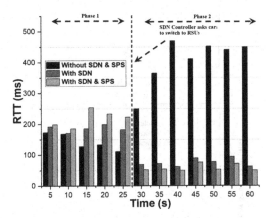

Fig. 2. Round Trip Time (RTT).

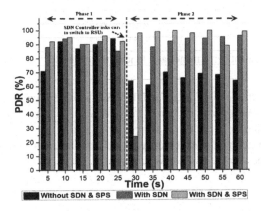

Fig. 3. Packet Delivery Ratio (PDR).

We also notice with the integration of the SPS that the performance of the network is improved, the average RTT is reduced by 51 ms and the PDR persists around 99%. We also notice that the PDR drops to 18% with the forwarding action between RSUs which has a network performance cost.

The consideration of the SDN paradigm as a key principle in the design of new vehicular network architectures poses again the challenge concerning the placement of controllers.

Figures 4(a) and (b) show respectively the overhead and the average FST as a function of the maximum number of jumps (tolerated by the placement strategy) and the number

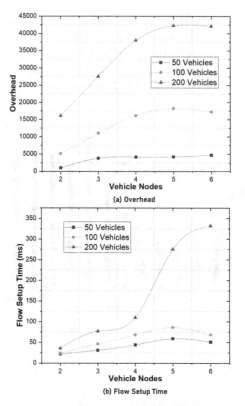

Fig. 4. Placement performance as a function of controller load and coverage.

of vehicles. As expected, the overhead and the FST increase according to the maximum number of hops between the controller and the vehicles. The increase in overhead mainly depends on the number of packet-in messages generated.

This increase in delay is due to increased load on the controller and the impact of increased load on the vehicle-to-RSU wireless links.

6 Conclusion

The contributions proposed in this paper aim at the development of a new security concept of vehicular network programmable via SDN. For the first contribution, we defined the vehicular network architecture based on the SDN paradigm. The combination of the properties of the SDN paradigm with the hybridization of vehicular networks makes the success of the proposed architecture. To further secure VANET networks, we have also come up with a second smart protection scheme. This scheme prevents and informs basic and compound attacks, and does more than react to the privacy and security conditions of the VANET network.

The definition of the view of the network to be shared and how it will be shared, as well as the operational mode of data exchange between the various actors of this system, can constitute a first perspective of architectural order.

References

1. Chen, B., Wu, L., Kumar, N., Choo, K.K. R., He, D.: Lightweight searchable public-key encryption with forward privacy over IIoT outsourced data. IEEE Trans. Emerg. Top. Comput. **9**(4), 1753–1764 (2021)
2. Drira, W., Ahn, K.H., Rakha, H., Filali, F.: Development and testing of a 3G/LTE adaptive data collection system in vehicular networks. IEEE Trans. Intell. Transp. Syst. **17** (2016)
3. Sellami, L., Alaya, B.: SAMNET.: self-adaptative multi-kernelclustering algorithm for urban VANETs. Veh. Commun. **29**, 1–15 (2021)
4. Ku, I., Lu, Y., Gerla, M., Gomes, R.L., Ongaro, F., Cerqueira, E.: Towards software-defined VANET: architecture and services. In: 13th Annual Mediterranean Ad-Hoc Networking Workshop (MED-HOC-NET), pp. 103–110 (2014)
5. Ji, X., Yu, H., Fan, G., Fu, W.: SDGR.: an SDN-based geographic routing protocol for VANET. In: IEEE International Conference on Internet of Things (iThings) and IEEE Green Computing and Communications (GreenCom) and IEEE Cyber, Physical and Social Computing (CPSCom) and IEEE Smart Data (SmartData), pp. 276–281 (2016)
6. Liu, Y.C., Chen, C., Chakraborty, S.: A software defined network architecture for geobroadcast in VANETs. In: IEEE International Conference on Communications (ICC), pp. 6559–6564 (2015)
7. Truong, N.B., Lee, G.M., Ghamri-Doudane, Y.: Software defined networking-based vehicular Adhoc Network with Fog Computing. In: IFIP/IEEE International Symposium on Integrated Network Management (IM), pp. 1202–1207 (2015)
8. Alaya, B., Sellami, L.: Clustering method and symmetric/asymmetric cryptography scheme adapted to securing urban VANET networks. J. Inf. Secur. Appl. **58**, 1–12. https://doi.org/10.1016/j.jisa.2021.102779
9. Heller, B., Sherwood, R., Keown, N.M.: The controller placement problem. In: ACM Proceeding of the First Workshop on Hot Topics in Software Defined Networks, HotSDN 2012, pp.7–12, New York, NY, USA (2012)
10. Wang, G., Zhao, Y., Huang, J., Duan, Q., Li, J.: A K-means-based network partition algorithm for controller placement in software-defined network. In: IEEE International Conference on Communications (ICC), pp. 1–6 (2016)
11. Hu, Y., Luo, T., Wang, W., Deng, C.: On the load balanced controller placement problem in Software defined networks. In: IEEE International Conference on Computer and Communications (ICCC), pp. 2430–2434 (2016)
12. Isong, B., Molose, R.R.S., Abu-Mahfouz, A.M., Dladlu, N.: Comprehensive review of SDN controller placement strategies. In: IEEE Access, vol. 8, pp. 170070–170092 (2020)
13. Mao, B., Tang, F., Fadlullah, Z.M., Kato, N.: An intelligent route computation approach based on real-time deep learning strategy for software defined communication systems. In: IEEE Transactions on Emerging Topics in Computing, vol. 9, no. 3, pp. 1554–1565, 1 July-Sept (2021)
14. Liyanage, K.S.K., Ma, M., Chong, P.H.J.: Controller placement optimization in hierarchical distributed software defined vehicular networks. Comput. Networks **135**, 226–239 (2018)
15. Zaidi, K., Milojevic, M.B., Rakocevic, V., Nallanathan, A., Rajarajan, M.: Host-based intrusion detection for vanets : a statistical approach to rogue node detection, IEEE Trans. Veh. Technol. **65**(8), 6703–6714 (2015)
16. Greenshields, B., Bibbins, J., Channing, W., Miller, H.: A study of traffic capacity, In Highway Research Board Proceedings, vol. 1935. National Research Council (USA), Highway Research Board (1935)
17. Rabah, K.: Theory and implementation of elliptic curve cryptography. J. Appl. Sci. **5**, 604–633 (2005)

18. Tseng, Y.M., Jan, J.K., Chien, H.Y.: Digital signature with message recovery using self-certified public keys and its variants. Appl. Math. Comput. 136(3), 203–214 (2003)

19. Grewe, D., Wagner, M., Arumaithurai, M., Psaras, I., Kutscher, D.: Information centric mobile edge computing for connected vehicle environments: challenges and research directions. In: Proceedings of the Workshop on Mobile Edge Communications, pp. 7–12 (2017)

20. Alaya, B., Laouamer, L., Msilini, N.: Homomorphic encryption systems statement: trends and challenges. Comput. Sci. Rev. 36, 1–14 (2021).https://doi.org/10.1016/j.cosrev.2020.100235

21. Yang, L., Li, H.: Vehicle-to-vehicle communication based on a peer-to-peer network with graph theory and consensus algorithm. In: IET Intelligent Transport Systems, vol. 13, no. 2, pp. 280–285 (2019)

22. Kalaiarasy, C., Sreenath, N.: An incentive-based co-operation motivating pseudonym changing strategy for privacy preservation in mixed zones in vehicular networks, J. King Saud Univ. – Comput. Inf. Sci. 34(1), 1510–1520 (2022)

23. Toshiyuki, I., Nguyen, M., Tanaka, K.: Proxy re-encryption in a stronger security model extended from CT-RSA2012. In: Proceedings of the Cryptographers' Track at the RSA Conference, pp. 277–292, San Francisco, CA, USA: Springer Berlin Heidelberg (2013)

24. Fontes, R.R., Afzal, S., Brito, S.H., Santos, M.A., Rothenberg, C.E.: Mininet-WiFi : emulating software-defined wireless networks, 11th International Conference on Network and Service Management (CNSM), pp. 384–389 (2015)

Implementation of Common-Use Electric Equipment in the Railway Environment with Respect to Electromagnetic Compatibility

Leszek Kachel[1][(✉)], Artur Dłużniewski[2], and Łukasz John[3]

[1] Institute of Communications Systems, Faculty of Electronics, Military University of Technology, Gen. Sylwester Kaliski Str. No. 2, 00-908 Warsaw, Poland
leszek.kachel@wat.edu.pl

[2] Cyberspace Defense Force Components Command, T. Buka. Str. No. 1, 05-120 Legionowo, Poland
artdluzniewski@mon.gov.pl

[3] Railway Institute – Signalling and Telecommunication Laboratory, Chlopickiego Str. No 50, 04-275 Warsaw, Poland
ljohn@ikolej.pl

Abstract. The article discusses problems that may occur during implementation of common-use devices in professional industrial environment based on the example of the railway environment. It discusses example problems associated with the process of implementation of common-use electric equipment in the dedicated railway environment. The article describes the method of testing railway traffic control system that include multimedia components. Differences in research Describes differences in research requirements for railway traffic control systems and multimedia systems. Show negative test results along with potential design errors are presented. Then, the introduced changes along with the final test results are presented.

Keywords: railway environment · electromagnetic compatibility · electromagnetic interference · source of interference

1 Introduction

Tests of electromagnetic compatibility may be considered in two aspects: resistance – defined as the system's or device's capability to maintain its quality of operation in the presence of electromagnetic interferences – and emissions – defined as the impact of the system or device via transmitted electromagnetic waves on other systems or devices located in an adjacent electromagnetic environment. For the last two and a half year, due to the epidemiological situation caused by COVID-19 and Russia's invasion on Ukraine, supply chains of various types of electronic components have been interrupted. As noted by Polish producers of electronic systems, deliveries of computers are irregular or other *"substitutes"* appear, the quality of which is worse compared to previously used elements. Due to the necessity to perform contract obligations against customers,

© The Author(s), under exclusive license to Springer Nature Switzerland AG 2024
K. S. Soliman (Ed.): IBIMA-AI 2023, CCIS 2101, pp. 119–130, 2024.
https://doi.org/10.1007/978-3-031-62843-6_13

manufacturers of industrial electronic systems decide to use other systems that meet functional requirements at a given moment; however, such systems are often intended for public environment, i.e., an environment that does not feature electromagnetic properties typical for the industrial environment, such as the railway environment. Use of so-called *"off the shelf"* computer or multimedia solutions in professional industrial systems, e.g., in computer systems that support control of railway traffic, may lead to unexpected problems during electromagnetic compatibility tests. This results mainly from the fact that electronic components used in dedicated professional construction solutions differ from such "off the shelf" elements. As a consequence, problems may occur during electromagnetic compatibility tests as a result of differences between the levels of allowed emissions and the levels of exposures specified in PN-EN 50121–4 [1] railway standard and dedicated standards for multimedia devices, i.e., PN-EN-55032 [2] and PN-EN 55035 [3].

2   Methodology of Measurements of Emission of Radiated Disturbances and Their Elimination

Radiated disturbance emissions are interferences transmitted in a form of electromagnetic waves. Measurements of emissions of radiated disturbances for computer and multimedia systems, as well as systems supporting the process of control of railway traffic, are carried out in accordance with the research method described in PN-EN 55016-2-3 [4]. Measurements of emissions of radiated disturbances are performed in a SAC type electromagnetically shielded chamber within an antenna measurement distance of 3 m from the tested object, which is illustrated in Fig. 1. Measurements of emissions of radiated disturbances of such systems are performed in the frequency band from 30 MHz to

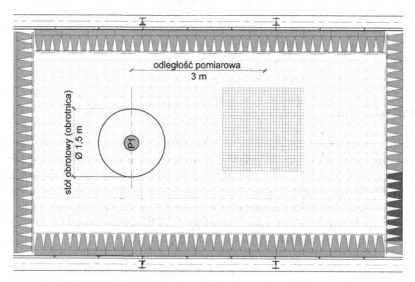

Fig. 1. Emission of radiated disturbances in SAC chamber

6 GHz, in line with provisions of PN-EN-55032 [2] and PN-EN 50121–4 [1], divided into three measurement subbands:

- 30 MHz ÷ 230 MHz – measurement of the vertical and horizontal electric component of the field strength using a biconical antenna,
- 230 MHz ÷ 1000 MHz – measurement of the vertical and horizontal electric component of the field strength using a log-periodic antenna,
- 1 MHz ÷ 6 MHz – measurement of vertical and horizontal the electric component of the field strength using a log-periodic antenna,

In the tests carried out by the Military Institute of Armament Technology in Zielonka, the measuring instruments presented in Table 1 were used.

Table 1. List of devices used to measure emissions of radiated disturbances

Instrument name	Type	Manufacturer
Measuring antenna	HK116	Rohde & Schwarz
Measuring antenna	HL223	Rohde & Schwarz
Measuring antenna	HF907	Rohde & Schwarz
Amplifier	BLMA 0118-0M	Bonn Elektronik
Measuring receiver	ESU-40	Rohde & Schwarz

The difference is in the allowed levels of emissions described for multimedia systems in PN-EN-55032 [2]; for railway traffic control systems, they are described in PN-EN 50121–4 [1]. A summary of allowed levels in the range of measurement of emissions of radiated disturbances for the measurement distance of 3 m is provided in Table 2.

Table 2. Summary of allowed levels of radiated emission for measurement distance of 3 m

Frequency range	Allowed levels as per PN-EN-55032	Allowed levels as per PN-EN 50121–4
MHz	dBμV/m	dBμV/m
30 ÷ 230	40 QP	50 QP
230 ÷ 1000	47 QP	57 QP
1000 ÷ 3000	70 PK, 50 AV	76 PK, 56 AV
3000 ÷ 6000	74 PK, 54 AV	80 PK, 60 AV

Devices are protected against radio and electric interference in order to prevent excessive emission. The basic measures used for this task are components that attenuate disturbances in the form of L and C elements, as well as shielding of circuits and individual blocks. Correct selection of L and C elements must be correlated with the range of attenuated frequencies and parameters of the circuit. This is due to resonance frequencies produced by given elements. The correct selection of components in terms of their frequency and disturbance elimination performance depends largely on whether the parameters of the circuit are known [5]. By using basic principles of elimination of radiated disturbances, we were able to acquire positive results from the previously obtained negative results. The obtained results of radiated emissions of the tested system for selected measurements are presented in separate Figures (Figs. 4, 5, 6, 7, 8). The results of polarisation of V vertical antenna are highlighted red on the chart, while the results for polarisation of H horizontal antenna are blue. The tests were carried out on a multi-element computer system, which had not initially meet the requirements of PN-EN 50121-4 [1], the purpose of which is supporting decision-making processes in railway traffic control in the railway environment. Due to the complexity of the system, the tests were divided into two stages, the implementation of which depended on the place of installation of particular components of the tested object. Due to the tight deadline for completion of the tests, the manufacturer of the computer system used to support railway traffic control replaced industrial computer components with solutions used in common-use multimedia systems. As a result, the allowed values of radiated emission

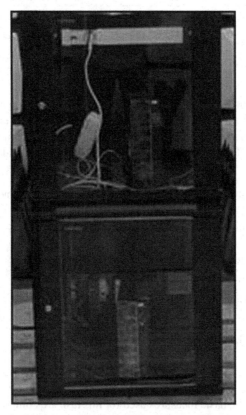

Fig. 2. Overview of the test object with computer elements

were exceeded and the resistance of the system to radiated RF electromagnetic field dropped. The overview of the object is presented in Fig. 2. The rack contains computer systems that support the dispatcher in making decisions regarding railway traffic control in the premises of the railway infrastructure administrator.

Fig. 3. Installation of components inside the rack

Figure 3 presents the method of installation of the system components in the rack, including incorrect routing of the structural cables and grounding made by the manufacturer of the system.

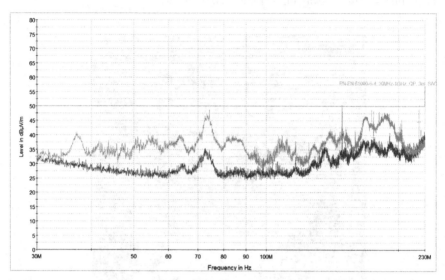

Fig. 4. Basic results of emission of radiated disturbances in the frequency band from 30 MHz to 230 MHz

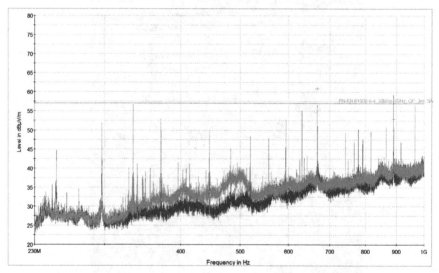

Fig. 5. Basic results of emission of radiated disturbances in the frequency band from 230 MHz to 1000 MHz

Figures 9, 10, 11 present the results of radiated emission after structural changes, i.e., reduction of the length of the structural cables and their routing, which allowed to

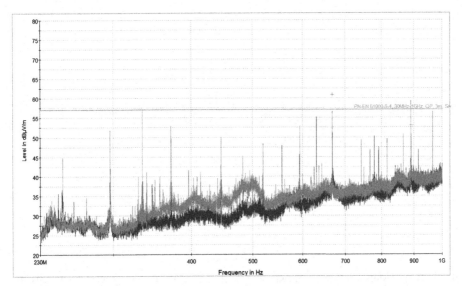

Fig. 6. Results of emission of radiated disturbances in the frequency band from 230 MHz to 1000 MHz after correction of the routing of cables

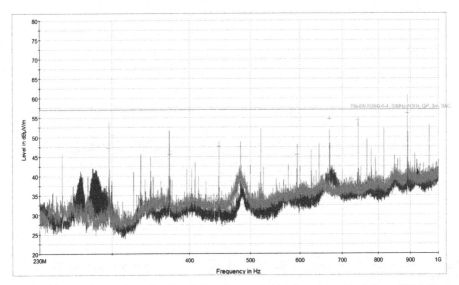

Fig. 7. Results of emission of radiated disturbances in the frequency band from 230 MHz to 1000 MHz after correction of the routing of cables consisting of shortening of the cables

meet requirements provided in PN-EN 50121–4 [1] applicable for railway traffic control supporting computer systems.

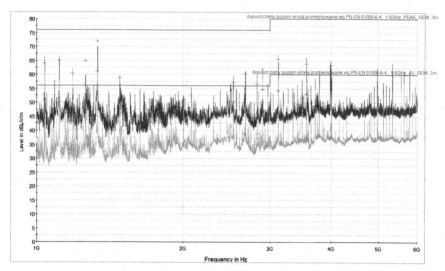

Fig. 8. Basic results of emission of radiated disturbances in the frequency band from 1 GHz to 6 GHz for polarisation of the horizontal antenna

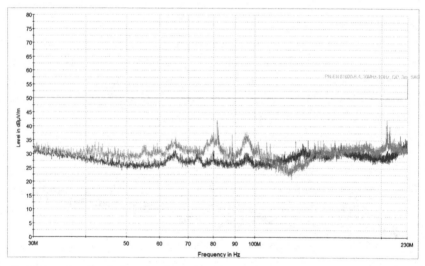

Fig. 9. End results of emission of radiated disturbances in the frequency band from 30 MHz to 230 MHz

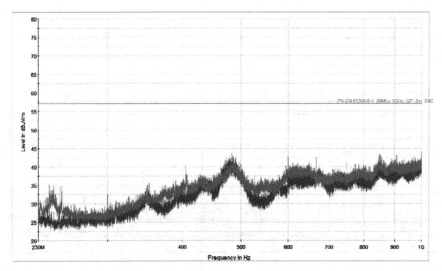

Fig. 10. End results of emission of radiated disturbances in the frequency band from 230 MHz to 1000 MHz

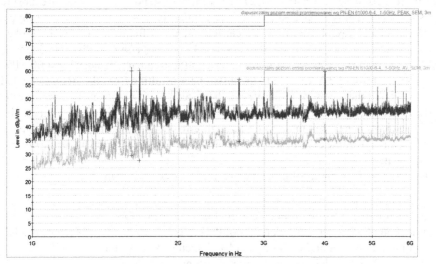

Fig. 11. End results of emission of radiated disturbances in the frequency band from 1 GHz to 6 GHz for polarisation of the horizontal antenna

3   Tests of Resistance to Radiated RF Electromagnetic Field

The test was carried out in a SAC type chamber shielded against electromagnetic fields. The test consisted of checking the resistance to radiated RF electromagnetic field (*with amplitude modulation using 1kHz signal and 80% depth*) in accordance with PN-EN 61000–4-3 [6], as well as the levels of exposures provided in PN-EN 50121–4 [1] railway standard; the levels of exposure for multimedia devices are described in PN-EN 55035

[3]. Differences between the exposure levels for both standards are provided in Table 3. The frequency was automatically increased in 1% increments; the duration of exposure at each frequency was 3 s.

Table 3. Exposure levels in the range of resistance to radiated RF electromagnetic field

Exposure level	PN-EN 50121-4					PN-EN 55035
	80 – 800MHz	800 – 1000 MHz	1.4 – 2 GHz	2 – 2.7 GHz	5.1 – 6 GHz	80 – 1000MHz
10V/m						
20V/m						
5V/m						
3V/m						

According to Table 3, the exposure levels and the frequency range for both standards are different. In case of PN-EN 50121–4 [1] railway standard, the defined exposure levels are significantly higher. Differences are noticeable also in the frequency range; therefore, for railway objects tests are carried out up to frequency of 6GHz, broken down into dedicated exposure subbands (Table 3 – *green fields*). In PN-EN 55035 [3] multimedia standard, tests are carried out only in the frequency band 80 – 1000 MHz and exposure level of 3 V/m. Due to the differences resulting from the frequency band and selection of the exposure level (*green*), the tested object was losing communication between particular elements of the system, which meant loss of the required functionality by the entire system. This manifested through error messages, which, in the light of dedicated railway traffic control standards, eliminated this system from use in the railway environment.

By using basic methods of protection of such a system through:

- application of additional shielding,
- application of a shielding film on the front pane of the rack,
- protection of other sensitive elements of the system by application of ferrite beads,
- use of additional grounding for particular elements of the system (Fig. 12),
- use of structural cables dedicated for professional solutions,

Fig. 12. Example of routed grounding in the device

We managed to obtain a positive results in the tests of resistance to radiated RF electromagnetic field. As a result, the public system elements were adapted to the requirements for computer systems used to support railway traffic control.

4 Summary

In the light of technical and logistic problems of today, we have to keep in mind structural assumptions of systems we plan to use in electromagnetic environments. Therefore, we should also remember that such systems require further work aimed to adapt them to the electromagnetic compatibility requirements for devices in terms of emissions, such as use of additional shielding, filtration, grounding, separation, as well as adjustment of the value of impedance of the circuit and selection of appropriate cables. Disturbance attenuation may be ensured by using appropriate components right at the source, as well as by eliminating the disturbance infiltration paths. In the end, the applied electromagnetic field shielding and attenuation methods allowed to successfully adapt a common-use computer system, in this case a railway traffic control supporting system, to the railway environment.

Acknowledgment. This work was financed by the Military University of Technology under research project no. UGB/22–854/2021/WAT on *"Applications of selected computer science, communication, and reconnaissance techniques in civil and military areas."*

References

1. PN-EN 50121-4:2017-04 + A1:2019-07 Railway applications - Electromagnetic compatibility - Part 4: Emission and immunity of the signalling and telecommunications apparatus Warsaw (2019)

2. PN-EN 55032:2015-09 + A1:2021-05 + A11:2020-07 Electromagnetic compatibility of multimedia equipment -- Emission Requirements, Warsaw (2021) r
3. PN-EN 55035:2017–09 + A11:2020–09 Electromagnetic compatibility of multimedia equipment -- Immunity requirements, Warsaw (2020)
4. PN-EN 55016-2-3:2017-06 + A1:2020-01 Specification for radio disturbance and immunity measuring apparatus and methods -- Part 2–3: Methods of measurement of disturbances and immunity -- Radiated disturbance measurements, Warsaw (2020) r
5. A. Dłużniewski, Ł.J.: Methods of radiated disturbance devices conducted in railway wagon converters", Przegląd Elektrotechniczny nr 11/2015
6. Charoy, A.: Disturbance in Electronic Devices , vol 1,2,3,4", Wydawnictwo Naukowo Techniczne, Warszawa (2000)

Exploring the Potential of OLSR Steganography for Confidential Communication

Gabriel Jekateryńczuk and Zbigniew Piotrowski[(✉)]

Military University of Technology, Warsaw, Poland
{gabriel.jekaterynczuk,zbigniew.piotrowski}@wat.edu.pl

Abstract. The article discusses potential use of the OLSR (Optimized Link State Routing) protocol for network steganography, which consists of hiding confidential data in Internet packages in order to ensure safe communication. The authors explore possibilities and limitations of steganography using OLSR. According to research results, the OLSR steganography may potentially ensure efficient and safe non-public communication; however, there are challenges associated with reliability and capacity of the method that must be faced. The purpose of the research is proposing a steganographic method that would be possible to implement and indicating the further direction of development of steganographic methods based on the OLSR protocol.

Keywords: Steganography · Optimized Link State Routing · Network

1 Introduction

In today's world, protection of communication became the basic requirement in order to protect confidential information against unauthorised access. Steganography, i.e. a method of hiding information inside other data, is one of the techniques used to ensure safe communication [1]. Network communication steganography consists of embedding secret information inside the network in order to send it without rising any suspicion [2]. The Optimized Link State Routing is widely used in **wireless mesh networks**, and the use of this protocol in steganography has grew in popularity in the recent years. One of the main advantages of the OLSR protocol in steganography is its scalability. OLSR was designed for efficient operation in large-scale wireless networks, which makes it suitable for embedding and sending secret information in networks with many nodes. Another advantage of the OLSR protocol is its ability to ensure reliable communication via use of many data transmission paths. This ensures successful sending of confidential information, even when certain paths fail due to interruptions or other network problems. However, use of the OLSR protocol for steganography also has certain disadvantages. One of its main limitations is its complexity, which makes it difficult to implement and maintain. Another disadvantage is its potential to overload the network, since use of the OLSR protocol for steganography may cause increased network traffic and slow down transmission rates. Moreover, the OLSR protocol is prone to certain types of attacks, such as routing, which may jeopardise confidentiality of hidden data [3, 4].

K. S. Soliman (Ed.): IBIMA-AI 2023, CCIS 2101, pp. 131–134, 2024.
https://doi.org/10.1007/978-3-031-62843-6_14

2   Protocols

In order to confirm the possibility of use of the OLSR protocols in implementation of the steganographic method, the first stage was establishing the stack of protocols. For this purpose, we chose the Internet Protocol Version 4 (IPv4) from the ISO/OSI Model network layer, as well as the User Datagram Protocol (UDP) from the transport layer [5]. IPv4 was selected due to easier implementation compared to the IPv6 protocol. As for the transport layer, there are two popular protocols – UDP and Transmission Control Protocol (TCP). In this case, we chose UDP due to [6]:

- **Performance**: UDP is a simpler protocol compared to TCP. OLSR was designed to operate in a low bandwidth and long delay environment, while UDP is better suited to such scenarios due to its minimum markup.
- **Speed**: OLSR was designed to quickly adapt to changes in the network topology, while UDP helps to achieve this goal by ensuring faster transmission of packages and shorter delays compared to TCP.
- **Connectionless**: OLSR uses a connectionless protocol, e.g. UDP, since it does not require an establishment markup and maintenance of connection between nodes. This makes OLSR more suitable for use in ad hoc networks, where nodes may join or leave the network at any time.
- **Scalability**: OLSR was designed to work in large and dynamic networks, while UDP helps to achieve this goal by ensuring a simpler and more scalable protocol compared to TCP.

In this method, the authors chose the approach based on modification of fields of headers of particular Internet protocol. The following fields were used to hide steganography information: identification, flags, time to live (TTL).

3   Implementation

The implementation was carried out using the Python programming language [7] and a popular library used to manipulate packages – Scapy [8]. It allows to capture, analyse and manipulate network packages in any layer of the OSI model and may be used to create own network tools, automate network tests and to test network security. It provides a simple interface for creation and sending of packages, allowing easy adaptation of the content of packages, setting various fields of a package, and even generating packages with random data. The capabilities of Scapy in terms of manipulation of packages are not limited to basic protocols, such as TCP/IP, as it also supports more advanced protocols, such as DNS, DHCP, SNMP, and even non-standard protocols.

As a part of implementation, the authors used previously implemented IPv4 and UDP protocols, as well as implemented the OLSR protocol from scratch, as it has not been defined in the Scapy library. The following messages were implemented:

- Hello,
- Host and Network Association (HNA),
- Multiple Interface Declaration (MID),
- Topology Control (TC).

Example packages sent by the server and received by the listening node were captured using Wireshark [9]; they are presented below (Figs. 1, 2, 3, 4).

```
Frame 7: 62 bytes on wire (496 bits), 62 bytes captured (496 bits) on interface lo, id 0
▶ Ethernet II, Src: 00:00:00_00:00:00 (00:00:00:00:00:00), Dst: 00:00:00_00:00:00 (00:00:00:00:00:00)
▶ Internet Protocol Version 4, Src: 127.0.0.1, Dst: 127.0.0.1
▶ User Datagram Protocol, Src Port: 698, Dst Port: 80
▼ Optimized Link State Routing Protocol
    Packet Length: 20
    Packet Sequence Number: 0
  ▶ Message: HELLO (1)
```

Fig. 1. OLSRv1 Hello Message

```
Frame 5: 66 bytes on wire (528 bits), 66 bytes captured (528 bits) on interface lo, id 0
▶ Ethernet II, Src: 00:00:00_00:00:00 (00:00:00:00:00:00), Dst: 00:00:00_00:00:00 (00:00:00:00:00:00)
▶ Internet Protocol Version 4, Src: 127.0.0.1, Dst: 127.0.0.1
▶ User Datagram Protocol, Src Port: 698, Dst Port: 80
▼ Optimized Link State Routing Protocol
    Packet Length: 24
    Packet Sequence Number: 0
  ▶ Message: HNA (4)
```

Fig. 2. OLSRv1 HNA Message

```
Frame 3: 74 bytes on wire (592 bits), 74 bytes captured (592 bits) on interface lo, id 0
▶ Ethernet II, Src: 00:00:00_00:00:00 (00:00:00:00:00:00), Dst: 00:00:00_00:00:00 (00:00:00:00:00:00)
▶ Internet Protocol Version 4, Src: 127.0.0.1, Dst: 127.0.0.1
▶ User Datagram Protocol, Src Port: 698, Dst Port: 80
▼ Optimized Link State Routing Protocol
    Packet Length: 32
    Packet Sequence Number: 0
  ▶ Message: MID (3)
```

Fig. 3. OLSRv1 MID Message

```
Frame 1: 78 bytes on wire (624 bits), 78 bytes captured (624 bits) on interface lo, id 0
▶ Ethernet II, Src: 00:00:00_00:00:00 (00:00:00:00:00:00), Dst: 00:00:00_00:00:00 (00:00:00:00:00:00)
▶ Internet Protocol Version 4, Src: 127.0.0.1, Dst: 127.0.0.1
▶ User Datagram Protocol, Src Port: 698, Dst Port: 80
▼ Optimized Link State Routing Protocol
    Packet Length: 36
    Packet Sequence Number: 0
  ▶ Message: TC (2)
```

Fig. 4. OLSRv1 TC Message

4   Research Results

The proposed steganographic method fulfils its role and allows sending of steganographic data via a hidden channel. This means that the OLSRv1 protocol may be used in steganographic methods. Further development of methods using this Internet protocol is based on use of other header fields or its newer version – OLSRv2. While OLSRv1 may be prone to steganographic attacks, the newer version of the protocol, i.e. OLSRv2, includes additional securities, which make it more resistant to this type of attacks. In particular, OLSRv2 includes a new type of message, known as TLV (Type-Length-Value) block, which ensures safe sending of additional data, including OLSR control messages.

The TLV blocks allow nodes to include additional information in their OLSR messages, such as safety certificates or other metadata. These additional data are encrypted and protected via an authentication code (MAC), which makes it significantly harder for the attacker to modify or capture messages without detection and increases the capacity at the same time.

References

1. Simplilearn: What is Steganography? Types, Techniques, Examples & Applications' 26 March 2023. https://www.simplilearn.com/what-is-steganography-article
2. Lubacz, J., Mazurczyk, W., Szczypiorski, K.: Principles and overview of Network Steganography. IEEE Commun. Mag. **52**(5), 225–229 (2014). https://doi.org/10.1109/mcom.2014.681 5916
3. Harleenk.: Optimized Link State Routing Protocol' 26 March 2023. https://www.geeksforg eeks.org/optimized-link-state-routing-protocol/
4. Palta, P., Goyal, S.: Comparison of OLSR and TORA routing protocols using OPNET modeler, Int. J. Eng. Res. Technol. (IJERT) **01**(05) (July 2012) (2012)
5. Cloudflare.: What is the OSI Model?' 26 March 2023. https://www.cloudflare.com/learning/ ddos/glossary/open-systems-interconnection-model-osi/
6. BasuMallick, C.: 'TCP vs UDP: Understanding 10 Key Differences' 26 March 2023. https:// www.spiceworks.com/tech/networking/articles/tcp-vs-udp/
7. Python, 'Documentation' 26 March 2023. https://www.python.org/
8. Scapy, 'Documentation' 26 March 2023. https://scapy.net/
9. Wireshark, 'Documentation' 26 March 2023. https://www.wireshark.org/

Recommendation Systems Techniques in Finance's Perspective: A Conceptual Research

Manal Alghieth[✉]

Department of Information Technology, College of Computer, Qassim University, Buraydah, Saudi Arabia
mgietha@qu.edu.sa

Abstract. Recommendation systems in general are being studied broadly in the literature. However, RS in finance sector have less attention in the literature than other sectors such as music, movies, advertisements and entertainment. This study explores recommendation systems in finance field that help customers dealing with overload information and choices available online. In addition, such systems can help the service providers by expanding customer access and boosting sales. The technology behind the recommender systems will be discussed including filtering approaches, challenges to the recommendation process, and their solutions. The recommendation system (RS) approach in financial services domain perspective will be examined too. The obstacles of using recommendation systems specific to the financial services domain will be investigated. The study summarizes the advantages and disadvantages of RS in financial domain focusing on previous studies that discuss the field of finance with regards to RS. It can be used as a guidance of using recommendation systems for the financial services domain such as banks and financial organizations.

Keywords: Recommendation Systems · Finance · Filtering approaches

1 Introduction

The explosive growth of digital content and the internet has created the challenge of information overload for the user. Recommendation systems deal with this challenge to a great extent by filtering the choices for the consumer and serving exclusive, personalized content and recommendations for products and services. Recommendation systems have been used successfully for e-commerce and entertainment. In the field of financial services, however, recommendation systems are still not that prevalent [8]. Although the technology and tools driving recommendation are largely domain-independent, there are several factors unique to the financial services and products that have limited the use of recommendation systems in financial services. This paper aims to analyze the opportunity and challenges of implementing recommendation systems in the finance domain.

© The Author(s), under exclusive license to Springer Nature Switzerland AG 2024
K. S. Soliman (Ed.): IBIMA-AI 2023, CCIS 2101, pp. 135–142, 2024.
https://doi.org/10.1007/978-3-031-62843-6_15

1.1 Recommendation Systems in Finance

Recommendation or recommender systems are software systems that filter dynamically generated information as per the user's profile, preferences, interests, and observed browsing or purchase behavior. Recommender systems benefit both the user and service providers. They assist the user in their purchase decisions by helping them find and select items for their purchase in less time and also help the service providers boost their sales revenue.

The filtering methods used in recommender systems are collaborative filtering content-based filtering or hybrid filtering. In collaborative filtering, other users having similar preferences are identified and their choices are recommended to the user. Content-based filtering utilizes the user's demographic information and purchase history to make recommendations, without using other users' information.

The collaborative and content-based techniques have certain limitations. The product rating data is sparse since most of the users do not give ratings. There are also the issues of overspecialization and cold-start where new users don't have a purchase history or new products don't have a sale history. Scalability is another issue with collaborative filtering. Hybrid filtering combines multiple filtering techniques in different ways to improve the accuracy of recommendations [6]. Very often, the content-based and collaborative approaches are combined. The hybrid is aimed at leveraging the strengths of the filtering techniques and smoothing out their weaknesses. There are several ways in which techniques could be combined - a weighted hybrid, mixed hybrid, switching hybrid, feature-combination hybrid, cascade hybrid, feature-augmentation hybrid, and meta-level hybrid [6].

The recommendation process broadly has three phases – Information Collection, Learning, and Prediction/Recommendation. In the information collection phase, a user profile is created using the user's demographic data, preferences, behavior, and the content the user accesses. This information can be explicit i.e. acquired directly from the user or implicit, i.e. inferred based on user behavior, purchase, or browsing history. Implicit feedback is less accurate as compared to explicit, however, it may be more objective as explicitly collected feedback may involve a bias with user responses. The learning phase involves a learning algorithm to filter and utilize the user attributes collection in the information collection phase [6]. The prediction or recommendation phase involves making predictions on what would the user's preferences be based on the information collected.

1.2 Content-Based Filtering

Content-based filtering relies on the analysis of the attributes of the items to make predictions. Recommendations are made based on user profiles using product features of items that have been rated by the user in the past. The similarity between the items rated positively by the users and another item is calculated using vector models such as Term Frequency Inverse Document Frequency (TF/IDF) or Probabilistic models such as Naïve Baise classifier, Decision Trees, and Neural networks.

Other users; profiles do not influence the recommendations in this technique. The technique is effective where product metadata, i.e. detailed product features descriptions are available. It is therefore very effective when recommending webpages, publications, news, etc. Using the product information, this technique can make recommendations when user preferences are not available, and can recommend similar products as well instead of the same product. Examples of recommendation systems using content-based filtering are News Dude, a personal news system, CiteSeer, an automatic citation indexing system, and LIBRA, a content-based book recommendation system [6].

1.3 Collaborative Filtering

The collaborative filtering technique is based on matching users by similar interests and preferencing and recommending items rated positively by the matching users. This technique is useful when the item descriptions are not easy to find, e.g. in the case of music and movies. Collaborative filtering is therefore a domain-independent technique where detailed product knowledge is not required. In this technique, a database of user preferences in the form of user-item matrices is built. The similarity between user profiles is calculated to make recommendations. Similar users are identified as neighborhoods or clusters. A positively rated item by one user in the neighborhood can be recommended to other users in the same neighborhood.

These techniques can further be of two types – memory-based and model-based. In memory-based techniques, the ratings made by a user in the past are used to find users in the neighborhood, i.e. with similar tastes. The similarity calculation could be user-based, where similar users are identified, or it can be item-based where similar items are identified. A model of item similarities is created by retrieving items rated by an active user from the user-item matrix. The retrieved items are compared to a target item. Top k-similar items are selected. Prediction is made using the weighted average of active users' ratings on similar items. The similarity measure is either correlation-based or cosine-based.

In model-based techniques, the previous ratings are built into a model using machine learning or data-mining techniques that identify relations between items in the user-item matrix and use these relations to predict items that would be most preferred for a user. Since they use pre-computed models, predictions can be made quickly. The model-based approach also resolves the scarcity and scalability issues. The modules get around the sparsity in the user-item matrix by using dimensionality reduction techniques like Singular Value Decomposition (SVD), Matrix completion techniques, Latent Semantics method, regression, and clustering. Once clusters have been constructed the user ratings in the cluster are averaged and used for recommendations for individual users in the cluster. Unsupervised machine learning techniques like k-means clustering and Self-organizing maps (SOMs) are commonly used. Some of the recommenders like Amazon also apply algorithms that can mine association rules and recommend items related to the one being transacted. Besides these, there are other classification methods like decision trees and Artificial Neural Networks (ANN) that recommenders use. The model-based systems, however, are computationally intensive.

Collaborative filtering methods have the advantage that they can be applied in areas where there is not much metadata associated with the product or it is difficult to create. Examples of Collaborative filtering is Amazon.com in e-commerce and Ringo, a music album and artist recommender system.

1.4 Demographic Filtering

Recommender systems based on demographic filtering use the demographic information of the users, like age, gender, occupation, income, nationality, etc. to make recommendations. Demographic data is a good indicator of similarity when classifying users although it is a somewhat stereotypical classification. Although it involves a people-to-people comparison like collaborative filtering, it does not depend on the users' preference history. The main issue with the demographic approach is that people are reluctant to share all their demographic data, especially for e-commerce applications. Also, demographic data needs updating from time to time. Demographic filtering is mostly combined with collaborative or other models in recommender systems [1].

2 Knowledge-Based Filtering

Knowledge-based recommender systems make recommendations based on specific queries made by the user. The system prompts the user to provide information through a dialogue that guides the system through a discrimination tree of product features to locate the item relevant to the user. [5] The user responses may be transformed into queries to locate an item in a database. These queries may not return any items in many cases, so these systems generally use similarity metrics as well to recommend similar items. Unlike collaborative filtering systems, knowledge-based systems do not require a large data of user preferences to work through and it bases their search on individual tastes rather than using a cluster's preferences.

2.1 Hybrid Filtering

Hybrid Filtering combines two or more filtering algorithms to overcome their shortcomings and utilize their strengths. A hybrid approach can be taken in the following ways.

Weighted hybridization integrates the scores of the individual techniques using a scoring system. The individual techniques are assigned equal waits first, and then the weights are adjusted depending on whether the user actions confirm or negate their predictions. An example of weighted hybridization is a recommender called P-tango [10].

Switching Hybridization uses a switching logic to switch from one technique to another to avoid the disadvantages specific to an individual technique. An example of a switching hybrid recommender system is DailyLEarner which switches between content-based and collaborative techniques based on the situation.

Cascade hybridization technique iterates between individual techniques where the recommendations made by one technique are further refined by another. The order of preference is fined tuned to get the best results. EntreeC is a cascade hybrid recommender that combines knowledge-based and collaborative techniques.

The mixed hybridization approach combines the outputs from the individual techniques at the same time. The individual techniques may be applied to separate data, and then the recommendations from the two are mixed. An example of a mixed hybrid system is PTV, a TV view schedule recommender that combines content-based and collaborative techniques.

3 Review of Previous Studies

The application of recommender systems in the financial domain is still quite low. However, there is a rising interest in the industry to harness this technology to provide better services to customers and boost revenues. Financial services companies have started using recommender systems to alert users on key market investment opportunities and events that may interest them [3].

Recommender systems are beings used by financial intermediaries in their online interactions with customers. These intermediaries utilize social networks to make recommendations to clients and potential clients [11].

Human financial advisors are generally not considered trustworthy by investors as they place their own or their financial firm's interest before their client's interest [4]. Therefore, there is a need for FinTech alternatives, Still, there is regulatory caution around AI applications in the industry. The European Commission considers recommender systems and related technology as high-risk as they can impact people's lives directly. It is feared that the technology could be unfairly used for predatory loan targeting [3].

A framework for a multiagent financial advice recommender system is proposed by researchers at Virginia Commonwealth University in the US. Named as FinPathLight, the framework presents a design for a personal financial goal recommender system that can cater to users across a wide range of financial situations. The framework designs and evaluates a hybrid recommender system using content-based, collaborative, and demographic filtering. The framework takes into account the customer's *financial capability* to manage personal finances which are determined by financial knowledge, confidence, and motivation. It also integrates a role-based agent design for the recommender. The agent function is designed based on ontology where the knowledge database is built using queries. The system must be able to translate the query responses into actionable data accurately [4].

Another study explores the use of multi-label classification techniques and recommender systems to cross-sell products in the financial services sector. The researchers used data from an international financial services provider and statistical analysis using multi-label classifiers along with recommender systems to recommend cross-sell opportunities. The study found collaborative filtering techniques to be most effective along with multi-label classification [2].

Researchers at Dalhousie University in Canada presented a hybrid recommender system for the Banking domain [8]. The products included savings accounts, checking accounts, investment products like fixed deposits, treasury bills, etc., loans like mortgages, student loans, lease financing, overdrafts, debit cards, credit cards, wealth management solutions, currency transfers, and so on. Since banks do typically ask customers to rate their products, the ratings were implicitly inferred from the customer's transaction data and a customer-product rating matrix was created. K-means clustering was performed on the customer demographic data to identify clusters of similar customers. The customer-product rating matrix and clusters were used to calculate the average product rating per cluster. Product similarity matrices were created using collaborative filtering. These matrices were then used to predict ratings for unrated products. Top n-rated products can then be recommended to a customer [8].

In a similar study, researchers developed a recommender system as a web application in Java that provides the user advice on financial products, information, and services on their explicit query. The system uses customers' bank statements to study purchase behavior and uses the k-nearest neighbor algorithm for collaborative filtering, fuzzy decision trees for knowledge-based filtering, and Singular value decomposition for dimensionality reduction. The system also uses implicit feedback on user preferences as the data on the transaction grows [7].

4 Recommender System Challenges

The advantages and disadvantages of the filtering approaches discussed above are summarized in Table 1.

Table 1. Summary of Filtering Approaches

Filtering Approach	Advantages	Disadvantages
Collaborative Filtering	• Can work across product niches • Domain knowledge is not required • Quality improves with data growth	• Cold start problem with both user and product • Grey sheep problem • Quality depends on a large historical dataset • Scalability issues
Content-based Filtering	• Domain knowledge is not required • Quality improves with data growth	• Cold start problem • Quality depends on a large historical dataset • Scalability issues • Requires product meta-data
Demographic Filtering	• Can work across product niches • Domain knowledge is not required • Quality improves with data growth	• Cold start problem • Quality depends on a large historical dataset • Scalability issues • Demographic data requires updating from time-to-time • Stereotyping tendency
Knowledge-based Filtering	• Does not require a large historical dataset • Cater to individual tastes • Does not have cold start problems	• Requires more participation from users • Required domain knowledge
Hybrid system	• Leverage the benefits of two or more approaches and overcome their weaknesses	• Added complexity of combining multiple approaches

There are several challenges that recommender systems encounter.

Cold start problem – this is the situation where the existing data is not adequate to make effective recommendations. This could be a user cold-start issue where there are new users with no browsing or purchase history. It can also be a product cold-start where a new product has no reviews or ratings in the system. Some of the solutions are to explicitly ask new users about their preferences or ask them to rate products. Other is to recommend based on demographic data [9].

Shilling attack problem – malicious users enter the system with fake ids to deliberately enter biased ratings to boost ratings or malign a product. Such attacks negatively impact the reliability of the recommender systems. To prevent this issue, the systems need to be monitored to identify fake profiles and ratings early on and remove them from the system.

Synonymy problem – this situation arises when the same or similar products have different entries in the system and are identified as different. To solve this, automatic term expansion and singular value decomposition techniques are used.

Latency problem – this problem is specific to collaborative filtering and happens when new items enter the system frequently and the system won't recommend them until they have been rated. To get around this, the ratings could be added offline before adding the item to the system or make content-based or demography-based recommendations in the meantime.

Data sparsity problem – this situation arises because the recommender systems work on large datasets but have too few items that are rated. There are some solutions like dimensionality reduction using singular value decomposition, demographic filtering, and model-based collaboration techniques.

Grey sheep problem – this is an outlier problem specific to pure collaborative filtering, where feedback from one user does not match any other in the cluster. The workaround for these situations is to use content-based filtering in such cases.

Scalability problem – this problem again happens due to large amounts of data and frequent addition of new users and items. The solution to the problem is applying dimensionality reduction techniques [9].

There is no standardized evaluation system for recommender systems. However, their performance is indicated by the percentage of recommendations that are followed up by the users.

5 Conclusion

Recommender systems are increasingly being used to recommend products to users online. They help the users to cope with the problem of information overload and help in making decisions. They are beneficial to the service provider as they boost sales.

Recommenders have been successfully used in e-commerce and entertainment. However, they are relatively prevalent in the domain of financial services. There are specific issues in the financial domain that need to be addressed. Therefore, the study analyzed the opportunity and challenges of implementing recommendation systems in the finance domain.

Consequently, it has been found out that Product knowledge plays a big role in the financial domain. Hence, any recommenders should have knowledge-based filtering.

Furthermore, there is a caution around AI-based financial decisions as these can impact the lives of people directly.

Finally, the future of recommender system research relies in the integration of proven deep learning models into hybrid filter approaches.

References

1. Al-Shamri, M.Y.: User profiling approaches for demographic recommender systems. Knowl.-Based Syst. **100**, 175–187 (2016). https://doi.org/10.1016/j.knosys.2016.03.006
2. Bogaert, M., et al.: Evaluating multi-label classifiers and recommender systems in the Financial Service Sector. Europ. J. Oper. Res. **279**(2), 620–634 (2019). https://doi.org/10.1016/j.ejor.2019.05.037
3. Bogers, T. et al.: FINREC: the 3rd international workshop on personalization & recommender systems in financial services. In: Sixteenth ACM Conference on Recommender Systems [Preprint] (2022). https://doi.org/10.1145/3523227.3547420
4. Bunnell, L., Osei-Bryson, K.-M., Yoon, V.Y.: FinPathlight: framework for a multiagent recommender system designed to increase consumer financial capability. Dec. Sup. Syst. **134**, 113306 (2020). https://doi.org/10.1016/j.dss.2020.113306
5. Burke, R.: Integrating Knowledge-based and Collaborative-filtering Recommender Systems (2000)
6. Isinkaye, F.O., Folajimi, Y.O. and Ojokoh, B.A.: Recommendation systems: principles, methods, and evaluation, Egyptian Inf. J. **16**(3), 261–273 (2015). https://doi.org/10.1016/j.eij.2015.06.005
7. Temitope, O., et al.: A model of intelligent recommender system with explicit feedback mechanism for performance improvement. Int. J. Innov. Res. Comput. Sci. Technol. **8**(2), 20–28 (2020). https://doi.org/10.21276/ijircst.2020.8.2.3
8. Oyebode, O., Orji, R.: A hybrid recommender system for product sales in a banking environment. J. Bank. Finan. Technol. **4**(1), 15–25 (2020). https://doi.org/10.1007/s42786-019-000 14-w
9. Roy, D., Dutta, M.: A systematic review and research perspective on Recommender Systems. J. Big Data **9**(1) (2022). https://doi.org/10.1186/s40537-022-00592-5
10. Sharaf, M. et al.: A survey on recommendation systems for Financial Services. Multimedia Tools Appl. **81**(12), 16761–16781 (2022). https://doi.org/10.1007/s11042-022-12564-1
11. Zatevakhina, A., Dedyukhina, N., Klioutchnikov, O.: Recommender Systems - the foundation of an intelligent financial platform: Prospects of development. In: 2019 International Conference on Artificial Intelligence: Applications and Innovations (IC-AIAI) [Preprint] (2019). https://doi.org/10.1109/ic-aiai48757.2019.00029

PC-Based Electronic Testbed for Comprehensive Security Evaluation of IoT Devices

Marek Michalski[✉]

Faculty of Computing and Telecommunications, Poznan University of Technology, Piotrowo 3,
60-965 Poznan, Poland
marek.michalski@put.poznan.pl

Abstract. LXI (LAN eXtensions for Instrumentation) protocol allows to control measurement devices from software via LAN (IP) connection. It allows to access screen and settings panel of oscilloscopes or another devices and also typical multimeters. Most commands are available from commandline interpreter and can be used by tools prepared by programmer, i.e. they are available as public API. In some cases, they require plugins for proper cooperation between software module and device. In this paper I will show example, where typical software does not allow to use full functionality (due to not working plugin or version conflict). I will give a solution which improves vendor software. It is available from commandline and it can be built in automated mechanism as Ansible/Jenkins or another scripts. Basing on this functionality, devices have been included into testing system which is controlled by typical SDN, since it is available in IP network and controlled by automated software tools. This system is very flexible, one example case is testing side-channel attacks in IoT devices in automated way.

1 Introduction

Modern electronic devices very often have many different interfaces. In IT world, typical interface is Web based GUI for convenient management. More advanced, professional devices, use also professional protocols. One of standard protocols which is used as a basis of such a interface is LXI (LAN eXtensions for Instrumentation) [1]. It allows to communicate with PC or another application with LAN access with electronic device with such a functionality run on Ethernet physical port. Professional applications are available for advanced and sophisticated tools. Unfortunately, they cost a lot of money. But older devices can be also plugged to LAN network with these protocols. However, in many cases, the problem occurs in versions of software or availability of libraries and plugins. In this paper I present case where it was possible to "reactivate" very useful functionality on old device. With this functionality this device can be treated as very modern and can be available as a measurement node in SDN environment.

Internet of Things (IoT) devices are very popular. One of their aspects is their security. Since they are present in our private space, wide spectrum of security tests should be performed. One of them is testing side-channel attacks vulnerabilities [2]. In this paper I will present equipment and mechanisms which are used in my laboratory for automated tests. I use oscilloscopes connected via IP network to testing system, advanced electronic

K. S. Soliman (Ed.): IBIMA-AI 2023, CCIS 2101, pp. 143–150, 2024.
https://doi.org/10.1007/978-3-031-62843-6_16

measurements (as current [5] and electromagnetic field probes [6]), set of simple switches and many scripts and software tools. When tests are planned, physical configuration of laboratory is fixed (i.e. cabling) and only logical configuration is changed. What is very flexible, it can be done via software, even remotely and without direct human management, via Internet. The tests can be realized also without any supervisor, they can take long time and test wide area of parameters controlled by scripts and software for automatization. The results are gathered, stored and available for off-line analysis.

The rest of the paper is organized as follows: Sect. 2 presents technical elements of my laboratory, next some problems and their solution is presented, Sect. 4 presents example scenario for usage of presented mechanisms, finally, I conclude and present future works.

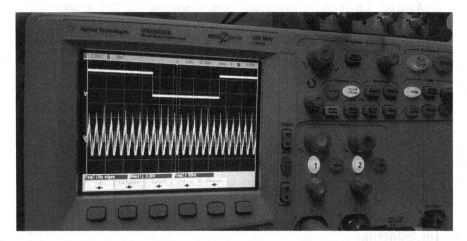

Fig. 1. MSO6032 oscilloscope - 2 analog channels (300 MHz)

2   Technical Background

In my laboratory I work with Agilent MSO6032A (Fig. 1) and DSO6054A (Fig. 2) oscilloscopes [3, 4]. They are old, not fully supported, but still powerful devices. The first one has 2 analog channels with 300 MHz bandwidth, 16 digital channels, second one - 4 analog channels with 500 MHz bandwidth. Nowadays, company Agilent is included in Keysight brand. It is possible to use their software to work with old models, but some functions are not available.

2.1 Available Functionalities in Oscilloscopes

I will mention only several functionalities available in Keysight tools. You can download for free huge pack of software (Command Expert) [7]. It is very powerfull tool, it extends functionality of your device. You can do automatization of your electronic measurement, you can create virtual model of your measurement environment and use it as element of your Software Defined Networking as lots of probes and devices with remote access. In my case, I use such a mechanisms implemented as script with Ansible [8] or Jenkins [9] software, which allows me to automate some actions in my laboratory, which is focussed on networking and electronics (to IoT devices). When many mechanisms can be controlled with software (as topology of network by vlan assignment, takeing measurement from Putty or automatic script) it is very easy and flexible to work remotely, which is very convenient in pandemic situation and remote teaching. On sub page [7] you can read about available functions. What is nice. All functions listed in the documentations [12], are available under GUI tool and also as command line commands, which allow use them in my own scripts and software.

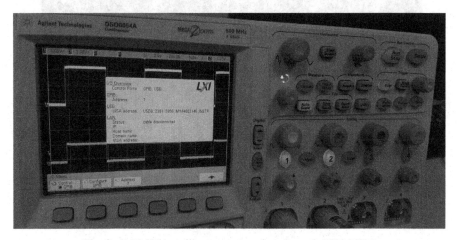

Fig. 2. DSO6054 oscilloscope - 4 analog channels (500 MHz)

2.2 Semi-supported Functionality of my Devices

When you connect via web browser to device, you will obtain web interface with some basic functionality. In theory, it is possible to run some sort of remote desktop and obtain full control - you can observe screen and with dedicated button it is possible to change settings. This functionality is realized with VNC plugin (very old version) and JavaScript. Unfortunately, it works only on Windows XP (I was not successful with another systems), IE6.0 and old version of Javascript. On modern realization I was able only to run actual version of VNC (with TCP connection to default TCP port) and only graphical content of screen was available without any control mechanisms. Some random actions related with mouse roller and some keyboard keys worked as control commands, but it was not useful due to only partial coverage of functionality of whole device. I found solution for this problem, it is described in further section.

In Linux operating system, you can install LXI client [10] and from command line you can read values or change settings. Unfortunately for me, the plugin for my model, is not available, hence I was able to use only basic functionality. Generally, it is possible to print screen with simple command, but not in this case. I found solution which allows me to do printscreen of actual state with command line tools. It is described in further section.

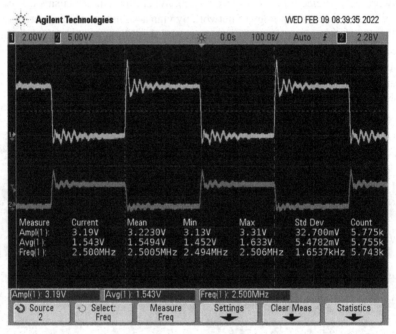

Fig. 3. PrintScreen taken from commandline command

2.3 Set of Switches

Basically, with two oscilloscopes mentioned above, I have 6 analog inputs. In some case it is to few. I decided to extend this set by adding 6 (in maximal) multiplexers composed of 8 relays each. The output of each of them is attached to signal input of oscilloscope, its inputs are connected to points in tested system. Since I can use up to 6 multiplexers with 8 inputs in each, I can serve 48 measurement points. What is more important, physical configuration of cables is fixed, logical configuration (i.e. active input source) is controlled by additional electronic board (ESP32 [11]) which is connected via wireless network to my LAN and it is available for scripts, where by prepared API and proper commands it is possible to change their state by software. Example on one set is presented in Fig. 4. 8 useful signals come with cables from top of the picture, blue switches chooses only one of them to probe and the chosen one is measured by oscilloscope. After saving results of measurements (mostly in png file with date, time and configuration of measured signal, see last command in Fig. 7), configuration and parameters can be changed by command sent to ESP32 and next measurement can be performed.

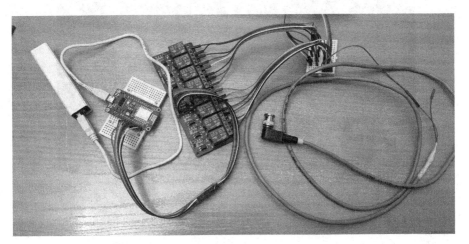

Fig. 4. One set of switches for one input channel in oscilloscope.

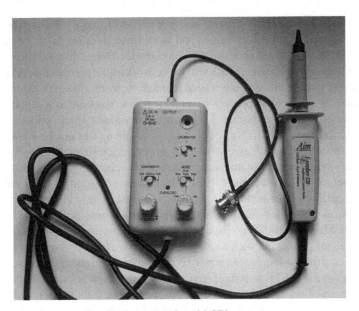

Fig. 5. Current probe with I/U converter.

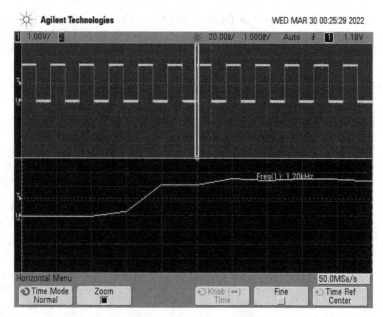

Fig. 6. Example of settings where LXI can extend basic panel functionality

3   My Approach to Some Shortcomings

First action related with extended functionality of my oscilloscope was to connect XVGA monitor. It allowed me to extend screen and work better. It is important to notice, that refresh rate on XVGA screen is the same as on embedded one. Different situation was in case of VNC screen - due to time consumed for network traffic preparation, those pictures was not fully actual and this way is not good for realtime work. However, external XVGA monitor has a copy only of screen, not panel for settings. You have to accept it or prepare your own panel. And it is possible. I used virtual machine (which works as a normal PC) connected to the same LAN as oscilloscope and run on this machine LXI protocol. With this protocol you can change settings of device which supports this protocol [12]. What was my surprise, witch commands we are able to change more settings than from original panel of the oscilloscope!!. I listed most interesting settings and shared them as scripts available under buttons on web page served by this virtual machine. With this mechanism I obtained fully customizable graphical interface to manage of LXI oscilloscope. Moreover, this web page is available for any www client, including web browser on smart phones. In such a case we obtained oscilloscope with 24 inch screen and remote control via handy. In proper IP routing configuration, this system is fully remote accessible - VNC is remote screen and prepared www server works as a remote panel. Command Expert is powerful tool, but it does not fully support older devices. My oscilloscope is such a case. But with command line it was possible to find a way to realize unsupported functions. Figure 3 presents view of screen taken as a picture with my script.

Figure 6 presents MegaZoom functionality, which allows to zoom (bottom shape) of signal (top shape). With LXI commands it is possible to change time scale in wider range and for more parameters than via physical panel.

Figure 7 presents example of Linux LXI commands which allow to change settings. There is also set of commands for reading parameters [12].

```
 1  lxi scpi --address 192.168.1.155   "*IDN?"
 2  lxi scpi --address 192.168.1.155   "CHANnel1:DISPlay off"
 3  lxi scpi --address 192.168.1.155   "CHANnel1:DISPlay on"
 4
 5  lxi scpi --address 192.168.1.155   ":DIGital1:DISPlay 1"
 6  lxi scpi --address 192.168.1.155   ":DIGital1:DISPlay 0"
 7  lxi scpi --address 192.168.1.155   ":DIGital5:DISPlay 0"
 8  lxi scpi --address 192.168.1.155   ":DIGital5:DISPlay 1"
 9
10  lxi scpi --address 192.168.1.155   ":CHAN1:RANG 8V"
11  lxi scpi --address 192.168.1.155   ":CHAN2:RANG 8V"
12  lxi scpi --address 192.168.1.155   ":CHAN1:RANG 8mV"
13  lxi scpi --address 192.168.1.155   ":CHAN1:RANG 8uV"
14
15  lxi scpi --address 192.168.1.155   ":TIMebase:SCALe 100us"
16  lxi scpi --address 192.168.1.155   ":TIMebase:SCALe 100ms"
17  lxi scpi --address 192.168.1.155   ":TIMebase:SCALe 1ms"
18  lxi scpi --address 192.168.1.155   ":TIMebase:SCALe 1ps"
19
20  lxi scpi --address 192.168.1.155   ":MEASure:FREQuency1"
21
22  lxi scpi --address 192.168.1.155   ":DISPlay:DATA? png , GRATicule ,
23  COLor" >> $(date +"%H-%M-%S").png -t 10
```

Fig. 7. Example of LXI commands

4 Example Usage of Test-Bed

Figure 8 shows FPGA module from Propox [13], which is developer board for Xilinx Spartan3 chip. In this chip there is implemented tested project, which is designated to IoT device. Each output is analyzed by presented test-bed. Generally oscilloscopes works with analog signal, the digital ones can be also gathered and measured by them. Such a case is considered here. System is configured for testing this device in a long time (about 36 h). Dedicated chip generate malicious signals and the reaction of chip is registered by oscilloscopes. As a result, set of screenshots with signal shape and parameters of incoming signals is gathered and saved. Parameters are changed and measurements are triggered by commands from scripts which runs under Ansible and Jenkins. With configuration of scripts it is possible to test many configurations where each of them is a Cartesian product of ranges of parameters. All results are stored in files and present as html file (to be visible in any web browser, which is very popular and convenient tool).

Fig. 8. IoT project on FPGA Xilinx Spartan3 chip under test.

5 Conclusions and Future Work

With manual usage of LXI commands and scripts it is possible to extend functionality not only for new devices. It is possible to add them as wide functional nodes available in SDN and automated actions. Basing on this mechanisms automated test-bed has been constructed. I performed many tests when topology of network for IoT devices were changed by SDN mechanism, I also plan to extend functionality of my lab with current and voltage measurement with 12 bit DAC which will be accessible via LAN protocols. Another area of development is the addition of mechanical support for probe (Fig. 5), which also will be controlled by automated software.

Acknowledgements. The work described in this paper was financed from the funds of the Ministry of Science and Higher Education (0313/SBAD/1310 for year 2023).

References

1. https://www.lxistandard.org/
2. https://en.wikipedia.org/wiki/Side-channel_attack
3. https://www.keysight.com/zz/en/product/MSO6032A/mixed-signal-oscilloscope-300-mhz-2-analog-16-digital-channels.html
4. https://www.keysight.com/zz/en/product/DSO6054A/oscilloscope-500-mhz-4-analog-channels.html
5. https://www.aimtti.com/product-category/current-probes/aim-i-prober-520
6. https://www.newae.com/chipshouter
7. https://www.keysight.com/zz/en/lib/software-detail/computer-software/command-expert-downloads-2151326.html
8. https://www.ansible.com/
9. https://www.jenkins.io/
10. https://snapcraft.io/install/lxi-tools/debian
11. https://www.espressif.com/en/products/socs/esp32
12. https://www.keysight.com/zz/en/assets/9018-08107/programming-guides/9018-08107.pdf
13. http://www.propox.com/download/docs/MMfpga02_pl.pdf

Analysis of Time Reaction During Different Approaches to Command Handling in NetFPGA Hardware

Marek Michalski[✉]

Faculty of Computing and Telecommunications, Poznan University of Technology, Piotrowo 3, 60-965 Poznan, Poland
marek.michalski@put.poznan.pl

Abstract. Simulations in typical software take a long time. To make them faster, it is possible to use hardware acceleration. Some people use graphical processors (GPU) which are faster than typical CPU (Central Processing Unit). Much more faster and more effective is to prepare Application Specific Integrated Circuit (ASIC). But it costs a lot of money and also takes time. Nowadays, optimal solution is to use FPGA chips (Field-Programmable Gate Array) which allow to prepare programmable hardware. It is flexible and fast. It requires specific treatment, tool chain for programming and testing, but finally, it gives powerful platform for calculation and data processing. In this paper I will show treatment of new architecture in terms of command handling. Commands are sent to hardware as IP packets and after calculation results should be collected. There are at least 3 ways for this.

1 Introduction

For internal structure of NetFPGA card you can use your own project or you can modify one of prepared demo projects which are available on website [1]. In my proposal I focus on efficient usage of FPGA chip performance. I assumed new internal structure of code, which allows me to realize more than one calculation in the same time. In hardware, you can dedicate particular part or several ones for some, very strict, defined tasks. If designer multiply hardware, the efficiency will be also multiplied. By simple multiplication of calculation part, we can obtain system of parallel calculating engines. We have to control them by sending parameters of tasks and collecting results of calculations. In this paper I will show three approaches for sending commands and receiving results, where both are placed in IP packets. I use NetFPGA card, which can be programmed for serving ethernet traffic. But, in new architecture, the programmable core will be changed, only the outer view will be realized as in primary assumption, i.e. with ethernet frames and IP packets. Due to strict timing, commands and mainly responses, should be processed in a proper way. The rest of this paper is organized as follows: Sect. 2 gives description of NetFPGA cards, Sect. 3 presents usage of NetFPGA cards as a calculating engine with proposed internal structure, Sect. 4 describes software tools, and Sect. 5 defines approaches to sending and receiving commands via IP packets, last section summarizes paper and signalize future works.

© The Author(s), under exclusive license to Springer Nature Switzerland AG 2024
K. S. Soliman (Ed.): IBIMA-AI 2023, CCIS 2101, pp. 151–158, 2024.
https://doi.org/10.1007/978-3-031-62843-6_17

2 NetFPGA Cards

NetFPGA cards (Fig. 1) have been developed by University of Cambridge and Stanford University networking groups as an "open hardware" project [1–3]. NetFPGA card is an extension card for PC, it has four physical network interfaces (4 × 1 Gbps or 4 × 10 Gbps electrical or optical (SFP+) Ethernet ports) and FPGA - programmable hardware as a main chip. More details about structure, architecture and usage of such a card can be found in the literature. What is very important, there is a public framework which implements basic network functionality (routers, switches and interface cards) and it is relatively easy to add our own functionality. In the literature, there is a lot of information about typical usage and projects prepared by NetFPGA community [4–7].

Fig. 1. NetFPGA 10G Card

In primary assumption which is presented in Fig. 2a, the main chip of NetFPGA card receives packets from physical ports (eth0–eth3) as input traffic, analyzes and modifies them, and sends them out to physical ports as output traffic. Functionality of main chip is programmable and can be very flexible. The source and destination of traffic can be also logical interfaces visible in operating system as nf0–nf3 interfaces. Very important fact is that this functionality is realized by hardware, hence, the performance of such an appliance allows to serve whole traffic with speed of line, in case of these Ethernet ports it can be 1 Gbps or 10 Gbps.

3   Hardware Part as a Simulator

In my approach [8], which schematic is presented in Fig. 2b, there is no typical modules in FPGA chip. Only communication with operating system through one interface is used, it is visible as one active interface in the operating system. All the traffic sent to this interface is visible by all modules, they identify traffic dedicated to them by given IP/MAC address or even VLAN ID or UDP port. The return path for data is realized analogically, each module sends traffic with given parameters. The control application on operating system serves this interface in promiscuous mode and receives all frames. Figure 3a presents primary pipeline, where 8 incoming queues and 8 outgoing queues are implemented, because they are related with serving traffic from two representation of 4 interfaces in two directions. In proposed architecture only one buffer is realized, because nature of transferred frame is different. In primary version, 8 incoming traffic streams was fully served thanks to internal speedup. The main difference between primary and proposed architecture is to use parallel custom modules (Fig. 3b), where each of them can calculate its task in the same time. The speedup is not necessary, the maximal speed of calculation is used by multiple modules in the same time, hence, the final performance of calculation it is a product of performance of one module and number of modules. Proper control and timing mechanisms should be use to send requests for particular modules and also adequate way of receiving responses has to be implemented (in module with name output module arbiter). It reflects on functionality realized in the software part.

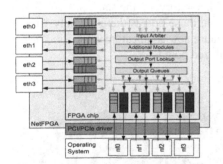 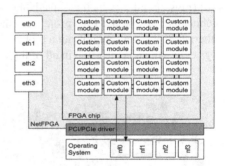

Fig. 2. Schema of modules on NetFPGA card and inside FPGA chip and modified schema of NetFPGA card - modification is only in FPGA chip

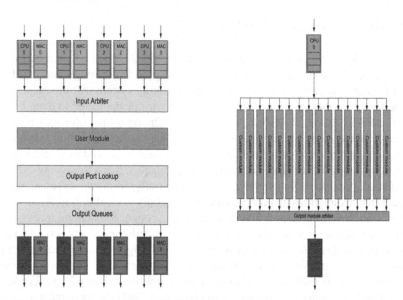

Fig. 3. Internal pipeline of modules on NetFPGA card and inside FPGA chip and modified schema of NetFPGA card - modification is only in FPGA chip

The same FPGA chip (Virtex 5) is used on developers boards ML555 [9] and ML505 [10] (Figs. 4 and 5) which are available in my laboratory. So the same procedure and architecture can be used for project for them. On those boards there are only 1 Gbps Ethernet SFP cages, but it is not a problem, because new architecture is focussed inside fpga chip, which is the same in all of three analyzed boards.

Fig. 4. ML555 developers board from Xilinx

4   Software Part of the System

Basic usage of this idea assumes that every custom module has its own MAC and IP address. All these addresses are in network which is related with nf0 interface. When operating system (basing on typical routing table) sends IP packet, proper module receives ethernet frame with this packet. Proper configuration of IP/MAC relation in ARP table of host should be realized, but it is realized automatically by script during addressing configuration. It is possible to control more than one card from the same control application (in my laboratory I have 5 NetFPGA 10G cards), proper configuration of IP addresses, IP networks and routing information has to be realized. In my case, first assumption was to use Omnetpp software and prepare software modules related with their hardware support, i.e. each module (node from Omnetpp) sends calculation commands for his own calculating module in FPGA via IP protocol. It was possible but actual version of my application is not related directly with Omnetpp, but many functionalities are copied and they are implemented in my own software (Fig. 3). In the Fig. 4 there is shown example of network which can be realized in one fpga chip. Each switch is represented by one module. In general case, this system is designated for analysing bigger topologies of IoT devices.

5   Commands and Results in IP Packets

To simulate some system its model has to be prepared. The calculating part will be realized in hardware, it means that in VHDL or Verilog modules have to be defined and implemented in FPGA chip. The software part should also reflect analyzed system in its internal structures, i.e. model in hardware has to reflects model in software and vice versa. This process is complicated and time consuming, it costs a lot of work. When the simulator is prepared and configured (i.e. IP/MAC addresses used in software part are also implemented in custom modules), tasks can be sent to hardware. When simulator decides to run some task and module for this task is ready, parameters of tasks are packed into IP payload and sent to NetFPGA card as typical IP packet packed in Ethernet frame. This block of data, after passing DMA in PCI bus, is placed in input buffer and it is visible by every custom module. There is only one module which has matching IP/MAC addresses, so, only one custom module will read this data. The content of IP payload is used as a parameters for calculations. After finishing calculations, when results are ready, they are packed into IP packet in order to be received by DMA and software part. But, the output of custom modules has to be served in proper way to omit problems. Different types of problems causes different approach to solving them, realization of different approaches is described further.

Fig. 5. ML505 developers board from Xilinx

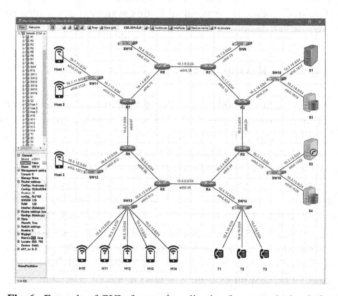

Fig. 6. Example of GUI of control application for network simulation

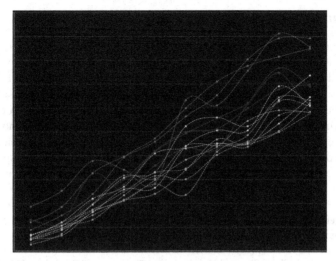

Fig. 7. Example of result view from software when second approach is realized

5.1 Approach 1: Ask One Module and Wait

The simples idea assumes that we will send request and wait for response. One module in FPGA receives tasks, after their realization it sends out results as IP packet. It will work, but not efficiently. In the same time only one module will realize calculations. This approach is relatively easy in implementation, it can be realized for project, where is no focus on parallel calculations.

5.2 Approach 2: Ask Dedicated Module and Monitor

Second approach assumes that simulator can send requests for modules before they finish their tasks. They respond with information about progress (for example "75% done") or final results if they are ready. This approach is quite good, it allows to run calculations on multiple modules in the same time. The software does not wait for end of calculations, just questioning for actual state of them. In this case control mechanism are more complicated, but efficiency is very good. All possible decisions and control of communications is realized in software. Figure 7 shows example view from software part of simulator which presents online gathered results.

5.3 Approach 3: Ask Dedicated Module and Wait

We can also imagine situation when module generates IP packet with results just after ending calculations. It looks interesting, but it is possible that more than one module will generate packet in the same time (or almost in the same time). For proper serving such a cases, dedicated output module arbiter is necessary. In my approaches, I prefer to use simple hardware and more sophisticated functionality is realized rather in software than in hardware for two reasons: 1) It is easier and faster, 2) and also I can save hardware resources for bigger number of modules in hardware. Moreover - in this case, software part has no full control of whole process, because some decisions are taken in hardware.

6   Conclusions and Future Work

The main chip of NetFPGA card can be programmed. Although, Designers of NetF-PGA cards assumed them to serve network traffic, it can be used as a almost general purpose hardware accelerator. When you have a practise with demo projects for network devices (as switch, card, router), which use MAC/IP addressing, registers, buffers and PCI operations, it is easy to implement your own functionality, which extends the already enormous possibilities even more. As my future work I plan to use another FPGA chips and prepare system of tools for convenient and user friendly simulator. Also automated procedure for huge amount of IoT devices organized in advanced topologies are considered. Additional user friendly functionalities will be implemented and added in software.

Acknowledgements. The work described in this paper was financed from the funds of the Ministry of Science and Higher Education (0313/SBAD/1310 for year 2023).

I would also like to thank (in alphabetical order):

• NetFPGA Teams from Stanford University and University of Cambridge [1] for their support and help in organizing NetFPGA workshop at "my anonymous uni" and overall work with NetFPGA cards;

• Xilinx University Program [11] for donating to My University of Technology five NetFPGA cards with 10G interfaces.

References

1. Website of community and NetFPGA project. http://www.netfpga.org
2. Gibb, G., Lockwood, J.W., Naous, J., Hartke, P., McKeown, N.: NetFPGA: an open platform for teaching how to build gigabit-rate network switches and routers. IEEE Trans. Educ. **51**(3), 364–369 (2008)
3. Zilberman, N., Audzevich, Y., Covington, G.A., Moore, A.W.: NetFPGA SUME: toward 100 Gbps as research commodity. IEEE Micro **34**(5), 32–41 (2014). https://doi.org/10.1109/MM.2014.61
4. NetFPGA reference projects. http://www.netfpga.org/project_table.html
5. Michalski, M.: The configurations for experimental study of the network performance. In: 8th IEEE, IET International Symposium on Communication Systems, Networks and Digital Signal Processing (CSNDSP 2012), 18–20 July 2012 (2012)
6. Michalski, M.: The system for delay measurement in Ethernet networks on NetFPGA cards. In: IEEE International Conference on High Performance Switching and Routing 2014, Vancouver, Canada, 1–4 July 2014 (2014)
7. Michalski, M., Sielach, T.: The analysis of time reaction in OpenFlow switches in NetF-PGA cards and ROFL. In: 2015 International Symposium on Networks, Computers and Communications (ISNCC 2015), 13–15 May 2015 (2015)
8. Michalski, M.: Elements of architecture of simulator realized on NetFPGA10G card. In: 2022 International Conference on Computer Communications and Networks (ICCCN), Honolulu, HI, USA, pp. 1–2 (2022). https://doi.org/10.1109/ICCCN54977.2022.9868941
9. Virtex-5 FPGA ML555 Development Kit for PCI and PCI Express Designs. https://docs.xilinx.com/v/u/en-US/ug201
10. ML505/ML506/ML507 Evaluation Platform User Guide. https://docs.xilinx.com/v/u/en-US/ug347
11. Xilinx University Program. http://xilinx.com/support/university.html

The Adoption of Spatial Information Technology in Precision Agriculture

Paolo Fetahu and Mukesh Srivastava[✉]

University of Mary Washington, Fredericksburg, USA
pfetahu@mail.umw.edu, msrivast@umw.edu

Abstract. This research paper analyses the adoption status of Spatial Information Technology via diffusion of innovations framework and diffusion variance model in the field of Precision Agriculture. This study explores four research questions; What is the landscape of spatial information technology diffusion and innovation in Precision Agriculture? How does Technical Compatibility impact SIT implementation in Precision Agriculture? How does the complexity of SIT impact Precision Agriculture? How does Relative Advantage of employed Spatial Information Systems influence (for example: remote sensing imagery) spatial innovation of agricultural technology? This study draws on cases of spatial technology acceptance and diffusion of innovation and highlights the significance of compatibility between hardware and software and complexity among these technology models utilized in PA. Developing an understanding of SIT adoption attributes and their relevant applications is crucial to better comprehend the innovation adoption perspective, as well as recognize any compatibility or complexity issues related to the advancement of spatial technologies integrated into agricultural activities to boost efficacy, productivity, and sustainability. Given the complexity of SIT technical practices and technical knowledge, it is principal to explore the leading dynamics and challenges present in the broader adoption of SIT in PA applications. The paper concentrates on specific spatial and remote sensing mode followed by comprehensive review that displays a wide range of insights considering the adaptation of spatial-technology-based systems to support agricultural productivity and sustainable development. If spatial technology solutions for PA progression do not address complexity and compatibility issues, adoption does not diffuse throughout PA, farmers are less likely to employ technologies if they consider the use as more complex, and there is less accuracy in agricultural analytics.

Keywords: Spatial Information Technology · Precision Agriculture · Remote Sensing Imagery · Geographic Information Systems

1 Introduction

The Diffusion of Innovation (DOI) Theory is used in this research to analyze how Spatial Information Technology was developed and utilized in the field of PA analyzing the case of saffron cultivation [12]. The DOI theory is often considered a valuable theoretical model for directing technological changes and innovations toward collaborating

© The Author(s), under exclusive license to Springer Nature Switzerland AG 2024
K. S. Soliman (Ed.): IBIMA-AI 2023, CCIS 2101, pp. 159–172, 2024.
https://doi.org/10.1007/978-3-031-62843-6_18

with several factors needed in shaping and advancing the overall IS process innovation adoption [9]. The theory strives to explain how, over time, a concept, system, or product moves faster as it keeps developing, gradually advances, and diffuses through a particular organization, society, or business environment [9]. The end goal of this theory is that individuals, societies, and other systems adopt brand-new ideas, ideologies, or functions.

Based on this theory, there can be distinguished two major series of activities that shape the innovation process: initiation and implementation. In between these two adoption milestones, there are five adopter categories followed by five major elements that impact the speed of innovation adoption, and each of these elements plays a distinct key role in each of the adopter groups as shown in Fig. 1, [4]. This research is focused on analyzing the first three core characteristics (compatibility, complexity, and relative advantage) that have been recognized as three dominant attributes required to strengthen and promote the establishment of Spatial Technologies in PA.

The latest advances in spatial information systems and precision agriculture technologies have empowered farmers to obtain principal site-specific data for their fields, with the objective to gather crucial information needed for farm management, enhance the decision-making process, and develop an economically and socially sustainable agriculture model that boosts profitability and productivity [2]. This study investigates the adoption and adoption intensity of SIT applied to PA. The paper presents literature research conducted on saffron cultivation case employing remote sensing information-intensive techniques through several implementation stages based on the level of innovativeness. The level of innovativeness is categorized as: innovators, early adopters, early majority, late majority, and laggards, Fig. 1, [11]. Each innovation stage consists of its time span and speed of spatial-technological adoption.

Adopter Categorization based on Innovativeness

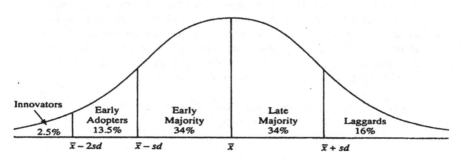

Fig. 1. Five Adopter Categories [4]

Research showed that precision farmers together with agricultural and GIS specialists have placed great importance on utilizing spatial technology, remote sensing, and geospatial techniques in terms of boosting their relative advantages and agricultural efficiency, particularly in the innovation, early adoption, and early majority stages [8]. However, these advantages might become less effective as new innovations flourish and certain impediments such as adoption flexibility, farmers' knowledge and perceptions towards specific technologies, and practical problems of the utilization of spatial information technology may appear along the process.

2   Research Framework

The goal of this research paper is to analyse the adoption of Spatial Information Technology via the diffusion of innovations framework and diffusion variance model in the field of Precision Agriculture through exploring the following research questions:

2.1   RQ1: What is the Landscape of Spatial Information Technology Diffusion and Innovation in Precision Agriculture?

This paper focuses on the diffusion of adoption of Spatial Information Technology with the objective to enhance the overall efficiency of precision agriculture practices and farm resources management optimization – as well as understanding how certain spatial techniques tackle spatial characteristics of precision agriculture to then transform agricultural systems towards a more sustainable model. To embrace transformation, it is beneficial to comprehend the adoption steps of spatial diffusion mechanisms and integration of spatial systems throughout PA.

2.2   RQ2: How Does Technical Compatibility Impact SIT Implementation in Precision Agriculture?

The relationship between technical compatibility and PA determines the degree to which the agricultural community is confronted with potential challenges in terms of implementing and utilizing new approaches and technologies to boost agricultural productivity growth, crop systems performance, optimizing crop disease mitigation, and other similar practices. These practices are unable to thrive without leveraging spatial technologies with complete hardware and software compatibility in connection with existing systems that are already built and operated in the area. Incompatible techniques which cannot operate satisfactorily with existing systems and structures or do not reach target goals hinder the diffusion process and provide obstacles for the adoption stage. If new spatial systems and technologies are successfully applied to PA practices and yield transformative results, the rate of adoption of the new systems and relative advantage will move forward and aid in speeding spatial agricultural intelligence.

2.3   RQ3: How Does the Complexity of SIT Impact Precision Agriculture?

As innovations boost the transition to sustainable agriculture on spatial technology framework, it is important to underline obstacles and factors of complexity (technical proficiency, socio-economic/cost-effective perspectives, etc.) that might restrict the broader use of spatial technologies across PA practices. A high rate of complexity for the innovations leads to a significantly diminished capability for technology adoption which eventually leads to diffusion failure.

2.4   RQ4: How Does Relative Advantage of Employed Spatial Information Systems Influence. (Example: Remote Sensing Imagery) Spatial Innovation of Agricultural Technology?

As SIT practices and new geospatial technologies strive in directing the future of precision agriculture toward a sustainable production model, relative advantage must be in conformity with these innovations and the way they function to be able to achieve the end goals and overcome competition. This process requires the effective collaboration of several components primarily involving competency in software and hardware machinery to support spatial technological models, spatial analysis experts, and other agricultural professionals utilizing knowledge, effort, and resources for the new innovations to experience rapid growth and develop more productive and competitive precision agricultural systems.

2.5   Approach for Spatial Information Technology Adoption in the Sphere of Precision Agriculture

The purpose of this study is to better understand, describe and analyze the unique spatial diffusion of precision agriculture practices. The study investigated the research how the adoption of SIT influences the improvement of farm management, productivity, and sustainability by evaluating four research questions. This study used a qualitative approach, and its results support previous works regarding the adoption and diffusion of spatial farming technologies.

2.6   Landscape of Spatial Information Technology Diffusion and Innovation in Precision Agriculture

The following model (illustrated in Fig. 2) indicates two significant innovation processes - Model A, portrays the workforce productivity for technology implementations that are uncomplicated and rather simple [4]. Authors claimed that this technology carries a higher knowledge adoption rate that experiences a climax but progressively becomes unlikely to change at a certain rate thus diminishing the innovation rate.

Model B is more complicated thus indicating more advanced technologies to be implemented. Complexity comes in terms of time required to absorb and practice the new knowledge, cost allocation, and derived results taking longer than in Model A since more complex technologies would involve more steps in the process [4]. Research has shown that PA applications are probable to employ processes as entailed in Model B,

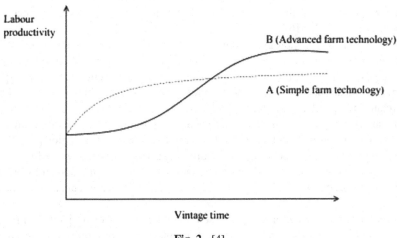

Fig. 2. [4]

since PA spatial activities are highly technical, demand savviness, and allocate a large amount of data that requires extremely large storage capacities [5].

The latest advances in information systems and technologies have given farmers the opportunity to gather great amounts of data utilized to locate, examine, and measure differences across fields, track these differences at locations, and employ such insights to enhance the decision-making process and transform major agricultural purposes for the better [11]. PA is a by-product of SIT implemented in agriculture. Spatial technologies help advance site-specific farming practices by accumulating and examining data relevant to different locations in a specific field to then assess the data to obtain key information regarding management decisions related to the different fields based upon spatial variations [7]. PA heavily relies on modern spatial technologies such as precision Global Positioning Systems, Geographical Information Systems, Remote Sensing Imagery, Variable Rate Technologies, and other technologies [7]. Spatial technologies collaborate with precision farming to aid decision-making by delivering key insights for crop and soil management in various field areas.

GIS, a primary technology in SIT, is regarded as an influential system that includes instruments for collecting, storing, analyzing, and illustrating spatial data for target objectives [6]. The authors state it is essential because it comprises specific spatial contexts and key insights on different spatial aspects serving as important stages in the overall process. There has been a tremendous expansion in the use of GIS practices for a variety of precision agricultural activities on a global scale. According to the authors, such practices entail the use of GIS in conjunction with other spatial systems to get a comprehensive picture of a specific location and to provide other needed procedures or actions needed for crops, soil, diseases, irrigation, and so on.

GPS serves as a navigation or positioning system centered around satellite networks that provide specific solutions in terms of where and under what conditions an agricultural location is faced with [6]. The precise location data retrieved by GPS, allows farmers and specialists to practice field monitoring and understand what areas are facing problems such as for instance crop diseases or irrigation issues [11]. This field mapping and monitoring system then allows farmers to work on site-specific issues and plan ahead to intervene where needed [6].

Remote Sensing technology collaborates with GPS and GIS to improve crop monitoring and classification activities, estimate crop yields, and tackle additional crop and soil changes such as fertility, soil moisture evaluation, the occurrence of pest species in particular locations, etc., [12]. This technology gathers data about objects and problems related to specific areas remotely far-off without directly interacting with what is being analyzed. To reach sustainable agricultural patterns, all factors that impact the agricultural sector must be determined and assessed on a spatial foundation [12]. Several research experiments have been conducted utilizing aerial videography and digital image processing techniques minimizing the large amount of agricultural spatial information needed by providing extra accuracy and precision in the measurements that it processes [8].

Spatial data is a key factor to be assessed in modern precision agricultural practices. Spatial technology processes revolve around computer systems monitored by computer-based algorithms that are related to cyber-physical attributes of spatial technology applied to farming practices [1]. Figure 3 displays how big data and spatial analysis collaborate to create a cycle where the focus is shifted toward farmers acting as data collectors by using a cloud-based infrastructure that oversees farm spatial activities such as smart sensing, remote monitoring, UAV devices, and so on, [1]. If the cycle is successful thus farmers can analyze spatial data that alerts, informs, or encourages them to take action according to what and how certain spatial variables alter due to certain factors (for example, forecast changes, disease presence, etc.).

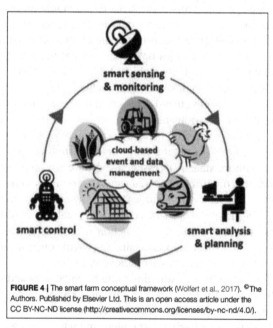

FIGURE 4 | The smart farm conceptual framework (Wolfert et al., 2017). ©The Authors. Published by Elsevier Ltd. This is an open access article under the CC BY-NC-ND license (http://creativecommons.org/licenses/by-nc-nd/4.0/).

Fig. 3. [1]

3   Remote Sensing System Analysis

This paper has analyzed certain practices of the above-mentioned spatial technologies in agriculture that consider major agricultural factors. SIT practices such as Remote Sensing Imagery in collaboration with precision agriculture have built different platforms that are capable to examine several agricultural measurements. One example is the OSI model which proposes a remote sensing system that heavily employs spatial insights through seven significant layers as illustrated in Fig. 4, [13]. This system allows farmers to form precise thoughts and decisions related to field operations through spatial innovative techniques backed up by data mining and advanced networking. Farmers can manage collected data to boost productivity, crop yield, and efficiently use resources to solve major problems through successfully employing the following layers [13]:

1. **The Sensor Layer:** several sensors are implemented deep within the soil, on aerial devices such as drones or other UAV objects (unmanned aerial vehicles), or on crops, to collect data and monitor activity such as physio-chemical features, soil parameters, etc. The UAV (such as thermal imaging drones) estimate environmental parameters varying from physical to chemical attributes and involve analysis of all needed elements to measure environmental quality.
2. **The Link Layer:** includes wireless networking among sensors to send important "messages" that eventually send signals related to the instant monitoring of crop quality and other above-mentioned attributes.
3. **The Encapsulation Layer:** the main goal is to translate and filter sensory field messages into smart data by allowing data to be enclosed in systems such as IPv6 that allows data identification and categorization before sending it to respective network servers.
4. **The Middleware Layer:** transfers generated sensor data to the next stage, as well as serves as an intermediary between devices to communicate and manage the data as it transitions from one stage to another.
5. **The Configuration Layer:** assists in the process by collecting other raw information streamed from outside sources (other farm equipment, geo-spatial data resources) selecting and transforming it into certain data contexts to enrich the overall process data quality.
6. **The Management Layer:** at this stage data is ready to be processed and analyzed via advanced database management and analysis systems to conclude results in the opted perspectives (for example crop infection identification, irrigation inefficiencies, etc.).
7. **The Application Layer:** the last stage to manifest the process completion. At this stage, farmers are ready to utilize all the processed data portrayed on advanced interfaces to assist farmers' decision-making, visualize what certain results shall be inspected, and guide in taking certain further actions.

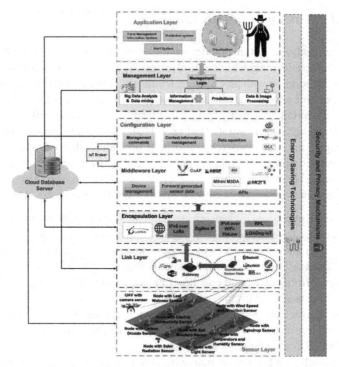

Fig. 4. [13]

4 Remote Sensing System Application – The DIAS System and Saffron Cultivation

The following case represents the application and realization of spatial information technology through a remote sensing model utilizing the DIAS platform (Drone Innovation in Agriculture Surveillance) in Saffron cultivation in Western Macedonia [13]. The core goal of this technology is to monitor the saffron cultivation process and protect the edible saffron crop from diseases, animal involvement, wild weeds or other cautions such as represented in Fig. 6. According to research done by the authors, this process is supported by UAV devices, spatial image analysis, and risk analysis systems assisted by sensor-based networks to provide instant feedback. Authors stated that this process utilizes the same remote sensing system architecture that was previously described (Fig. 5).

Saffron harvesting.

Fig. 5. [13]

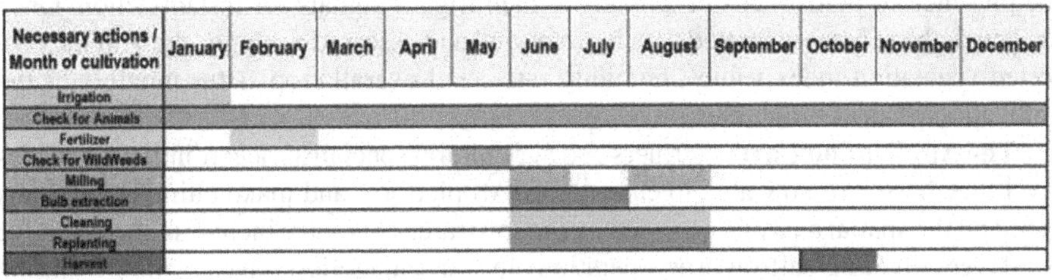

Necessary actions / Month of cultivation	January	February	March	April	May	June	July	August	September	October	November	December
Irrigation												
Check for Animals												
Fertilizer												
Check for WildWeeds												
Milling												
Bulb extraction												
Cleaning												
Replanting												
Harvest												

Saffron cultivation yearly stages.

Fig. 6. [13]

The Sensor layer: UAV devices and thermal cameras cooperate with several wireless nodes and sensors placed on the ground or on the leaves to gather and analyze how data varies each month and respond to weather changes, humidity, temperature, animals, soil moisture, level of chemicals needed.

The Link and Encapsulation layer: the sensor-generated data proceeds through advanced technology such as LoRaWAN - the DIAS system equips the sensor nodes with IP addresses to transfer encrypted data to the particular LoRa Gateways to the respective network systems to store and process the data.

The Middleware layer: the MQTT-SN platform controls information going through all the networks guided by the FIWARE's context broker which then assorts and categorizes the data into particular messages that signify the level of risk, importance, and alert.

The Configuration layer: the obtained data is aggregated and formulated to enter the information management unit transitioning through the FIWARE NGSI API with the end goal to generate an ideal model that represents insights on saffron data.

The Management layer: records, manages, and interprets the acquired data, generating estimates for crop health and information on its present status. The data management system launches the related operations employing specific algorithms to conclude insights on the development and health of saffron crops. Such an algorithm is instantly practiced on the data of pictures obtained by UAV devices, meanwhile, the analysis of retrieved geospatial imagery concentrates on providing the appropriate vegetation indexes for assessing the status of saffron crops. Vegetation indexes developed from images with multiple spectral channels (for instance NDVI) allows the observation of diseases. The thermal cameras electronically linked to the algorithm, surveil and identify the presence of wild weeds or animals to then trigger signals for instant action. Once analyzed, the sensor-generated data is structured and assessed analogously with the projected vegetation index values, humidity rates, and overall crop status monthly as the cultivation process progresses.

The Application Layer: farmers and agricultural specialists according to the access level they have, are now able to enter the DIAS platform and make ultimate decisions based on the spatial analysis provided by the software. This stage includes four executive sub-layers dividing saffron crop operations in four categories: Visualization Unit, the Data Management Unit, the Prediction Unit, and the Data collection Unit. The Data Collection Unit allows farmers to gather and edit sensor data of particular fields, review remote sensing imagery captured during the process, and estimate vegetation indexes based on particular data in particular saffron areas using spatial imagery tools. The Visualization Unit is responsible for displaying findings and infographics for each saffron area, whereas the Prediction Unit applies the previously stated data mining technologies to generate a proper review of the obtained information (Fig. 7, 8).

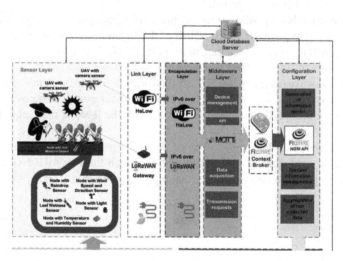

Fig. 7. [13]

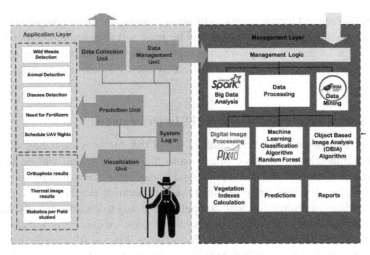

Fig. 8. The DIAS architecture

5 Results and Discussions

5.1 Technical Compatibility Impact on SIT Implementation

There are significant limitations to establishing and upholding a space remote sensory monitoring system in precision agriculture. One critical aspect lies in the sensor stage which accounts for sensor nodes to operate effectively and continuously in a particular environment for an extended period while accounting for weather variability and animal activities, [13]. The battery performance of sensor nodes is not deemed adequate, while it is important to establish and apply energy-efficient procedures with the maximum achievable system performance.

Furthermore, based on the kind of technology implementation, challenges that occur may be diverse - for example, using sensors, transmitters, or networks from various suppliers, limits connectivity and complicates interaction with other devices that control other agricultural elements on the DIAS platform, [13]. Another issue related to maintaining a crop monitoring system utilizing wireless sensor networks in the network stages comprises sensor nodes' low processing capacity. Authors described that the limited memory makes it impossible for the nodes to manage significant volumes of data transmission and reception, thus causing large data queues to line up in each node, resulting in longer transmission delays. The extended communication intervals across sensor nodes delay the overall process. A central challenge that routing algorithms should address in these instances is the large amount of energy demand that affects the network's feasibility, [13].

As stated by the authors, routing mechanisms exchanging routing information between routers to make decisions about the saffron crops should have a lower latency rate through the sensor nodes. The routing protocol's efficiency is influenced by capability in terms of storage (the number of nodes in the network) and speed communication that channels employ, [13]. Correspondingly, network performance impacts the system compatibility required for the saffron cultivation process. Yet, the incompetency of such ultramodern monitoring systems can as well be attributed to agricultural specialists facing knowledge or financial gaps when going through the decision-making process to either design, implement, or purchase specific systems for their agricultural activities, [13].

5.2 Technical Complexity Impact on SIT Implementation

In terms of innovation complexity, authors stated that the network bandwidth, which is used for transmitting signals captured from the sensory nodes, can be limited in certain areas in the world where computational advancement, industrial bases, and other standards are less developed in comparison to other countries. For the innovation process to thrive, authors recommended edge computing as a way to save bandwidth and utilize a framework that brings agriculture applications and derived data faster and closer to the sources of data and respective networks. For instance, Microsoft's FarmBeats low-cost system whose goal is to provide user-friendliness and faster functionality encourages technology adoption (particularly for farmers performing agricultural activities on a limited scale) by building a very simple system that utilizes the same spatial devices and sensors but through a simplified and much cheaper process (Farmbeats Microsoft, 2022). Figure 9 illustrates how this system employs cheap devices and simple software to work with field sensors and spatial devices to capture field variables (such as soil moisture, etc.).

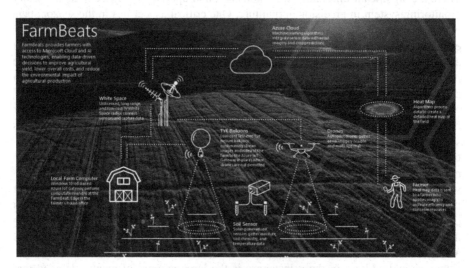

Fig. 9. (Farmbeats Microsoft, 2022)

5.3 Relative Advantage Impact on SIT Implementation

The cost of implementing such systems is a significant limiting issue for farmers to advance their processes and move forward in the industry in comparison to competitors who might afford such technology [13]. Authors stated that such systems may vary from affordable to very pricey depending on features, network arrangement of nodes, capacity, and energy-saving schemes. The inability to provide considerable analytical proficiency is another factor–farmers' educational background should be considered as a booster in using human capital to achieve results through effectively utilizing remote sensing imagery and analyzing its derived data. Another factor is age – older farmers tend to rely more on traditional methods that employ a narrower technological perspective rather than modern spatial computerized methods.

6 Conclusion

The SIT practices, such as remote sensing, has significantly improved the effectiveness of precision agriculture in dealing with large amount of agricultural data, considering production implications and take precautions for creating sustainable agricultural models. Spatial imagery and other related technologies have played an important role in managing crop monitoring to simplify the decision-making process related to the establishment of spatially variable agricultural activities. Due to the latest technical advances, remote sensing practices enable utilization of high-dimensional data, aerial and satellite images that alert farmers on important issues.

It is important to note that, however, innovation is unlikely to thrive if the creation of a system that promotes the use of new technologies is hindered due to certain factors. As a result, sustainable development of PA practices is reliant on innovation and the crucial part that farmers play when utilizing knowledge and resources that contribute to the process. As illustrated by the research conclusions, given the complexity of several factors such as sensory nodes capability, storage capacity, expertise demanded for application, specialists should further explore existing spatial systems or design simpler structures for real-time spatial applications. Establishment of accurate, user-friendly systems gravitates toward greater adoption of spatial remote sensing technologies in agricultural practices.

References

1. Delgado, J.A., Short, N.M., Roberts, D.P., Vandenberg, B.: Big Data Analysis for sustainable agriculture on a geospatial cloud framework. Front. Sustain. Food Syst. 3 (2019). https://doi.org/10.3389/fsufs.2019.00054
2. Fanelli, R.M.: The spatial and temporal variability of the effects of agricultural practices on the environment. Environments 7(4), 33 (2020). https://doi.org/10.3390/environments7040003
3. Farmbeats: Ai, Edge & IOT for Agriculture. Microsoft Research, 28 November 2022. https://www.microsoft.com/en-us/research/project/farmbeats-iot-agriculture/. Accessed 26 Feb 2023
4. Fountas, S., Pedersen, S.M., Blackmore, S.: ICT in Precision Agriculture – diffusion of technology. In: Gelb, E., Offer, A. (eds.) ICT in Agriculture: Perspective of Technological Innovation (2005). http://departments.agri.huji.ac.il/economics/gelb-main.html
5. Griffin, T.W., Lowenberg-Deboer, J., Lambert, D.M., Peone, J., Payne, T., Daberkow, S.G.: Adoption, profitability, and making better use of precision farming data. Staff Paper #04-06. Department of Agricultural Economics, Purdue University (2004)

6. Ghosh, P., Kumpatla, S.P.: GIS applications in agriculture. In: Geographic Information Systems and Applications in Coastal Studies (2022). https://doi.org/10.5772/intechopen. 104786

7. Kolady, D.E., Van der Sluis, E., Uddin, M.M., Deutz, A.P.: Determinants of adoption and adoption intensity of precision agriculture technologies: evidence from South Dakota. Precis. Agric. **22**(3), 689–710 (2020). https://doi.org/10.1007/s11119-020-09750-2

8. Masi, M., De Rosa, M., Vecchio, Y., Bartoli, L., Adinolfi, F.: The long way to innovation adoption: insights from precision agriculture. Agric. Food Econ. **10**(1) (2022). https://doi.org/10.1186/s40100-022-00236-5

9. Mitchell, S., Weersink, A., Erickson, B.: Adoption of precision agriculture technologies in Ontario crop production. Can. J. Plant Sci. **98**(6), 1384–1388 (2018). https://doi.org/10.1139/cjps-2017-0342

10. Precision Agriculture: an overview. In: Handbook of Precision Agriculture, pp. 33–48 (2006). https://doi.org/10.1201/9781482277968-11

11. Roberts, D.P., Short, N.M., Sill, J., Lakshman, D.K., Hu, X., Buser, M.: Precision agriculture and geospatial techniques for Sustainable Disease Control. Indian Phytopathol. **74**(2), 287–305 (2021). https://doi.org/10.1007/s42360-021-00334-2

12. Shanmugapriya, P., Rathika, S., Ramesh, T., Janaki, P.: Applications of remote sensing in agriculture - a review. Int. J. Curr. Microbiol. Appl. Sci. **8**(01), 2270–2283 (2019). https://doi.org/10.20546/ijcmas.2019.801.238

13. Triantafyllou, A., Sarigiannidis, P., Bibi, S.: Precision agriculture: a remote sensing monitoring system architecture †. Information **10**(11), 348 (2019). https://doi.org/10.3390/info10110348)

Identifying Critical Success Factors (CSF) for Cyber Supply Chain Risk Management (CSCRM): A Qualitative Study Using Agency Theory

Ryan Firth and Mukesh Srivastava[✉]

University of Mary Washington, Fredericksburg, USA
{rirth,msrivast}@umw.edu

Abstract. This research paper shall analyze the relationship of Cybers Supply Chain Risk Management (CSCRM) between Principals and their Agents via Agency Theory, and the critical success factors perceived in maintaining a CSCRM process. The goal is to outline the complex constraints of maintaining CSCRM structure, and assess organizations, whether acting as the Principal or Agent, comprehensive relationship when balancing the risk factors & governance throughout the Principal/Agent relationship and the implications of regulatory requirements associated with CSCRM.

Keywords: CSF · CSCRM · Agency Theory · Cyber Supply Chain · Risk Management

1 Overview

The ecosystem of CSCRM relies on a multifaceted, international, and interconnected supply chain network that has thousands of compounding strata layers necessary to ensure the deliverable required for an organization's mission. This Information Communication Technology (ICT) CSCRM network, made up of a vast number of governments and industries entities, innovations, regulations, policies, procedures, and practices that interact to identify, design, assess, execute, monitor, control, and distribute ICT goods and services. ICT CSCRM is the process of identifying, assessing, and mitigating the risks associated with the cyber supply chain on an international level within ICT products and services supply chains. The system of ICT CSCRM constantly needs to adapt to provide quality, cost-effective, reusable ICT solutions. Organizations throughout multiple industries have rapidly adopted varying solution options, internal and external to their corporate structure, which has increased the dependance on commercially available goods, services, integration support, and external resources. This shift has created and will continue to create a wineglass effect on industry competition. Before, an immense number of suppliers along the supply chain existed but as risks and nefarious entities increase their complexity and impact on the cyber supply chain, industry organizations will need to evolve to maintain to continue to provide products, goods, and services to their clients [10].

K. S. Soliman (Ed.): IBIMA-AI 2023, CCIS 2101, pp. 173–186, 2024.
https://doi.org/10.1007/978-3-031-62843-6_19

Authors' goal is to identify and rank the key critical success factors (CSF) with the perspective of Agency Theory focused internal to an organization and their vendors, by asking five research questions:

1. What is the need of a Principal and Agent relationships within Cyber Supply Chain Risk Management?
2. What are the types of Principle and Agent relationships within Cyber Supply Chain Risk Management?
3. What are the perceived risks to the Principal/Agent relationship associated with CSCRM? And how do those perceived risks impact the Principal and Agent Relationship?
4. What is the Level of Effort (LOE) from varying areas within an organization regarding supply chain? And which area in an organization has the greatest impact on CSCRM procedures, considering the Principal/Agent relationship?
5. What are the required changes by an organization from a regulatory perspective? And how do the regulatory CSCRM requirements impact diametrically diverse industries that rely on their Principal/Agent, and the integration of CSCRM requirements?

There will be a focus on governance/regulatory compliance and that impact on the Principal/Agent relationship, as that has one of the largest driving effects on the three areas I will be focusing on, manufacturing, insurance, wholesale/retail, technology, utilities, healthcare, communication, aerospace & defense, and transportation. This data is from a sample of 205 organizations sourced from Hampton et al., *Cyber Supply Chain Risk Management: Toward an Understanding of the Antecedents to Demand for Assurance,* 2021. Due to the nature of the accessible data, and the premise of this topic, there are admittedly considerable constraints to the scope of data provided. However, I will be using examples of the federal mandates that impact these the industries to review the level of CSCRM requirements. The dependent variables are as follows: the industries listed above, that each organization has some level of cyber supply chain, each organization has an IT division, and all variable data artifacts shall be sourced between 2007 and 2023. Outline source material e.g., Agency Theory references, will range from 1932 to 2023.

Some of the cyber/ICT supply chain risks could include insertion of counterfeit products, unauthorized production, tampering, theft, insertion of malicious software and hardware, as well as poor manufacturing and development practices in the ICT supply chain [10]. Those risks have a high probability of being attributed with a lack of understanding of the potential that foreign entities have on that organizations supply chain. Technology that an organization acquires, integrates, and maintains in their systems needs to be vetted to assure the security, integrity, safety, and quality can provide the services they require. Vulnerabilities in a system could be something simple or something highly advance that poses to risk to the organization. It is impossible to completely remove, insider threats and ransomware being a prevalent risk in today's society, however an often-neglected risk is the own organizations willfulness to purposely be ignorant or complacent in understanding and battling cyber supply chain risks. The relationship between the Principal (e.g., owner/primary organization) and the agent (e.g., CSCRM Managers/vendors), is often complex and fraught with complex relationships and requirements from each party, reference Fig. 1 *Example of CSCRM Principal/Agent Relationship* for a very simplistic example of a potential relationship structure. However, later in the document we will explore the complexity of Agency Theory, and how this example is more than likely a predominate structure throughout large and small organizations.

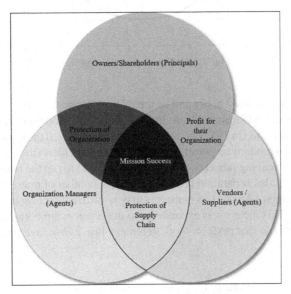

Fig. 1. Example of CSCRM Principal/Agent Relationship

2 Agency Theory Perspective

Agency theory is a branch of economics that studies the relationship between two parties: the principal, who delegates decision-making authority to an agent to act on their behalf, and the Agent, who is responsible for making decisions and carrying out actions that align with the principal's goals.

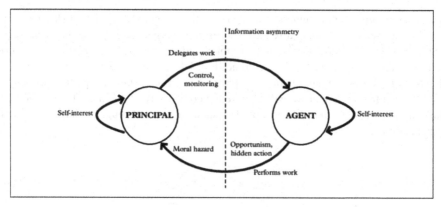

Fig. 2. Principal Agent Relationship

The origins of Agency Theory can be traced back to the work of economist Adolph Berle and legal scholar Gardiner Means in their book "The Modern Corporation and Private Property" published in 1932 [7]. In this book, they analyzed the separation of ownership and control in modern corporations, where the shareholders (the owners/Principals) delegate decision-making power to managers (the agents) to run the company. Berle and Means argued that this separation created a potential conflict of interest between shareholders and managers (Agents), as managers may prioritize their own interests over those of shareholders. This theory was expanded into the relationship between those that delegate work, and those that perform work, reference Fig. 2 *Principal Agent Relationship* (Table 1).

Table 1. Agency Theory Overview [5].

Agency Theory Overview	
Key Idea	-Principal-Agent relationships should reflect efficient organization of information and risk-bearing costs
Unit of Analysis	-Contract between Principal and Agent
Human Assumption	-Self-interest -Boundary rationality -Risk aversion
Organizational Assumption	-Partial goal conflict among participants (non-equicautious HARA-class utilities). -Efficiencies as the effectiveness criterion. -Information asymmetry between Principal and the Agent
Information Assumption	-Information as a purchasable commodity, e.g., a trade between time and resources for information
Contracting Problems	-Agency (moral hazard and adverse selection) -Risk sharing
Problem domain	-Relationship in which the Principal and agent have partially differing goals and risk preferences (e.g., regulations, whistle-blowing, vertical integration, mitigation strategies, etc.)

3   Research Questions

Q1: What is the need for a Principal and Agent relationship within Cyber Supply Chain Risk Management? In a CSCRM context, the principal, such as an organization or person, may delegate responsibility for cybersecurity to an agent, such as a vendor/supplier, or role within an organization. This delegation of responsibility can create a potential risk if the agent is not properly equipped to manage cybersecurity risks. Trust being a defining factor in this delegation to follow through with a capable and comprehensive CSCRM, however the guiding principle should be "trust but verify" of every organization and entity that engage with supply chain partnerships, or an internal role. The relationship of the principal verifying and validating that the Agent has a sustainable CSCRM structure with immediate and direct indicators to validate the trust established through either contractual or organizational obligations [2].

Above a list of job functions and industries sampled by Clark Hampton, Steve Sutton, Vicky Arnold, and Deepak Khanzanchi in an independent survey. Hampton et al., sourced 1,021 companies via an e-mail based survey company (EMPanel, EMPanelonline.com; "EMPanel solicits potential respondent groups at industry conferences and through online connections to develop panels for a broad range of industries and positions within those industries." [2] who solicited potential respondents based on their job titles. With pretested questions, conducted in *Cyber Supply Chain Risk Management: Toward an Understanding of the Antecedents of Demand for Assurance* by. Of the 1,021 respondents, 205 were deemed usable based on the following questions:

1. Does your organization have experience in working with trading partners (e.g., suppliers, customers, outsourcers, etc.) in a B2B e-commerce relationship?
2. Does your organization repeatedly transact with any such trading partners?
3. Do you have a basic understanding of the technological and IT-driven components of B2B e-commerce?
4. Do you have a reasonable understanding of any of your trading partners' B2B e-commerce capabilities and your firm's relationship with this partner?

Most of the respondents (92.2%) worked for publicly traded companies, with greater than 90% evaluating cyber supply chain, and the dependencies between the organizations. CSCRM, in relations to the Agency Theory, involves the Principal delegating responsibility for cybersecurity to an Agent, such as a vendor or supplier. This delegation of responsibilities creates risk within an organization from both the perspective of the Agent and the Principal. The first being the reliance on each other to maintain a hygienic system of correspondence and maintain the necessary hardware and software to manage cybersecurity. Second, is that the Principal would not have in every instance complete information about the Agent's cybersecurity systems, practices, and controls, this would cause information asymmetry. Third would be the risk management practices, day-to-day, of both the Principal and Agent. Finally, would be accountability of both parties, ultimately, the Principal having the greater risk and accountability in the relationship based on their customer/clientele requirements. Ranking the CSFs identified above that have the greatest influence on the need for a Principal/Agent relationship within CSCRM would be CSF4: Collaboration and Communication, CSF1: A Comprehensive Risk Assessment, CSF2: Strong Contractual Obligations, CSF3: Continuous Monitoring and Evaluation, CSF6: Incident Response Planning, and CSF5: Employee Awareness and Training.

Figure 3 Experience of Positions & Organization Cyber Supply Chain, Years [2] presents an interesting curve with regards to the relationship of experience of personnel at their assessed roles (**Error! Reference source not found.**), and the number of years that their Cyber Supply Chain has been in use. In De Groot's, *The History of Data Breaches* they define data breaches occurring as far back as the 1980s, with increased frequency occurring in the 1990s and 2000s. Data integrity and breaches not being a foreign concept for most working and depending on electronics to store and communicate their data. With less than 1% of the 205 sample organizations responding that they have had an established cyber supply chain starting in the 1980s, several of the sampled organizations potentially were at risk. Hampton et al., categorized the varying stages of cyber supply chain management as follows:

Adoption: Incoming business documents are electronically received and printed. A staff member is required to key in outgoing messages. B2B applications run on a standalone PC/workstation or terminal.

Integration: Incoming business documents are received electronically, stored in files, and can be printed on demand. Outgoing business documents are also created as files by internal applications and are electronically sent. B2B applications are either run on a PC/workstation or are based in a mainframe/minicomputer where internal business applications are run. This setup replaces the keying-in and printing-out of messages with files, speeding up the process and makes incoming messages particularly useful, since they do not require re-keying prior to use by another system (e.g., production scheduling or accounting);

Infusion: B2B transaction processing is seamlessly integrated with internal business applications such as purchasing, order entry, production scheduling, inventory management, accounts receivable/payable, shipping, and so on. Business documents are exchanged internally and externally (with trading partners) in a nearly "paperless" environment with little human intervention; and (Fig. 4)

Strategic: B2B applications are viewed as strategic ICT and are instrumental in reengineering (changing) internal business processes and functions with trading partner(s) and redefining organizational structure. B2B is seen as an integral part of the organizational context and is a major factor in strategic and information systems planning. Sharing databases, participating in just in time/quick response (JIT/QR) programs are examples of this top-down, organization-wide, strategic view of B2B and other related information technologies."

With the majority of the sample in the adoption and integration stages of CSCRM, a precedent requirement of the Principal enacting and collaborating (CSF4) the requirement of a CSCRM plan or contingency within their contractual obligations between themselves and their Agent (CSF2), to drive the safety and security of their respective organizations, thereby removing the 'trust' factor from the relationship and building a more dynamic secure bond to operate with one another.

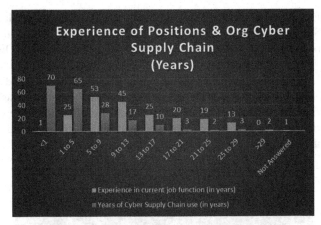

Fig. 3. Experience of Positions & Organization Cyber Supply Chain, Years [2].

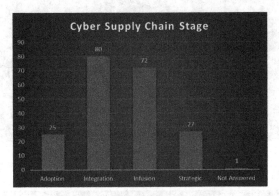

Fig. 4. Cyber Supply Chain Stage [2]

Q2: What is the current perceived relationship of the Principal and Agent with supply chain organizations partners? The current perceived relationship of the Principal-Agent relationship with supply chain organizations partners is often seen as one of mutual dependence and shared responsibility for cybersecurity. As mentioned previously, those external agencies depend on one another to provide goods and services to fulfill their client's needs, or to remain within compliance to create and produce deliverables. Within the previously aforementioned data sets by Hampton et al., they identify the varying types of supply chain partners working with the sampled organizations (Fig. 5 Organization Supply Chain Partners [2]) and the cyber functions those supply chain providers provide for the organizations [2].

On the one hand, supply chain partners (Agents) are typically responsible for implementing cybersecurity controls within their own organizations and for ensuring that their products and services meet certain security standards. Referencing Fig. 1 Example of CSCRM Principal/Agent Relationship, the relationship of the Agent and the Principal has many critical dependencies, that could change based on the nature and structure of the organization. For example, the Principal could be the Organization Managers, with the Vendors/Suppliers acting as the Agents. Or, as the graphic depicts, the Organization Managers and Vendors/Suppliers report directly to the Principals/Owners of the organization. This is all dependent on how the organization is structured to handle the perceived and unperceived risks of an organization. Another example could be that those Organization Managers and Owners (Agents) are expected to work closely with their customers (Principals) to ensure that their products and services integrate well with the customer's existing security infrastructure. The fluidity of the relationship is dependent on the overall risk and accountability factors that flow along the supply chain route (Fig. 6).

Fig. 5. Organization Supply Chain Partners [2]

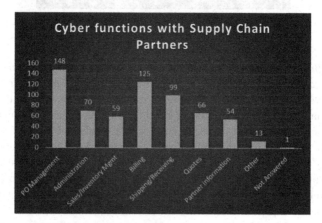

Fig. 6. Cyber Functions with Supply Chain Partners [2]

Management of the supply chain organizations cybersecurity risks fall on both the Principal and the Agent to perform their set obligated duties to ensure the safety of their organizations and that little-to-no disruption or nonconforming outputs impact the inputs and eventual outputting deliverables of their organizations. This could include, but is not limited to, assessing the security posture of their partners, establishing clear security requirements for their partners, and monitoring their partners' compliance with those requirements.

The relationship between principals and agents in the supply chain is one of inter-dependence and shared responsibility for cybersecurity. Both parties have a role to play in ensuring the security of the supply chain, and both must work together to manage the risks associated with their partnership.

Q3: What are the perceived risks to the Principal/Agent relationship associated with CSCRM?

March 2020, the Association of International Certified Professional Accountants (AICPA), one of the world's most influential body of professional accountants that combines the American Institute of CPAs (AICPA) and The Chartered institute of Management Accountants (CIMA), released its system and organization control (SOC) for Supply Chains—an assurance service designed to help organizations assess the risks and associated controls in place among its trading partners within their supply chain. This tool gives organizations an understanding of the potential risks associated with other entities production, manufacturing, or distribution of goods. These risks include, "management objectives, planning associated with supply chain activities, core business processes, and the systems utilized to facilitate production, manufacturing, disruption activities, and the risks that exudes from establishing IT connectivity with the trading partner" [2] by those external entities. The last risk mentioned obviously being a major impactor to the CSCRM planning of any organization apart of AICPA.

Q3.a: How do those perceived risks impact the Principal and Agent Relationship?

Referencing back to the data presented by Hampton et al., in *Cyber Supply Chain Risk Management: Toward an Understanding of the Antecedents to Demand for Assurance* the below graphic Fig. 7 Cyber Supply Chain Purchase Orders & Sales, Dollars [2] presents how those 205 sample industries work and operate with their vendors/suppliers/partners with regards to the purchase orders or sales to/from those vendors/suppliers/partners. The immense amount of value that transfers through just a sample of organizations should present a clear indication as to why those above risks would impact the relationships between the Principal and Agent. However, outside of the fiduciary impactors to an organizations CSCRM planning, other facets can be impacted. Trust is a critical component of the Principal-Agent relationship, and the risks associated with CSCRM can erode trust between the two parties. For example, if the Principal does not trust the Agent's cybersecurity practices, they may be hesitant to share sensitive information with them and slow down the effectiveness of the product or service.

Additionally, effective communication is essential for managing cybersecurity risks in the supply chain. However, the perceived risks associated with CSCRM can create barriers to communication between the Principal and the Agent. Like the example above, the principal may be hesitant to share information with the agent if they do not trust the Agent's ability to protect that information. If a principal or Agent does not have or meet any of the required compliance areas associated to CSCRM to function and operate within the industry, it can make it difficult for the principal to ensure that their supply chain partners are complying with relevant cybersecurity regulations and standards.

Fig. 7. Cyber Supply Chain Purchase Orders & Sales, Dollars [2]

This compliance standard can also work in the opposite direction for vendors, suppliers, stakeholders, or even employees within an organization working for a Principal entity. This can create legal and regulatory risks for all parties working in and around the cyber supply chain.

Q4: What is the Level of Effort (LOE) from varying areas within an organization regarding cyber supply chain risk management?

The level of effort (LOE) required from areas or divisions within an organization for CSCRM can vary depending on the organization's size, complexity, and industry. However, here are some typical areas within an organization that have greater involvement in the CSCRM planning and coordination internal and external to an organization. First being the Procurement Division. This division is often responsible for selecting and vetting potential supply chain partners, in essence working to find those Agents that can supplement requirements needed to fulfill the organization's intended mission. The LOE required from procurement may include, but is not limited to, conducting due diligence on potential partners' cybersecurity practices, reviewing security policies and procedures, and incorporating cybersecurity requirements into supplier contracts. This would be followed by the Legal or Contracts Division within an organization. They are responsible for the initial review of supplier contracts and ensuring that they include appropriate cybersecurity language. The LOE required from legal may include reviewing cybersecurity requirements, assessing legal risks associated with the supply chain, and negotiating contractual terms. Both the Procurement Division and Legal/Contracts Divisions would need to work with external certification agencies, such as DCMA, to ensure that their own systems are meeting the standards set by an industry. The IT Security division is often responsible for managing the organization's cybersecurity posture. IT Security LOE should include assessing the cybersecurity risks associated with supply chain partners, developing security requirements for partners, and monitoring partners' compliance with those requirements. The day-to-day activities related to supply chain management is often managed by the Operations Division. Their role does include coordinating with supply chain partners to ensure that security requirements are being met, monitoring the performance of supply chain partners, and responding to cybersecurity incidents within the supply chain. If an organization is large enough, they may have a Risk Management Division that would be responsible for assessing the organization's overall risk posture, including supply chain risks. Their LOE would include working with all the above divisions to identify, assess, and plan for supply chain risks, while developing risk mitigation strategies, and monitoring supply chain risks over time.

An external impactor that counteracts the potential of diluting risk aversion is the regulatory requirements of local/federal governments. Published 5 May 2022 by the National Institute of Standards and Technology [10] SP 800-161r1 provides guidelines for protecting the United States government and its suppliers supply chain from cybersecurity threats. Titled "Supply Chain Risk Management Practices for Federal Information Systems and Organizations" it provides the blueprints for organizations to protect their information systems and data by identifying, assessing, and either avoid, mitigate, transfer, or accepting the potential risk events. Additionally, it provides guidance on how organizations can evaluate suppliers and vendors, how to ensure the security of an organization's information systems software and hardware components, and how to respond to Cybersecurity Supply Chain threats.

Q4.a: Which area in an organization has the greatest impact on CSCRM procedures, considering the Principal/Agent Relationship?

Unequivocally, the area in an organization that has the greatest impact on CSCRM procedures is the Procurement Division, or agency that acts as the procurement hand in an organization. Procurement is responsible for selecting and vetting potential supply chain partners, negotiating contracts, and ensuring that suppliers meet the organization's cybersecurity requirements. Often the first line of defense in managing cybersecurity risks in the supply chain, and their decisions can have a significant impact on the organization's overall cybersecurity posture. Their role is critical due to the fact that they are responsible for establishing and maintaining the Principal/Agent relationship with supply chain partners. Procurement must ensure that potential partners have robust cybersecurity practices and controls in place to protect the organization's sensitive information and assets. They must also negotiate contractual terms that clearly establish the cybersecurity responsibilities of each party and provide a framework for managing cybersecurity risks in the supply chain. Finally, procurement must monitor supply chain partners' compliance with cybersecurity requirements, manage any disputes that arise, and work closely with the Legal Division to ensure that contracts include appropriate cybersecurity language.

Q5: what are some major changes required by an organization to adopt a CSCRM structure?

The first steps of a mid-small organization to start the adoption process of a CSCRM focused organization can be daunting due to the excessive costs and resource requirements. Significant changes would need to occur throughout an organization, not just within their cybersecurity program, but throughout the entirety of an organization and their overall supply chain management practices. The organization initially should conduct a comprehensive risk assessment (CSF1) to identify potential cybersecurity risks within the supply chain. Potentially, using either internal Subject Matter Experts (SMEs), or preferrable using an experienced and vetted third party entity to provide an unbiased report of the potential risks to that organization. The assessment should include identifying critical assets, potential threats, and vulnerabilities. Additionally, future incident response planning (CSF6) thereby assessing the potential impact of a cybersecurity incident on the organization's operations. Second, the organization needs to establish cybersecurity requirements for supply chain partners that align with the organization's overall cybersecurity policies and standards. These requirements should address security controls, incident response procedures, reporting requirements, and compliance requirements. A supplier vetting process needs to be established early in the integration of a CSCRM plan, essentially to evaluate potential supply chain partners' cybersecurity practices and controls. The contractual agreements (CSF2) with supply chain partners should be vetted to include appropriate, and necessary cybersecurity language. Establishing how (CSF4) those organizations monitor (CSF3) and report their capabilities, procedures, and ensure that their vendors/suppliers are complying with cybersecurity requirements and identifying potential cybersecurity risks. The organization needs to provide training (CSF5) and awareness programs for employees to integrate the knowledge of how a hygienic cyber supply chain functions and subsequently ensure that all stakeholders understand the requirements and capabilities of their supply chain partners management of cybersecurity risks in the cyber supply chain.

Q5.a: How do the regulatory CSCRM requirements impact diametrically diverse industries that rely on their Principal/Agent, and the integration of CSCRM requirements?

Government bodies and regulatory agencies establish laws and regulations, such as HIPAA or the PCI Data Security Standard, to provide guidelines for organizations when handling certain types of sensitive consumer information. This acts as a framework for the required safeguards, storage, and use practices for handling data, but these rules do not exist in all industries, nor do they definitively stop data breaches from occurring (De Groot, 2022). Additionally, there is a significant impact of regulatory CSCRM requirements on industries that, often have little-to-no similarity, rely on their Principal/Agent relationship to ensure the integration of CSCRM requirements. Different industries face different cybersecurity risks, depending on the nature of their operations, the type of data they handle, the publicity/sociological perspective, and the technologies they use. Regulatory CSCRM requirements must consider any and all industry-specific risks to be effective. Different industries may have different supply chain partners, ranging from large established companies, to small, specialized vendors. Regulatory CSCRM requirements (contractual or regulatory) must be flexible enough to accommodate this supplier diversity and ensure that cybersecurity risks are effectively managed across the supply chain. As mentioned, compliance with regulatory CSCRM requirements can be costly, particularly for smaller suppliers. Regulators, or even Principals when negotiating initial contractual obligations/costs, must consider the impact of compliance costs on small businesses and take steps to mitigate these costs, such as providing guidance, financial assistance, or even insurances that can offset or transfer the risks to their cyber supply chain. Different industries may have existing cybersecurity requirements or standards that they must comply with, such as HIPAA for healthcare, United States Major Procurement/Regulatory bodies e.g., DCMA Procurement Policies ([10] SP 800-161) for government contracting, or PCI DSS for payment card processing. Ideally, regulatory CSCRM requirements would be integrated with these existing requirements to avoid duplication, varying levels of requirements for the same or similar ICT configurations and ensure that suppliers can effectively comply with all requirements. However, at least in the United States, this is not always a tenable perspective. Regulatory CSCRM requirements may be new to some industries, and suppliers may need education and awareness training to understand their obligations and how to comply with these requirements effectively.

4 Conclusion

In conclusion, this research paper has highlighted the importance of understanding the relationship between Principals and their Agents in the context of CSCRM. The application of Agency Theory provides a framework for examining the inherent complexities in maintaining CSCRM structures, and the CSFs necessary for organizations to effectively manage supply chain risks. The paper has shown that CSCRM is a challenging process that requires collaboration, communication, and transparency between Principals and Agents (internally and external to the organization). Additionally, the regulatory requirements associated with CSCRM increase the levels of complexity to the process. Organizations, and their suppliers/vendors, must continuously evaluate their CSCRM process to ensure that it remains effective in mitigating risks and compliant with regulatory requirements. Ultimately, a strong CSCRM process will not only protect an organization from cyber threats, but it will also enhance the trust and collaboration between Principals and Agents, leading to a more successful business relationship.

References

1. Amershi, A.H., Stoeckenius, J.H.W.: The theory of syndicates and linear sharing rules. Econometrica **51**(5), 1407–1416 (1983). https://doi-org.umw.idm.oclc.org/10.2307/1912281
2. Hampton, C., Sutton, S.G., Arnold, V., Khazanchi, D.: Cyber supply chain risk management: toward an understanding of the antecedents to demand for assurance. J. Inf. Syst. **35**(2), 37–60 (2021).https://doi-org.umw.idm.oclc.org/10.2308/ISYS-19-050
3. Creazza, A., Colicchia, C., Spiezia, S., Dallari, F.: Who cares? Supply chain managers' perceptions regarding cyber supply chain risk management in the digital transformation era. Supply Chain Manag. **27**(1), 30–53 (2022). https://doi-org.umw.idm.oclc.org/10.1108/SCM-02-2020-0073
4. Boyson, S.: Cyber supply chain risk management: revolutionizing the strategic control of critical IT systems. Technovation **34**(7), 342–353 (2014). https://doi-org.umw.idm.oclc.org/10.1016/j.technovation.2014.02.001
5. Eisenhardt, K.M.: Agency theory: an assessment and review. AcadeAuthors' Manag. Rev. **14**(1), 57–74 (1989). https://doi-org.umw.idm.oclc.org/10.5465/AMR.1989.4279003
6. AICPA. https://www.aicpa.org/about/landing/about. Accessed 20 Feb 2023
7. Lee, F.S.: The modern corporation and Gardiner Means's critique of neoclassical economics. J. Econ. Issues **24**(3), 673–693 (1990). https://doi-org.umw.idm.oclc.org/10.1080/00213624.1990.11505066. (Association for Evolutionary Economics)
8. Smith, V.L.: Essays in the theory of risk-bearing (book). J. Bus. **47**(1), 96–98 (1974). https://doi-org.umw.idm.oclc.org/10.1086/295615

9. Wilson, R.: The theory of syndicates. Econometrica **36**(1), 119 (1968). https://doi-org.umw. idm.oclc.org/10.2307/1909607

10. National Institute of Standards and Technology, Cybersecurity Supply Chain Risk Management Practices for Systems and Organizations. (Department of Commerce, Washington D.C.), Computer Security Division Information Technology Laboratory, NIST SP 800-161r1, May 2022 (2022). https://doi.org/10.6028/NIST.SP.800-161r1

11. De Groot, J.: The history of data breaches (2022). https://digitalguardian.com/blog/history-data-breaches. Accessed 22 February 2023

12. Farahbod, K., Shayo, C., Varzandeh, J.: Cybersecurity indices and cybercrime annual loss and economic impacts. J. Bus. Behav. Sci. **32**(1), 63–71 (2020)

13. Wu, Y., Tayi, G.K., Feng, G., Fung, R.Y.K.: Managing information security outsourcing in a dynamic cooperation environment. J. Assoc. Inf. Syst. **22**(3), 827–850 (2021). https://doi-org.umw.idm.oclc.org/10.17705/1jais.00681

VLSM Techniques for Optimizing Real IPv4 Networks

Marek Michalski[✉]

Faculty of Computing and Telecommunications, Poznan University of Technology, Piotrowo 3,
60-965 Poznan, Poland
marek.michalski@put.poznan.pl

Abstract. In this paper, some mechanisms of IPv4 Variable Length Subnet Mask are mentioned, and a tool for their demonstration and explanation is presented. This tool is a graphical user interface software that allows users to create a table with a given range of IP addresses and show the relation between subnets with different sizes (length of subnet mask or prefix). It also solves cases where given IPv4 spaces have to be efficiently calculated for subnetworks with different sizes. The most useful function is to draw maps and topologies with dynamically assigned IP addresses. This tool allows users to create demo topologies and readdress them in real-time. Despite its primary teaching purpose, it is also a useful tool for network professionals.

1 Introduction

Despite the fact that we have a well-known and fully defined IPv6 protocol, IPv4 remains very popular due to the costs associated with implementing the newer version, backward compatibility, and user convenience. Teaching IPv4 addressing and subnetting, especially with variable length subnet masks, is not easy. That is why, after many years of different teaching and practical experiences [1–6], I decided to create a tool to aid in this area. While there are many IP calculators available [7], their functionality is often limited, and they do not work with VLSM. In this paper, I will present a tool with a user-friendly GUI that allows users to create graphical maps and represent topologies with addresses in a convenient way. Additionally, variable subnetting problems can be solved using this tool. In the following sections, I will explain particular problems and present their solutions with example topologies.

1.1 Subnetting

In general case we can treat IP addressing space as a continuous range of 32 bit numbers. But their usage and purpose assume some hierarchy. We distinguish network part and host part.

K. S. Soliman (Ed.): IBIMA-AI 2023, CCIS 2101, pp. 187–194, 2024.
https://doi.org/10.1007/978-3-031-62843-6_20

1.2 Subnetting with Classful Mask

Due to the binary representation of this number, it is more convenient to treat the 32 bits as four groups with 8 bits in each (octets). This allows for the network part to be placed in the same location as the dot in the decimal representation of IPv4 addresses. Hence, we have 8, 16, or 24 bits in class A, B, and C respectively. Further details will not be discussed here, as they are well known among network professionals.

1.3 Subnetting with Classless Mask but Fixed Subnet Mask Length

In Table from Fig. 1, we see fragment of IP space divided with different masks. It is easy to identify columns for masks 255.255.255.0 (24 bits), 255.255.255.128 (25 bits), 255.255.255.192 (26 bits), 255.255.255.224 (27 bits), 255.255.255.240 (28 bits), 255.255.255.248 (29 bits), 255.255.255.252 (30 bits) and 255.255.255.254 (31 bits). Each rectangle represents space with given first and last IP address of this subnet. Also column for 255.255.255.255 (32 bits of prefix) is presented, where such a space contains exactly one address. It is easy to notice and show to the students, that sizes of subnets with different prefix lengths are strictly related with number of bits included in network prefix; for example, subnet with prefix 26 is two times bigger than subnet with 27 bit subnetwork. What is more important, we can notice, that subnet 10.0.0.8/29 (which contains 8 addresses) can be divided into two subnets with mask 30 bits (10.0.0.8/30 and 10.0.0.12/30) (4 addresses in each) or into four subnets (10.0.0.8/31, 10.0.0.10/31, 10.0.0.12/31, 10.0.0.14/31) (2 addresses in each). What is also important, it is easy to shown space 10.0.0.18/31 is not included in space 10.0.0.8/29, while it is included in 10.0.0.16/29. The software can generate table with given size of biggest and smallest

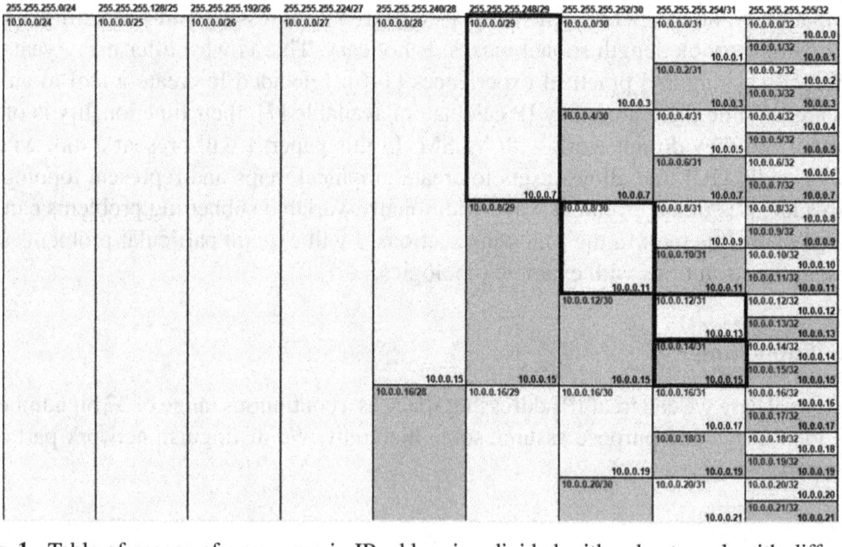

Fig. 1. Table of spaces of some area in IP addressing divided with subnet mask with different length

prefix and given number of subnet with biggest size. It can be huge, it can be stored in bmp file. Future usage will save it also in html, csv format.

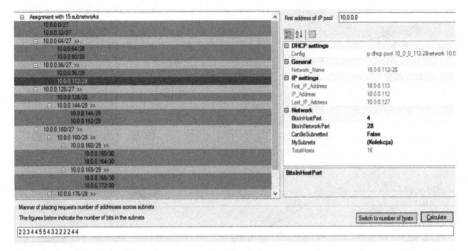

Fig. 2. Presentation of solution for networks with different size (required number of addresses for hosts)

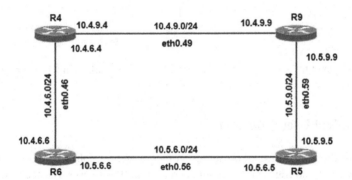

Fig. 3. A schema for automatic addressing networks between nodes with given IDs

1.4 Subnetting with Variable Length Subnet Mask (VLSM)

In many real cases, when we have to save IP addresses, IP spaces (subnetworks) have to be assigned to the networks according to real size of network (number of required hosts). Lets assume that we need IP subnets for 8, 3, 2 and 2 addresses. We can notice in the Table 1, that we can use spaces marked with bolded rectangle. In general case, we can several algorithms for such an optimal assignment. In this tool there is implemented one of them. In Fig. 2, an example IP assignment for some requested subnets is presented using the implemented algorithm.

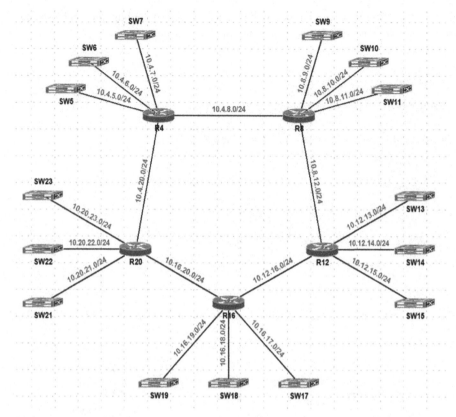

Fig. 4. Example of topology and addressing where route summarization with short prefixes can be explained

2 Graphical User Interface

The GUI of this tool allows to create topologies as their graph, where nodes represent routers, switches and edges between routers represent IP networks. Users can add routers or switches by clicking the mouse with the left or right button. By typical mouse gesture, it is possible to connect routers and switches. The software automatically assigns an IP subnet to a new link according to chosen addressing schema. Created topologies can be customized by showing/hiding some information as interface names, IP addresses or hostnames. Prepared topology can be stored in files for sharing or future usage. In the Fig. 3 there is presented simple network with 4 routers and 4 networks. Addressing schema used here assumes 24 bits as length of mask for each network. Addresses are automatically created where value 10 is used as first octet, on the second and third octet two IDs of adjacent nodes are used, where the lower value is used for the second octet and the higher value is used for the third octet of the network part. Last octet, which is a host part, is filled with host ID. It's easy to notice, that gray color is used for network addresses, whereas addresses for interfaces of particular devices are printed with black.

3 Route and Prefix Summarization

To make more granular and matched to real size of structures, some IP networks are divided into smaller one. To reduce number of information in routing tables, the reverse process is carried out. i.e. several networks are represented by one common entry. The Fig. 4 shows example of topology and network addresses, where 20 different and separated IP networks can be represented in routers routing table by 4 dynamic (or static) aggregated entries.

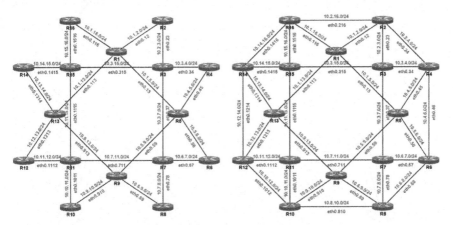

Fig. 5. Topologies based on ring, where each router has 4 neighbors and shortest path can be searched for different routers pairs

4 Secondary Functionality

Dynamic maps with automatic addressing can be used to quickly prepare lab topologies for students. The number of nodes on the topology can be adjusted based on the number of students in the class, and each student can be assigned a different router ID to encourage intellectual effort and improve test results. Figures 5 and 6 show example topologies with addressing that can be used as configuration tasks for students. Depending on their knowledge, experience, and level of advancement, they can configure static or dynamic routing, work with different types of VPNs, and analyze shortest path searching algorithms and the multi-path behavior of IP packets. With automatic and meaningful addressing, it is easy to identify the administrator responsible for missing or problematic networks. One common mistake is using the default network mask instead of the proper 24-bit mask.

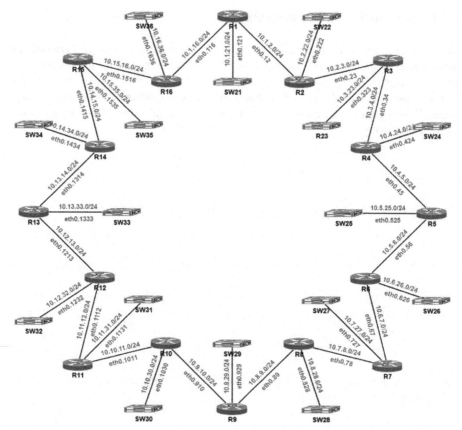

Fig. 6. Ring of 16 routers witch local network attached to each router. Each router can advertise 3 IP networks in dynamic routing. Each router should have 32 networks in its routing table.

Apart from its IP configuration and analysis functionality, the tool also has another more advanced functionality, where it is connected to a virtualization system. Adding a new node to the topology results in activating a new virtual machine that is created as a clone of the base template, and the configuration of node created here is applied as a configuration of virtual machine created in the laboratory network. Some figures include names of interfaces, which correspond with VLAN interfaces created in the server and in the real network, making it possible to connect virtual machines between them and with real devices attached to proper VLANs. Double-clicking on an icon opens Putty and SSH terminal to the pointed device 7. Double-clicking on a link opens a window that allows for the analysis or change of parameters of interfaces that are the two ends of this link 8. Data from Figs. 7 and 8 correspond to situation from topology from Fig. 6.

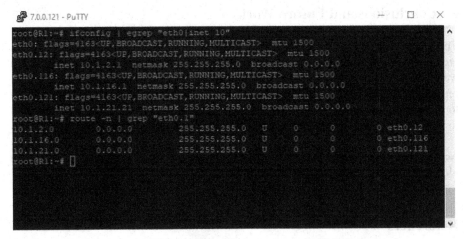

Fig. 7. Pytty SSH terminal with connection to VM in laboratory

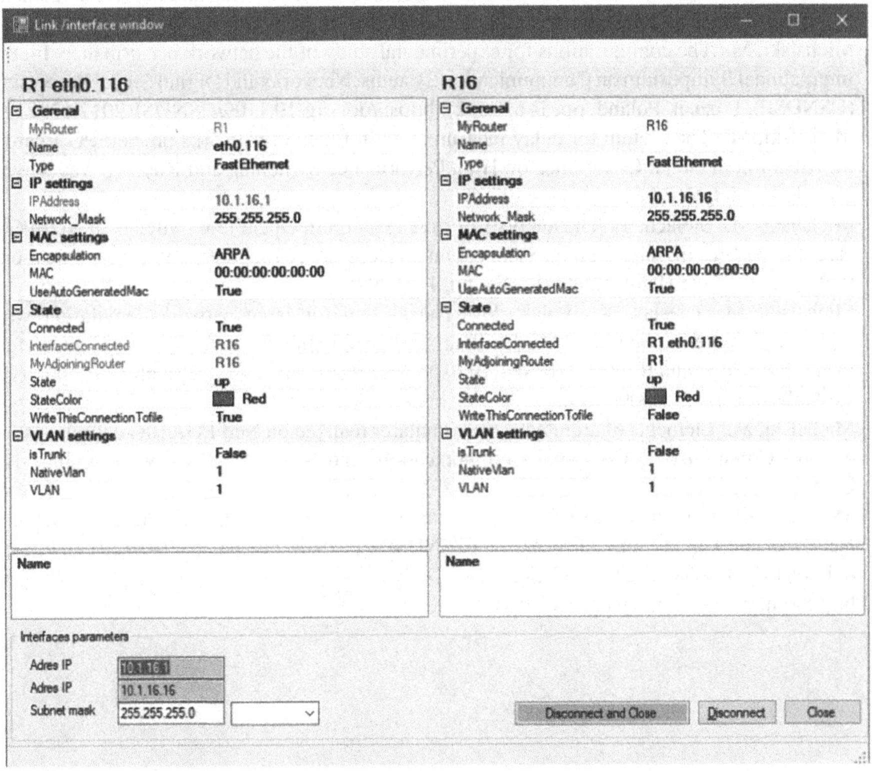

Fig. 8. Window with parameters of link R1-R16

5   Conclusions and Future Works

This tool is widely used for teaching and networking activities, as it allows for the creation of demo topologies. Its demo version can be downloaded from the author's webpage [8], which also includes example files with many topologies and their graphical representations in jpg/pdf formats, along with explanations of interesting features. As the tool continues to be developed by the main user, more advanced versions are expected to be released soon, with the natural step being to include functionality for IPv6.

Acknowledgements. The work described in this paper was financed from the funds of the Ministry of Science and Higher Education (0313/SBAD/1310 for year 2023).

References

1. Michalski, M.: A software and hardware system for a fully functional remote access to laboratory networks. In: 2009 Fifth International Conference on Networking and Services, Valencia, Spain, pp. 561–565 (2009). https://doi.org/10.1109/ICNS.2009.104
2. Michalski, M.: The configurations for experimental study of the network performance. In: 8th International Symposium on Communication Systems, Networks and Digital Signal Processing (CSNDSP), Poznan, Poland, pp. 1–6 (2012). https://doi.org/10.1109/CSNDSP.2012.6292790
3. Michalski, M.: The system for delay measurement in Ethernet networks on NetFPGA cards. In: IEEE International Conference on High Performance Switching and Routing, Vancouver, Canada 1–4 July 2014 (2014)
4. Michalski, M., Sielach, T.: The analysis of time reaction in OpenFlow switches in NetFPGA cards and ROFL. In: International Symposium on Networks, Computers and Communications (ISNCC), Yasmine Hammamet, Tunisia, pp. 1–5 (2015)
5. Michalski, M., Cieslak, K., Polak, M.: The system for large networks emulation with OSPF/BGP routers based on LXC. In: IEEE 16th International Conference on High Performance Switching and Routing (HPSR), Budapest, Hungary, pp. 1–4 (2015). https://doi.org/10.1109/HPSR.2015.7483091
6. Michalski, M.: Elements of architecture of simulator realized on NetFPGA10G card. In: International Conference on Computer Communications and Networks (ICCCN), Honolulu, HI, USA, pp. 1–2 (2022)
7. Michalski, M.: IP pool manager. In: 8th International Symposium on Communication Systems, Networks and Digital Signal Processing (CSNDSP), Poznan, Poland, pp. 1–5 (2012). https://doi.org/10.1109/CSNDSP.2012.6292791
8. http://mm.et.put.poznan.pl/ipcalc/

Review and Criteria for Selecting Open-Source Tools for Managing Wireless Local Networks

Piotr Augustyniak[(✉)], Jakub Skóra, and Piotr Zwierzykowski

Institute of Communication and Computer Networks, Faculty of Computing and Telecommunications, Poznań University of Technology, Poznan, Poland
piotr.augustyniak@doctorate.put.poznan.pl,
jakub.skora@student.put.poznan.pl,
piotr.zwierzykowski@put.poznan.pl

Abstract. This article provides an overview of open source administrative tools for wireless LANs. The following areas of software operation are covered: management, automation, backup and disaster recovery, version and software control, resource mapping, print server, monitoring, authorisation, link performance, log management, ticket management, packet analysis, network scanning and software for routers. The article provides numerous summaries and comparisons and suggests software that could be included in a WLAN administrator's toolbox.

Keywords: administration · WLAN · open-source

1 Introduction

The dynamic and continuous development of computer networks constantly poses new challenges to network administrators. The exponentially increasing number of devices capable of communicating with each other raises problems that few previously realised existed. In addition, the variety of possible configurations, their requirements and their complexity pose new questions for administrators and force them to seek innovative answers. Modern challenges require well thought-out, cleverly planned and proven solutions. In professional applications, there is no room for half-finished products that only work partially or hardly at all. Optimal configuration processes are a challenging issue. There are many types of networks, physical and logical topologies, while the combinations and possible configurations of hardware and software are even more numerous, so administrators need to select solutions according to their needs. In many applications, they use hardware from a single manufacturer, which helps with integration and management. Sometimes, more universal solutions are also used, which very often have the required functions.

K. S. Soliman (Ed.): IBIMA-AI 2023, CCIS 2101, pp. 195–209, 2024.
https://doi.org/10.1007/978-3-031-62843-6_21

There are many solutions to support the work of engineers. Their number is also growing rapidly. One group is software developed for the products of a particular manufacturer. These have closed code - not available to everyone. The second group are open-source solutions, i.e. with open source code, usually free of charge. These are developed by groups of enthusiasts, researchers, students, individuals and even large organisations. Open-source tools are in most cases more versatile, but thus less powerful.

The software belonging to each of these groups can be divided according to many different criteria. The principle and speed of operation, the number and range of functions and capabilities offered are important. Scalability, reliability, security and level of user-friendliness are also important. It should not be forgotten which systems are supported, the support of the developers and/or the community and the hardware requirements.

Therefore, the authors of this article decided to collect, compare a set of open source software that can be used to administer a wireless local area network. As a result of our work, a proposal for a universal set of tools for a wireless local area network administrator was developed.

The article is divided into four sections. Section 2 presents a summary of the compared solutions in terms of basic administrative functionality. Section 3 provides a brief summary of trends in the development of WLAN management tools. The article concludes with a brief summary.

2   Discussion and Selection of the Software for the Toolbox

When creating a toolbox, we are aware that many solutions develop dynamically. Sometimes the passage of a few months can make some proposals obsolete or inferior. However, others are gaining popularity and interest in the industry, which translates into increased publicity, but also opportunities for development. Certain new tools are based on older, well-known solutions, but in a newer, refreshed, usually expanded and much more accessible form, which ideally corresponds to current trends in technological development. Therefore, we were guided by a number of criteria when selecting the software in question. The analysis thus took into account, among other things, ease of use, configuration, supported platforms and the customisability of the solution, i.e. flexibility.

The software under consideration is characterised by a wide variety of functions. The survey was conducted in the following areas: management, automation, backup and disaster recovery, version and software control, resource mapping, print server, monitoring, authorisation, link performance, log management, ticket management, packet analysis, network scanning and router software. The test procedure involved selecting representatives, installing (this was not always possible) and checking the functionality of the software, establishing comparison criteria and selecting the software for the toolbox.

OpenWISP [1] was selected for the **management** (Table 1). This is the most complete of the solutions analysed [2, 3]. It has significant support and community, which is a major advantage, especially for inexperienced administrators. This is a modular system, which means that it can be freely extended by adding further modules, not necessarily related to management. The system has a clear and intuitive user interface.

The solution chosen for **automation** was Ansible [4]. The main advantage of this solution is that it does not need agents on the end systems to operate, it connects to them via SSH or PowerShell. Additionally, it uses a very simple storage format (YAML). The benefit of using Ansible is also the idempotency of the target state (Table 2).

The **backup creation** chosen was Bacula [5] (Table 3). Due to its good scalability, Bacula can be used in large and small environments. It is a mature solution (it has good scalability, supports TLS encryption, allows for data compression and also data integrity verification) that can compete with commercial solutions. A major advantage is the availability of advanced storage management features to help recover damaged and/or lost files.

An overview of the **software enabling version and software control** is given in Table 4. In this category, the software Oxidized [6] was selected. Its major advantage is the ease of adding new device models and its good integration with network monitoring tools.

For **resource mapping**, Samba [7] was chosen (Table 5). The solution is cross-platform, easy to configure and uses the very well-known, widely used SMB protocol. TrueNAS CORE, on the other hand, will be selected as the operating system for the NAS [8]. It is modular in design, so it can be expanded with additional functionality. Supports all popular file systems and OpenZFS [9].

Operation of the **print server** was entrusted to CUPS [10]. Although this software only runs on Unix systems, through Samba it can also handle printers on Windows. The software allows the computer to become a print server and manage basic print jobs. With a graphical web interface, configuration is intuitive and easy. It is worth noting that this software offers the most features and has extensive documentation (Table 6).

For the **network monitoring**, Zabbix [11] was chosen (Table 7). It gathers, analyses and visualises data. Detects anomalies and notifies the administrator with alerts. Installation and configuration of the application is not difficult thanks to extensive documentation and the support of the software user community. All data is visualised on easy-to-read dashboards. Zabbix supports multiple communication protocols and offers the possibility to run scripts. It can be integrated with other solutions, e.g. for data visualisation.

The **authorisation** will be the responsibility of FreeRadius [12]. This is the most commonly implemented and most popular RADIUS server. Among all the solutions analysed, it has the most features and the largest documentation. FreeRadius is fast, feature-rich, scales well and has a modular design (Table 8).

Link performance will be tested using Iperf3 (Table 9). It is a very commonly used tool that can measure TCP, UDP and SCTP throughput. The software has relatively low hardware requirements and is easy to use. It works on many platforms.

The **logs will be managed** by Graylog [13]. There is a leading and reliable tool for the centralised capture, storage and analysis of logs. It allows easy management of unstructured and structured logs. A major advantage of the software is the use of the Elasticsearch database, which searches the records very quickly (Table 10).

For the **management of tickets**, OSTicket [14] was selected (Table 11). This software is one of the easiest to use and configure. Many features are available to help communicate with submitters and to help manage submissions. A number of these are automated, such as sending acknowledgements when a request is opened. OSTicket permits customisation of everything we need from email templates to the permissions of ticket agents. It scales well.

Wireshark [15] (Table 12) will be the best solution for **packet analysis**. It features a very powerful and clear graphical interface and a command-line counterpart (TShark). The intercepted traffic can be sorted and filtered according to the parameters searched for.

The **scanning of the network** (Table 13) will be performed by Nmap [16]. The software has a graphical interface called Zenmap. This is very flexible and has a syntax that is easy to learn. Its operation consists of creating packets and sending them to the target and analysing the response to them. This allows it to, for example, detect hosts in the network, calculate open ports and detect the targets' operating systems.

In the category of **router software**, OpenWRT [17] was selected (Table 14). This is the oldest alternative operating system for SOHO routers. Is based on Linux. It has many different functions, i.e. support for VPN tunnels, data server, support for an external 3G modem, QoS support or collection of statistics on the device's operation. A major advantage is the size of its user community and is regularly updated.

3   Trends and Developments

The number of open source projects will continue to grow in the future, this form of business model has proved successful for many suppliers. The move towards open-source software will continue, it is likely that a significant number of companies will continue to distribute the basic version of their software in this way, giving the option to purchase paid add-ons and support. In new solutions, ease of use, and therefore clarity and functionality of the graphical interface, is increasingly important. A trend has been observable for many years among many administrators to prefer a graphical interface to a text-based interface (CLI). This is mainly due to the ease of work, and therefore the intuitiveness of use of the GUI is one of the main factors in favour of a particular solution. However, this is sometimes at the expense of the number of functions or performance. When choosing open solutions, it is worth remembering that open source communities are often the source of many innovations, for example: the containerisation platform - Docker; the platform for managing, automating and scaling containerised applications

- Kubernetes; GNOME 3; the cloud and cloud solutions; the Chrome OS operating system; or ubiquity in IoT solutions. Currently, many well-known global companies are investing in open source software and solutions. The software currently in use is getting older which often translates into better performance, a larger community and a multitude of features. It is worth noting that also the role of cloud environments is growing and integration with it is becoming more and more important.

4   Conclusions

The aim of the article was to present a comparison and selection of open source programs that can constitute a set of applications used by the administrator of wireless local area networks. For this purpose, the authors, using their own experience, defined the areas of administrators' activities, as well as the types and scopes of functions of individual tools. Then, they identified solutions that meet most of the conditions presented.

While choosing open source applications, it is worth bearing in mind that many of them develop dynamically. Occasionally, the passage of a relatively short period of time can cause some to become obsolete. However, others are gaining popularity and interest in the industry, which is reflected in an increase in reputation and development opportunities. It is worth remembering that many new tools are based on older, often well-known tools and offer them in a newer, refreshed, usually expanded and much more accessible form, which may be ideally suited to current trends in technological development. Therefore, the selection of the software in question was guided by, among other things, ease of use and configuration, supported platforms and the ability to adapt the solution to current needs, i.e. flexibility and adaptability.

When describing the various tools, the authors tried to present a natural and objective approach to the demonstrated programs/tools, not to suggest known and already used solutions. It is also worth emphasising that an additional aim of the work carried out was the desire to test solutions different from those commonly used in production networks. The authors hope that such a slightly different approach from the commonly used one will allow to draw attention to less popular solutions with promising features.

Acknowledgments. The authors thank the Polish Ministry of Education and Science for financial support (Applied Doctorate Program, No. DWD/6/58/2022). This research was funded in part by the Polish Ministry of Science and Higher Education (No. 0313/SBAD/1310).

Appendix. Tables Comparing the Functions of Selected Open-Source Software

Table 1. Comparison of open-source software performing the management function

Open-source software	OpenWRT Remote Manager	OpenWISP	Cardinal
GUI/CLI	CLI	GUI	GUI
Supported devices	OpenWRT instances	OpenWRT instances + ability to write configuration backends for any type of network operating system	SSH-enabled Cisco access points in standalone mode
Main functions	Manage remote OpenWRT installations that operate as routers	Managing a network built on OpenWRT	Access point controller
Strengths	Simple management of ports, users and network interfaces, configuration backup, all written in Python	Integration with RADIUS, creation of VPN tunnels, configurable mesh and wireless networks, support for WPA2, WPA3 802.1x and others, multipath notification, modular design	User-friendly interface, simple installation, requires only MySQL, Python3 and Nginx to operate
Weaknesses	No support, development or GUI	The initial overwhelming number of modules, the complex installation	Only supports Cisco access points in standalone mode
Documentation and community support	Medium	Large	Small

Table 2. Comparison of open-source software implementing the automation function

Open-source software	Ansible	Terraform	Chef	Puppet	SaltStack
Supported platforms - server	Unix	Linux	Linux	Linux	Linux
Supported platforms - clients	Does not require	Does not require	Unix, Windows	Unix, Windows	Unix, Windows
Best used for	Configuration management	Management of infrastructure resources	Configuration management	Configuration management	Configuration management
Infrastructure	Variable	non-variable	Variable	Variable	Variable non-variable
Language	Procedural	Declarative	Procedural	Declarative	Declarative

(*continued*)

Table 2. (*continued*)

Open-source software	Ansible	Terraform	Chef	Puppet	SaltStack
Strengths	User-friendly, no agent, YAML-based Playbooks, Ansible Galaxy content portal for Ansible	Highly flexible, ability to generate dependency charts	Well integrated with the cloud, high flexibility and maturity	Reliable for managing server status, easy and robust module testing	High performance for large deployments, agent-based and agentless operation
Weaknesses	Insufficient user interface	Lack of an undoing function	In the current situation well adapted only to AWS, recommended knowledge of Ruby	No comprehensive reporting functions, difficult for beginners, knowledge of Ruby recommended	The network interface offers limited possibilities and functions
Documentation and community support	Large	Medium	Medium	Large	Medium

Table 3. Comparison of open-source software implementing the backup and disaster recovery

Open-source software	Amanda	Duplicati	Bacula	BackupPC	luckyBackup	Box Backup	BURP
GUI/CLI	CLI	GUI, CLI	GUI (Baculum), CLI	GUI	GUI, CLI	GUI (Boxi), CLI	CLI
Supported platforms - clients	Windows, Linux, macOS	Windows, Linux, macOS	Windows, Linux, macOS	Windows, Linux, macOS	Linux	Windows, Linux, macOS	Windows, Linux, macOS
Supported platforms - server	Linux	Linux	Linux	Linux	Linux	Linux	Linux
Required client-side software	Yes	Yes	Yes	No	Yes	Yes	Yes
Backup schedule	Yes	Yes	Yes	Yes	Yes	Yes	Yes
Strengths	Extensive configuration options	Encryption can be omitted	Custom implementation of the files created	Resume when interrupted, no client-side software required	Extremely easy to operate	Delivers reliability without complex configuration or expensive equipment	Resume when interrupted

(*continued*)

Table 3. (*continued*)

Open-source software	Amanda	Duplicati	Bacula	BackupPC	luckyBackup	Box Backup	BURP
Weaknesses	Occasionally unrefined interface	Weak support	Complex to configure, no incremental copies	Only GUI	No longer being developed	Absence of more advanced features available from others	Absence of more advanced features available from others
Documentation and community support	Medium	Medium	Large	Medium	Small	Small	Medium

Table 4. Comparison of open-source software implementing the version control function and software

Open-source software	Rancid	Oxidized	rConfig v3	Netshot
GUI/CLI	CLI	CLI, partially GUI	GUI	GUI
Supported platforms	Unix	Linux, Docker	Centos 7 +	Linux, Docker
Number of network operating systems supported	over 30	over 130	over 15	over 25
Strengths	Highly mature and well-performing software, good scalability	Highly scalable, supports pull and push for configuration changes, good scalability, frequent updates	Web-based user interface, embedded reporting, compliance monitoring	Web-based intuitive interface, quickly resolved issues, actively developed, integration possible - REST API
Weaknesses	Operates only on pull model, no GUI	Lack of GUI	The newer version is payable, no support or updates for this version	Smooth and problematic configuration of certain devices
Documentation and community support	Large	Medium	Small	Medium

Table 5. Comparison of open-source software implementing the resource mapping function – software and NAS

Main task	Mapping of resources	Mapping of resources	Mapping of resources	Mapping of resources	Mapping of resources	NAS	NAS	NAS
GUI/CLI	CLI	CLI	GUI, CLI	GUI, CLI	CLI	GUI, CLI	GUI, CLI	GUI, CLI
Supported platforms	Windows, Linux, macOS	Unix (there is a port on Windows)	Windows, Linux, macOS	Windows	Windows, Linux, macOS	VM	VM	VM
Supported protocols	SMB	SFTP	SFTP, FTPS, FTP	SFTP, SCP, FTP	NFS	SMB, AFP, NFS, iSCSI, SSH, rsync, FTP/TFTP	SMB, FTP, NFS, SSH, rsync, iSCSI, AFP, TFTP	SMB, AFP, NFS, FTP/TFTP, rsync, SCP, iSCSI, Unison
Strengths	Simple configuration for Windows as well as Linux	SSH access is sufficient for operation	Not all advanced features are included in the paid version	Integrated text editor, user-friendly interface	Very simple configuration	Encryption on ZFS volumes, offers a number of useful plug-ins	Includes support for link aggregation, IPv6 and Wake on LAN	Encrypting drives with support for cryptography-enabled hardware acceleration
Weaknesses	No manufacturer support, use of netbios - not an efficient protocol	Inefficiency of operation for long delay	A higher entry threshold compared to others	Poor performance	Not very safe without a firewall	Needs a large amount of RAM, especially when using ZFS	Lack of Enterprise-NAS functionality	Interface is not user-friendly
Documentation and community support	Medium	Medium	Large	Medium	Small	Large	Medium	Medium

Table 6. Comparison of open-source software that perform the print server function

Open-source software	CUPS	LPRng	PyKota
Supported platforms	Unix	Unix	Unix
Main tasks	Offers print server functionality	Offers print server functionality	Management of printing
Operation with Windows printers	With the help of Samba	With the help of Samba	With the help of Samba
Strengths	Includes GUI for operation, integration of multiple authentication methods, compatibility with other printing systems, modular architecture, integration with LDAP, support for SSL3 and TLS encryption	Includes GUI (LPRng Tool), automatic job maintenance, highly detailed diagnostics, multiple printers supporting one queue, compatibility with other print buffers and network printers that use LPR	Operates with CUPS and LPRng, allocation, queue and user management, print accounting
Weaknesses	Pay version for Apple devices, command line configuration Pay version for Apple devices, command line configuration	GUI is not working perfectly, sometimes does not want to print from theoretically supported printers	Lack of support, tool no longer being developed
Documentation and community support	Large	Medium	Small

Table 7. Comparison of open-source software performing the monitoring function

Open-source software	Zabbix	Cacti	Prometheus	Nagios Core	Icinga	LibreNMS	Checkmk Raw Edition	NetXMS	OpenNMS
Supported platforms - clients	Windows, Linux, macOS, Docker and others (SNMP)	Windows, Linux and others (SNMP)	Windows, Linux and others (SNMP)	Windows, Linux and others (SNMP)	Windows, Linux and others (SNMP)	Windows, Linux and others (SNMP)	Windows, Linux, macOS and others (SNMP)	Windows, Linux and others (SNMP)	SNMP
Supported platforms - server	Linux, Docker	Linux	Linux, Docker	Linux	Windows, Linux	Linux, VM	Linux, Docker, VM	Windows, Linux	Linux, Docker
Strengths	Highly efficient at low levels	Extremely adaptable	Perfect for container networks, very fast database	Very extensive plug-in library, simple interface	Technical enhancement of Nagios, most Nagios plug-ins and extensions work	Highly configurable alert module, well scalable	More intuitive configuration and troubleshooting than others	Simple installation, pleasant and flexible user interface	Elastic and powerful tool, integrates well with alert systems
Weaknesses	Performance above 1000 nodes, limited support	Weak scaling, lack of other popular features present in other software	Problematic and time-consuming first configuration, mainly used for metrics	Qualitatively worse than the paid version	Higher, steeper learning curve compared to other	Comparatively high memory consumption	Shortcomings and outdated documentation	Commercial version not available, sometimes not very intuitive	Steep learning curve, non-intuitive user interface
Documentation and community support	Large	Medium	Medium	Large (free implementation support)	Large	Medium	Medium	Large	Large

Table 8. Comparison of open-source software performing the authentication function

Open-source software	FreeRadius	freeDiameter	tac_plus	Kerberos
Supported platforms - server	Unix	Unix	Linux	Unix, Windows
Main tasks	Authentication, authorisation and access control	Authentication, authorisation and access control	Authentication, authorisation and access control	Authentication
Protocol	RADIUS	Diameter	TACACS +	Kerberos
Strengths	Integration with other management tools, better access control compared to TACACS +, Vendor Specific Attributes for nearly 100 vendors, support for failover, load balancing	Support for SCTP and TCP, peer-to-peer architecture for high flexibility, built-in failover mechanisms, RADIUS/Diameter translation support	Supported by most manufacturers, high scalability, uses TCP protocol, entire packet is encrypted	Multiple operating system support, mutual authentication, strong cryptography, secret keys are shared - more efficient than sharing public keys

(continued)

Table 8. (*continued*)

Open-source software	FreeRadius	freeDiameter	tac_plus	Kerberos
Weaknesses	Lower reliability than TACACS + - UDP, password only encryption	Lack of active support and updates, no encryption - secure transmission via TLS or IPSec	Only Linux, support for access control than RADIUS, little support	Strict time requirements, lengthy set-up, authentication only
Documentation and community support	Large	Small	Small	Medium

Table 9. Comparison of open-source software performing the link performance test function

Open-source software	Iperf3	Netperf	Packet Sender	Mausezahn	nping
GUI/CLI	GUI(PPerf), CLI	CLI	GUI	CLI	CLI
Supported platforms	Linux, Windows (informally)	Windows, Linux, macOS	Windows, Linux, macOS	Linux	Windows, Linux, macOS
Main tasks	Measuring network performance and throughput	Measuring network performance and throughput	Sending and receiving packets for testing purposes	Creation of packets for testing purposes	Packet sending and analysis of test responses
Strengths	Very simple operation, many parameter adjustments, multithreading, multicast and IPv6 support	Offers a range of predefined tests, support for IPv6, provides CPU utilisation data	Automation and scripting of the network environment, built-in ASCII and HEX readers, scaling up and down	Possibility to create almost every possible and impossible packet, developed within netsniff-ng	Custom generation of ARP, TCP, UDP and ICMP packets, traceability, flexible and customisable
Weaknesses	Lack of backward compatibility with Iperf2	Low support, no updates to add new features	Worse reliability than commercial solutions, not tailored to business needs	Only available for Linux and no Windows version planned	Experimental support for IPv6
Documentation and community support	Large	Small	Medium	Small	Medium

Table 10. Comparison of open-source software performing the log management function

Open-source software	Octopussy	Graylog	AlienVault OSSIM	SIEMonster Community Edition	Prelude OSS
Supported platforms	Linux	Linux, Docker	VM and physical	VM, Docker	Unix
Main tasks	Management of events	Management of events	SIEM	SIEM	SIEM
Strengths	Plug-in support, multilingualism, custom notifications, extensive built-in incident report tool	Highly flexible, fast, can be integrated with other solutions, scales easily, can process large amounts of data	Correlation of SIEM events, asset detection, vulnerability assessment, behaviour monitoring, intrusion detection	Real-time risk analysis and reporting	Multiple log formats are supported, correlation, filtering, alerting, analysis and visualisation capabilities
Weaknesses	Low support, no longer developed, has security-related bugs	Dashboards and charts are no longer as flexible, they cannot use the whole ELK ecosystem	Limited log management features, performance problems on a large scale, deployable only for one server	Limited to 100 end devices, many features missing from the community version, weak online documentation	Weaker performance, scalability and fewer features compared to other SIEMs, mainly intended for testing and/or research purposes
Documentation and community support	Small	Large	Large	Small	Medium

Table 11. Comparison of open-source software implementing the ticket management function

Open-source software	OTRS Community Edition	OTOBO	osTicket	Zammand	UVdesk
Supported platforms	Unix	Linux, Docker	All	Linux, Docker	Windows, Linux, macOS
Strengths	Process and workflow automation, mobile user-friendly, customisable customer and agent portals, support for 38 different languages	Dashboards with a variety of important information, compact and clear ticket overview, lots of statistics and reporting possibilities, simple customisation, ability to switch from OTRS	Extensive filtering and sorting options, HTML-formatted e-mails, custom fields in submissions, configurable auto-reply scheme	Frequent updates, external authentication, history of changes to requests, high performance and flexibility, enables generation of reports	Simple installation and configuration, high flexibility, speed and configurability, multiple contact channels

(*continued*)

Table 11. (*continued*)

Open-source software	OTRS Community Edition	OTOBO	osTicket	Zammand	UVdesk
Weaknesses	In January 2021 development and support ends, somewhat old user interface, many useful features in paid version	New software - relatively little documentation, many useful features in paid version	Any change of personalisation required to fill in the form again, no reporting	Complex configuration, no paid version, relatively new software	Weak identification of spam
Documentation and community support	Medium	Medium	Large	Large (support in over 30 languages)	Medium

Table 12. Comparison of open-source software performing the packet analysis function

Open-source software	Wireshark	tcpdump	EtterCap	netsniff-ng	Ngrep	EtherApe	TCPTrace	Xplico
GUI/CLI	GUI, CLI (TShark)	CLI	GUI, CLI	CLI	CLI	GUI	CLI	GUI, CLI
Supported platforms	Unix, Windows	Unix, Windows (WinDump)	Unix, Windows	Linux	Unix, Windows	Uniksowe	Linux	Linux. VM
Main tasks	Packet capture and analysis	Packet capture and analysis	Packet capture and analysis	Traffic analyser + network tool kit	Network packet analysis	Graphical representation of traffic + monitoring	Analysis of TCP and UDP dump files	Network forensic analysis
Strengths	Collection and analysis of packets in one, user-friendly interface	Quick and lightweight application, numerous customisable parameters, no GUI required	Penetration tests, offers endpoint isolation methods	Powerful multi-programme tool, fast-acting analyser	Compatible syntax with grep, data presented in a friendly manner	Graphic approach to show traffic volumes, reading live and file traffic	Generate several types of input data, create graphs	Data storage limit is the limit of the hard disk, customisation possibilities
Weaknesses	Steep learning curve, collects everything by default, which can be overwhelming	Complicated filtering query language	Slightly outdated interface	Runs only on Linux, no GUI	Produces more false alarms, slower performance than other sniffers	Not easy to use	Lack of support and updates, minimal UDP processing since version 5	Works only on Linux, limited by hard disk access time
Documentation and community support	Large	Large	Medium	Medium	Medium	Medium	Small	Medium

Table 13. Comparison of open-source software performing of network scanning programs

Open-source software	Nmap	Zmap	p0f	Masscan
GUI/CLI	GUI(Zenmap), CLI	GUI, CLI	CLI	CLI
Supported platforms	Unix, Windows	Linux, macOS	Unix, Windows	Windows, Linux, macOS
Scanning mode	TCP SYN, TCP, UDP	Stateless	Passive	Stateless
Typical applications	Detection of hosts, scanning of open ports	Scanning and discovering an open port - single port	Fingerprinting the TCP/IP stack	Scanning and discovering an open port - multiple ports
Detail of scanning	Large	Small	Medium	Small
Strengths	Very versatile tool, can be used to audit network systems, bypass firewalls and/or IDS,	Ultra-fast scanning - full address space in under 45 min (Gigabyte link) or 5 min (10 Gigabyte link and PF_RING)	No traffic generation, making it more difficult or impossible to detect, support for full tcpdump-style filtering expressions, high speed	Capable of transmitting up to 10 billion packets per second, Nmap-compatible
Weaknesses	Port scanning leaves its mark - it is "noisy"	Probing only one port, can only scan IPv4 spaces	Remote/scanned host must initiate TCP connection - passive scanning	Only IP addresses and simple ranges are supported (no DNS)
Documentation and community support	Large	Medium	Medium	Medium

Table 14. Comparison of open-source software programs for routers

Open-source software	DD-WRT	Tomato	OpenWRT
Strengths	Supports a large number of routers, has numerous options and features for advanced customisation, supports OpenVPN and QoS	Rapid operation, modern interface, support for OpenVPN and live monitoring, take up little space	Large number of control and customisation options, OpenVPN and QoS support
Weaknesses	Lack of new versions, can be overwhelming for new users	Limited functionality, support for fewer routers than competitors	Less number of routers supported than DD-WRT, less user-friendly than others
Documentation and community support	Large	Medium	Large

References

1. https://medium.com/@williamchoudhury/openwisp-blog-post-ac6987d6b734. Accessed 2 May 2022
2. https://github.com/jumpscale7/openwrt-remote-manager. Accessed 2 May 2022
3. https://dataiku-research.github.io/cardinal/. Accessed 2 May 2022
4. https://www.ansible.com/. Accessed 2 May 2022
5. https://www.bacula.org/. Accessed 2 May 2022
6. https://github.com/ytti/oxidized. Accessed 2 May 2022
7. https://www.samba.org/. Accessed 2 May 2022

8. https://www.truenas.com/truenas-core/. Accessed 2 May 2022
9. https://www.openzfs.org. Accessed 2 May 2022
10. https://www.cups.org/. Accessed 2 May 2022
11. https://www.zabbix.com/. Accessed 2 May 2022
12. https://freeradius.org/. Accessed 2 May 2022
13. https://www.graylog.org/. Accessed 2 May 2022
14. https://osticket.com/. Accessed 2 May 2022
15. https://www.wireshark.org/. Accessed 2 May 2022
16. https://nmap.org/. Accessed 2 May 2022
17. https://openwrt.org/. Accessed 2 May 2022

Laboratory Studies of Infrared Radiation Transmission of Camouflage Net Materials Used on the Battlefield

Krzysztof Szajewski[1(✉)], Paweł Kalinowski[2], Anna Szajewska[3], and Paweł Szczepaniak[2]

[1] Cybernetics Faculty, Military University of Technology, gen. Sylwestra Kaliskiego 2 Street, 00 -908 Warsaw, Poland
krzysztof.szajewski@wat.edu.pl

[2] Air Force Institute of Technology, Księcia Bolesława 6 Street, 01-494 Warsaw, Poland
{pawel.kalinowski,szczepaniak}@itwl.pl

[3] The Main School of Fire Service, Faculty of Security Engineering and Civil Protection, 52/54 Słowackiego Street, 01-629 Warsaw, Poland
aszajewska@sgsp.edu.pl

Abstract. The paper presents the results of testing the properties of several different camouflage net materials. These means are not weapons, so their distribution is carried out on a general basis without licenses or permits. In contemporary armed conflicts, the means of direct camouflage are being used intensively. Frequently, the quality of the camouflage nets supplied in terms of thermal masking is not defined and there is therefore a strong need for an objective examination before they are used. The conflict in Ukraine and the lack of literature data in this area became the motivation to assess the quality of the camouflage net material and to propose a method for its quick qualitative assessment. Their transmission was examined in visible light and in infrared light. The infrared transmission study consisted in testing radiation reaching the measuring camera, derived from the black body standard and human body. The correlation between visible light transmission and infrared transmission has been investigated. Test results of the studies indicate that the level of transparency is not directly reflected in thermal contrast. Hence, the conclusion that the thermal properties of the nets cannot be assessed on the basis of visual observation. The transparency of the net in visible light is not proportional to infrared transparency. The degree of perforation cannot determine the effectiveness of thermal masking.

Keywords: emission factor · thermal camouflage · infrared imaging

1 Introduction

Reconnaissance is a key element in conducting combat operations. It provides commanders with information on the surrounding area as well as the location and movements of the opponent, his actions, forces, combat capabilities and equipment. Conducting reconnaissance is the basis for planning tactical and strategic operations, through which optimal use of forces and resources is possible. The variety of ways to conduct reconnaissance

© The Author(s), under exclusive license to Springer Nature Switzerland AG 2024
K. S. Soliman (Ed.): IBIMA-AI 2023, CCIS 2101, pp. 210–223, 2024.
https://doi.org/10.1007/978-3-031-62843-6_22

has contributed to the development and use of camouflage to counter reconnaissance. Camouflage on the modern battlefield involves replacing real information with a false image. In military applications, the quality of camouflage is crucial because it determines people's lives. Camouflage at tactical level is intended to counteract ImageryIntelligence (IMINIT). IMINIT is an intelligence discipline consisting in obtaining information using imaging devices and systems. IMINIT subcategory, which acts directly with camouflage measures, is optoelectronic imaging (ElectroopticalImageryIntelligence – EO IMINIT) – information is obtained by remote sensing using body's own radiation (emission) and reflecting radiation. The aim is to detect an emission or reflective contrast between the object and the background. This results in data transmitted by the earth's atmosphere in the visible, infrared and ultraviolet bands [4]. Currently, human senses are replaced by advanced technology for the detection of camouflaged real images. The latest technologies are used, such as image analysis by discriminators based on neuron networks [9]. Analysers of this type can be taught to detect hidden images effectively. However, regardless of the method of detecting camouflage, infrared radiation contrasts are one of the most important sources for disclosing actual information and are the basis for optoelectronic reconnaissance. An image without differences in infrared radiation is difficult to detect by thermal cameras working with analysers on which machine vision algorithms have been installed. The emission factor is one of the most important parameters used to assess the characteristics of thermal camouflage materials in the image reconnaissance, as it depends on the ratio of the amount of radiation reflected and absorbed, which in turn has a direct impact on the thermogram contrast. The article presents an analysis of infrared radiation transmission of twelve different camouflage net materials and compares their thermal properties. The method presented in the article may be useful for a rapid qualitative assessment of the camouflage net material. The test is limited to the necessary measuring equipment. The article describes the results of this method based on the measurement of radiation of the black body standard.

1.1 Electro-optical Imaging Methods

In the conflicts that have recently engulfed Ukraine, Syria, Armenia and Nagorno-Karabakh, reconnaissance measures based, among others, on optoelectronic sensors, including thermal cameras that record electromagnetic radiation in the NIR (Near Infrared), MWIR (Midwave Infrared) and LWIR (Long Wave Infrared) bands, are leading the way. UAVs (Unmanned Aerial Vehicle) or polar satellites are currently used for reconnaissance. In the second case, access to remote sensing information is generally limited due to long revisit times, spatial resolution and high system maintenance costs. The development of thermal imaging sensors on the battlefield has led to the fact that their use is not just the domain of highly specialized, sophisticated reconnaissance assets but is part of the soldier's individual equipment. In the case of UAVs, relatively low costs and mobility have made them 'eyes' of the modern battlefield. The Russian invasion of Ukraine led to the first war, in which the military and commercial use of the UAVs is observed on such a large scale by both sides of the conflict. The range of UAVs used in Ukraine is impressive. Large UAVs, e.g., Bayraktar TB2 carrying combat assets capable of hitting, for example, logistics subdivisions under conditions of air superiority. Small UAVs turn out to be crucial for expanding the situational awareness of infantry and maneuvering units. Despite the fact that the invasion started a year ago, many publications have already been published, which describe the large share of the UAVs in this conflict [1, 8, 10]. In the area of thermal cameras integrated with UAVs, in addition to specialized and expensive military solutions, the civilian market offers, for example, the DJI MATRICE 30 T drone with an uncooled LWIR thermal camera with a resolution of 640×512 px, which cost is a fraction of the price of military solutions. The literature [6] describes an example of a UAV equipped with an LWIR KTX high-resolution 1024× 768 px thermal imaging camera head, which could certainly be used for reconnaissance operations on the modern battlefield.

Large-scale thermal reconnaissance necessitates the reduction of heat emissions to the environment by humans and equipment. For equipment, there is a need to reduce heat emissions mainly from the engine, power transmission parts, wheel hubs, brakes and armament components. The most commonly used means of camouflage are camouflage nets (Fig. 1), or artificial masks, which are used to camouflage troops, objects and equipment. There are also mobile camouflage measures, which are an integral part of military vehicles and limit the detection of vehicles in motion and at a standstill.

Fig. 1. Multiscope camouflage covering on a military vehicle – a photograph in visible light [photo by Miranda]

Manufactured camouflage nets are often made of aramid, carbon or metallic fibers. These fibres typically allow thermal masking. The net shape shall be designed to have perforations of different sizes and shapes. The openings should be large enough to allow for a convective flow of air and reduction the temperature around the camouflaged object and at the same time small enough to ensure thermal masking. The size of openings is a result of a compromise between these two opposite features. In order to improve thermal masking properties, the nets are additionally covered with materials with altered emissivity, such as special paint, ceramic coatings or polyvinyl chloride [7]. These coatings change the absorption and emission properties of the net, because the design aims to make it reveal a minimum of incoming energy from the object being masked. Work is currently underway on nanophotonic materials of structures [13] by which radiation spectrum can be reduced in the requested area. Silicon is used to produce structures on a 'micro' scale. Work is also underway on adaptive materials with variable emissivity in the spectral ranges from 3–5 μm and 8–14 μm of thermal camouflage. These materials may be electrically modulated and shall be made in a multi-layer form where graphene forms part of the layers [3].

1.2 Imaging Reconnaissance

Natural background radiation is usually irregular, as it consists of various natural components of the image, the composition and characteristics of which are most often diverse. However, in the case of artefacts, the materials are usually homogeneous and often synthetic, thus having uniform thermal radiation. There are four basic features of infrared image recognition: temperature, texture, shape and statistical distribution of thermal radiation. In addition, 11 auxiliary image indicators may be specified which may contribute to the recognition of the object being sought in the image stage [12]. These are:

1) Average radiation difference
2) Standard deviation of radiation
3) Radiation contrast
4) ASM indicator (image texture stability measure)
5) CON indicator (measure of contrast of texture)
6) COR indicator (similarity of texture in rows and columns)
7) ENT indicator (entropy of texture)
8) Characteristics of shape
9) MSE indicator (average square error between object and background)
10) PSNR indicator (signal/noise ratio between background and object)
11) R indicator (degree of homogeneity of thermal image)

To evaluate the effectiveness of nets, a frequently used criterion is the minimum distance from the target at which the camouflaged object can be recognized. The detection distance is sought to be the smallest, because the performance criterion is met, if the distance between the observer and the object, at which the diagnosis took place, is less than the range of the hidden object. This measure is based on actual field research, which is costly and dependent on prevailing environmental conditions. Another measure of the effectiveness of the camouflage is the average difference in background and hidden object temperatures [5]. In this method, it is possible to create tables of average temperatures for the background at a certain time of year for the current conditions and then compare the tabulated value with the average temperature of the observation field. Still another method of evaluating effectiveness is the multifractal method, which involves comparing the spectrum of the background and the camouflaged object [2]. It is worth noting that, apart the NO-10-208:2014 standard, the generally accepted method for assessing the effectiveness of camouflage and the final assessment criteria have not yet been developed. However, it is certain that this effectiveness depends primarily on the contrast between the background and the object and, secondly, on the imaging method.

The contrast depends on the emissivity coefficient of the camouflage net. The emissivity coefficient can be determined using a spectrophotometer operating in the infrared spectrum or with a measuring thermal imaging camera. The spectrophotometric method consists of measuring the absorption of infrared radiation with different wavelengths and comparing it with the actual source emission. This method is based on the phenomenon of absorption. The result of a spectrometric measurement is information about the material under study in the form of a spectrum, i.e. a graph of the dependence of the magnitude of absorption on the energy of radiation, most often expressed by a wave number that is the inverse of the wavelength, which is derived from Planck's relation:

$$E = \frac{hc}{\lambda} \tag{1}$$

where: h = Planck's constant, c = light speed [m/s], E - energy [J].

Referring to the total radiation emitted by the black body, it should be assumed that the total energy flux under the law of Stefan-Boltzmann is:

$$M = \sigma \cdot T^4 \tag{2}$$

where: σ − Stefan − Boltzmann constant 5.670×10^{-8} W/m^2 ·K^4, T - temperature [K].

It should be noted that a black body is a theoretical creation, so in real conditions the observer has to deal with bodies similar in their properties to a gray body in which only part of the energy is given off to the environment. In the thermal imaging method, the emissivity coefficient can be calculated from the difference between the incoming radiation to the detector from the masking net and the incoming radiation from an observed object of the same temperature and wavelength. Measurement with a thermal imaging camera is usually done in one of two spectral ranges MWIR or LWIR. The use of these ranges is due to the fact that the earth atmosphere is not uniquely transparent for all infrared spectrum. LWIR and MWIR are ranges within atmospheric windows that slightly suppress radiation with these wavelengths [14]. Figure 2 indicates the two most commonly used infrared observation ranges in relation to the surface atmospheric permeability windows. At this point, it is worth noting that developers of modern camouflage net materials strive for thermal emission to occur precisely in the range of greatest attenuation by the atmosphere, i.e. 5–8 μm [11].

Measuring the amount of radiation with a measurement camera is subject to many errors due to the fact that the infrared detector receives the sum of radiation coming from the observed object, reflected radiation and scattered radiation from the atmosphere appearing on the object-detector path. It is important that measurements be carried out under controlled conditions, where measurement errors related to temperature differences, humidity or other environmental factors are likely to be small.

The components of the total radiation reaching the infrared detector are shown in Fig. 3. The total energy flux that hits the detector has the following components:

1. The energy component of the object $M_1 = \varepsilon_{obj} \cdot \tau \cdot M_{obj}$ where ε_{obj} means the emissivity of the object, τ means transparency of the atmosphere, and M$_{obj}$: exitance of the radiation of the object.
2. Energy component of all reflected radiation sources $M_2 = k \cdot \tau \cdot M_{ot}$ where M$_{ot}$ is the total existence of all radiation sources k − reflection factor $(1 − \varepsilon_{obj})$.

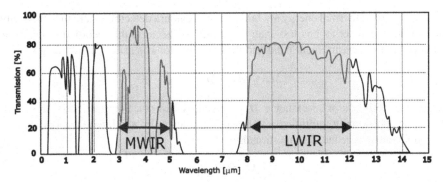

Fig. 2. Infrared atmospheric windows (own elaboration)

3. The component of the atmosphere's diffuse $M_3 = (1 - \tau) \cdot M_{atm}$ exitance, where M_{atm} is the atmosphere's exisitance, assuming that ε of the atmosphere $= 1$.

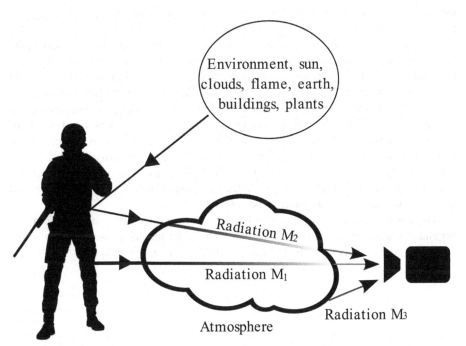

Fig. 3. Schematic of the radiation detection system reaching the infrared sensor from different sources. M_1- energy component of the object, M_2- energy component of all reflected radiation sources, M_3-energy component of diffuse atmospheric exitances (own elaboration)

The total M_r thermal flux reaching the detector is the sum of components M_1, M_2, M_3 [15].

The recorded thermal energy M_r falling on the camera detector, where the emissivity factor ε has been set to 1 is less than the actual (3) because the recorded radiation is narrowed to the measurement band and the actual factor ε is usually less than unity.

$$M_r \leq M_1 + M_2 + M_3 \tag{3}$$

For a blackbody, the total exitance M_r is given by Eq. (4). For grey body, the result should be additionally multiplied by the emission level, in which case the radiation in the whole range is reduced proportionally.

$$M_r \approx \sigma \cdot T_w^4 \tag{4}$$

In contrast, the spectral emissivity ε_λ is the ratio of the spectral power of an object's radiation to that of a black body of the same temperature and wavelength (5).

$$\varepsilon_\lambda = \frac{M_{\lambda ob}}{M_{\lambda black}} \tag{5}$$

where: $M_{\lambda ob}$ − radiation of an object for a wavelength of λ, $M_{\lambda black}$ − detector radiation for the same wavelength.

In practice, the majority of observed materials in nature exhibit non-linear emission properties as a function of wavelength. It follows from the above relationships that knowledge of the black body temperature and the temperature measured with the camera is required to determine the emissivity coefficient. In practice, knowledge of the emissivity coefficient alone is not a practical determinant of the effectiveness of camouflage because the camera receives the sum of the reflected, radiated radiation, but also radiation that enters through the perforations of the net. For this reason, it is necessary to know the transparency of the net. Figure 4 shows the sources of radiation reaching the detector using a camouflage net. In the case of a thermogram of an object obscured by a net, the component M_1 will be the sum of the radiation of the object behind the net that has penetrated it and the radiation of the net itself.

The component, M_2 similarly, will be the sum of the radiation reflected from the net and the radiation reflected from the object that reflected and passed through on the source-object-net-detector path. The component M_3 remains unchanged.

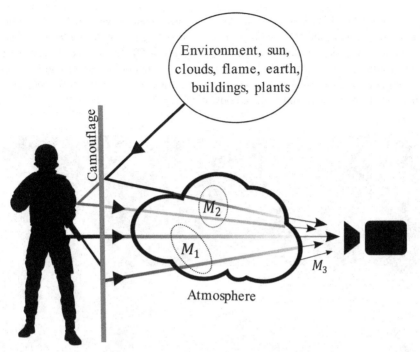

Fig. 4. Schematic of the radiation detection system reaching the infrared sensor using a masking net. M_1-energy component of the object, M_2-energy component of all reflected radiation sources, M_3 energy component of scattered atmospheric exitance (own elaboration).

2   Methodology of the Research

The subject of the research was 12 camouflage nets made available by Miranda Spółka z o.o. from the Lubawa S.A. group. View of the nets in the visible light is presented in Fig. 5. Examination of the characteristics of the nets consisted in testing transparency in visible light and conducting a series of LWIR radiation measurements for various cases. The degree of perforation was first examined, i.e. the ratio of the actual surface area of the net material per 1 m^2 of the observed surface. The perforation of the net means that heat accumulating underneath the net finds an outlet and air heated through convection currents can circulate freely through the openings. The degree of net perforation is associated with the proportion of radiation reaching the infrared detector from the net and the camouflaged object. The degree of perforation was assumed to be identical with transparency in visible light. Testing the transparency of the nets involved calculating the ratio between the amount of light falling on the net and the amount of radiation penetrating it. Transparency testing has been carried out in the scope of the visible light spectrum of white light LEDs with a colour temperature of 4000 K. The measuring instrument was the luminous intensity meter UT383S. The test was carried out by testing the proportion of light intensity between the light source and the light passing through the net. Measurements were taken on both sides of each net and then the arithmetic mean was found. The second and third studies examined the transparency of the net for the infrared in the LWIR range. The test was carried out at two black body standard temperatures: 50 °C and 90 °C. The temperature settings were due to the fact that the lowest adjustable black body standard temperature was 50 °C. The second temperature (90 °C) is due to the fact that the surfaces of masked vehicles normally do not exceed this temperature. The tests were performed on a measuring station (Fig. 6) equipped with a measuring camera and a black body standard.

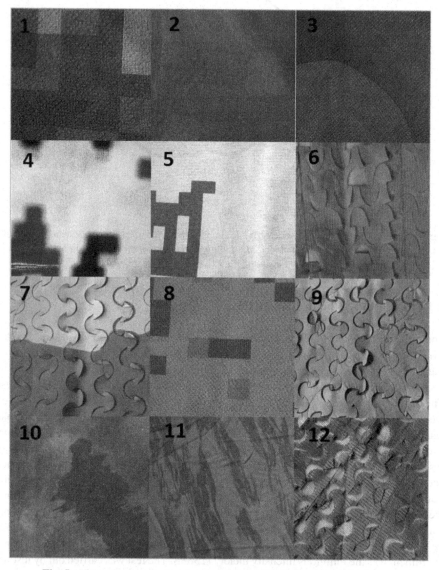

Fig. 5. View of camouflage net materials in visible light (own elaboration).

Fig. 6. Measuring station 1- black body standard, 2-Flir SC550 measuring camera, 3 - temperature meter, 4 - recorder (PC) (own elaboration).

The standard of the black body was set at a distance of 1 m from the net. The thermovisual camera was set at 4 m from the net. The tests were carried out at a constant ambient temperature of 18 °C, without exposure to atmospheric conditions and without the presence of direct sunlight on the observed stage. The fourth and fifth studies examined the contrasts between the radiation of the net behind which a person was standing and the net behind which there were no heat sources. In the first case, the radiation was determined by the average of a 20-cm diameter thermogram circle measured at the height of a person's chest located behind the net. In the second case, the radiation was determined by the average temperature from the designated measurement circle of the thermogram of the net behind which there was no heat source. The list of tests and the description are set out in Table 1.

Table 1. List of conducted tests with a short description

Test number	Test description
1	Visible light transparency test of nets [%]
2	Measured temperature of the net behind which the blackbody standard was set at 50 °C
3	Measured temperature of the net behind which the blackbody standard was set at 90 °C
4	Measured temperature of the net behind which a person was set. Breast height measurement (average temperature from 20 cm diameter circle)
5	Net temperature without heat source placed

3 Results

Table 2 shows the results of measuring the permeability of the net materials for visible light and for infrared light. The test numbers are in accordance with Table 1. The last three columns show the differences in temperatures recorded by the measurement camera.

Table 2. Results of the 5 tests described in Table 1 and temperature contrast between the results of the selected tests.

Net number	Study 1 [%]	Study 2 [°C]	Study 3 [°C]	Study 4 [°C]	Study 5 [°C]	Contrast[a] [°C]	Contrast[b] [°C]	Contrast[c] [°C]
1	18.29	20.2	28.0	21.9	19.2	1.2	2.7	8.8
2	3.56	25.1	37.9	22.5	18.8	0.8	3.7	19.1
3	21.16	23.6	32.3	22.0	19.3	1.3	2.7	13.0
4	3.51	19.8	22.1	20.8	19.5	1.5	1.3	2.6
5	2.22	18.8	20.2	20.5	19.7	1.7	0.8	0.5
6	21.13	22.5	33.4	22.5	19.7	1.7	2.8	13.7
7	9.40	19.3	24.5	20.2	19.9	1.9	0.3	4.6
8	25.12	24.3	37.0	22.3	19.4	1.4	2.9	17.6
9	6.00	18.7	20.4	20.6	19.4	1.4	1.2	1.0
10	14.33	21.2	28.2	20.8	19.4	1.4	1.4	8.8
11	21.75	21.4	29.6	21.1	19.6	1.6	1.5	10.0
12	23.81	30.2	34.3	23.7	18.9	0.9	4.8	11.3

a - *Average temperature difference between study 4 and ambient temperature (the difference between the man behind the net and the ambient temperature).*
b - *Difference between study 4 temperature and study 5 temperature (difference between the man behind the net and net radiation itself)*
c - *Difference between study 3 temperature and study 5 temperature (difference between black body standard 90 °C and net radiation itself)*

Figure 7 shows thermograms of a man placed behind the net. Two areas were delineated on each thermogram: an area located at the height of a person's chest with a diameter of 20 cm, and an area with a diameter of 20 cm outside the human silhouette. Based on the results of averaged temperatures from these areas, the temperature difference was determined (Contrast[b] Table 2). Intuition would suggest that thermal contrast is strongly dependent on the transparency of the net material in visible light, but from measurements of 12 different camouflage net materials, it appears that the level of transparency is not directly reflected in thermal contrast.

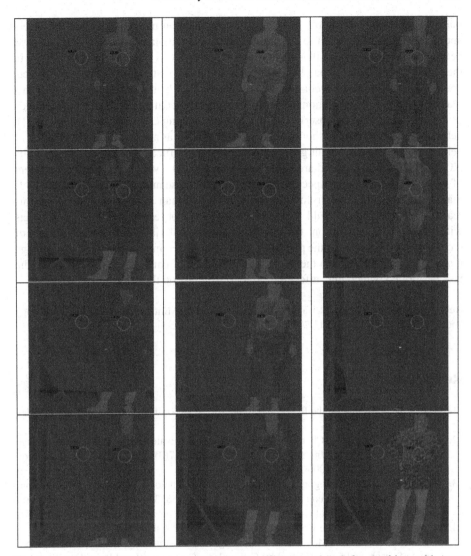

Fig. 7. Summary of thermograms with a human silhouette placed for masking grid (own elaboration). Sequence of nets analogous to Fig. 5

For example, nets No. 5 and 9 which have a transparency in visible light of 2.2% and 6% showed a temperature difference between the net without a heat source and the net with a heat source behind it at the level of measurement error (0.5 and 1 °C). Net material No. 2 also had low transparency in visible light (3.56%) while the measured thermal contrast was 19 °C. Some of the tested net materials had high transparency in visible light and at the same time moderate thermal contrast (materials No. 3 and 10). Hence, the conclusion that the thermal properties of the nets cannot be assessed on the basis of visual observation. The degree of perforation must not be such as to render thermal masking effective. During the test, the path the radiation traveled between the object and the camera was parallel to the ground plane and the plane of the net material was perpendicular to the ground plane. For this reason, there was no heat convection effect in the study, which, with the parallel orientation of the net material to the ground surface, could cause warm air to accumulate under the net and heat it by convection. For this reason, the angle of observation of the object is important with regard to the transparency of the net, because when observed with a thermal imaging camera from ground level, a net with small perforations should not heat up as quickly as a net placed over a soldier or vehicle where rising warm air gives off heat to the net. Efficacy studies according to the NO-10-A208:2014 standard are based solely on ground level observations assessment of several observers. This aspect is very important because modern observation methods mainly use imaging taken from altitude (UAV) rather than from ground level. For this reason future research should focus on the aspect of observing camouflaged objects with UAVs so as to confront the properties of net materials with modern means of reconnaissance. The use of the presented method to determine the quality of camouflage materials may contribute to the appropriate selection of camouflage depending on the task performed, which may affect the safety of soldiers on the battlefield.

Acknowledgment. This work was financed/co-financed by Military University of Technology under research project UGB 811/2023.

References

1. Chávez, K.: Learning on the fly: drones in the Russian-Ukrainian war. Arms Control Today **53**, 6–11 (2023)
2. Cheng, X.P., Shu, B.W., Chang, Y.J., Li, X., Yu, D.B.: Evaluation of infrared camouflage effectiveness via a multi-fractal method. Def. Technol. **17**(3), 748–754 (2021). https://doi.org/10.1016/j.dt.2020.05.006
3. Ding, P., et al.: Multilayer graphene-based radiation modulator for adaptive infrared camouflage with thermal management. J. Phys. D Appl. Phys. **55**, 345103 (2022). https://doi.org/10.1088/1361-6463/ac7484
4. D2: Doktryna rozpoznanie wojskowe. Warsaw. p. 11 (in Polish) (2013)
5. Frode Berg Olsen, F.B.: Methods for evaluating thermal camouflage. In: RTO SCI Symposium on Sensors and Sensor Denial by Camouflage, Concealment and Deception, Brussels, Belgium, 19–20 April 2004, RTO-MP-SCI-145 (2004)
6. Kalinowski, P., Szczepaniak, P., Ułanowicz, L.: Zastosowanie aerofotogrametrii w podczerwieni do śledzenia dzików w ich naturalnym środowisku oraz identyfikacji osobników zarażonych Afrykańskim Pomorem Świń. Cz. I – architektura systemu i metodyka identyfikacji, Mechanika w lotnictwie (2022). https://doi.org/10.15632/ML2022/165-183 (in Polish)
7. Kastek, M., Piątkowski, T., Dulski, R., Chamberland, M., Lagueux, P., Farley, V.: Multispectral and hyperspectral measurements of soldier's camouflage equipment. In: Proceedings of SPIE - The International Society for Optical Engineering, 8382. 83820 K (2012). https://doi.org/10.1117/12.918393
8. Kunertova, D.: The war in Ukraine shows the game-changing effect of drones depends on the game. Bull. At. Sci. **79**(2), 95–102 (2023). https://doi.org/10.1080/00963402.2023.2178180

9. Kuznetsov, A., Gashnikov, M.: Increasing the size of the camouflage area for remote sensing images. In: Ural Symposium on Biomedical Engineering, Radioelectronics and Information Technology (USBEREIT). Yekaterinburg. Russia, pp. 0312–0315 (2021). https://doi.org/10.1109/USBEREIT51232.2021.9455113

10. Kreps, S., Lushenko, P.: Drones in modern war: evolutionary, revolutionary, or both? Def. Secur. Anal. **39**(2), 271–274 (2023). https://doi.org/10.1080/14751798.2023.2178599

11. Lee, N., Kim, T., Lim, J.S., Chang, I., Cho, H.H.: Metamaterial-selective emitter for maximizing infrared camouflage performance with energy dissipation. ACS Appl. Mater. Interfaces **11**(23), 21250–21257 (2019). https://doi.org/10.1021/acsami.9b04478

12. Lv, Q., Ding, B., Li, L.: Research on evaluation of target thermal infrared camouflage effect based on image features. In: IEEE 2nd International Conference on Information Systems and Computer Aided Education (ICISCAE) (2019)

13. Moghimi, M.J., Lin, G., Jiang, H.: Highly absorptive nanophotonic structures on flexible substrates for infrared camouflage. In: Proceedings of the 12th IEEE International Conference on Nano/Micro Engineered and Molecular Systems, 9–12 April 2017. Los Angeles, USA (2017)

14. Szajewska, A.: Termowizja w ochronie przeciwpożarowej, SGSP (2018). ISBN 978-83-88446-87-0 (in Polish)

15. Więcek, B., De Mey, G.: Termowizja w podczerwieni. Podstawy i zastosowania, PAK Publishing House, Warsaw 2011 (in Polish) (2011)

Theoretical and Practical Aspects of the Evil Twin Attack. The Attacker's Perspective and Defense Methodology

Piotr Augustyniak[✉], Olgierd Rogowicz, and Piotr Zwierzykowski

Institute of Communication and Computer Networks, Faculty of Computing and
Telecommunications, Poznań University of Technology, Poznan, Poland
piotr.augustyniak@doctorate.put.poznan.pl,
piotr.zwierzykowski@put.poznan.pl

Abstract. This article provides an analysis of an attack on wireless networks
referred to as Evil Twin. In addition to a theoretical description, the article discusses the hardware and system combination used, while pointing out its relatively low complexity, and the complimentary nature of the solutions used, both
the operating system and the software used are presented. This clearly translates
into the potential when attempting to break through security and gain specific
data. Furthermore, the authors present the individual phases of the attack, including the proposed subsequent optimisations, in order to make the attack practically
applicable in most cases, regardless of the location and shape of the network under
investigation. The paper additionally presents methods for tuning the functionality
itself, in order to ultimately increase the probability of success of the attack itself.
The article is the result of work devoted to reviewing the literature on the subject
and conducting experiments with various scripts including their optimisation.

Keywords: evil twin · wireless LAN · MITM (Man in the Middle) · WLAN
Security

1 Introduction

Following a pragmatic approach to attacks, this article was guided by the principle of
rational management, both of time and available resources. The main aspects of this
approach were to try to get as much effect as possible with as little effort as possible.
Taking an approach close to phishing attacks, the main goal was to reach as many
potential victims as possible. As a result, the analysis of the attack can be used in
virtually most cases regardless of the location and shape of the network under study.

The purpose of the article is to show how relatively uncomplicated the execution
of the attack is, which as a result may lead to frequent use of this method, especially
by people who do not necessarily have expert knowledge of technologies and protocols
used in wireless networks. The article consists of five sections: introduction, description
of the concept of the attack, and analysis of the various phases of the attack, followed
by a discussion of the logic of the attack. The article ends with a summary.

© The Author(s), under exclusive license to Springer Nature Switzerland AG 2024
K. S. Soliman (Ed.): IBIMA-AI 2023, CCIS 2101, pp. 224–236, 2024.
https://doi.org/10.1007/978-3-031-62843-6_23

2 Attack Evil Twin

Evil Twin, or ET for short, is an attack that involves creating a fake WLAN impersonating an already existing network in order to intercept traffic [1–8]. Disconnecting a user from a real AP will in most cases trigger an attempt to reconnect to the network, at which point the ET will respond to the resulting opportunity by taking over the connection, providing an advantage in this field if only through a stronger signal than the real AP (Fig. 1).

Based on the mechanism of automatic connection of devices to the network or users' lack of vigilance in selecting available networks, it is possible to imperceptibly take over the network traffic, becoming the headquarters of communication between users and the original network, creating a classic MiTM attack. The second possibility is to mediate between the users and an alternative Internet access provided by the attacker and under his control, provided, for example, by GSM. In both cases, an attempt is made to redirect network traffic so that it passes through a device under the attacker's control. Traffic redirected in this way can be interfered with passively by collecting and reading the information in it, or actively by interfering with it directly.

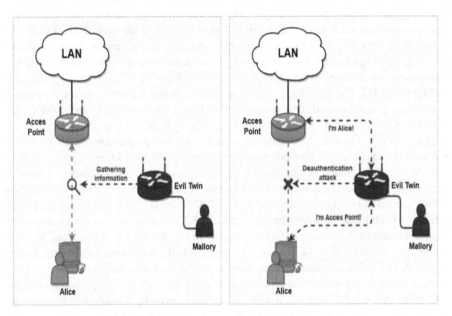

Fig. 1. Evil Twin's scheme of operation in two phases

Target of Evil Twin attacks are WLANs, in this case under consideration Wi-Fi networks, which by their very nature are always exposed in the radio band. Although their traffic can be encrypted, their presence will always be noted by surrounding devices capable of receiving a 2.4 GHz or 5 GHz Wi-Fi signal. Even when a network administrator decides to hide the network by disabling the SSID broadcasting an attacker who listens to the Wi-Fi band is able to catch the moment a user connects to the hidden network. Because at the moment the connection is established, the user broadcasts who he is connecting to, betraying the presence of the hidden network. Of particular interest by attackers are all kinds of shared Wi-Fi in malls, stores, bars and cafes, which want to offer their customers a service that is basic by the standards of today's world - the Internet. It is also increasingly common to see places with free public Wi-Fi in public use areas such as parks or city squares. Attackers tempted by the number of potential victims often encounter networks created sparingly, without expertise and with inadequate security, through which hundreds or thousands of users connect every day. A part of it may not even be aware that it is connected to such a network. Mechanisms for remembering networks with which a device has already once connected, whether in phones, tablets, laptops or other devices when a re-memorized network is detected will automatically try to switch to Wi-Fi in most cases in order not to overload mobile data transmission. As in many attacks such as this, there is no rigid framework within which the attack is to take place or by what means it is to be carried out. For this reason, the degrees of its sophistication and complexity can vary from case to case. When an attacker creates an Evil Twin, the first of the challenges he faces is to make the ET as similar as possible to the real AP. The resemblance must be high enough that the chosen target or targets will switch from the real AP to the ET without suspicion. Simultaneously, the attacker must keep in mind that the seemingly simple network he is attacking may have some mechanisms to detect this type of threat. The next element in the overall attack is access to the target network, be it the Internet or an intranet. In the case of Internet access, an attacker configuring the ET can provide this functionality in a number of ways. For example, the device can support mobile Internet, making it available to the victim connecting to the ET. The advantage of such a solution is that the entire attack is easier to process and ignores the real AP focusing only on taking over its identity. In the event that, in addition, the potential victim communicates through the AP with the intranet of the service provider where he is a customer or employer, being an employee, this solution will exclude the possibility of permanent interception of the victim's communication with the resources shared on the intranet. In such a case, there will be a need to develop the ET attack into a more complete MiTM attack. Instead of sharing its own connection to the external network, a connection to a real AP is used. The victim's traffic will be redirected back to the real AP. On one hand, the ET presents itself to the victim as the trusted AP and to the trusted AP as the victim. Being the intermediary of the wireless connection, the ET attack assumes the status of a fully developed MiTM attack. It is this model of ET attack that is more precise and allows it to lull vigilance, not only on the side of the victim, which can continue using network resources, but also on the side of the AP, whose connection with the victim returns to normal after a temporary disconnection.

3 Phases of the Attack

In order to carry out an attack, it is necessary to know several important parameters of the Wi-Fi network that is being targeted, as well as a basic knowledge of the potential security features within it. Attackers will first start by scanning the area where the attack is to be carried out. However, one of the easiest options they can do is in the network coverage area, pretending to be a customer busy with his own business, to use a personal laptop with the necessary software. Nowadays there are more discreet options-for example, using a less conspicuous cell phone. By using freely available applications that provide a satisfactory range of collected network information, or more advanced solutions like obtaining root privileges on the phone and then, through a terminal emulator such as Termux, using network scanning software packages modeled on the equivalents found for GNU/Linux. The attack can take on an even more cautious character and, using a micro device capable of scanning networks, be ingeniously hidden in objects or a closet without casting suspicion on the individual who collects the needed information.

The most important information to get is the SSID, or Service Set Identifier. This is a unique name that can consist of uppercase letters, numbers and special characters such as dashes, periods and spaces. In accordance with the 802.11 standard for wireless local area networks, the SSID can consist of 32 characters. Access points broadcast their identifiers so that they can be detected and distinguished. A similar identifier is the BSSID, Basic Service Set Identifier. By convention, the MAC address of an access point is used to designate it. Therefore, knowing the MAC address means knowing the BSSID, and since all packets that participate in traffic contain this identifier, it is possible to track them easily. The BSSID is unique for each access point in a wireless network, which means that in a network where several access points are used, each access point has its own unique BSSID MAC address. This allows wireless devices to identify exactly from which access point the wireless network is accessible. The ESSID, or Extended Service Set Identifier, meanwhile, is an extended version of the SSID and is used in wireless networks where more than one access point is configured to work together on a single network. In such a situation, the ESSID is used to identify a network consisting of several access points that operate in a single infrastructure mode. The ESSID is the same string as the SSID, for practical reasons, but in the case of a network where several access points are used, the ESSID must be identical across all of these devices. Each access point in such a network has its own unique BSSID, which are grouped into a single ESSID. This allows devices to move freely within the network range and automatically switch to the next access point without losing connection, which can be exploited.

The next important parameter is the channel on which the AP transmits. This is the radio frequency band that is used to transmit wireless data between devices. Obtaining information on what specific channel is used by the AP is very simple using specialized toolkits, and is not a problem for the average attacker. Typically, this information will be available along with the SSID.

The final step in gathering information is to find out the authentication method. Like the previous cases, this information is easily obtained by scanning the network. It is much more difficult to try to break the authentication. In the case where the target of the attack is an open system, that is, the wireless devices connecting to it have access to the network without the need for authentication, attackers can already be sure that they will have no difficulty in carrying out the attack. A similar approach can be taken if WEP, or Wired Equivalent Privacy, authentication has been used on the network. This method of authentication is heavily outdated these days, and you can find many articles confirming the ease of breaking it. The case is different when WPA or WPA2, Wi-Fi Protected Access II, is used on the network. WPA2 is a currently promoted standard that can reliably secure a network against uninvited guests. In this case, one of the more reasonable options for attackers who are not professionals with a large background may be to attempt a dictionary attack, a Captive Portal attack or possibly try to use cloud computing, but if these attempts do not yield quick results, attackers will most likely abandon the whole enterprise, considering it too dangerous and challenging.

Due to the robustness exhibited by WPA2 and the already high difficulty of circumventing this security at this level, an even newer method, WPA3, which is slowly beginning to appear in wireless solutions, will not be addressed. In the case of WEP, it is relatively simple to obtain the required network password. A number of ready-made solutions and tools exist to make this possible. For example, using the tools from the aircrack-ng package, you just need to capture enough packets visible to all around that are exchanged between the user and the real AP. Then with the right command, the software will do everything for the attacker, effectively breaking the encryption and displaying the extracted password. In the case of WPA/WPA2, attackers will try to intercept the four-step WPA handshake that is sent when the user connects to the AP. Attackers will use deauthentication packets to temporarily disconnect the user from the network, which will immediately try to automatically reconnect, at which point the WPA handshake will be intercepted, allowing them to continue acting on it. Attackers can try a dictionary attack or even a Brute force attack on such an intercepted handshake. In the case of WPA/WPA2 by the improved design with respect to the previous version, attackers will only try their luck with a dictionary attack, if the complexity of the password is too complicated for this type of attack, they can try a much more interesting option, which is the Captive Portal attack.

The method of carrying out an Evil Twin attack is not the most subtle. It assumes a certain degree of carelessness on the part of network users. The attacker creates a Fake AP that mimics an existing network with the difference that it operates without any authentication method, i.e. as an open AP. In addition, a web server is run on the Fake AP. The attacker can try to disrupt the real AP, and users, seeing problems with the network, will try to connect to it again. When selecting a network, they will see two identical entries. Due to different authentication methods, they will appear separately, the system handling network listing will not merge them into one network in most cases. Attackers hope that someone will mistakenly connect to the Fake AP, in which case the victim will be redirected to a web page that the Fake AP provides. The page will be crafted in such a way as to not arouse suspicion, while at the same time trying to get the victim to enter sensitive data into the login field, for example, the password of the network they are connected to, suggesting to the victim that this is a normal Wi-Fi login step. There are pre-made page templates that are made available to the public and that attackers are eager to use. Available are sites mimicking popular social media, online stores, as well as configuration pages of various router vendors. One option for how an attack using a Fake AP can be carried out is that the moment the fake login is typed and approved, the Fake AP disconnects from the user and shuts down the shared network, the confused user will try to reconnect, this time choosing the only available original AP, returning to their business and most likely forgetting about the momentary inconvenience. The attacker, the moment the user typed and validated the password on the substituted page, acquired the password, in a time incomparably faster than if he had decided to do it with a forceful attack. This may raise the question of whether the mere establishment of a Fake AP to which an inattentive user has connected is not enough, being already in an advantageous situation that can be exploited. If the attackers are time sensitive and do not have a specific user selected as a target, this is a method that may be perfectly sufficient for them. However, there are several problems with this, firstly, in the lists of available networks, in most systems, you will see two networks with identical names. One open the other with a requirement to authenticate the connection through a password. This may draw the attention of people in the area who decide to inform the owner of the original network. Secondly, in such a case, attackers have to rely on whoever connects to the Fake AP, they can't try to use the automatic reconnection mechanism and take over the users of the trusted AP, because most systems will connect to the network with the authentication method memorized before disconnection. Likewise, it is not possible to precisely pick a target, only to rely on randomness.

The effectiveness of the next discussed method of getting the password of the attacked Wi-Fi network may seem a bit frivolous. Attackers should first check whether the Wi-Fi network password has been changed from the default to their own at all. The lists used in dictionary attacks may not contain all the default passwords of network equipment manufacturers, so attackers often use online databases of such passwords that are made publicly available. After identifying the vendor and device model, attackers have the default password at their fingertips. Unfortunately, all too often this method is successful.

However, if the previous method of obtaining a password may have seemed frivolous, the next one may seem absurd, unfortunately mainly because of its high effectiveness. The vulnerability used in this method occurs at layer 8. In jargon, layer 8 is referred to, among other things, the user's operation, referring to the ISO/OSI model, the last 7 layers of which are the application layer, and over which the user is assumed to operate. Social engineering is a tool eagerly used by all criminals, regardless of the area in which they operate. Social engineering is also readily used in digital security. This is caused by the much greater ease of getting the information needed or getting people to perform certain actions, often obtaining this without much effort. Without examining the vast topic of social engineering, it is worth noting that attackers can simply ask for a password.

3.1 Hardware and Software Configuration

The establishment of an Evil Twin requires the provision of several key elements that, working together, enable the Evil Twin and the network it spreads to function properly. The number of these services that support the Evil Twin necessitates some automation of the entire process via scripts if attackers care about executing the attack efficiently. A simpler option, instead of using separate tools, is to use software built specifically for Evil Twin, which runs the entire process of creating and taking over traffic in a few clicks. If you opt for personal configuration and use custom scripts, the basis is to create a WLAN that takes on the parameters of the network under attack. Then this network must provide support for new users, so running DHCP within it is required. The next element is the operation of DNS, the creation of its configuration compatible with the network to be created and the script that the process will run at the right time will be necessary for the entire attack to work. In many cases with DNS, log collection will be triggered, so attackers can actively track the victim's actions. Finally, the newly established network must provide access to the Internet. Therefore, the device that will be used for Evil Twin should be able to support two Wi-Fi networks simultaneously, whether using built-in cards or using external Wi-Fi cards. The first card will impersonate the real network, while the second card will be connected to the real one. In this way, the intercepted traffic will be redirected back to the real AP. The other solution is to redirect the traffic to another output to the Internet if only by implementing a GSM network in the device used.

It is also worth checking at this stage whether the network cards you have, on which the attack will operate, work with the software selected for the attack. It may happen that the drivers do not fully support all the necessary operations. This is quite a common occurrence, especially when it comes to the ability to put the card into a monitoring state, which involves collecting all visible wireless traffic in the environment. Frequently, the problem also lies in the software itself, which may not have been developed for a long time, or which does not work in certain cases for certain types of hardware. Appropriate matching of the software used is crucial when launching an attack.

3.2 Creation of Evil Twin

As with the reconnaissance, the Evil Twin can be created through the use of a laptop computer, sitting at a table in a café that is being targeted, or what is most common in reports of similar attacks, through specially concealed micro devices, giving no reason for suspicion by those around. Appearance of a new item on the premises, which the autonomous Evil Twin stores inside, will in most cases be considered an interesting interior design instead of a security-threatening premeditated attack. In the case of choosing a micro device, it is currently not a problem to provide it with a power source that will last for a considerable amount of time. There are a variety of small compact batteries sufficient to satisfy the time available for use by most attackers. If planning a longer attack, finding an unoccupied electrical outlet in such a place that a plugged-in Evil Twin would not be conspicuous should not be a problem either. Evil Twin can even mimic the network device in use at the company, which may even reduce the interest in it, and the possibility of cutting it off.

The attackers' communication with the Evil Twin on the micro-device can be done either through the network that the victims will connect to, or using a completely different approach of leaving the automated Evil Twin in the perimeter of the network, and then taking it back after a certain period of time, and reading from it any information gained during that time. Definitely easier, and less prone to errors that will stop the whole attack, is the approach with communication and management over the wireless network, thanks to the ability to connect to the ET and correct configuration errors.

The process of creating the Evil Twin itself is lichen-free, especially if it has been automated by scripts or using readymade tools. In this stage there should be no major problems, if any, related to incorrect preparation of configuration files and scripts in the previous stage or errors related to incompatible hardware.

3.3   Tuning the Functionality of the Evil Twin

After creating the impersonating WLAN, it is required to run all services one by one to ensure the proper operation of the network. Before that, the network interfaces must still be properly configured and, depending on the exact plan of attack, routing and firewall must be set up, and interfaces must be connected to allow data forwarding. Next, using previously created scripts and configurations to take care of DHCP and DNS on the network, Software specialized in such an attack will do most of these activities for the attacker himself.

3.4   Increasing the Chances of Attack

Signal strength plays an important role in the attack. During the attack, the real AP, as well as the Evil Twin, in a way compete with each other for the attention of users. The network that the victim will connect to, in the case that there are two identical ones, will generally be the one with the highest signal strength in the area. It is possible to increase the signal strength of an Evil Twin either by shortening the distance between it and the victim, or by increasing the distance between the victim and the real AP. There is also a third option, which is to increase the transmit power itself programmatically. It is done by changing the country profile of the network card to a country that has higher limits in this area than the limits in the current location. Simply changing the transmit power is prohibited and penalized, even in private use.

3.5   Interruption and Interception of Traffic

At the point when the fake duplicate network is ready, the attackers will start the process of taking over the users of the real AP. At this stage, two networks, indistinguishable at first glance, are in operation at the site of the attack. The attackers will want to disconnect users from the real AP at all costs, using all sorts of sabotage to hinder or even prevent its continued operation. This is most easily achieved through an attack by invalidating authentication. The simple method of severing the connection between the user and the real AP involves sending a de-authentication frame on behalf of the user to the real AP, which, reading it, will stop receiving sent data from the user and also send the user a de-authentication frame, which will inform the user that the connection has been severed. Immediately after the attack, most of the user's devices that were still connected to the real AP a moment ago will start automatically connecting to the known station. In some cases, users themselves can also be counted on to manually renew the connection. The moment the attackers have taken care of the signal strength advantage, all devices trying to renew connectivity will connect to Evil Twin, which will unfortunately end the successful attack.

3.6 Network Internal Reconnaissance

The attack that has been completed in this way, which is a great example of the MiTM family of attacks, is just a foundation that an experienced criminal can expand upon with the many capabilities available, so that he can nullify the successive layers of security he encounters, each time entangling the victim more and more. Intercepting data and injecting their own, seizing passwords, blocking access or redirecting to fake sites, just as in the case of the successful Rogue AP attack, are all available from now on for the attacker to exploit. And like the Rogue AP, more attacks are starting from this point, for which Evil Twin is merely the platform from which they will be derived.

4   The Logic of Attack

The process of establishing a connection between a device and a Wi-Fi network, is divided into three overlapping stages (Fig. 2). First, the device must discover APs in the area, this is achieved by scanning. If a network is discovered that the device wants to connect to, device authentication takes place, that is, checking the compatibility and capability of the network and the device. Finally, the association, i.e. binding to a single selected AP, takes place at the very end.

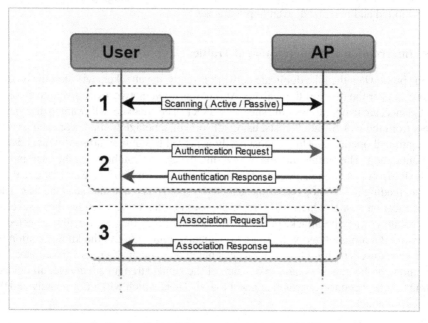

Fig. 2. Stages of establishing a connection to a Wi-Fi network

In order to join a network, a device must first find it. In Wi-Fi, this requires identifying a compatible network before the connection process can begin. This process of identifying a network is referred to as scanning. In the scanning process, network parameters must be learned. These parameters are BSSType, which determines the type of BSS to be included in the scan, the specified BSSID, SSID, activeScan, which determines whether to perform an active or passive scan, ChannelList which tells the list of channels to be scanned, ProbeDelay which determines the delay in seconds used before a probe frame is transmitted during an active scan, and MinChannelTime and MaxChannelTime which determines the minimum and maximum time to be spent on each channel during a scan [9]. These default parameters are set according to the Wi-Fi driver manufacturer, but can be modified by the user. If a hidden network is required, the user can set the boolean activeScan parameter to False, as active scanning will lead to SSID disclosure. The active and passive scans are two methods of network scanning. The default is for the transmitter to perform both types of scanning on all channels allowed in a given country. In Europe, 13 channels are used, while in the United States the standard is 11 channels.

In passive scanning (Fig. 3), the user device goes to each channel according to the channel list and waits for Beacon frames. Beacon frames are used by access points to communicate or announce themselves. The access point tries to send Beacon frames at a certain interval. This interval is called Target Beacon Transmission Time, or TBTT for short.

However, access points must respect the availability of the medium. They cannot send if the network is busy. In case an AP wants to send a Beacon frame and the network is busy, the AP will delay Beacon transmission until it can access the medium. In the 802.11 standard, the CSMA/CA protocol is responsible for supervising medium availability. Its operation involves the transmitting device checking whether the channel is free or busy to avoid collisions. If the channel is busy, the transmitting device waits for a random time and checks again whether the channel is idle or not. If the channel is free, it sends a frame. The information contained in the frame is used not only by potential clients during passive scanning, but also by clients that are already assigned to the BSS [10, 11].

In active scanning (Fig. 3), devices still go through each channel in turn, but instead of passively listening for signals from APs, they send a Probe Request management frame, whose purpose is to ask what network is available on that channel. If any AP uses that frequency, it should respond with a Probe Response frame. After the request is sent, by the emitting device, the Probe Timer starts counting down and waiting for a response. The Probe Timer value is usually much shorter than the Beacon frame interval. Most often the values are in the 10-ms range. After that time has elapsed, the device processes the responses it has received. In case no response has been received, the station moves to the next channel and repeats the same process [10].

The primary form of the attack gathers information about the network through one of two scanning methods available to ordinary network users. Use of specially prepared tools in this regard, simplifies and speeds up the whole process. If the targeted network is encrypted, attackers in order for Evil Twin to work properly must also acquire the key used in the encryption.

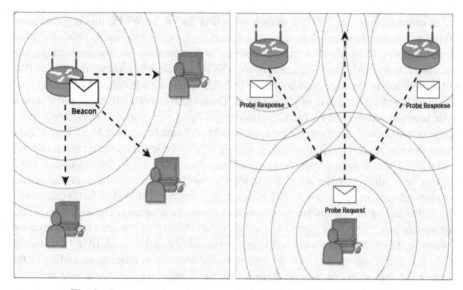

Fig. 3. Demonstration of the operation of passive and active scanning

In the case of using WEP, attackers have the ability to reconstruct the key using passively eavesdropped network communications. The attacker can rapidly acquire the key by acquiring the required number of packets from the traffic between the device and the AP [12]. The result is from the use of RC4 symmetric cipher for this purpose, which is vulnerable to attacks involving analysis of data encrypted with the same key. The modification of the encryption and the use of a socalled initialization vector did not improve the situation. More work on WEP security has shown the possibility of an attack termed "related key," which exploits similarities and mathematical relationships regarding the keys used. If the network is secured with WPA with TKIP encryption and WPA2 with CCMP encryption, vulnerabilities known to WEP cannot be exploited. Attackers in this case have a choice of offline force attacks, online force attacks, dictionary attacks and attempting to exploit cryptographic vulnerabilities in TKIP. The Pairwise Transient Key, abbreviated PTK, used to secure transmissions is created using the Pairwise Master Key, abbreviated PMK, which in turn is built based on the PreShared Key, abbreviated PSK, and certain data transmitted during 4-way handshake. In the situation where the attacker does not know the PSK after capturing additional values during the 4-way handshake, the attacker can try to launch a brute force attack aimed at guessing the PSK, which will result in gaining access to the network. In the attack, different PSK values are tried and then PMK and PTK are calculated for them to check if it is a valid value, using the acquired data from the 4-way handshake. During the ongoing 4-way handshake process in a wireless network, an attacker can intercept various types of information. While sending the first message from the access point to the client, the attacker can capture the access point's MAC address and ANonce ID. Then, when sending the second message from the client to the access point, an attacker can capture the client's MAC address and SNonce ID and key authentication, which has been encrypted using a WPA2 encryption key. However, even gaining this information, the size of the PSK's space of possible values, which ranges from 8 to 63 ASCII printable characters, makes it impossible for the average attacker to check all options. Therefore, the only option he is left with is a dictionary attack based on lists of known and frequently used passwords or an attack using rainbow tables. In case of failure to get the key, the main attack cannot be carried out, at least not in the form of Evil Twin.In order to improve the whole operation, attackers can use deauthorization frames. The frame is used when all communication is terminated, for instance because the AP has to be rebooted or because a station has stopped Wi-Fi communication. This is also used when a frame is received before authentication is completed. For example, a station attempting to send an association request or data frame before the authentication sequence is executed will then receive a deauthentication frame from the AP, indicating that authentication must be performed first. Attackers use specially crafted deauthentication frames to temporarily disconnect the victim from the network, so it will have to go through all three steps of connecting to the network from the beginning, but this time the Evil Twin will be waiting for the victim.

Another mechanism used by Evil Twin is Preferred Network List (PNL). Whenever the device searches for Wi-Fi, it scans its surroundings and shows a list of available networks within range. If a device detects a network that is on its PNL, it will automatically connect to that network, if only available. Network goes to the PNL list when a device connects to a network that is not yet on the list. When the Evil Twin pretends to be a trusted AP appearing on the PNL, it is treated exactly the same manner and with the same priority as the original network.

The last issue is the method by which the selection between Evil Twin and the real AP is made. When the device tries to reconnect to an AP in its PNL list and is confronted with a choice between the two options, the network with the stronger signal will be selected. The scheme of operation is based on the signal-strength-first assumption, and the device will choose the AP with the best signal-to-noise ratio. Evil Twin can increase its signal strength relative to the victim by reducing the distance from the victim to the Evil Twin, by using a better transmitter and antenna, or through software level manipulation of the transmit power settings.

5 Summary and Future Works

The article presents the logic and method of carrying out the Evil Twin attack, which, despite its presence in cyberspace for many years, remains a major and real threat. This is due not to the weakness of the technologies under attack, but primarily to the insufficient attention paid to network security issues by both network administrators and users. This is worth bearing in mind, especially in the context of easy access to hardware and free software that make such an attack possible.

The article is a kind of introduction, both theoretical and practical, in future research taking into account different methods of attacks and its different variants. The planned research will be qualitative in nature - it will seek to determine the degree and extent of the implementation of the various functions and their practical use, as well as quantitative in nature - it will seek to determine, among other things, the time required to prepare and execute an attack, and determine the factors that have a direct effect on the effectiveness of the chosen method of attack.

Acknowledgments. The authors thank the Polish Ministry of Education and Science for financial support (Applied Doctorate Program, No. DWD/6/0058/2022). This research was funded in part by the Polish Ministry of Science and Higher Education (No. 0313/SBAD/1310).

References

1. Shrivastava, P., Jamal, M.S., Kataoka, K.: EvilScout: detection and mitigation of evil twin attack in SDN enabled WiFi. IEEE Trans. Netw. Serv. Manage. **17**(1), 89–102 (2020). https://doi.org/10.1109/TNSM.2020.2972774
2. Asaduzzaman, M., Majib, M.S., Rahman, M.M.: Wi-Fi frame classification and feature selection analysis in detecting evil twin attack. In: 2020 IEEE Region 10 Symposium (TENSYMP), Dhaka, Bangladesh, pp. 1704–1707 (2020). https://doi.org/10.1109/TENSYMP50017.2020.9231042
3. Nakhila, O., Zou, C.: User-side Wi-Fi evil twin attack detection using random wireless channel monitoring. In: 2016 IEEE Military Communications Conference (MILCOM 2016), Baltimore, MD, USA, pp. 1243–1248 (2016). https://doi.org/10.1109/MILCOM.2016.7795501
4. Wasil, D., Nakhila, O., Bacanli, S.S., Zou, C., Turgut, D.: Exposing vulnerabilities in mobile networks: a mobile data consumption attack. In: 2017 IEEE 14th International Conference on Mobile Ad Hoc and Sensor Systems (MASS), Orlando, FL, USA, pp. 550–554 (2017). https://doi.org/10.1109/MASS.2017.76
5. Agarwal, M., Biswas, S., Nandi, S.: An efficient scheme to detect evil twin rogue access point attack in 802.11 Wi-Fi networks. Int. J. Wirel. Inf. Netw. **25**(2), 130–145 (2018). https://doi.org/10.1007/s10776-018-0396-1
6. Wang, C., et al.: Detecting Evil-Twin attack with the crowd sensing of landmark in physical layer. In: Vaidya, J., Li, J. (eds.) Algorithms and Architectures for Parallel Processing (ICA3PP 2018). LNCS, vol. 11337, pp. 234–248. Springer, Cham (2018). https://doi.org/10.1007/978-3-030-05063-4_19
7. Louca, C., Peratikou, A., Stavrou, S.: A novel Evil Twin MiTM attack through 802.11 v protocol exploitation. Comput. Secur. **130**, 103261 (2023). https://doi.org/10.1016/j.cose.2023.103261
8. Hsu, F.H., Hsu, Y.L., Wang, C.S.: A solution to detect the existence of a malicious rogue AP. Comput. Commun. **142**, 62–68 (2019). https://doi.org/10.1016/j.comcom.2019.03.013
9. OpenSim: INET framework: https://doc.omnetpp.org/inet/api-4.4.0/neddoc/inet-ieee80211-Ieee80211Prim_ScanRequest.html. Accessed 10 Apr 2023
10. BBC News: How the Dutch foiled Russian 'cyber-attack' on OPCW. https://www.bbc.com/news/world-europe-45747472. Accessed 10 Apr 2023
11. Greenberg, A.: How Russian spies infiltrated hotel Wi-Fi to hack victims up close. https://www.wired.com/story/russian-spies-indictment-hotel-wi-fi-hacking/. Accessed 10 Apr 2023
12. Esser, A.: Evil-Twin framework. https://repositorio.iscte-iul.pt/bitstream/10071/15151/1/evil-twin-framework%283%29.pdf. Accessed 10 Apr 2023

UAVs Communication Redundancy Checking Graph Algorithm

Stanisław Skrzypecki[✉]

Faculty of Cybernetics, Military University of Technology, Warsaw, Poland
stanislaw.skrzypecki@wat.edu.pl

Abstract. In the paper UAVs communication redundancy checking graph algorithm is presented. Algorithm consists of several steps including vertex labelling and using known algorithms as Suurballe's and Breadth-First Search's (BFS). It may be applied to check whether between every two aircrafts of UAV swarm communication with redundancy is provided at the moment. The assumption is that solving the mentioned problem will allow us to identify UAVs configurations that may be susceptible to single points of failure.

Keywords: UAVs communication redundancy · UAVs network · graph algorithm · vertex disjoint paths

1 Introduction

Providing communication is crucial to operate with many UAVs (Unmanned – or Uncrewed Aerial Vehicles) such as swarms, UAVs networks, FANETs. Only effective communication is able to provide UAVs with the necessary performance parameters, such as coordination, situational awareness (which allows the swarm to adapt to dynamic situations and make informed decisions), task allocation, safety, redundancy, division or optimize overall mission performance (e.g. for energy or path of optimization). One of the key issues (both theoretical and practical) is to provide redundancy in communication between network-forming or swarm-forming UAVs. Communication characteristics may vary depending of purpose of UAVs usage such as for internet delivery or disaster communication (with fixed position, with low mobility, low probability of delays and disruptions with centralized control), for reconnaissance or tacking missions (with more coordinated movement, with medium mobility, medium probability of delays and disruptions with centralized or distributed control), for combat missions (with fixed position, with low mobility, low probability of delays and disruptions with centralized control) [4]. Within UAVs networks with ground station, there are many types and topologies of networks designed to provide communication within UAVs: star, multi-star, mesh or hierarchical mesh. Star stands for topology when UAVs connects directly to one or more ground stations, multi-star when one UAV from group connects to ground station; mesh topology is applicable when aircrafts are connected with each other and some also connects to ground station, in case of hierarchical mesh aircrafts are combined in groups.

© The Author(s), under exclusive license to Springer Nature Switzerland AG 2024
K. S. Soliman (Ed.): IBIMA-AI 2023, CCIS 2101, pp. 237–249, 2024.
https://doi.org/10.1007/978-3-031-62843-6_24

The main problem which is considered in the paper is following:

In the air there is a group of unmanned aerial vehicles. Every UAV is equipped with a short-range communication module. It shall be verified that each ship has redundant communication with any other aircraft through at least two different communication paths consisting of unique aircrafts.

Presented problem of neighbor-based communication, where each UAV maintains communication with its neighboring UAVs within a certain range may be considered as a unidirected graph, where the vertices are aircrafts and the edges indicate the possible connection between two ships within range of their communication modules. The one of assumptions is that is possible to store information's from aircrafts in one place basing on their locations and communication ranges to build such graph. Moreover, the problem will be resolved in the manner of the current state of aircrafts. The assumption is that the identification of UAVs configurations which might be vulnerable to single points of failure. So this is particularly relevant for more static networks, but also may be temporarily applicable to dynamic and self-organizing mesh networks or UAV swarms in order to check current configuration. Solution may be used both in ad-hoc networks and with infrastructure-based if base station will be presented as another vertex in the graph. The solution in the presented problem does not require to find shortest paths, but only to confirm that exist at least two between every two pairs of aircraft. The solution does not need to cover all routing issues in the UAV networks itself like in routing protocols in UAVs or FANET networks such as proactive, reactive, hybrid protocols (e.g. BABEL, B.A.T.M.A.N., AODV or TORA) [4]. It also does not necessarily have to address the challenges specific to FANET networks, such as: variations in communication distance, ground reflection effects, shadowing resulting from the electronic equipment, the effect of aircraft attitude, environmental conditions or interferences and hostile jamming [2].

Moreover, the presented paper address problem of redundant communication between UAVs which stands for problem of finding at least two disjoint paths in graph multiply times for every two vertices. In literature problem finding K disjoint shortest paths can be found with many algorithms solving it. Although it was considered as NP-complete [6], there are algorithms where complexity was found as $O(n^3)$ [7] or even $O(n^2)$ [5]. In the paper of [10] provides short survey of other algorithms starting of starting with Suurballe algorithm which solves the discussed problem as a special case of the minimum-cost flow problem and utilizes two efficient implementations of the Dijkstra's algorithm to find the shortest path from a single vertex [9]. They mentioned works by [8] and [3] of finding two disjoint paths between in directed acyclic graphs (DAGs) which can be generalized to find a bundle of d disjoint paths between specified endpoints. They also presented their own modification of Edmonds-Karp method to solve problem of finding vertex-disjoint shortest paths passing through selected vertices in grid-structured networks.

2   Redundancy Checking Algorithm

The presented problem could be solved by using known algorithms for searching for disjoint paths as presented in introduction by search for them between every two aircrafts (vertices). However, the idea of proposed redundancy checking algorithm is basing on assumption that if there exists at least two vertex disjoint paths between two randomly chosen vertex (the beginning vertex and ending vertex), then from each vertex on this paths there exist two vertex disjoint paths to any other vertex in this paths. The vertices in this initial paths are labelled as confirmed. Moreover, if any next vertex from unconfirmed set has disjoint path for to the two different vertices from confirmed set it imply that there is also at least two vertex disjoint paths to every vertex in confirmed set and this vertex can be also to the confirmed set added. After checking in this manner each unconfirmed vertex it can be concluded that between every two vertices at least two vertex disjoint paths can be found.

The algorithm is as follows:

1. Choose two random vertex from the graph.
2. Find two vertex-disjoint path between chosen vertices (e.g. using the Surballe's algorithm and by transition to directed graph).
3. The vertices belonging to the found vertex-disjoint paths label with C (as confirmed).
4. Remove the edges belonging to the found vertex-disjoint paths.
5. As long as remain vertices which are unlabeled with C repeat:

   a Select any unlabeled with C vertex which is incident with an already labeled with C vertex and remove the edge between them.

   b Find path from the selected vertex to any other vertex which is labeled with C (e.g. using the BFS algorithm).

   c Label with C the selected vertex and all vertices in found path and remove the edges in this path.
6. If there is no more unlabeled vertices left, then each vertex in the initial graph has two vertex disjoint paths to any other. In the other case or if failed in complete any previous step there is no solution for such graph.

The most complex in the redundancy checking graph algorithm is step 2, however two vertex disjoint paths between two vertices can be found using Suurballe's algorithm [9], which is as follows.

Let G be a weighted directed graph with a set of vertices V and edges E. Let s be the starting vertex and t be the ending vertex. Each edge between any vertices u and v has a weight $w(u,v)$. Let $d(s,u)$ represent the cost of the shortest path from vertex s to any vertex u in the shortest path tree T with the root at the starting vertex s. The procedure is as follows:

1. Find the shortest path tree T with the root at the starting vertex s using Dijkstra's algorithm. The tree T contains the shortest path from the starting vertex s to each vertex u. Let P1 be the shortest path from the starting vertex s to the ending vertex t.
2. Modify the cost $w(u,v)$ of each edge (u,v) in the graph according to the equation:

$$w'(u, v) = w(u, v) - d(s, v) + d(s, u).$$

     With the function w', all edges in the tree T will have a cost of 0, and the remaining edges will have a non-negative cost.

3. Create the residual graph Gt based on the graph G by removing the edges from the path P1 that are directed towards the vertex s and reverse the direction of edges with a cost of 0 along the path P1.
4. Find the shortest path P2 in the residual graph Gt using Dijkstra's algorithm.
5. Remove opposite edges from both paths P1 and P2. The remaining edges in paths P1 and P2 form a subgraph that has two outgoing edges from s, two incoming edges to t, and one incoming and outgoing edge from each remaining vertex in this subgraph. The subgraph consists of two edge-disjoint paths from s to t, and additional cycles with a cost of 0 may appear within this subgraph. The result of the algorithm is two disjoint paths.

     In order to find path in step 5. b) in redundancy checking algorithm the BFS algorithm can be used. The well-known algorithm explores the graph in a breadth-first manner, visiting all vertices at the current level before moving to the next level. It guarantees that vertices are visited in increasing order of their distance from the starting vertex.

     Computational complexity of presented algorithm is about $O(V^2 + EV + E\log_{(1/-E/V)}V)$ basing on single application of the Suurbale's algorithm with complexity of $O(E\log(1 + E/V)V$ [10] and the multiply usage (V-2) of the BFS with complexity $O(V + E)$ algorithm.

3   Algorithm's Example Solution

In order to explain how works the proposed algorithm, an example solution for a graph G consisting of set of 17 vertices and 23 edges (on Fig. 1) is discussed and graphically presented in this chapter.

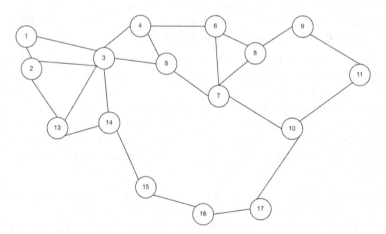

Fig. 1. UAVs swarm presented as graph G.

1. Choose two random vertex from the graph, e.g. vertices 3 and 9. (step no. 1 on Fig. 2)

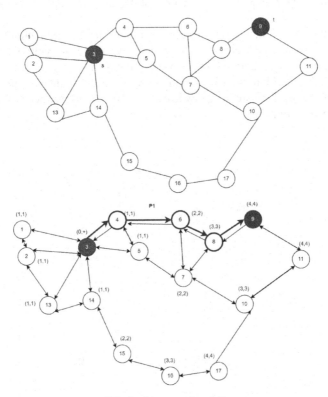

Fig. 2. Steps no. 1 and 2.

2. Find two vertex-disjoint path between chosen vertices (Suurballe's algorithm can be used; if there are no paths, there is no solution; due to the lack of weights, we assume that the weight of each edge is 1; during the execution of the Suurballe's algorithm, we convert the graph G into a directed graph, and after its application, we restore the graph to its undirected form).

   a Suurballe's algorithm (step 1) – finding the first path P1 using Dijkstra's algorithm. (step no. 2 on Fig. 2)

   b Suurballe's algorithm (step 1 continued) – based on Dijkstra's algorithm, the shortest path tree T is determined with the calculated distance $d(s, u)$ to each vertex u. (step no. 3 on Fig. 3) c Suurballe's algorithm (step 2) – calculation of edge weights $w'(u,v)$. (step no. 4 on Fig. 3)

d Suurballe's algorithm (step 3) – creation of the residual graph G_t. (step no. 5

e on Fig. 4)

f Suurballe's algorithm (step 4) – determination of the shortest path P2 using Dijkstra's algorithm Algorytm Suurballe (krok 4) – wyznaczenie najkrótszej ścieżki P2 z wykorzystaniem algorytmu Dijkstry. (step no. 6 on Fig. 4)

g Suurballe's algorithm (Step 5) – obtaining two vertex-disjoint paths that are P1 and P2. In this case, there are no opposite edges in both paths that need to be removed. (step no. 7 on Fig. 5)

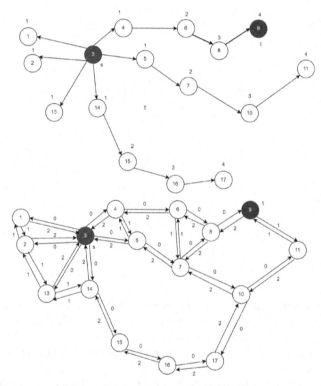

Fig. 3. Steps no. 3 and 4.

3. The vertices belonging to the found vertex-disjoint paths label with C (as confirmed). (step no. 8 on Fig. 5)

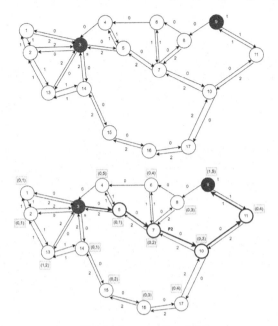

Fig. 4. Steps no. 5 and 6.

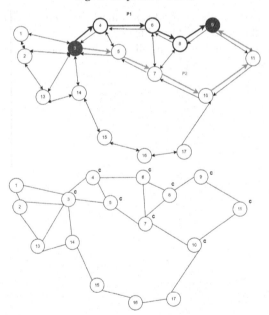

Fig. 5. Steps no. 7 and 8.

4. Remove the edges belonging to the found vertex-disjoint paths. (step no. 9 on Fig. 6)
5. (Repeat no. 1) As long as remain vertices which are unlabeled with C repeat:
   a Select any unlabeled with C vertex which is incident with an already labeled with C vertex and remove the edge between them. (step no. 10 on Fig. 6)

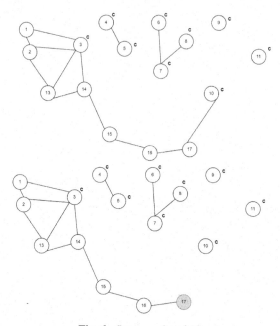

Fig. 6. Steps no. 9 and 10.

b Find path from the selected vertex to any other vertex which is labeled with C using the BFS algorithm. (step no. 11 on Fig. 7)

c Label with C the selected vertex and all vertices in found path and remove the edges in this path. (step no. 12 on Fig. 7)

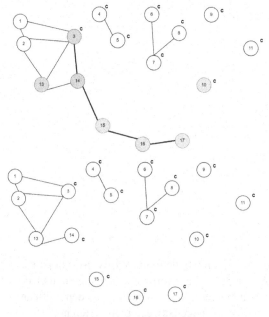

Fig. 7. Steps no. 11 and 12.

6. (Repeat no. 2) As long as remain vertices which are unlabeled with C repeat:
   a Select any unlabeled with C vertex which is incident with an already labeled with C vertex and remove the edge between them. (step no. 13 on Fig. 8)
   b Find path from the selected vertex to any other vertex which is labeled with C using the BFS algorithm. (step no. 14 on Fig. 8)
   c Label with C the selected vertex and all vertices in found path and remove the edges in this path. (step no. 15 on Fig. 9)

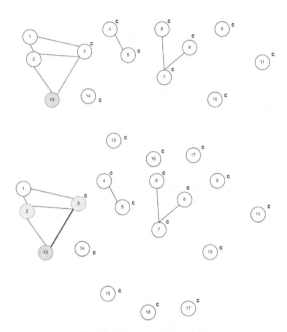

Fig. 8. Steps no. 13 and 14.

6. (Repeat no. 3) As long as remain vertices which are unlabeled with C repeat:
   a Select any unlabeled with C vertex which is incident with an already labeled with C vertex and remove the edge between them. (step no. 16 on Fig. 9)
   b Find path from the selected vertex to any other vertex which is labeled with C using the BFS algorithm. (step no. 17 on Fig. 10)
   c Label with C the selected vertex and all vertices in found path and remove the edges in this path. (step no. 18 on Fig. 10)

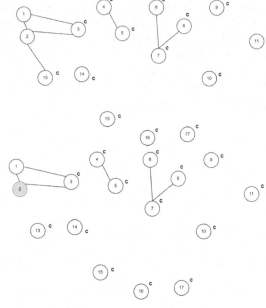

Fig. 9. Steps no. 15 and 16.

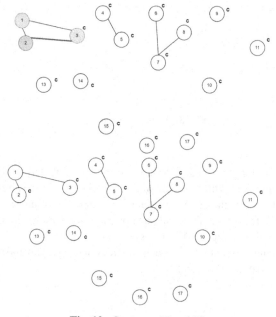

Fig. 10. Steps no. 17 and 18.

7. (Repeat no. 4) As long as remain vertices which are unlabeled with C repeat:
   a Select any unlabeled with C vertex which is incident with an already labeled with C vertex and remove the edge between them. (step no. 19 on Fig. 11)
   b Find path from the selected vertex to any other vertex which is labeled with C using the BFS algorithm. (step no. 20 on Fig. 11)
   c Label with C the selected vertex and all vertices in found path and remove the edges in this path. (step no. 21 on Fig. 12)

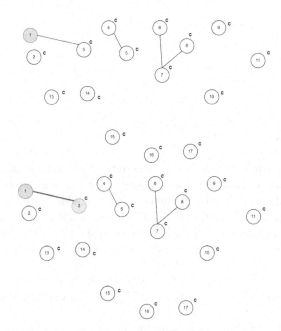

Fig. 11. Steps no. 19 and 20.

9. In the end on Fig. 12 in the remaining graph there is no more unlabeled vertices left, then each vertex in the initial graph has two vertex disjoint paths to any other. There is redundant communication between any two aircrafts in UAV network.

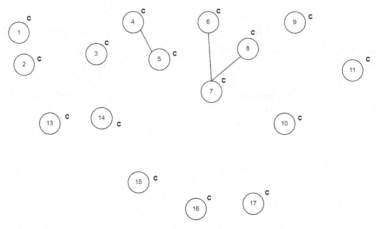

Fig. 12. Step no. 21.

4   Conclusion

The algorithm can only be used to determine the redundancy in the communication of the current state of the UAV swarm, which is on the one hand its assumption, but on the other hand also a crucial limitation. The algorithm does not provide the shortest paths, or even energy optimal ones, but is to designed to fulfill the simple task of confirming redundancy in communication. It is not complicated or computationally expensive according to one-time application of the Suurbale's algorithm and multiple usage of the BFS algorithm. Algorithm can be applied not only to UAVs but also to every case where vertex disjoints paths between all vertices in graph should be found. It can be also applied to configuration infrastructure-based configuration where both UAVs and base station should be presented as vertices in graph.

The algorithm works only in static manner and does not provide dynamic behavior to maintain such communication (e.g. selecting ships – vertices – which are crucial to maintain redundancy or determining which ones lost communication and where should be moved to provide it with the lowest cost). Examples of future works for the proposed algorithm may present implementation of algorithm with experimentations (both simulation and real life), wider analysis of computational complexity, and comparative analysis with other algorithms.

References

1. Adoni, W.Y.H., Lorenz, S., Fareedh, J.S., Gloaguen, R., Bussmann, M.: Investigation of autonomous multi-UAV systems for target detection in distributed environment: current developments and open challenges. Drones **7**, 263 (2023). https://doi.org/10.3390/drones704 0263
2. Bekmezci, İ, Sahingoz, O.K., Temel, Ş: Flying ad-hoc networks (FANETs): a survey. Ad Hoc Netw. **11**, 1254–1270 (2013). https://doi.org/10.1016/j.adhoc.2012.12.004
3. Eppstein, D.: Finding common ancestors and disjoint paths in DAGs. Department of Information and Computer Science University of California, Irvine (1995)

4. Gupta, L., Jain, R., Vaszkun, G.: Survey of important issues in UAV communication networks. IEEE Commun. Surv. Tutor. **18**, 1123–1152 (2016). https://doi.org/10.1109/COMST.2015.2495297

5. Kawarabayashi, K., Kobayashi, Y., Reed, B.: The disjoint paths problem in quadratic time. J. Comb. Theory Ser. B **102**, 424–435 (2012). https://doi.org/10.1016/j.jctb.2011.07.004

6. Middendorf, M., Pfeiffer, F.: On the complexity of the disjoint paths problem. Combinatorica **13**, 97–107 (1993). https://doi.org/10.1007/BF01202792

7. Robertson, N., Seymour, P.D.: Graph minors. XIII. The disjoint paths problem. J. Comb. Theory Ser. B **63**, 65–110 (1995). https://doi.org/10.1006/jctb.1995.1006

8. Shiloach, Y., Perl, Y.: Finding two disjoint paths between two pairs of vertices in a graph. J. ACM **25**, 1–9 (1978). https://doi.org/10.1145/322047.322048

9. Suurballe, J.W.: Disjoint paths in a network. Networks **4**(2), 125–145 (1974). https://doi.org/10.1002/net.3230040204

10. Tarapata, Z., Wroclawski, S.: Methods for solving the problem of finding vertex-disjoint shortest paths passing through selected vertices in grid-structured networks. In polish: Metody rozwiązywania problemu najkrótszych dróg wierzchołkowo rozłącznych przechodzących przez wybrane wierzchołki w sieciach o strukturze kraty. Biuletyn Wojskowej Akademii Technicznej **60**, 201–229 (2011)

Computer-Aided Design of Electric Drives with FEA Software

Michał Manka[1,2(✉)], Grzegorz Karpiel[1,2], and Daniel Prusak[1,2]

[1] RIOT Sp. z o.o., ul. M. i B. Wysłouchów 26/26, 30-612, Kraków, Poland
[2] Faculty of Mechanical Engineering and Robotics, Department of Robotics and Mechatronics, AGH University of Krakow, Al. Mickiewicza 30, 30-059 Kraków, Poland
{mmanka,gkarpiel,daniel.prusak}@agh.edu.pl

Abstract. The rapid development of new technologies in recent years leads to a significant reduction in time-to-market. It requires a significant increase in research and development expenditure or a change in the design process. Such a change was the introduction of virtual prototyping techniques, i.e.: Finite Element Analysis (FEA). Initially, FEA was limited to mechanics, however, the introduction of multi-domain simulation, allows to study other physical phenomena, such as thermal or electromagnetic, which are of interest to us in this case. Often in commercial applications, time pressure limits the scope of research for an optimal solution to shorten the research time, which leads to suboptimal solutions. In the case presented in the paper, virtual prototyping techniques were used in the design process of the BLDC direct drive using FEA techniques, the main criterion of which was to shorten the design time while maintaining a wide range of tests and high test accuracy. The proposed methodology assumes using 2D simulations for approximate tests and then accurate 3D simulations only for selected, most promising configurations. Approximate 2D tests are several times faster than 3D tests, which means that it can be tested significantly more configurations at the same time, which increases the chance of finding the global optimum of the structure. The use of FEA 3D tests for selected constructions significantly improves the accuracy of the results obtained and allows for the final selection of the best solution. The example presented in the paper allowed for the design of the BLDC motor, taking into account the testing of 31 different BLDC drive configurations, and thus determining its optimal design, confirmed by the construction of the final prototype.

Keywords: Simulation · FEM · FEA · Electric Motors

1 Introduction

Virtual prototyping techniques allow you to test various product concepts and optimise them in a much shorter time and at lower costs. Only the best constructions are next selected for physical prototyping, which significantly affects the products' quality. The article proposes a method for selecting the best BLDC drive design based on the simulation of its operation using the finite element method. FEM environments that also

K. S. Soliman (Ed.): IBIMA-AI 2023, CCIS 2101, pp. 250–263, 2024.
https://doi.org/10.1007/978-3-031-62843-6_25

consider electromagnetic phenomena allow for simulation testing of the impact of various motor parameters, e.g., the number of magnets and windings and the air gap and magnet thickness on the density of the electromagnetic field and the cogging and electromagnetic torque. Three-dimensional FEM (3D-FEM) simulations, especially taking into account the Multiphysics approach, are a very resource-intensive and time-consuming process. On the other hand, analysis performed only in two dimensions with FEM (2D-FEM) allows for a significant simplification of calculations and, thus, their considerable acceleration. Unfortunately, this is burdened with the deterioration of the accuracy of the obtained results.

1.1 Electric Motors

Currently, many different types of drives are available on the market; however, electric drives are most often used in mechatronics due to their flexibility. In addition to the well-known and commonly used electric drives such as brushless motors, stepper motors or electric linear motors, more and more popular become multi-pole direct motors, which are a variety of brushless DC motors (BLDCM) and a very specialised and narrow group of piezoelectric drives [5].

Direct BLDC motors significantly simplify the construction of the device itself and increase its failure-free operation, thus improving the designed devices' reliability. In addition, the increasing possibilities of controlling such motors, both in terms of hardware and software, allows for the development of multi-pole solutions in which both the speed of the motor and the torque generated by it can be smoothly regulated.

These types of motors will be discussed and simulated in the following chapters of this article.

1.2 The Finite Element Method in the Modelling of Electromagnetic Phenomena

Finite element methods (FEM) are computational methods that allow to obtain approximate solutions of differential equations. They are widely used in various fields of technology and science to solve both linear and non-linear problems in steady and transient states. This type of method is most often used in static and dynamic simulations of mechanical systems, strength calculations, and modal analyses, as well as in calculations related to fluid dynamics or electromagnetic phenomena, which will be described in more detail in this publication.

Currently, a whole range of different numerical tools, both commercial and free, are available on the market. The most widely used tools include ANSYS [5], ADAMS, COMSOL [3], and FLUX3D. These solutions are most often dedicated to simulations using the finite element method. Still, some solutions extend the capabilities of CAD/CAE environments that primarily use the multi-body modelling methods with FEM solvers, such as LMS Virtual.Lab, for the CATIA software or EMS, for the SolidWorks package or Autodesk Inventor.

In addition to a wide range of commercial tools, there are also partially free tools with limited functionality in which more advanced functions are available only after purchasing a paid license or entirely free of charge, which the perfect example is the FEMM (Finite Element Method Magnetics) calculation package presented below.

2 Methodology of the Design Process Using FEM Analysis

The initial stage of research related to the selection of the optimal geometric distribution of magnets in the motor was the theoretical analysis of possible solutions. For this purpose, various motor configurations were tested.

The main guidelines for the selection of engine parameters, and thus the tested solutions, were:

- Three-phase motor;
- Number of coils below 20;
- Number of pole pairs below 10;
- Supply current 10A;
- Only balanced configurations were considered.

As a result of preliminary analytical considerations, the parameters having the most significant impact on the operation of the BLDC motor were selected for the initial simulations [1, 4]. The tested configurations, meeting the initial requirements presented earlier, are shown in Table 1.

Table 1. Geometric configurations of the engine tested during the simulation

Analysis of the impact of magnet distribution (Number of Coils × Number of Magnets)	Analysis of the influence of coil distribution (Number of Coils × Number of Magnets)	Study of the effect of the gap width
12 × 8	3 × 20	0,5 [mm]
12 × 10	6 × 20	1,0 [mm]
12 × 16	9 × 20	1,5 [mm]
12 × 20	12 × 20	2,0 [mm]
	15 × 20	2,5 [mm]

Then, the optimal three-phase motor power supply configuration was defined for each design. Examples of power supply diagrams obtained using the online tool available [9] are shown in Fig. 1.

Configuration 3x20	Configuration 6x20	Configuration 9x20
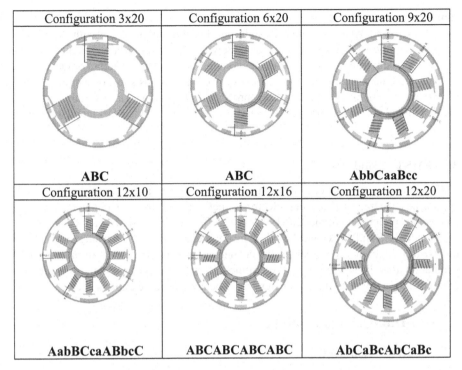		
ABC	**ABC**	**AbbCaaBcc**
Configuration 12x10	Configuration 12x16	Configuration 12x20
AabBCcaABbcC	**ABCABCABCABC**	**AbCaBcAbCaBc**

Fig. 1. Example configurations of the BLDC drive

Then, such selected configurations were implemented in simulation environments using the MES Multiphysics approach.

2.1 FEA Computing Environments

During the simulation tests, two FEM environments were used to allow for the inclusion of electromagnetic phenomena in the simulation process. In the first step, coarse simulations, the 2D-FEM environment was used, FEMM 4.2. Then, after determining the motor's geometric structure based on the simulation results, 3D-FEM simulations were carried out to determine the remaining parameters of the motor, for example, the type of windings. These simulations were carried out in a SolidWorks environment with an additional EMS toolbox.

2.2 FEMM 4.2 Environment

The FEMM package is software that allows the use of the finite element method in solving two-dimensional problems concerning electrostatic, magnetostatic and electromagnetic phenomena for low frequencies as well as problems related to thermal flows in steady states. Simplified Maxwell equations [7] are used to solve these problems. The program also has an implemented LUA scripting language [2], which allows for significant automation of the model creation process, its optimisation and simulation, as well as the analysis of results. In addition, the libraries provided with the FEMM software and the LUA scripting language allow for the integration of calculations also with external environments for numerical computations, such as Matlab or Octave.

The modular structure of the FEMM environment, consisting of a preprocessor, MESH mesh generator, solver and postprocessor, allows for extensive automation of computational processes through the use of scripts created in the LUA language at each stage.

2.3 EMS for SolidWorks

EMS is an electromagnetic field simulation software using multi-domain FEM approaches capable of modelling electromagnetic fields, circuit parameters as well as mechanical parameters of modelled systems [8]. This tool is available as an extension to the CAD/CAE SolidWorks and Autodesk Inventor environments. This integration allows the use of full geometric models of the created systems in the process of multi-domain simulation as well as parameterisation of models and a series of simulations examining the impact of a given model parameter on the behaviour of the entire system.

3   Two-Dimensional Analysis

3.1   Model Development

The FEMM environment allows you to directly build 2D models, which are then used in further calculations, but it is a tedious and time-consuming process. Therefore, the SolidWorks environment was used to create the models, and then the resulting sketches were exported to the DXF format and imported to FEMM 4.2.

Preparation of the model in the FEMM environment included:

- Defining the research topic.

    All analyses were carried out for a flat case of magnetic analysis; however, these results were scaled by the postprocessor to a motor having a length of 15 mm.
- Definition of materials for individual elements of the modelled motor.

    To carry out the simulation, the individual elements of the engine were given physical properties by assigning them appropriate materials from the program's library:

Rotor housing: 316 Stainless Steel
Permanent magnets: NdFeB 40 MGOe with radial magnetisation direction, placed alternately
Winding cores and stator: 1010 steel
Windings: Copper wire with a diameter of 0.4 mm, wound in the form of 100 windings
Gaps between rotor and stator: Air

- Boundary conditions were defined as Dirichlet conditions on an arc determined by the outside diameter of the casing. In this case, the magnetic field generated by the motor does not go beyond its housing.

- The model also defines the motor power supply and assigns the individual power supply phases to the appropriate windings.
- Then, the model was digitised, a triangular MESH mesh was generated, and simulations were performed.

Since the FEMM environment can perform calculations of the magnetic field only in steady states, the capabilities of the LUA scripting language were used to obtain the transient conditions prevailing in the rotating motor. As a result, in each step of the simulation, the position of the rotor relative to the stator and the power parameters of individual coils changed. The results obtained for each step were saved in the form of graphic files showing the distribution of the magnetic field (Fig. 2) and a text file with the received data, which was then used in the Matlab environment to analyse the results.

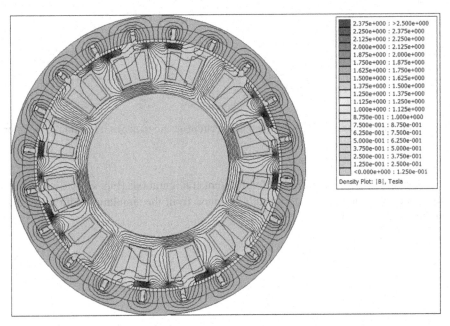

Fig. 2. Example distribution of the magnetic field in the engine

3.2 Analysis of the Obtained Results

The first step in the analysis was to compare the variability of the cogging torque (Fig. 3) and the electromagnetic torque as a function of the angular position and the calculation of the maximum torque for the supply current of 10A.

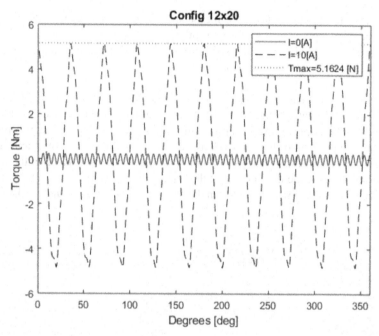

Fig. 3. Variation of the cogging torque and the electromagnetic torque as a function of the rotor position

Then the results were compared for different configurations (Fig. 4). A similar analysis was also carried out for the results obtained from the simulation with a variable number of magnets (Fig. 5).

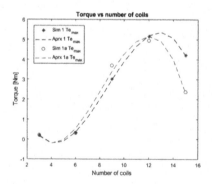

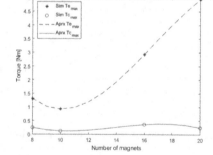

Fig. 4. The influence of the number of coils on the torque generated by the motor

Fig. 5. Influence of the number of magnets on the torque generated by the motor

Based on the analysis, a configuration consisting of 12 coils and 10 pairs of magnetic poles was selected for further research.

In the course of further research, the influence of the variability of the size of the air gap and the thickness of the magnet on the obtained electromagnetic torque was examined. The tests were limited only to the 12 × 20 configuration, in which the configurations assuming the width of the slot: 0.5; 1; 1.5; 2; 2.5 mm and the thickness of the magnets from 20 to 50 mm in 5-mm steps were tested. The obtained results are presented below (Figs. 6 and 7).

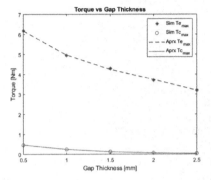 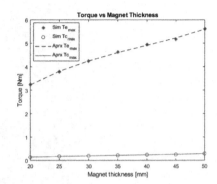

Fig. 6. Influence of the width of the gap on the torque generated by the motor.

Fig. 7. Influence of the thickness of the magnet on the torque generated by the motor.

The simulations and analyses of the results obtained in the FEMM 4.2 environment allowed for the initial selection of the optimal geometry of the designed BLDC motor. The 12 × 20 configuration was chosen for further testing.

4 Three-Dimensional Analyses

In the next step, the pre-designed drive was designed as a 3D object in the Solid-Works environment. And then, the selected geometric configuration was tested during simulations.

4.1 Model Development

As in the previous step, the first step was to prepare the engine geometry in the SolidWorks environment. The preparation of the EMS-SW model included:

- Building a 3D engine model (Fig. 8).
- The range of the electromagnetic field is defined by additional 3D objects covering the regions around the engine components.
- Defining the research topic.

  All analyses were carried out for the 3D model in the "Magnetostatic analysis" type.
- Definition of materials for individual elements of the modelled motor.

  To carry out the simulation, individual motor's components were given physical properties by assigning them appropriate materials from the EMS program library, which also took into account the electromagnetic properties:

Rotor housing: Stainless steel

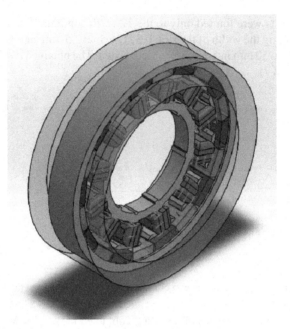

Fig. 8. Model of the designed BLDC motor in the 12 × 20 configuration modelled in the SW-EMS environment

Permanent magnets: S2818 with radial magnetisation direction, placed alternately
Winding cores and stator: 1010 steel
Windings: Copper wire of variable diameter depending on the simulation (Table 2), wound on the core. The number of turns relies on the thickness of the wire to obtain a constant filling factor.
The gaps between the rotor and the stator and the space around the motor: Air.

- The method of virtual work was chosen to calculate the electromagnetic force.
- The model also defines the motor power supply and assigns the individual power supply phases to the appropriate windings.
- Then, the model was discretised, a MESH mesh was generated (Fig. 9), and simulations were performed.

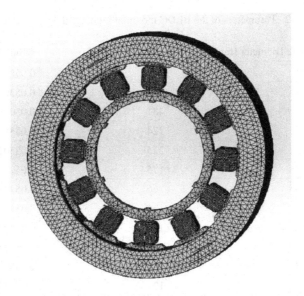

Fig. 9. Model of the designed BLDC motor with the mesh imposed in the SW-EMS environment

The SW-EMS environment allows you to carry out similar simulations as the previously conducted 2D simulations in the FEMM environment, with the difference of using 3D geometry. Previously, the research indicated a relatively high qualitative convergence of the obtained 2D-FEM (FEMM) and 3D-FEM (SW-EMS) simulations; therefore, in the presented research, it was decided to proceed immediately to optimise the coil winding parameters.

During the simulation, various configurations of the wire diameter of the coil and the number of wings were tested, however, while maintaining a similar degree of filling. The parameters of the coil and the calculated degree of filling are presented in Table 2.

An example of the visualisation of the obtained results superimposed on the meshed FEM model is shown in Fig. 10.

Table 2. Parameters of the BLDC motor coil modelled during the tests.

No.	Wire Diameter [mm]	Number of wings	Filling Factor
1	0,1	2025	0,053014376
2	0,15	900	0,053014376
3	0,2	481	0,050370202
4	0,25	324	0,053014376
5	0,3	225	0,053014376
6	0,34	175	0,052962016
7	0,35	166	0,053236906
8	0,36	156	0,052929553
9	0,37	148	0,053043698
10	0,39	134	0,05335838
11	0,4	127	0,053197636
12	0,41	121	0,053250257
13	0,43	110	0,053247378
14	0,45	100	0,053014376
15	0,5	81	0,053014376
16	0,55	67	0,053060191
17	0,6	56	0,052778757

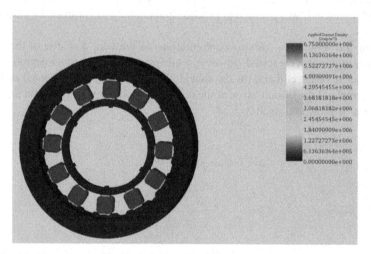

Fig. 10. Example visualisation of simulation results in the SW-EMS environment

As part of the conducted research, it was compared to what energy the motor can generate with the same geometrical parameters and 1 V voltage applied to the coils. The obtained results are presented in the chart below (Fig. 11).

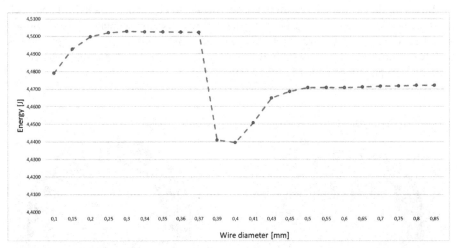

Fig. 11. The amount of energy generated on the motor obtained during the simulation in the SW-EMS environment

As you can see, the motor can generate the highest energy at small cross-sections of the wire from which the coil is made. The maximum energy is generated for a wire with a diameter of 0.37 mm and 148 wings; above this value, we observe a sharp decrease in the generated energy.

5 Summary

The simulations and analyses of the results obtained in the 2D-FEM and 3D-FEM environments presented in this article allowed for the initial selection of the optimal construction of the designed BLDC motor. The use of free tools such as the FEMM 4.2 environment will enable you to significantly reduce the costs associated with the purchase of appropriate software as well as through 2D simulations; they reduce the requirements related to the resources of the computer used, which is also not without significance when it comes to costs. In addition, using simplified two-dimensional models and scripting languages allows for a significant reduction in the time necessary to prepare the model and its simulation compared to three-dimensional models. Thanks to this, it is possible to test a much larger number of configurations at the same time.

Using a Multiphysics approach in a three-dimensional FEM environment allows for taking into account a much larger number of different phenomena affecting the formation of the electromagnetic field inside the motor and thus the obtained more accurate results of numerical simulations. However, it is burdened with a significant extension of the time of the tests. While the quantitative results between the 2D and

3D simulations may differ, the qualitative results and the observed trends of changes in engine parameters when changing its geometry are preserved, which allows the selection of the best configuration among those considered without the need to involve significant hardware and time resources.

Based on the conducted research, the best seems to be the use of a hybrid approach in which preliminary, coarse tests are carried out in a 2D environment using simplified models, and only selected structures are simulated in 3D environments. Then prototypes of only the most promising configurations are made. In the presented case, it was a drive with 20 permanent magnets and 12 coils (Fig. 12).

Fig. 12. The prototype of the designed BLDC drive

Acknowledgment. The research was carried out as part of the project entitled "Hybrid ultra-precise drive system based on DirectDrive and piezo technology" (POIR.01.01.01-00-0102/17-00).

References

1. Cabuk, A.S., Sağlam, Ş, Üstün, Ö.: Impact of various slot pole combinations on an in-wheel BLDC motor performance. IU-J. Electr. Electron. Eng. **17**(2), 3369–3375 (2017)
2. Ierusalimschy, R., Celes, W., de Figueiredo, L.H.: Programming Language Lua 4.0. http://www.lua.org. Accessed 26 May 2023
3. Modreanu, N.M., Andrei, M.I., Morega, M., Tudorache, T.: Brushless dc micro-motor with surface mounted permanent magnets. Rev. Roum. Sci. Techn.–Électrotechn. et Énerg. **59**(3), 237–247 (2014)
4. Ocak, C., Tarimer, I., Dalcali, A., Uygun, D.: Investigation effects of narrowing rotor pole embrace to efficiency and cogging torque at PM BLDC motor. TEM J. **5**(1), 25–31 (2016)
5. Prusak, D., Karpiel, G., Manka, M.: Przegląd rozwiązań napędów do zastosowań w mechatronicznych napędach hybrydowych. In: Projektowanie mechatroniczne. Manka, M. (ed.) Krakow (2018). ISBN: 978-83-949477-1-2

6. Rupam, S.M., Marwaha, A.: FEA based design of outer rotor BLDC motor for battery electric vehicle. Int. J. Electr. Electron. Res. **10**(4), 1130–1134 (2022)
7. Sikora, J.: Numeryczne metody rozwiązywania zagadnień brzegowych. Wyd. Politechniki Lubelskiej, Lublin (2011)
8. https://www.emworks.com/product/ems. Accessed 26 May 2023
9. http://www.bavaria-direct.co.za/scheme/calculator/. Accessed 20 May 2023

Software Engineering

ABAP Unit Testing Performance and Quality Analysis in SAP HANA

Marek Gałązka[✉] and Jerzy Szymański

Adam Mickiewicz University, Poznań, Poland
{galazka,jesz}@amu.edu.pl

Abstract. The development of large software systems is a complex and error prone process. Faults might occur at any development stage and they must be identified and removed as early as possible to stop their propagation and reduce verification costs. In this paper, we present some technical insights into Unit Testing in ABAP, including some practical rules for better performance and quality of unit testing.

Keywords: Unit testing · ERP systems · SAP S/4HANA · Software Testing Life Cycle · Software Testing strategies · Software Testing Techniques

1 Introduction

Today, software testing is an integral part of the software development process [2, 6, 10] to gain information about the quality of the software under test and to subsequently improve it if needed. Software testing is motivated by the experience that software programs can contain defects. These defects, if they are encountered during software execution (failure), can lead to undesirable results ranging from unimportant details to hundreds of million dollars in costs or even loss of life [7] Loss of trust from users also translates to financial costs. Therefore, avoiding such costs is a strong motivation for software testing.

Software testing strategies are very important in order to construct software successfully [8, 9]. Software testing strategies combines test cases design methods. This leads to planned systematic steps for carrying out successful testing of software. Software testing strategies are developed by software tester and project manager. Four types of testing strategies are there: Unit testing, Integration testing, System testing, Acceptance testing [3].

K. S. Soliman (Ed.): IBIMA-AI 2023, CCIS 2101, pp. 267–279, 2024.
https://doi.org/10.1007/978-3-031-62843-6_26

Enterprise Resource Planning (ERP) and Business Intelligence (BI) systems are a fundamental part of today's enterprise IT applications portfolio. They provide a set of standardized software packages that capture interdisciplinary business processes across the entire value chain of an enterprise in a streamlined fashion [4] ERP and BI systems integrate business functions with a centralized data repository shared by all business processes in the enterprise. The information provided by these systems drive daily business operations and provides for the development of new business ideas.

One of the most popular ERP systems is the SAP system [5]. For several years, we have had a newer database technology (i.e. SAP HANA) and the latest generation of the ERP system - S/4HANA.

In this article are described some practical rules for better performance and quality of unit testing that can significantly improve S/4HANA system robustness [1]. The paper is organized as follows: ABAP Unit Test are described in Sect. 1. In Sect. 2 we present ABAP unit-testing frameworks that improve test quality and efficiency. We conclude the paper in Sect. 3.

2 ABAP Unit Test

A unit test is an automated test of individual program units. Typically, methods and classes are tested with it. A unit test is also referred to as a module test.

The benefit of unit testing is automation. When creating unit tests, expected outputs from program units are tested for correctness. If the expected result occurs, the unit test is successful. If an unexpected result occurs, this indicates an error in the programming.

Once you have developed a unit test, you can quickly and easily identify faulty program without having to manually test each program again. Unit tests are therefore used to test individual components in isolation. A method of a test class can look like this as an example:

```
METHOD sum_2_numbers.

DATA: lv_result TYPE int8_lew.

CALL METHOD f_cut->sum_2_numbers
EXPORTING
  i_number_1 = 15
  i_number_2 = 3
IMPORTING
  e_result  = lv_result.

cl_abap_unit_assert=>assert_equals(
act = lv_result
exp = 18
).

ENDMETHOD.
```

This example tests a method that adds two numbers. The result as a result is compared with an expected value.

An ABAP unit test class is required for an ABAP unit test. A test class tests the methods of another ABAP class. You can recognize an ABAP test class by the addition "FOR TESTING" in the definition. In addition, the type of duration and the risk level are given. The actual ABAP unit tests are executed in the methods of the test class. A test class can also test a function module. Then the test class must be implemented in an include of the function group.

The addition "FOR TESTING" declares the ABAP class as a test class and uses the Unit Test Framework. This automatically makes the following methods available to the class (Table 1):

Table 1. Methods of the Unit Test Framework

Method	Description
CLASS_SETUP	static method Runs once when the test run starts
SETUP	instance method Runs when each test method is called
CLASS_TEARDOWN	static method Executed once when the test run ends
TEARDOWN	instance method Runs when each test method exits

Of course, if the methods are to be used, they must be declared in the class definition. These methods do not have to be implemented.

In this example we want to create an ABAP test class for a simple ABAP class. In addition to a getter and a setter method, this class has a method sum_2_numbers that adds two numbers and returns the result.

```
METHOD sum_2_numbers.
  e_result = i_number_1 + i_number_2.
ENDMETHOD.
```

This method can now be easily tested with an ABAP test class. The definition and implementation of the ABAP test class could look like this:

```
*-------------------------------------------------------------------
* Definition zcl_erp_up_test
*-------------------------------------------------------------------
CLASS zcl_erp_up_test DEFINITION FOR TESTING
  DURATION SHORT
  RISK LEVEL HARMLESS

  PRIVATE SECTION.
   DATA:
    f_cut TYPE REF TO zcl_erp_up. "class under test
   METHODS: setup,
        sum_2_numbers FOR TESTING.
ENDCLASS.     "zcl_Erp_Up_Test
*-------------------------------------------------------------------
* Implementation zcl_erp_up_test
*-------------------------------------------------------------------
CLASS zcl_erp_up_test IMPLEMENTATION.
  METHOD setup.
   f_cut = NEW zcl_erp_up( ).
  ENDMETHOD.
  METHOD sum_2_numbers.
   DATA: lv_result TYPE int8_lew.
   CALL METHOD f_cut->sum_2_numbers
    EXPORTING
     i_number_1 = 15
     i_number_2 = 3
    IMPORTING
     e_result  = lv_result.
   cl_abap_unit_assert=>assert_equals(
   act = lv_result
   exp = 18
   ).
  ENDMETHOD.
ENDCLASS.
```

In this example, the method sum_2_numbers is tested with the input values 15 and 3. The return value should be 18.

3 New ABAP Unit-Testing Frameworks

Better performance and quality of unit testing is an important factor during the SAP system testing process. In this Section we present 2 new ABAP unit-testing frameworks: CL_ABAP_TESTDOUBLE and CL_OSQL_TEST_ENVIRONMENT.

3.1 ABAP Test Double Framework (CL_ABAP_TESTDOUBLE)

In object-oriented programming, mock objects are simulated objects that mimic the behavior of real objects in controlled ways, most often as part of a software testing initiative. In a unit test, mock objects can simulate the behavior of complex, real objects and are therefore useful when a real object is impractical or impossible to incorporate into a unit test. If an object has any of the following characteristics, it may be useful to use a mock object in its place:

- the object supplies non-deterministic results (e.g. the current time or the current temperature);
- it has states that are difficult to create or reproduce (e.g. a network error);
- it is slow (e.g. a complete database, which would have to be initialized before the test);
- it does not yet exist or may change behavior;
- it would have to include information and methods exclusively for testing purposes (and not for its actual task) (Fig. 1).

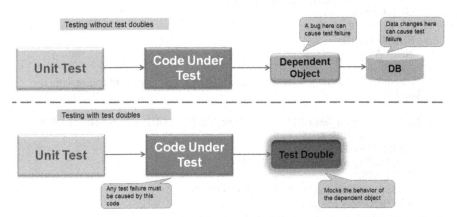

Fig. 1. Comparison of the Test Double framework with the standard ABAP Unit Testing framework

Until now test doubles classes had to be written by hand. This can be quite a tedious process. The ABAP Test Double Framework solves this problem and makes it easier to write unit tests for your code.

Let's go to an example. Let's implement the ZCL_ACTION class

```
CLASS zcl_action DEFINITION.
  PUBLIC SECTION.
    METHODS constructor IMPORTING actor TYPE REF TO zcl_actor.
    METHODS who_am_i RETURNING VALUE(rv_name) TYPE string.

  PRIVATE SECTION.
    DATA: mo_actor TYPE REF TO zcl_actor.
ENDCLASS.

CLASS zcl_action IMPLEMENTATION.
  METHOD constructor.
    mo_actor = actor.
  ENDMETHOD.

  METHOD who_am_i.
    rv_name = mo_actor->get_name( ).
  ENDMETHOD.
ENDCLASS.
```

The ZCL_ACTOR class looks like this.

```
CLASS zcl_actor DEFINITION .
  PUBLIC SECTION.
    METHODS: get_name RETURNING VALUE(rv_name) TYPE string.

ENDCLASS.

CLASS zcl_actor IMPLEMENTATION.
  METHOD get_name.
    rv_name = 'Real value'.
  ENDMETHOD.
ENDCLASS.
```

Required: Write a unit test for the ZCL_ACTION class. You can of course write it like this:

```
CLASS lcl_action_test DEFINITION FOR TESTING DURATION SHORT RISK
LEVEL HARMLESS.
  PUBLIC SECTION.
    METHODS who_am_i FOR TESTING.
ENDCLASS.
CLASS lcl_action_test IMPLEMENTATION.
  METHOD who_am_i.

    DATA(lo_action) = NEW zcl_action( NEW zcl_actor( ) ).

    DATA(lv_return) = lo_action->who_am_i( ).

    cl_abap_unit_assert=>assert_equals( act = lv_return
                                        exp = 'Real value' ).

  ENDMETHOD.
```

But it's not entirely fair here. Each unit test should test its own class and be conditionally independent of other classes. Moreover, the dependent class may be at the same time under development by another developer or contain cumbersome initialization. According to the standard rules, we must write a mock object for the ZCL_ACTOR class and use it in ZCL_ACTION tests. And since such an exercise can be somewhat tedious, using the Test Double framework, we can create a mock object on the fly and slip it into our test class. That is where the profit lies.

The implementation must meet the following requirements:

- a dependent class must be made a global interface, a call to the dependent class must be made through this interface
- the number of uses at a time is somewhat limited, since this framework temporarily generates a real ABAP class representing the required interface (GENERATE SUBROUTINE POOL with all the consequences)
- only supported in versions 7.40/7.50 and higher

First, let's deal with the auxiliary class, take out the external interface:

```
CLASS zcl_actor DEFINITION .
 PUBLIC SECTION.
   INTERFACES: zif_actor.

ENDCLASS.

CLASS zcl_actor IMPLEMENTATION.
 METHOD zif_actor~get_name.
   rv_name = 'Real value'.
 ENDMETHOD.
ENDCLASS.
```

Let's adapt the interface inside the main class:

```
CLASS zcl_action DEFINITION.
 PUBLIC SECTION.
   METHODS constructor IMPORTING actor TYPE REF TO zif_actor.
   METHODS who_am_i RETURNING VALUE(rv_name) TYPE string.

 PRIVATE SECTION.
   DATA: mo_actor TYPE REF TO zif_actor.
ENDCLASS.

CLASS zcl_action IMPLEMENTATION.
 METHOD constructor.
   mo_actor = actor.
 ENDMETHOD.

 METHOD who_am_i.
   rv_name = mo_actor->get_name( ).
 ENDMETHOD.
ENDCLASS.
```

And hello-world in our case will be like this:

```
CLASS lcl_action_test DEFINITION FOR TESTING DURATION SHORT RISK
LEVEL HARMLESS.
 PUBLIC SECTION.
   METHODS who_am_i FOR TESTING.
ENDCLASS.
CLASS lcl_action_test IMPLEMENTATION.
 METHOD who_am_i.

   DATA: lo_actor TYPE REF TO zif_actor.
   lo_actor ?= cl_abap_testdouble=>create( 'zif_actor' ).
```

```
cl_abap_testdouble=>configure_call( lo_actor )
                ->returning( 'Fake value' ).
lo_actor->get_name( ).

DATA(lo_action) = NEW zcl_action( lo_actor ).

DATA(lv_return) = lo_action->who_am_i( ).

cl_abap_unit_assert=>assert_equals( act = lv_return
                                    exp = 'Fake value' ).
  ENDMETHOD.
  ENDCLASS.
```

Let's sum up:

Step 1: lo_actor ?= cl_abap_testdouble=> create('zif_actor')
Creates and returns a mock object with the required interface.
Step 2: cl_abap_testdouble=> configure_call(lo_actor)->returning('Fake value')
Sets the configuration, prepares the output parameters for the expected call.
Step 3: lo_actor->get_name( )
Initializes the method to be hooked to the given configuration.

And then you can safely use this mock object in tests.

3.2   Open SQL Test Environment (CL_OSQL_TEST_ENVIRONMENT)

Since of ABAP 7.52, database tables can be mocked using the CL_OSQL_TEST_ENVIRONMENT class. The mocked tables replace the originals in Open SQL statements without any changes to the productive coding, so that productive data is not used in the test case. With this framework it is very easy to foist manipulated data on the database. We will show you how this works in detail here.

Let's imagine we have an application that is to determine the material type for a material and is to use the material type to check whether a specific action is permitted or not.

The class for determining the material master data could look like this:

```
CLASS mat DEFINITION.
 PUBLIC SECTION.
  METHODS check_usage
   IMPORTING
    matnr TYPE matnr
   RETURNING
    VALUE(result) TYPE abap_bool.

 PRIVATE SECTION.
  METHODS get_type
   IMPORTING
    matnr TYPE matnr
   RETURNING
    VALUE(mtart) TYPE mtart.
ENDCLASS.
CLASS mat IMPLEMENTATION.
 METHOD check_usage.
  IF get_type( matnr ) = 'FERT'.
   result = abap_true.
  ENDIF.
 ENDMETHOD.

 METHOD get_type.
  SELECT SINGLE mtart FROM mara INTO mtart WHERE matnr = matnr.
 ENDMETHOD.
ENDCLASS.
```

We can use the CHECK_USAGE method to determine whether or not a given material is allowed for any use that is not defined here.

If we have two materials in the test system with which we can test this, then the unit tests could look like this:

```
CLASS test DEFINITION FOR TESTING
DURATION SHORT
RISK LEVEL HARMLESS.
PRIVATE SECTION.

DATA f_cut TYPE REF TO mat.
METHODS: setup.
METHODS: check_allowed FOR TESTING.
METHODS: check_forbidden FOR TESTING.
ENDCLASS.

CLASS test IMPLEMENTATION.

METHOD setup.
 f_cut = NEW #( ).
ENDMETHOD.

METHOD check_allowed.
 cl_abap_unit_assert=>assert_equals(
  act  = f_cut->check_usage( 'MAT-2277' )
  exp  = abap_true ).
ENDMETHOD.

METHOD check_forbidden.
 cl_abap_unit_assert=>assert_equals(
  act  = f_cut->check_usage( 'MAT-565' )
  exp  = abap_false ).
ENDMETHOD.
ENDCLASS.
```

As a result, the material MAT-2277 in the database is a material of type "FERT" and the material MAT-565 has a different type.

However, one must not rely on master data. These are often changed or deleted, especially in a development system. In a unit test, however, we need to be able to rely on the data. We can only do that if we give them firmly.

With the oSQL Test Environment we can do this very comfortably. And as follows: An instance must be created using the method CL_OSQL_TEST_ENVIRONMENT=> CREATE. We give this instance the table names that we want to influence. In addition, we give exactly the data that should be fooled into the database. In this example we use the material FAKEMAT1 as a test material for FERT and FAKEMAT2 as a test material for a material not equal to FERT.

CLASS test DEFINITION FOR TESTING

```
DURATION SHORT
RISK LEVEL HARMLESS.
PRIVATE SECTION.
  CLASS-DATA: osql TYPE REF TO if_osql_test_environment.
  CLASS-METHODS: class_setup.
  CLASS-METHODS: class_teardown.
  DATA f_cut TYPE REF TO mat.
  METHODS: setup.
  METHODS: check_allowed FOR TESTING.
  METHODS: check_forbidden FOR TESTING.
ENDCLASS.
```

CLASS test IMPLEMENTATION.

```
  METHOD class_setup.
  osql = cl_osql_test_environment=>create( VALUE #( ( 'MARA' ) ) ).
  DATA(materials) = VALUE mara_tab(
    ( mandt = '100' matnr = 'FAKEMAT1' mtart = 'FERT' )
    ( mandt = '100' matnr = 'FAKEMAT2' mtart = 'HALB' ) ).
  osql->insert_test_data( materials ).
ENDMETHOD.

  METHOD class_teardown.
  osql->destroy( ).
ENDMETHOD.

  METHOD setup.
  f_cut = NEW #( ).
ENDMETHOD.

  METHOD check_allowed.
  cl_abap_unit_assert=>assert_equals(
    act = f_cut->check_usage( 'FAKEMAT1' )
    exp = abap_true ).
ENDMETHOD.

  METHOD check_forbidden.
  cl_abap_unit_assert=>assert_equals(
    act = f_cut->check_usage( 'FAKEMAT2' )
    exp = abap_false ).
ENDMETHOD.

ENDCLASS.
```

4 Conclusion

Software testing has been an active research area for many decades, and today quality engineers can benefit from many results, tools and techniques. However, challenges are far from being over: while many traditional research areas are still open, advances in design and applications open many new problems. Available testing techniques are certainly useful, but not completely satisfactory yet. We need more techniques to address new programming paradigms and application domains, but more important, we need better support for test automation. The ABAP unit-testing frameworks presented in the article are certainly a step in the right direction and significantly facilitate and increase the effectiveness of testing.

References

1. Bach, T., Andrzejak, A., Seo, C., et al.: Testing very large database management systems: the case of SAP HANA. Datenbank Spektrum **22**, 195–215 (2022). https://doi.org/10.1007/s13 222-022-00426-x
2. Arban, A., Bourque, P., Dupuis, R., Moore, J.W., Tripp, L.: The guide to the software engineering body of knowledge. IEEE Softw. **16**(6), 35–44 (1999)
3. Babar, H.: Software testing: techniques and test cases. Int. J. Comput. Appl. Robot. **5**(3), 44–53 (2017)
4. Booth, P., Matolcsy, P., Wieder, B.: Economic benefits of enterprise resource planning systems: some empirical evidence. Account. Finance **45**(3), 439–456 (2005)
5. Brockman, C., Mirzoev, T.: SAP HANA and its performance benefits. Inf. Technol. J. **2**(1), 13–21 (2013)
6. Dai, H., Hu, T., Li, X., Zhang, X.: Software development methodologies, trends and implications: a testing centric view. i-Manage. J. Inf. Technol. **9**(8), 1747–1753 (2010)
7. Huckle, T., Neckel, T.: Software, environments, and tools. SIAM J. Comput. Philadelphia (2019)
8. Pathak, B., Taley, S.H.: Comprehensive study of software testing techniques and strategies: a review. Int. J. Eng. Res. Technol. **9**(8), 46–58 (2020)
9. Pavithra, L., Sandhya, S.: Survey on software testing. J. Netw. Commun. Emerg. Technol. **9**(3), 7–10 (2019)
10. Pyhäjärvi, M., Rautiainen, K.: Integrating testing and implementation into development. Eng. Manage. J. **16**(1), 33–39 (2004)

The Use of Random Methods in the Process of Generating a Set of Test Cases

Kazimierz Worwa[✉]

Institute of Computer and Information Systems, Faculty of Cybernetics, Military University of Technology, 46, gen. S. Kaliskiego St. 2, 00-908 Warsaw, Poland
kazimierz.worwa@wat.edu.pl

Abstract. The paper discusses the issue of using random methods for the purposes of generating a set of test cases, which is the basis for the implementation of the software testing process. Two methods, most often used in practice, were characterized: random testing and partition testing. Presented characteristics include a description of the conditions for which one of the above-mentioned random testing methods is better than the other, in terms of the probability of detecting at least one error using equally numerous test data sets created on their basis. Particular attention was focused on the analysis of how to generate a set of test cases for the partition testing method. Contrary to the majority of works related to this issue, the presented considerations include the cost of determining such a set. The main result of this work is to obtain the method of determining the partition testing strategy, which can be the basis for the implementation of the program testing process. This strategy is obtained as a result of solving the problem of two-criteria optimization, with the following component criteria taken into account as the component criteria: probability of an event that the set of test cases will allow to detect at least one error and the cost of extracting a certain number of partitions from the domain of the tested program and drawing some sets of test cases from them.

Keywords: random testing · partition testing · set of test cases

1 Introduction

Despite the constant development and improvement of design and implementation methods used in the practice of software production, their current level still does not fully guarantee the development of a complex software product completely error-free. These errors, detected after a shorter or longer period of use of the software, expose the user to specific losses, depending on the nature and purpose of the software. Bearing in mind the minimization of these losses, the user requests the software producer to create software that fully meets the requirements, maximally proven and reliable, even if it is associated with a significant increase in the costs incurred.

According to the IEEE Standard Glossary for Software Engineering Terminology (1990), software reliability is understood as the probability of its correct functioning

© The Author(s), under exclusive license to Springer Nature Switzerland AG 2024
K. S. Soliman (Ed.): IBIMA-AI 2023, CCIS 2101, pp. 280–295, 2024.
https://doi.org/10.1007/978-3-031-62843-6_27

within a specified period of time and under specified conditions. Software reliability is a basic aspect of software quality, and this term is used to describe a set of features and characteristics that describe the extent to which the software meets the specified requirements.

The concept of software reliability is directly related to the concept of software error (fault, bug). In the presented considerations, a program error is understood as a defect in the program code that may cause incorrect, i.e. non-compliant, operation of the program. A software error is a result of a human error (e.g. a designer or programmer), committed at one of the stages of the program development process. An example of a programming error can be a faulty program instruction, but also the absence of a specific instruction or group of instructions. If a faulty piece of code is activated during program execution, the program may fail. A programming error is the reason for the incorrect operation of the program, while the incorrect operation of the program is the result of errors in its code.

The occurrence of software errors, which in certain cases result in incorrect functioning of the software, has a direct qualitative dimension (influencing the reduction of the level of software reliability) and cost (increasing, often very serious, time and financial outlays). For these reasons, the fight against software errors is an important factor in the development and improvement of design and implementation techniques as well as methods of work organization used in the software development process. The practice of modern software engineering shows that the testing stage has the largest share in the error detection process.

The basic problem to be solved at the planning and preparation stage of the software testing process is to determine such a subset of all possible input data sets that would maximize the probability of detecting all errors committed in the earlier stages of the software development process. This problem arises due to the fact that, due to the time and cost of the testing process, it is generally impossible to test the software against the entire set of all possible test cases. The problem of determining the subset mentioned is the problem of designing a set of test cases (tests). Each test is an acceptable combination of values that may be assumed by the input variables of the tested software product, required for its single run, where input variables are those variables whose values are determined directly from the input data, e.g. as a result of executing a input data instruction. The method of creating a set of test cases, on the basis of which the software testing process will be carried out, depends on the adopted testing method, each of which is based on a specific criteria for the selection of a set of test cases.

Depending on the approach to the problem of designing a set of test cases, the testing methods used in practice can be divided into two classes:

- deterministic methods,
- random methods.

Deterministic testing methods assume that a set of test cases is created in an exclusively deterministic way, i.e. without the participation of a random factor. Individual sets of input data, which are elements of the designed set of test cases, are determined on the basis of an analysis of the requirements specification or an analysis of the source code of the tested program.

Unlike deterministic methods, in random methods, some of the set test cases (or even all) used in the software testing process are created using a random factor, i.e. by random sampling, wherein the random sampling method most often used in the practice is sampling without return.

This article, inspired by the results obtained by [12] and [2, 3], contains some generalizations of these results, as well as some new results in terms of comparing the effectiveness of two fundamental methods of random testing in software engineering practice.

2   Characteristics of Random Testing Methods

The method of creating a set of test cases based on sampling is very commonly used in testing practice. This is primarily due to its simplicity (e.g. it does not require a very laborious analysis of the logical structure of the tested program), a direct consequence of which is the low cost of the testing process and its high susceptibility to its automation. The second feature of the random method, determining its wide practical use, is its high efficiency, measured by the number of errors detected in the testing process. Studies conducted to compare the effectiveness of the most commonly used testing methods in practice have shown that for a wide class of programs testing based on random generation of a set of test cases is more effective than other methods, with particularly good results obtained by random generation of test cases based on the probability distribution described by the operational profile of the tested program, specifying the probabilities of occurrence of individual test case of the considered program in the conditions of its actual exploitation.

The analysis of random testing literature allows for the division of the methods of its implementation into strategies, the essence of which is:

- random testing,
- partition testing, i.e. random testing within selected subsets of the input data set.

Random testing consists in using, in the program testing process, a set of test cases, created by random sampling (usually without returning) its successive elements from the entire set of set of test cases of the tested program. The basic problem here is to determine the probability distribution with which individual data sets are drawn, which make up the test data set created in this way. In the absence of appropriate premises as to the nature of this distribution, an uniform distribution over the entire set of input data of the tested program is often assumed.

A very common variant of random testing is testing in which a set of test cases is created on the basis of the entire set of input data of the tested program, but the randomization of successive test cases is based on the probability distribution determined by the operational profile of the program.

Differences in the approach to determining the probability distribution according to which individual test cases are randomized in the random testing variants that have been described result in differences in their effectiveness. In particular, the use of the operating profile of the tested program makes it possible to direct the testing process to detecting all errors that are most likely to occur during the use of the program in real conditions.

In turn, the use of a set of test cases, determined by random methods without taking into account the operational profile of the tested program, directs the testing process to detecting all program errors, regardless of the probability of their disclosure during the usable operation of the program.

The second of the previously mentioned groups of random testing methods are methods in which subsequent elements of the created set of test cases set are randomly selected from certain subsets of the entire program input data set, called partitions. Therefore, the described approach requires - before starting the actual process of drawing individual test cases - partitioning the set of all possible set of test cases into partitions. As a consequence, the testing process is carried out on the basis of a certain number of test cases (corresponding to the number of separated partitions), and the sampling of individual test cases within the separated partitions is most often based on an uniform distribution.

[4] same as [6] conducted a series of experiments and simulation studies to compare the effectiveness of random testing and partition testing. The analysis of the obtained results showed that in a number of cases, the cheaper random testing turned out to be more effective strategy (in terms of error detection capability) than the more expensive partition testing.

The evaluation of the effectiveness of random and partition testing methods is the subject of many publications, e.g.: [1–6, 12]. [12] conducted a formal comparative analysis of the effectiveness of both random testing techniques. The results of this analysis indicate that partition testing can be better or worse technique than random testing, depending on how the error-producing test cases are distributed among the individual partitions.

The comparative analysis of random testing and partition testing in the following part of the article will be carried out using the notation adopted in [12] same as [2, 3].

Let for the considered program under the testing process, the set of all its possible test cases be denoted by D, and its size - i.e. the number of input datasets forming it - by d, $d > 0$. The elements of the set D corresponding to the incorrect operation of the program will be called erroneous set of test cases (abbreviated: incorrect tests) and their number will be denoted by m, $0 \leq m \leq d$. The remaining set of test cases will be called valid set of test cases (abbreviated: valid test), and their number will be denoted by c, wherein $m + c = d$.

Let θ mean the so-called error coefficient, defined as $\theta = m/d$. For the purposes of comparing the effectiveness of both considered random testing techniques, it is assumed that in each of these testing techniques the total number of randomly selected tests is n. In the case of random testing, the set of test cases D is divided into k subsets, denoted by D_i, where $i = 1, 2, ..., k$. A subset of D_i has size d_i and contains m_i wrong tests, $0 \leq m_i \leq d_i$ and $c_i = d_i - m_i$ correct tests, having an error factor $\theta_i = m_i/d_i$. The number of tests drawn from the i-th subset is n_i, $n_i \geq 1$. Of course it takes place

$$\sum_{i=1}^{k} n_i = n. \tag{1}$$

In accordance with the earlier assumption, the comparison of the effectiveness of both random testing techniques will be carried out for the same total number of randomized tests. Assuming that the subsets of D_i are disjoint, we can write:

$$\sum_{i=1}^{k} d_i = d, \quad \sum_{i=1}^{k} m_i = m, \quad \sum_{i=1}^{k} c_i = c. \tag{2}$$

In further considerations, it is assumed that the tests are drawn without replacement, according to an uniform distribution, i.e. that all tests are drawn with the same probability. Specifically, this means that when a test is drawn from either D or D_i the probability that the drawn test is an invalid test is θ or θ_i, respectively.

For the purposes of comparing the effectiveness of both considered random testing techniques, the probability of an event that among the randomly selected tests there is at least one incorrect test will be considered, which means that, based on the set of test cases generated in this way, in the testing process of the considered at least one error is detected. This probability will be denoted by P_r for random testing and P_p for structured random testing, respectively. These probabilities are defined as follows [12] or [2]:

$$P_r(n) = 1 - (1 - \theta)^n \text{ and } P_p(n) = 1 - \prod_{i=1}^{k}(1 - \theta_i)^{n_i}, \tag{3}$$

where $n = (n_1, n_2, ..., n_k)$, $k > 1$, is a vector of the number of tests drawn from the i-th subset of the program's input test cases (partitions).

For the case of only one partition, i.e. for $k = 1$, we have $P_p = P_r$.

Likewise, if $\theta_1 = \theta_2 = ... = \theta_k = \theta$ we have

$$P_p(n) = 1 - \prod_{i=1}^{k}(1 - \theta_i)^{n_i} = 1 - \prod_{i=1}^{k}(1 - \theta)^{n_i} = 1 - (1 - \theta)^{n_1 + n_2 + \cdots + n_k} = 1 - (1 - \theta)^n = P_r(n) \tag{4}$$

that means that the probabilities P_r and P_p are equal.

It might seem that from the point of view of the number of errors detected, partition testing should be more effective than random testing. However, studies by [4] as well as [6] show that the differences in the effectiveness of both methods are very small and very often random testing can be even more effective than structured random testing.

It is easy to see that, intuitively, partition testing will be superior to random testing if most of the tests come from partitions with higher error coefficient. The fulfillment of this condition, however, does not guarantee the occurrence of this effect, which is illustrated by example presented in Table 1. In this example, 3 variants of testing strategies are considered, each of which is based on $k = 3$ partitions and in each case the total number of tests and the total number of incorrect tests are the same. For the first strategy, partition testing is better than random testing, i.e. $P_r < P_r$; for the second strategy the opposite is true, i.e. $P_r > P_r$ while in the third strategy both probabilities are equal, i.e. $P_r = P_r$.

It is obvious that in practice it is impossible to have a priori accurate information about the distribution of invalid tests of the program under testing that could be used in partition testing process. Despite the lack of such information, [12] found a way of dividing the set of all possible program inputs into partitions that guarantees that partition testing will not be worse than random testing. The authors of the cited paper showed that if $d_1 = d_2 = \cdots = d_k$ and $n_1 = n_2 = \cdots = n_k$ then $P_p \geq P_r$. If, furthermore, the

Table 1. Example of testing strategies giving different results of comparing the values of probabilities P_p and P_r

Strategy number	d_i		m_i		n_i		θ_i		θ	P_r	P_p
	d_1	3500	m_1	30	n_1	30	θ_1	0,0086			
1	d_2	1500	m_2	21	n_2	21	θ_2	0,0140	0,01	0,4528	0,4704
	d_3	1000	m_3	9	n_3	9	θ_3	0,0090			
Total		6000		60		60					
	d_1	3500	m_1	33	n_1	39	θ_1	0,0094			
2	d_2	1500	m_2	21	n_2	9	θ_2	0,0140	0,01	0,4528	0,4337
	d_3	1000	m_3	6	n_3	12	θ_3	0,0060			
Total		6000		60		60					
	d_1	3500	m_1	35	n_1	39	θ_1	0,0100			
3	d_2	1500	m_2	15	n_2	9	θ_2	0,0100	0,01	0,4528	0,4528
	d_3	1000	m_3	10	n_3	12	θ_3	0,0100			
Total		6000		60		60					

invalid tests are uniformly distributed across the partitions, i.e. $m_1 = m_2 = \cdots = m_k$ than $P_p = P_r$. Therefore, partition testing will never be worse than random testing if the partitions have the same cardinality, i.e. $d_1 = d_2 = \cdots = d_k$ and the same number of test cases are drawn from each of them, i.e. $n_1 = n_2 = \cdots = n_k$. Table 2 illustrates this effect. This condition is a sufficient for partition testing to be more effective than random testing. However, it is very difficult (if at all possible) to meet this condition in testing practice, because it is very difficult to obtain equally numerous partitions based on the currently used techniques of structural design of test cases.

In Table 2, 3 variants of testing strategies are considered, each containing $k = 3$ partitions. In the first two strategies $d_1 = d_2 = d_3$ and $n_1 = n_2 = n_3$. Then it occurs that $P_p \geq P_r$. In the third strategy, the condition $m_1 = m_2 = m_3$ is additionally fulfilled and then the values of probabilities P_p and P_r are the same.

[2] made the following generalization of the previously discussed condition indicated by [12]: when partitions are disjoint, partition testing will be more effective than random testing if the number of test cases drawn from each partition is proportional to the cardinality these partitions. Formally, this means that if $k \geq 2$ and $n_1/d_1 = n_2/d_2 = \cdots = n_k/d_k$ than $P_p \geq P_r$. This effect is illustrated by example presented in Table 3, where $k = 3$ and $n_1/d_1 = n_2/d_2 = n_3/d_3 = 0,05$. For each of this three cases, the total number of tests remains the same $n = 2500$, the total number of incorrect tests is different for each case. It is easy to see that in each of the three strategies considered in Table 3, partition testing is not more effective than random testing. It can also be seen that an increase of the number of incorrect tests $m = m_1 + m_2 + m_3$ entails an increase in the values of both probabilities P_r and P_p. For the third strategy among those presented in Table 3, for which additional condition $m_1 = m_2 = m_3$ is met we have $P_p = P_r$.

As noted earlier, partition testing requires the division of the set of all possible test cases (domains) of a program into a number of subsets called partitions. This process, sometimes called the partitioning process, is often very time-consuming and expensive, because modern software engineering does not offer unambiguous ways of proceeding (effective methods) in this regard. In practice, the partitioning process can be implemented with the use of some methods used for the purposes of designing sets of test cases, which are the basis for the implementation of the testing process. In particular, in the group of methods of designing set of test cases based on a functional approach (black box testing), the equivalence partitioning method or the cause-effect graphing method may be useful to isolate individual partitions. On the other hand, in the group of methods for designing sets of test cases based on a structural approach (white box testing), the logical path coverage method can be used to identification of individual partitions. The characteristics of the above methods for designing a set of test cases can be found e.g. in the work of Roman (2015).

Table 2. Example of a test strategy with equal partition sizes from which the same number of test cases were drawn

Strategy number	d_i		m_i		n_i		θ_i		θ	P_r	P_p
						k=3					
1	d_1	1000	m_1	17	n_1	30	θ_1	0,0170			
	d_2	1000	m_2	15	n_2	30	θ_2	0,0150	0,0150	0,743398	0,743429
	d_3	1000	m_3	13	n_3	30	θ_3	0,0130			
Total		3000		45		90					
2	d_1	1000	m_1	15	n_1	30	θ_1	0,0150			
	d_2	1000	m_2	14	n_2	30	θ_2	0,0140	0,0150	0,743398	0,743406
	d_3	1000	m_3	16	n_3	30	θ_3	0,0160			
Total		3000		45		90					
3	d_1	1000	m_1	15	n_1	30	θ_1	0,0150			
	d_2	1000	m_2	15	n_2	30	θ_2	0,0150	0,0150	0,743398	0,743398
	d_3	1000	m_3	15	n_3	30	θ_3	0,0150			
Total		3000		45		90					

It is worth noting that the probabilities P_p in the examples in Tables 1, 2 and 3 are only slightly higher than the probabilities P_r. This is due to the fact that the probability values P_p determined in these examples are very far from the best cases for partition testing. Best and worst case analysis for partition testing with $k > 1$ partitions is presented in [12]. The most important results of this analysis are presented below.

Let $k > 1$, $\sum_{i=1}^{k} n_i = n$. Suppose partitions are numbered such that $\theta_1 \leq \theta_2 \leq ... \leq \theta_k$. Then the following inequality is true

$$\prod_{i=1}^{k} (1 - \theta_i)^{n_i} \geq \prod_{i=1}^{k-1} (1 - \theta_i)(1 - \theta_k)^{n-k+1}, \tag{5}$$

which means that we have

$$P_p(1, 1, ...1, n - k + 1) = \max_{n \in \mathcal{N}} P_p(n), \tag{6}$$

wherein $n \in \mathcal{N} = \{n = (n_1, n_2, ..., n_k) : n_i \geq 1, n_1 + n_2 + ... + n_k = n\}$.

Let $k > 1$, $\sum_{i=1}^{k} n_i = n$. Suppose partitions are numbered such that $\theta_1 \geq \theta_2 \geq ... \geq \theta_k$. Then the following inequality is true

$$\prod_{i=1}^{k} (1 - \theta_i)^{n_i} \leq \prod_{i=1}^{k-1} (1 - \theta_i)(1 - \theta_k)^{n-k+1}. \tag{7}$$

what means that

$$P_p(1, 1, ...1, n - k + 1) = \min_{n \in \mathcal{N}} P_p(n), \tag{8}$$

wherein $n = (n_1, n_2, ..., n_k) \in \mathcal{N}$.

The correctness of the above observations is illustrated in Table 4, which presents the most and least favorable cases of probability P_p for $k = 3$, $n = 20$ i $\theta_1 \leq \theta_2 \leq \theta_3$, respectively. According to the previous remarks, the probability P_p reaches a maximum for $n = (1, 1, 18)$ and a minimum for $n = (18, 1, 1)$ respectively. It is worth noting that for $n = (4, 10, 6)$ we have $n_1 / d_1 = n_2 / d_2 = n_3 / d_3 = 0, 02$, which means compliance with the conditions formulated by [2]. The row that corresponds to these conditions has been shaded. As noted earlier, the fulfillment of this condition guarantees that $P_p \geq P_r$ however, the value of the probability P_p is only slightly greater than the probability P_r.

Table 3. Example of a testing strategy with the number of test cases drawn from each partition proportional to the size of these partitions

Strategy number	d_i		m_i		n_i		θ_i		θ	P_r	P_p
	d_1	2500	m_1	30	n_1	125	θ_1	0,0120			
1	d_2	1000	m_2	21	n_2	50	θ_2	0,0210	0,012	0,9511	0,9513
	d_3	1500	m_3	9	n_3	75	θ_3	0,0060			
Total		5000		60		250					
	d_1	2500	m_1	30	n_1	125	θ_1	0,0120			
2	d_2	1000	m_2	30	n_2	50	θ_2	0,0300	0,018	0,9893	0,9894
	d_3	1500	m_3	30	n_3	75	θ_3	0,0200			
Total		5000		90		250					
	d_1	2500	m_1	40	n_1	125	θ_1	0,0160			
3	d_2	1000	m_2	60	n_2	50	θ_2	0,0600	0,026	0,9986	0,9987
	d_3	1500	m_3	30	n_3	75	θ_3	0,0200			
Total		5000		130		250					

k=3

Table 4. Example of testing strategies illustrating the most and least favorable case of probability P_p for $k = 3$ and $\theta_1 \le \theta_2 \le \theta_3$

n	d	m	θ
20	1000	220	0,22

m_1	30
m_2	100
m_3	90

d_1	200
d_2	500
d_3	300

θ_1	0,15
θ_2	0,2
θ_3	0,3

n_1	n_2	n_3	P_p	P_r
1	1	18	0,9989	
1	2	17	0,9987	
1	3	16	0,9986	
1	4	15	0,9983	
1	5	14	0,9981	
...				
4	8	8	0,9950	
4	9	7	0,9942	
4	10	6	0,9934	
4	11	5	0,9925	0,9931
4	12	4	0,9914	
4	13	3	0,9902	
4	8	8	0,9950	
...				
16	2	2	0,9767	
16	3	1	0,9734	
17	1	2	0,9753	
17	2	1	0,9717	
18	1	1	0,9700	

3   The Cost of Implementing the Partition Testing Strategy

The process of partitioning the set of all possible set of test cases of the program under testing, called the program domain, is usually very time consuming and expensive. In software engineering practice, the process of extracting the partition of the tested program can be carried out on the basis of the requirements specification analysis or on the basis of the source code analysis.

In most works devoted to the comparison of random testing methods, including, above all, the comparison of random strategy and partition testing strategy the aspect of the cost of determining the set of test cases for both strategies is completely omitted. Only one criterion is used for the purpose of comparing the random testing and partition testing strategies. That criterion is the probability of an event that the set of test cases will allow to detect at least one error.

Currently, the problem of determining the optimal partition testing strategy will be considered, i.e. the optimal number of tests drawn from individual k partitions in the partition testing process, maximizing the probability of detecting at least one error and minimizing the cost of the process of isolating individual partitions and drawing a certain number of test cases from them.

Let $C(k, n)$ mean the cost of extracting k partitions, $k > 1$, from the domain of the tested program and drawing sets of test cases defined by the strategy $n = (n_1, n_2, ..., n_k)$ from them. It is assumed that this cost has a following form

$$C(k, n) = \alpha e^{\beta k} + \sum_{i=1}^{k} \gamma_i n_i, \tag{9}$$

where the values of the coefficients α, β depend on the complexity of the tested program and value of the coefficient γ_I depends on the size of the set of test cases that make up the k-th partition and the difficulty in obtaining the i-th test case drawn from this partition. The nature of the dependence of the cost $C(k, n)$ on the number of partitions k and the number of tests drawn from individual partitions in accordance with the partition testing strategy n presents Fig. 1.

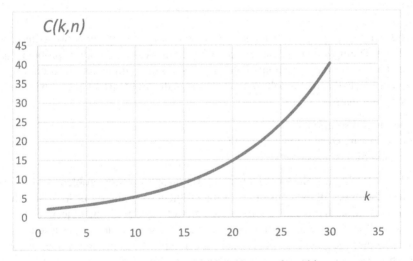

Fig. 1. Plot of the cost function of extract k partitions

Determination of an optimal partition testing strategy, assuming the division of its domain into partitions and drawing a certain number of tests from each partition, can be made as a result of solving the formal problem of two-criterion optimization with two objective functions as follows:

$$\text{maximize} \quad P_p(n) = 1 - \prod_{i=1}^{k} (1 - \theta_i)^{n_i}, \tag{10}$$

$$\text{minimize} \quad C(k, \boldsymbol{n}) = \alpha e^{\beta k} + \sum_{i=1}^{k} \gamma_i n_i, \tag{11}$$

wherein $\boldsymbol{n}$ is the partition testing strategy, $\boldsymbol{n} \in \mathcal{N} = \{\boldsymbol{n} = (n_1, n_2, ..., n_k): n_i \geq 1, n_1 + n_2 + ... + n_k = n\}$, θ_i mean the i-th partition error coefficients, $i = 1, 2, ..., k$ and the values of the coefficients α, β depend on the complexity of the tested program and value of the coefficient γ_i depends on the size of the set of test cases that make up the k-th partition and the difficulty in obtaining the i-th test case drawn from this partition.

The complexity of the problem of determining the testing strategy $\boldsymbol{n} = (n_1, n_2, ..., n_k)$ strongly depends on the cardinality of the set $\mathcal{N}$ of all testing strategies for a given number k of partitions. It can be shown that the cardinality of the set $\mathcal{N}$ for a fixed number of partitions k and the sum of all n tests drawn from individual partitions is equal to the number of solutions to the diophantine equation of the form

$$n_1 + n_2 + ... + n_i + ... + n_k = n, n_i \in \{1, ..., n\} \tag{12}$$

which can be defined as follows (see e.g. Martin (2001))

$$|\mathcal{N}| = \binom{n-1}{k-1}. \tag{13}$$

The optimization problem of the partition testing strategy is a two-criteria optimization problem with nonlinear objective functions. A solution of this problem can be obtained by using well known methodology of solving multiple optimization problems [8]. According to that methodology as a solution of the problem that has been formulated can be determined:

- a dominated solution set,
- a non-dominated solution set,
- a compromise solution set.

The set of feasible solutions of the multi-criteria optimization problem is a set of such solutions that meet all the constraints of the problem. If in the set of feasible solutions there is a solution that is the best from the point of view of all the objective criteria, it is the so-called dominated solution. We say that a solution s_1 dominates a solution s_2 if all of s_1's objective values are better than the corresponding objective values of solution s_2. In that case, we can also say that solution s_2 is dominated by a solution s_1 if all of s_2's objective values are worse than the corresponding objective values of s_1.

A non-dominated solution set also considered as Pareto optimal solution set is a set of such feasible solutions, those are not dominated by any other feasible solutions. Generally speaking, in multi-objective optimization there is a single best solution for each objective value. However, in all the other objective values this solution might not fare that well. Therefore, in multi-objective optimization, the non-dominated solutions are the ones that form the set of most interesting solutions. In the absence of any preference regarding the objectives, all non-dominated solutions are assumed equivalent or indifferent. However, in practice, the multi-objective decision problems often require that a single non-dominated alternative (or a subset of non-dominated alternatives) is selected from the set of non-dominated solutions.

As the set of non-dominated solutions is very numerous, in practice various methods of its narrowing down are used. In order to narrow down that non-dominated solution set we will determine a compromise solution of this problem, i.e. such solution that belongs to the non-dominated solution set that and is nearest (in sense Euclidean distance) to the so-called an ideal objective point. For this reason both objective functions $P_p(n)$ and $C(k, n)$ will be normalized by means of the following formulae:

$$\overline{C(k, n)} = \frac{C(k, n) - C_{min}(k, n)}{C_{max}(k, n) - C_{min}(k, n)}, \quad \overline{P_p(n)} = \frac{P_p(n) - P_{p\,min}(n)}{P_{p\,max}(n) - P_{p\,min}(n)}, \quad (14)$$

where

$$C_{min}(k, n) = \min_{n \in \mathcal{N}} C(k, n), \quad P_{p\,min}(n) = \min_{n \in \mathcal{N}} P_p(n), \quad (15)$$

$$C_{max}(k, n) = \max_{n \in \mathcal{N}} C(k, n), \quad P_{p\,max}(n) = \max_{n \in \mathcal{N}} P_p(n). \quad (16)$$

Taking into account the fact that the component criterion functions appearing in the formulated problem $P_p(n)$ and $C(k, n)$ are conflicting objectives (in sense that if the value $P_p(n)$ is increased, the value $C(k, n)$ is increased, too) it is reasonable to expect that the dominated solution set will be empty. In a such situation practically recommended approach is to determine a non-dominated solution set. If this set is very numerous we can narrow it down by determining a so-called compromise solution using the distance metric-based multi-objective methods aim at minimizing a function of the distance between the desired (usually unachievable) and achieved non-dominated solutions.

The optimal partition testing strategy n^* that to be obtained after the solving the optimization problem will both maximizing the probability of detecting at least one error and minimizing the cost of the process of isolating individual partitions and drawing a certain number of test cases from them.

4 Numerical Example

The methodology of determination of the optimal partition testing strategy that has been presented can be illustrated by the following numerical example.

For the purpose of formulating the previously discussed optimization problem, it is assumed that values of the parameters $k, n, \alpha, \beta, \Theta_i$ and γ_i, $i = 1, 2, ..., k$, be defined as in Table 5.

Due to the nature of the criterion functions $P_p(n)$ and $C(k, n)$ of the two-criteria optimization problem that has been formulated, there are no dominant solutions. The solution to this problem should therefore be sought in the set of non-dominated solutions.

Table 5. Values of parameters k, n, α, β, Θ_i and γ_i used for considered numerical example

k	n	α	α
3	20	0,1	0,3

i	1	2	3
Θ_i	0,15	0,3	0,2
γ_i	0,3	0,4	0,5

For the data presented in Table 2, the cardinality of the set of all possible partition testing strategy is $|\mathcal{N}| = \binom{19}{2} = 171$. The criterion space of the formulated two-criteria optimization problem for normalized criterion functions is presented in Fig. 2. The set of non-dominated solutions is marked with a red contour. Every point of the contour is a non-dominated solution.

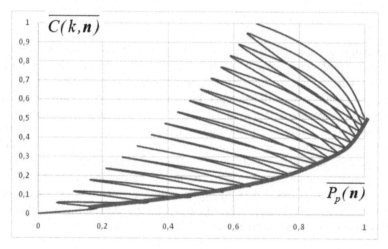

Fig. 2. The set of non-dominated solutions of the formulated two-criteria optimization problem

In order to narrow the set of non-dominated solutions down to e.g. a single-element set, a compromise solution will be determined which is the closest (in terms of the Euclidean space) to the so-called ideal point [8].

Table 6. A compromise solution of the formulated two-criteria optimization problem

Lp.	n	n_1	n_2	n_3	$P_p(n)$	C(k,n)	$\overline{P_p(n)}$	$\overline{C(k,n)}$	$d[\overline{P_p(n)}, \overline{C(k,n)}]$
1	20	1	1	18	0,9893	9,94596	0,667829	1	1,05372544
2	20	1	2	17	0,9906	9,84596	0,714134	0,970588	1,011810574
3	20	1	3	16	0,9918	9,74596	0,754651	0,941176	0,972629995
4	20	1	4	15	0,9928	9,64596	0,790104	0,911765	0,935612825
					...				
10	20	1	10	9	0,9968	9,04596	0,926894	0,735294	0,738919438
130	20	10	4	6	0,9876	7,84596	0,610014	0,382353	0,546152544
131	20	10	5	5	0,9892	7,74596	0,663546	0,352941	0,487615221
132	20	10	6	4	0,9905	7,64596	0,710387	0,323529	0,434220171
133	20	10	7	3	0,9917	7,54596	0,751372	0,294118	0,385124713
134	20	10	8	2	0,9927	7,44596	0,787234	0,264706	0,339615169
135	20	10	9	1	0,9936	7,34596	0,818614	0,235294	0,297093107
136	20	11	1	8	0,9803	7,94596	0,359054	0,411765	0,761814761
137	20	11	2	7	0,9828	7,84596	0,443956	0,382353	0,67481744
138	20	11	3	6	0,9850	7,74596	0,518245	0,352941	0,59720604
139	20	11	4	5	0,9868	7,64596	0,583248	0,323529	0,527591897
140	20	11	5	4	0,9885	7,54596	0,640126	0,294118	0,464773564
					...				
165	20	15	4	1	0,9832	6,84596	0,458377	0,088235	0,548762942
166	20	16	1	3	0,9734	6,94596	0,118557	0,117647	0,889259825
167	20	16	2	2	0,9767	6,84596	0,233521	0,088235	0,771541137
168	20	16	3	1	0,9796	6,74596	0,334114	0,058824	0,668478678
169	20	17	1	2	0,9717	6,74596	0,061075	0,058824	0,940766149
170	20	17	2	1	0,9753	6,64596	0,183224	0,029412	0,817305315
171	20	18	1	1	0,9700	6,54596	0	0	1

In terms of the discussed two-criteria optimization problem, the ideal point $(P_p(n), C(k, n))$, being an element of the so-called extended standardized criterial space, is in the form of *(1, 0)*.

The solution of the two-criteria optimization problem that has been formulated is presented in Table 6. The green table row corresponds to compromise solution, being the closest to the ideal point *(1, 0)*, where distance function $d[(\overline{P_p(n)}, \overline{C(k, n)}), (1, 0)]$ is defined by the following formula

$$d[(\overline{P_p(n)}, \overline{C(k, n)}), (1, 0)] = \sqrt{[\overline{P_p(n)} - 0]^2 + [\overline{C(k, n)} - 1]^2}. \qquad (17)$$

Table 6 shows that value $n* = (10, 9, 1)$ is a compromise solution of the two-criteria optimization problem that has been formulated for the numerical values assumed in the considered example. This value corresponds to the following point in the criterion space

$$(\overline{P_p^*(n)}, \ \overline{C^*(k, n)}) = (0, 818614, 0235299).$$

This means that the Euclidean distance between the ideal point *(1,0)* and the point (0, 818614, 0235299) is the smallest among all points of the criterion space and is corresponding to the partition testing strategy $n* = (10, 9, 1)$.

5 Summary

It can be generally stated that almost all program testing strategies are based on the following approach: a set of program test cases is divided into subsets (partitions) from which a certain number of test cases are then selected. The set of test cases created in this way is then used in the program testing process. Assuming that the selection of test cases from individual partitions is carried out randomly leads to a strategy which in the presented considerations is called partition testing. This strategy was confronted with the strategy based on the so-called random testing, according to which individual test cases were randomly selected from the entire set of input data of the considered program.

Simulations and empirical work by [4], aimed at comparing the effectiveness of partition testing and random testing, show that the effectiveness of both methods is comparable, and under certain conditions random testing can be even more effective - especially in terms of cost - than partition testing.

[12] formulated the conditions under which the effectiveness of partition testing will not be lower than the effectiveness of random testing. To satisfy these conditions, it is enough that the following equality: $d_1 = d_2 = \cdots = d_k$ and $n_1 = n_2 = \cdots = n_k$. [2] extended and generalized the results of [12] by formulating more general conditions under which one testing strategy is superior to another. The most important result of [2] is the observation that if the number of test cases drawn from individual partitions is proportional to the size of these partitions, the efficiency of partition testing will not be lower than the efficiency of random testing.

The main result of this work is to obtain the method of determining the partition testing strategy, which can be the basis for the implementation of the program testing process. This strategy is obtained as a result of solving the problem of two-criteria optimization, with the following component criteria taken into account as the component criteria:

– probability of an event that the set of test cases will allow to detect at least one error;
– the cost of extracting a certain number of partitions from the domain of the tested program and drawing some sets of test cases from them.

References

1. Boland, P.J., Singh, H., Cukic, B.: Comparing partition and random testing via majorization and Schur functions. IEEE Trans. Softw. Eng. **29**(1), 88–94 (2003)
2. Chen, T.Y., Yu, Y.T.: On the relationship between partition and random testing. IEEE Trans. Softw. Eng. **20**(12), 977–980 (1994)
3. Chen, T.Y., Yu, Y.T.: A more general sufficient condition for partition testing to be better than random testing. Inf. Process. Lett. **57**(3), 145–149 (1996)
4. Duran, J.W., Ntafos, S.C.: An evaluation of random testing. IEEE Trans. Softw. Eng. **10**(4), 438–444 (1984)
5. Gutjahr, W.J.: Partition testing vs. random testing: the influence of uncertainty. IEEE Trans. Softw. Eng. **25**(5), 661–674 (1999)
6. Hamlet, R., Taylor, R.: Partition testing does not inspire confidence. IEEE Trans. Softw. Eng. **16**(12), 1402–1411 (1990)

7. IEEE Std 610.12-1990, IEEE Standard Glossary for Software Engineering Terminology. IEEE, New York (1990)
8. Keller, A.A.: Multi-Objective Optimization in Theory and Practice I: Classical Methods, Bentham Science Publishers (2017)
9. Martin, G.E.: Counting: The Art of Enumerative Combinatorics. Springer, Cham (2001)
10. Roman A.: Software testing and quality. Models, techniques, tools. PWN, Warsaw (2015)
11. Weyuker, E.J., Jeng, B.: Analyzing partition testing strategies. IEEE Trans. Softw. Eng. **17**(7), 703–711 (1991)
12. Worwa, K.: Optimization of test case allocation scheme in program partition testing. In: Proceedings of the 36th International Business Information Management Association Conference (IBIMA), 4–5 November 2020 (2020)

The Architecture of the Mobile Application for Android with the Use of the MVVM Pattern and the HILT, Livedata, Room, Retrofit and Kotlin Coroutines Libraries

Paweł Kaczmarek and Zbigniew Piotrowski[✉]

Faculty of Electronics, Institute of Communications Systems, Military University of
Technology, Kaliskiego 2 str., 00-908 Warsaw, Poland
{pawelk.kaczmarek,zbigniew.piotrowski}@wat.edu.pl

Abstract. The paper describes the recommended practices used in Android application development. The paper solves the issues related to the selection and application of modern technologies and libraries on the example of a mobile application. The application architecture was proposed using the MVVM design pattern and the HILT, LiveData, Room, Retrofit and Kotlin Coroutines libraries. As a result, a generic application architecture model will be presented, which can be used and implemented in many other applications depending on their functionality.

Keywords: Software architecture · Android · Android application design

1 Introduction

The creators of the Android operating system - Google - during periodic presentations present a number of libraries, components and mechanisms that software authors can use when developing applications for Android OS. From the very beginning of the Android system, developers had at their disposal the basic components of the application. They include: Activity, Intent, Broadcast Intent Receiver, Service and Content Provider. They are described in more detail in [2]. Not all components are required for the application to run, but some of them will be used at least once. When designing and creating an application, one should bear in mind many aspects that permeate the entire production process, including fragmentation of available devices and their heterogeneity on the market, complexity and variety of APIs and components, effective management of physical resources of devices, multithreading and synchronization. In addition to the above, an important issue are also the functional requirements for applications that are required to perform tasks intended for web applications. An analysis in (App Analytics and Data Company) shows that there were 204 billion downloads of mobile applications in 2019, compared with 178 billion in 2018. It is estimated that the number of downloads of applications by 2022 will be 260 million (App Analytics and Data Company). With all of the above factors in mind, developing the right architecture for your mobile application is critical to your success. By identifying all prior components at the development

K. S. Soliman (Ed.): IBIMA-AI 2023, CCIS 2101, pp. 296–307, 2024.
https://doi.org/10.1007/978-3-031-62843-6_28

stage, it is easier to scale, test, develop, maintain, and understand and reuse your application's source code. When asked about the appropriate architecture for an Android OS application, the creators of the development toolkit answer that there is no single way to write an application that will be best for each scenario (Modern Android development: Android Jetpack, Kotlin, and more).

2 Design Pattern MVVM – Model-View-ViewModel

Model-View-ViewModel is a software architecture design pattern that allows for separations in the production of GUI views (Graphical User Interface) – View (V-View) - from the source codes of the business logics or server layer (backend) – Model (M-Model). The pattern assumes that the developed application or system will have separate layers that will allow for the division of tasks and responsibilities. Thanks to this, the non-functional requirement for the ease of maintenance and care (maintainability) of the entire source code is fulfilled [4]. The information exchange between the model and the view is accomplished through the view model (VM-ViewModel). The view model is responsible for exchanging information with the model and making these data available to the view. It allows you to determine from where the view is supplied with data and notifies this view in the event of a model state change. In addition, it also implements data conversion logic in order to prepare them for presentation on view. Figure 1 shows the communication between the layers of the pattern.

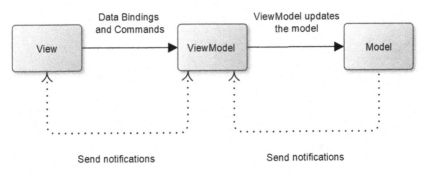

Fig. 1. Layers communication in the MVVM pattern (own work)

Figure 2 shows the life cycle of activities and fragments. Taking into account the life cycle of activities and fragments is very important due to the fact that it applies to both creating and destroying user views. The complexity of this process is a big problem when it comes to application design. If the system destroys or recreates the user interface view, any transient user interface data stored in it will be lost. This situation will occur whenever the user rotates the device from a horizontal to a vertical position or vice versa. The Android SDK (Software Development Kit) tools provide appropriate methods to preserve and restore model data after device rotation, but their use is limited to small data sets, which can also be serialized and deserialized. Another problem is asynchronicity. Time-consuming asynchronous method calls must be managed from within the view to prevent memory leaks. Considering in this case also the possibility of changing the device screen orientation, actions should be taken in order not to execute the time-consuming and resource-intensive call that has already been made. Assigning over-accountability to UI views can cause a single class to try to handle all application functionality on its own, rather than delegating work to other classes. For mobile applications for Android, a dedicated solution was created that allows you to manage model data intended for the user interface, taking into account the complex life cycle of application components (activities or fragments) - class ViewModel (ViewModel overview I Android Developers) The class is designed to store user interface data and manage them taking the life cycle into consideration. The ViewModel class allows you to preserve data after configuration changes, such as rotating the screen. This solution, which implements the MVVM pattern and which is the controller of the interface logic, while enabling the separation of views from the model, is efficient and effective.

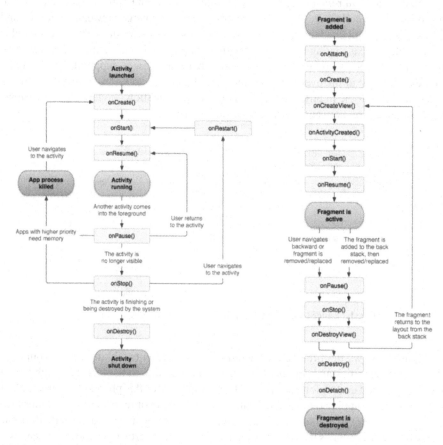

Fig. 2. Activity life cycle (left) (Fragments I Android Developers) and fragment life cycle (right) (The activity lifecycle I Android Developers)

3   The LiveData Class - Storing Data Using the Observer Pattern

In order to fully implement the MVVM pattern, the last issue must be considered - informing the view about the delivery of the model and updating the model after changes to the view. Tracking the life cycle of components is very important in this case as well. The creators of the Android mobile system provide developers with a ready-made solution in the form of LiveData class. LiveData is a class that implements data storage using the observer pattern. Contrary to a properly implemented observer pattern, this solution depends on the components life cycle, so observers notification takes place only for active and registered observers in the process of starting or resuming components. The process for damaged components is similar - observers are removed and do not handle subsequent notifications. This solution offers a number of advantages. The user interface is always up to date with the data without having to react manually to changes in application data. The association with the components life cycle ensures no memory leaks, and the data provided by LiveData are always up to date, also after a configuration change (e.g. device rotation or activity closure).

4   Dependency Injection Using the Hilt Library

In order for the model views to provide data, they must have dependencies on repositories - a design pattern that enables the separation of the data access layer from the layer implementing the business logic of the application. The assumption is that the repositories will obtain data from the default Android SQLite database and remotely via REST API, using the HTTP protocol. In the first case, the Room (Save data in a local database using Room | Android Developers) library was used for data sources, and in the second, the Retrofit (Retrofit) library. Data sources also have dependencies, among others, configuration dependency. The multitude of dependencies - the greater the more functionalities the application has - makes it difficult to change the implementation of classes without modifying the classes that depend on them and limits the testing of individual classes without providing their dependencies. The solution to this problem is to use the Dependency Injection design pattern. This pattern is to remove direct dependencies of components in favour of delivering them through the dependency space. Deployment of dependency injection as an implementation of reverse control is described in [2]. Hilt is a dependency injection library for Android that limits the scheme for performing manual dependency injection in a project, providing a standard way to use DI in an application, providing containers for each Android class, and automatically managing their life cycle. The library's advantages include dependency checking at the compilation stage, delivery by the constructor, as well as performance and scalability. The implementation and configuration of the library is carried out with the use of defined annotations and the Hilt module, for cases where dependencies cannot be specified directly - primarily for the injection of interfaces or classes from external libraries.

5 Data Access: Room and Retrofit Libraries

As mentioned, repositories deliver data from local and remote sources. Such solution allows for two scenarios. The first is to save the data locally, and then send them to a remote data source. Such a situation occurs when the user uses the application without access to the network, in order to synchronize data when joining the network. In the second case, the data downloaded from the remote repository are saved in a local source, from where they are presented to the application user. This example is implemented by the cache mechanism. Developing the entire software in one component is wrong, therefore various functionalities and tasks are separated into separate components and modules, which is exemplary shown in Fig. 3.

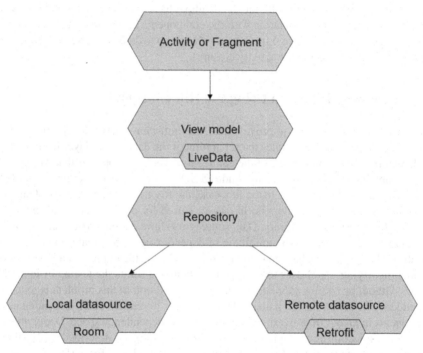

Fig. 3. Android application architecture components (own work).

Local data can be accessed smoothly through the SQLite database abstraction layer while taking full advantage of it through the Room library. The library not only provides access to data, but also their caching and synchronization. Its use is based on three elements, which include: database, entities and DAO (Data Access Object) components. The database element serves as the primary access point for connecting to the database. An entity represents a table in the database according to the ORM mapping (Object-Relational Mapping) facilitating the downloading and preservation of objects stored in a relational database [12]. DAO components are interfaces that contain methods that access a database. The implementation of the interfaces is carried out by the library. The use and operation of the Room library is based on the fact that the application, using a database element, accesses DAO components, to then download the entities through them and save them. Changing attributes in an entity changes individual columns in the table that reflects it. The configuration of elements is based on the provided annotations [12].

The remote repository in many cases is located on the server, where communication takes place via the HTTP protocol using the basic methods in the REST API pattern. The classic approach to the implementation of the HTTP client on the Android system side is laborious due to the large amount of code to be produced and is complicated due to the complexity of the issue. To simplify the data exchange with API, the Retrofit library was used instead of the standard approach. The library provides a secure HTTP client for Android implemented through an interface whose implementation is generated by the library. Annotations describe specific HTTP requests that can be sent synchronously or asynchronously, ensuring the replacement of URL parameters, handling of query parameters, conversion of objects into the request body (e.g. JSON, buffers) or file transfer (Retrofit).

6 Kotlin Corotuines

At the 2017 Google I/O conference, Kotlin statically typed object-oriented programming language was officially announced as the default and supported programming language for the Android platform. It is a language fully interoperable with Java, running on the Java Virtual Machine (Developer Keynote (Google I/O). The studies described in [14] show that the code written using the Kotlin language is concise, reduces the amount of code to be written and is safer due to the reduction of errors related to the lack of a pointer to variables (exception NullPointerException). It has been adopted in the described architecture as the default application development language.

The final technical consideration related to application architecture is asynchronicity. When an application component starts and no other component of the application runs in the background, a new process with a single thread of execution starts. If any component is already running, the application runs under an already existing process. By default, all components of one application run in the same process and thread, called the main thread. This thread is very important as it is responsible for sending events to the appropriate UI widgets, including drawing events, and thus is also called UI thread. All components run in the same process, so the application's complex and time-consuming work causes the user interface to be blocked. In this situation, no events are sent, including drawing events, which implies a blockage of the entire user interface, simulating an application crash. In addition, UI package widgets are not thread-safe, so they only need to be manipulated from the main thread. Two conclusions should be drawn from the above. First, long and laborious operations cannot be performed on the UI thread. Second, the UI Toolkit cannot be accessed from the main thread (Processes and threads overview I App quality I Android Developers). Multithreading and concurrency are the main challenges that developers of mobile applications have to face in their daily work. The ultimate solution to asynchronicity and multithreading should be simple, comprehensive, and robust. This issue can be solved via LiveData, but the mere storage of the data in the observer pattern is incomplete. LiveData is not designed for multithreading, but for accessing data from the main thread. The implementation of the RxJava library, described in [2] using the observer pattern, allowing the development of asynchronous, event-based applications using observable sequences, is a powerful solution, but often misused, and it is perceived as an exaggerated concurrency solution. The target solution described in the article is the use of Kotlin Coroutines. Coroutines simplify asynchronous code generation by replacing callbacks with suspended computations. By using Coroutines, you can create secure code that will never block the main thread, and that supports cancellation of calls. Kotlin Coroutines cooperates with WorkManager, Room or Retrofit libraries, which additionally supports its use. The support for LiveData added by the developers of the Android system through the liveData() extension method allows the use of a Coroutine block inside a function, returning the implementation of this class and allowing the emission of events and data for this pattern.

Coroutines functions are realized by adding two keywords for common functions or methods:

- suspend – interrupts the execution of the current program, saving all local variables,
- resume – continues program execution from where it was interrupted.

Functions marked with the suspend modifier can only be called from other suspend functions or through the Coroutine Builder mechanism. Kotlin Coroutines use dispatchers to determine which threads are used to execute a program. To run the code outside the main thread, select the Default or IO dispatcher. In Kotlin, all programs must run in the dispatcher, even while running on the main thread. Coroutines may suspend their work and the dispatcher is responsible for resuming them. To determine where Kotlin programs should run, three basic dispatchers are available:

- Dispatchers.Main – a dispatcher launching Coroutine in the main Android thread. It should only be used to interact with the user interface or perform quick work. Examples include calling suspend functions, starting Android UI functions, and updating LiveData objects.
- Dispatchers.IO – this dispatcher is optimized to perform I/O operations on a physical disk or network outside of the main thread. Examples of use include components of the Room library, reading or writing data to files, and running any network operation, including those using the Retrofit library.
- Dispatchers.Default – a dispatcher focused on performing processor-intensive work outside the main thread. Exemplary use cases include sorting lists and parsing JSON.

To use a given dispatcher, use the withContext() function that takes the dispatcher parameter, which allows you to create a block that works on a specific pool of threads. This function does not add a computational overhead compared to callback based solutions. Note that using Dispatchers.IO or Dispatchers.Default does not guarantee that the block will execute on the same thread from start to finish. In some situations, Kotlin Coroutines may move execution to another thread after suspend and resume. This means that thread-local variables may not point to the same value for the entire withContext() block (Use Kotlin coroutines with lifecycle-aware components I Android). To call Coroutine functions, one of the functions should be used: runBlocking(), launch(), async(). The first one – runBlocking() – blocks the current thread until all Coroutines have been executed. This solution is advisable when writing tests. The launch() function does not block the current thread, and it does not expect to return a result when it is called. It returns a Job class object that implements methods to cancel invoked Coroutines or block related Coroutines until all are completed. The async() function differs from the launch() function with the returned object - Deferred class. It is a promise of a future Coroutine output, which can be obtained by suspending further execution of the instruction with the await() function. Kotlin Coroutines are operating within the scope. Within the specified structure hierarchy, the scope is the Coroutine executable space. This enables the management of all Corotutines within a given scope. Any class that implements CoroutineScope interface and overwrites coroutineContext becomes a scope. On Android, some libraries provide their own CoroutineScope for specific life cycle classes. For example, ViewModel class has viewModelScope, and Lifecycle – lifecycleScope. CoroutineContext defines behaviour of Coroutine transferring its calling to an appropriate thread (Use Kotlin coroutines with lifecycle-aware components | Android).

7   Application Architecture Implementation

The application allows you to save data in the format of sheets to which you can add expenses and income. As intended, the application writes data to the database first and then tries to save them on a remote server. In the case of no network access, the application sets the status of no synchronization for new items. Synchronization takes place after reconnecting the mobile device to the Internet when restarting the application or it can be triggered manually. In the first step of the practical implementation of the architecture of the described application, dependencies to the libraries described above were collected and configured. Gradle is the default tool for managing dependencies and automating the process of compilation and building source codes by creating an output file with the.apk extension. Dependencies are added in the build.gradle file, where apart from the library name, their versions should be indicated. The data model was saved using the Room library, and then the DAO data access layer is used for the specific model in the repositories. Repositories are included in model views for fragments and activities that manipulate the model. The data access layer has methods using Coroutines, thanks to the keyword suspend before the method signature. The above model dependencies to the model view are managed by the Hilt dependency container, which injects the appropriate classes based on the module configuration class. Dependencies are provided by the constructor. Figure 4 presents two views that show the added data model saved to the database when there is no Internet access. The added sheet on the left has a red synchronization icon, which means that the data were not transferred to the remote server. The right side shows a similar case for the cost-benefit ratio of a given sheet. Again, the data are not synchronized with the remote server.

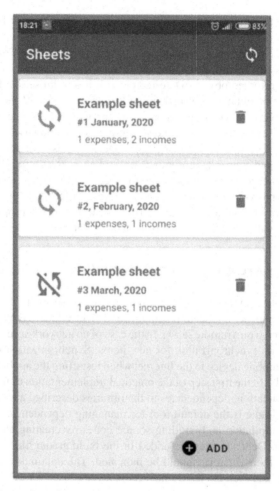

Fig. 4. An example of the application's operation for the lack of access to the Internet (own work)

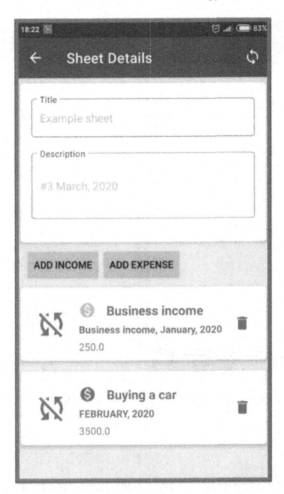

Fig. 4. (*continued*)

In the next stage, access to the Internet on the mobile device was enabled, so that the repository collecting the data synchronized with the server automatically. Figure 5 shows the case after automatic synchronization. The image on the left shows the successful completion of the synchronization, and by using the LiveData classes, the view was automatically updated based on the current, synchronized data in the application database. The update also took place in the sheet-dependent model - for the expense and cost model entities - the figure on the right.

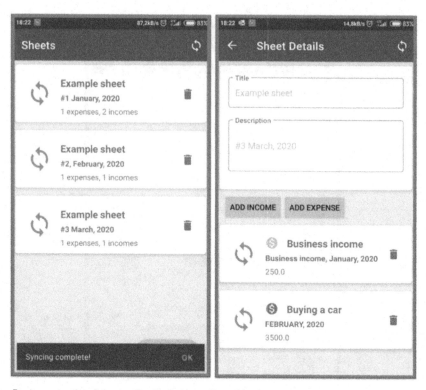

Fig. 5. An example of the application's operation with access to the Internet - synchronization (own work)

8 Summary

All the libraries described above constitute a complementary set of tools and programming solutions that enable the creation of a reliable mobile application for the Android operating system. The use of the MVVM pattern separated the view from the data model, making it easier to maintain the source codes. The used repositories and LiveData classes provide data, manage them and automatically update views. The data access layer is easy to implement and maintain with the help of the Room and Retrofit libraries. All components are created and managed by the dependency injection library and work asynchronously thanks to Coroutines, which makes the application multi-threaded, efficiently delivering data. The developed application architecture can be used and implemented in many other applications depending on their functionality.

Acknowledgment. This research was funded by the Military University of Technology, Faculty of Electronics, grant number UGB 22 864 on "Watermark embedding and extraction methods as well as aggregation and spectral analysis methods using neural networks".

References

1. Online. https://www.youtube.com/watch?v=IrMw7MEgADk. Accessed July 2023
2. Kaczmarek, P., Piotrowski, Z.: Designing a mobile application on the example of a system for digital photos watermarking (2020). https://doi.org/10.1117/12.2565225
3. Online. https://www.data.ai/en/about/. Accessed July 2023
4. Saifan, A., Al-Rabadi, A.R.: Evaluating maintainability of Android applications (2017). https://doi.org/10.1109/icitech.2017.8080052
5. Online. https://developer.android.com/topic/libraries/architecture/viewmodel. Accessed July 2023
6. Online. https://developer.android.com/guide/fragments. Accessed July 2023
7. Online. https://developer.android.com/guide/components/activities/activity-lifecycle. Accessed July 2023
8. Online. https://developer.android.com/topic/libraries/architecture/livedata. Accessed July 2023
9. Online. https://kosi-libs.org/kodein/7.19/index.html. Accessed July 2023
10. Online. https://developer.android.com/training/data-storage/room. Accessed July 2023
11. Online. https://square.github.io/retrofit/. Accessed July 2023
12. Vial, G.: Lessons in persisting object data using object-relational mapping. IEEE Softw. **36**(6), 43–52 (2019). https://doi.org/10.1109/ms.2018.227105428
13. Online. https://www.youtube.com/watch?v=EtQ8Le8-zyo. Accessed July 2023
14. Ardito, L., Coppola, R., Malnati, G., Torchiano, M.: Effectiveness of Kotlin vs. Java in android app development tasks. Inf. Softw. Technol. (2020)
15. Online. https://developer.android.com/kotlin/coroutines/coroutines-best-practices. Accessed July 2023
16. Online. https://kotlinlang.org/docs/coroutines-overview.html. Accessed July 2023
17. Online. https://developer.android.com/guide/components/processes-and-threads. Accessed July 2023
18. Online. https://developer.android.com/topic/libraries/architecture/coroutines. Accessed July 2023

Common Problems in Application Development

Filip Majerik[(⊠)] and Monika Borkovcova

University of Pardubice, Pardubice, Czech Republic
{filip.majerik,monika.borkovcova}@upce.cz

Abstract. The aim of this article is an introductory familiarization with the results of the first case studies dealing with the evaluation of the object-oriented paradigm in collaboration with the data layer [16]. From the conducted survey of ORM Framework possibilities and subsequent consultation with companies implementing these frameworks, various questions have arisen that form the main basis for this article. We focused primarily on whether it is possible to prevent the decrease in performance of applications implementing ORM Frameworks with an increasing amount of managed data [10]. What is the most suitable implementation of an ORM Framework in terms of performance and availability of the resulting software, and how can the required memory for processing large volumes of data be reduced with the help of an ORM Framework. It also explores if it is possible to eliminate the need for custom data consistency checks or validations. ORM issues are often addressed due to their extensive use [5]. [11] investigates the impact of transactional cache and object cache on application performance and application behavior, [13] focuses on ORM issues at the schema level. A description of the underlying ORM issues of Hibernate can then be found in [9], while they also mention issues related to object unserializability, missing access methods, simple paging and more. From the area of design patterns, one can also point to one-to-many antivorms in Hibernate, where each antivor is described including the implications and recommended solution [15].

Keywords: ORM · data layer · relational database · optmization of databases

1 Introduction

Database systems are currently one of the most widespread storage spaces for application data. This software is sufficiently sophisticated compared to earlier versions, allowing developers to use a variety of indexing methods, data partitioning, data merging, data modification, and many other tools or additions. However, with this comes great responsibility for developers who often fail to exploit all the features of database systems, and due to this ignorance, they often create sub-optimal software solutions. Such software solutions then manifest themselves in common phenomena such as overly slow response, unnecessarily long data loading, low performance, a low number of handled requests per unit of time, and others. This fact is related to the current boom in ORM development, which brings significant problems with heavy loads. Given that the current trend of developers, associated with the increasing frequency of IT innovations, is to look for

K. S. Soliman (Ed.): IBIMA-AI 2023, CCIS 2101, pp. 308–317, 2024.
https://doi.org/10.1007/978-3-031-62843-6_29

the simplest approaches. The growing demand for new functionalities has allowed for a fairly fundamental development of ORM Frameworks in recent years. These frameworks typically aim to simplify working with a database and create a certain abstraction, which then, for example, allows for easy replacement of the database system with another. Given this effort, the developers of such frameworks often do not focus directly on performance, but try to cover as many database systems as possible. This effort to cover everything possible, such as unifying access to SQL and noSQL databases, then leads to a decrease in data throughput and thus to a decrease in the performance of the application as a whole [2]. The study we are concerned with focuses on removing inefficient parts of the software and incorrect database accesses in the application source code. The theoretical insights derived from general software development practices are further validated in practice in various software development companies. The outputs of the study in the final phase are summarized query optimization, deadlock analysis using source code analysis, DB schema enhancement, and reduction in query response latency. We try to describe the problem of automatically recompiled SQL using ORM, which often leads to performance degradation and inability to optimize. As part of these solutions, we also describe the actual problem of retrieving data from the database, where we address the required data versus the retrieved data. A natural part of this research is the area of transactional code processing.

2 Literature Review

[4] describes an automated framework that is capable of troubleshooting ORM problems. It tries to describe the problems that developers do during development where they don't address performance implications and again focuses mainly on the issue of one-to-one processing, where they pull data out of the database line by line. As another work, they describe the problem of Design-Level Performance Antipatterns. [3] focus on the issue of MVCs and their controllers, where often MVC frameworks implement some ORM API. Developers then often use e.g. loops, frequent updates or inmemory entity collections. They try to link relational algebra with ORM so that it is easier to optimize the database approach. They try to simplify accesses to subobjects and their data and consequently reduce the complexity of SQL. [8] They address the issue of application performance degradation versus using hand-written SQL. Their article also describes the advantages and disadvantages of using ORM such as speed of development, implementation in the language, no need for SQL knowledge, no need to write SQL queries, reducing the amount of code, reducing performance, using ORM and native SQL. It also describes for example the object-server layer of the application, where much of the database-related issues are combined into their own layer. The main output is the observation of application performance degradation when using ORMs. In contrast to these studies, where individual researches always focus on a selected area in relation to the use of ORM frameworks, we want to achieve an appropriate use of these frameworks and validate these recommendations in practice in order to develop a comprehensive methodology. The research is currently in its first phase, where we are verifying the current state of use of these frameworks in practice and testing our initial hypotheses, which are described later in this paper.

3   Database Software Architecture and Design

The basis of well-functioning and fast software is an appropriate database design, as well as the architecture of the software itself. Unfortunately, this step is greatly underestimated today, and many companies abandon software design and analysis because it costs additional resources. As a result, situations often arise where a company works with developers who understand the basic principles of everything, but the depth of their talent is not sufficiently developed. Such a developer then tries various frameworks, adds knowledge gained from professional community forums, and the result is often software that works until the first major load [14]. This can only be prevented, unfortunately, by investing in good software analysts or at least spending costs on some initial self-analysis of the resulting software. Often even basic analysis can reveal various pitfalls that may occur in future software. When designing a database application, it is always necessary to devote enough time to requirement analysis, and subsequently to the analysis and architecture of the resulting database. All of this results in better or worse data throughput, possibly the speed of handling database requests, and overall the result of the response of the entire application.

3.1   Object-Oriented Software Architecture

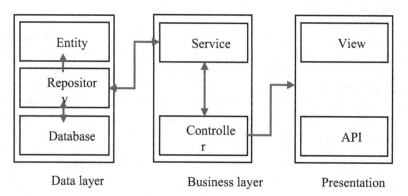

Fig. 1. Software Architecture

In Fig. 1, the model of the currently most commonly used software architecture is displayed. This architecture is based on the classic MVC model.

3.2   Data Layer

The data layer of this architecture serves to prepare data that is retrieved from the database. The repository in this layer ensures that data is appropriately stored in or retrieved from the database. It also has all the necessary information about what the data in the database looks like and how to potentially work with it. Subsequently, this data is mapped to an entity. Nowadays, the classic approach, where data is not mapped to an entity, is rarely used. ORM Frameworks, which are subsequently placed in the data layer between repositories and the database, have served for this. They work there as an abstraction between the application and the database, allowing, for example, to change the database for another one or even to migrate to a completely different category of database. Several critical points that can have a significant impact on the performance of the entire application can be listed within this layer. Communication of the repository with the database, where in the case of non-optimally written queries, there may be a significant delay both in terms of data processing and on the part of the database, can be primarily mentioned. And another critical point can be the database itself, which can already have a very bad design prepared by itself.

3.3 Business Layer

This layer serves as a mediator between the data and the final output of the application. All calculations and all business logic that needs to be implemented into the application are done here. Often this is the most extensive part of the application, where there is also the potential to create many so-called bottlenecks or non-optimal algorithms that can reduce the performance of the entire software. The biggest bottleneck on this layer can be that data from the database is not obtained optimally. For example, data is obtained that the final logic does not need at all, data is being joined that are not needed in the end, and so on. These mentioned problems are often caused by inappropriate implementation or poor knowledge of the frameworks that developers implement into applications.

3.4 Presentation Layer

The last layer in our architecture serves to present data to the user, or through an API to some other component that may be tied to the software. Here it might come to mind that it is impossible to influence the performance of the application, but unfortunately the opposite is true. The most common problem of the presentation layer is that users often want extreme results. A common case is, for example, printing out all available data from the database, displaying data that they actually do not need at all, excessively long pages, and the like. Here too, it is always necessary to think about what the final presentation layer should look like and whether everything that appears at the output is really necessary.

4 Software Architecture Design

Even the design of the application itself can significantly influence performance at all layers of such an application. Therefore, it is always appropriate to conduct at least a basic design. This design should be based on requirements analysis, which should clearly show what the final software should look like.

Unfortunately, there is no unified design on how exactly to design applications or there is no unified architecture that could be applied without problems to any problem. However, various methodologies are available that try to help with this issue and the result should always be the most complete, but at the same time the smallest model of software architecture. This model is then converted by the developer during the implementation phase of the project into source code. One of the primary benefits of good software architecture design is that various methodologies (both agile and non-agile) allow so-called incremental delivery of functionalities. As a result, the software client gradually receives implemented parts of the software and does not have to wait for the result as a whole.

5   Data Sources and Data Storage Selection

Currently, almost every application requires some source of data for its proper functionality. The most widespread sources of data are currently databases, which perform several tasks. These include, for example, data storage, maintaining data consistency, data security against misuse, etc. The vast majority of these tasks can be influenced by the developer during the implementation of the data layer. As part of the application design, it is necessary to consider what source of data, or possibly database, the application should use and which database is ideal for a given use case from the perspective of their properties. In general, data can be accessed using various methods. The most common methods for working with data are direct access to file data, storage in local databases or access to remote databases using pre-defined APIs. No less important is the database design. This chapter will describe a general database design that is independent of the use of a relational or non-relational database, or the use of a file database or a classic database system [6]. The API does not apply at all in the general database design, because in such a data source the database design is left to an external source, which can often not be influenced at all within the newly developed application.

6   Data Access on the Data Layer

Choosing the appropriate data access on the data layer is always influenced by several factors. The most common factor is the target device where the developed application will run. Often, especially with modern applications, embedded devices are used. These devices typically do not have substantial performance or large storage, so they use access to remote databases via APIs. On the other hand, there are traditional desktop or server applications that have sufficient performance and can therefore maneuver in some way with the selection of suitable storage and data access. However, even these traditional applications can use remote APIs, which can provide them with supportive data for their operation and proper functionality.

Historically, the most common and widely used are files or file databases. Nowadays, the use of files or file databases is very limited. They were replaced by the use of APIs, which are much more flexible, although they may be slower for solving certain things. The advantage of files and file databases is primarily that they can be easily backed up, delivered directly with software, can run independently of the internet. The disadvantage is the need to know complex data structures, or the implementation of some service module, for file databases. Also, there may be additional requirements for performance, memory, or storage size, if such a database would process a large amount of data. In general, it can be said that files and file databases are suitable to use where relatively little data will be worked with.

Database systems are currently the most commonly used data sources. These data sources are often based on extensive DBMS. These DBMS themselves implement many tools for working with data, optimize access to such data, decide on strategies for selecting data from data files, and often implement various security mechanisms that prevent data misuse. All mentioned are quite fundamental advantages of why not to use file databases or files in general. As part of the data layer design, it is also always necessary to decide what type of database is suitable. In the first place, there is a choice between relational and non-relational databases. Non-relational databases can be further divided into object, graph, key-value, document, and others [12]. Each of the mentioned databases has a relatively specific use case. Modern software often uses several databases. Usually one, which serves as primary storage, and others, which serve as secondary in the role of cache. The choice of primary and secondary database, or possibly the use of a secondary database at all, is always the subject of a general database design when all use cases for the given software are known.

The last type of data source are APIs. This source has been experiencing quite a boom in recent years, as developers are trying to shift a large part of the performance to user workstations. This idea is quite historical, however, with the expansion of web software and a massive shift in JavaScript, which runs directly in browsers on end stations, it is becoming more and more substantial [7]. All the more, there is a need for necessary optimizations on the API server side to handle as many clients as possible. Generally, one can speak relatively only in superlatives about accessing data via API, as its disadvantages are almost non-existent. Basically, only two can be defined - a nonfunctional or unavailable remote server or an unexpected incompatible change in the remote API, which makes almost all clients unavailable, at least until they update their client applications. However, even this second disadvantage is quite quickly solvable these days even at the level of long-running applications, which take care of their own upgrade. At the same time, it should be mentioned that the API is as powerful as the data layer and business layer under this API. If the design of these layers is sloppy, poorly done, and not optimal, the end application can work as well as possible and the result will only be a poorly responding, or even unstable and unusable application. Therefore, special attention must be paid to the implementation of the data layer in the API and choose the most suitable approaches that will allow the greatest throughput and the fastest data handling with high security.

7   General Database Design

When designing a database, it is often not known at the beginning what type and specific database will be needed for the software. This is determined over time when the relationships and associations between entities are clear and the database functionalities required to serve the entire database model are identified. In modern applications, where hardware performance is less of a concern, multiple primary databases or secondary databases are often used. For example, a data cache can be implemented using a key-value store (Redis) or a document database (MongoDB). Alternatively, there may be a need to process large amounts of text data, perform searches within this data, apply grammar rules, and prefer various word combinations. In such cases, a non-relational document database like Elasticsearch, which is built on a RESTful interface, can be used. Selecting the appropriate database system should receive roughly the same amount of attention as the rest of the database design process. It is often an irreversible step that can require significant effort and financial resources if not done properly. An inappropriate database selection can lead to complications in the performance of the database application.

8   Design Patterns

In modern software development, design patterns are often utilized. These patterns serve as guidelines that define specific behaviors, logics, or structures. Design patterns are closely associated with object-oriented programming, which has brought many new possibilities to the world of programming. In simplified terms, design patterns are created to ensure that different programmers do not solve the same problems differently. Knowledge of design patterns allows developers to streamline their work, as they can easily decide which design pattern is appropriate given their understanding. The result can be faster and more accurate implementation of new functionalities.

9   The Most Common Problems in Development

9.1   Low Performance

As the number of entities increases, the response time of the system starts to slow down. This deteriorating performance is mainly attributed to the ORM and entity manipulation. When processing a large number of entities, the ORM framework has to handle a significant number of change sets, leading to performance degradation. Similarly, when retrieving data from the database, the ORM framework has to hydrate numerous relational data that ultimately remain unused.

9.2   Low Throughput

With an increasing number of new entities and tables, the throughput of the database significantly decreases. This is primarily due to the current model layer not allowing the retrieval of only the necessary data from the database. This problem is closely related to the issue of low performance in the model layer.

9.3   Entity Joins

Due to the current design and limited knowledge of relational databases among developers, there are several poorly implemented joins in the relational database. For example, an entity called Service may contain two attributes, id_channel_packages and id_channels, which store comma-separated values representing the corresponding parent entities' IDs. The ORM framework allows and even indirectly supports such join implementation. However, this kind of join results in performance and throughput degradation, particularly because such fields cannot be indexed in commonly available relational databases.

9.4 Security and Data Integrity

The aforementioned issue also poses a potential security problem. As the comma-separated data cannot be intelligently verified as foreign keys at the database level, unwanted data can be stored in these attributes. Moreover, data integrity is compromised, as the deletion of parent keys cannot rely on deletion restrictions. Ensuring data security and integrity is "shifted" to the application's model layer. However, in this model layer, there is no guarantee that all programmers will use the same implementation. It solely relies on the human factor.

9.5 Data Validation

Due to the mentioned implementation in the previous points, the deployment companies were forced to move some validations directly to the model layer. For example, the attributes id_channels and id_channel_packages in the Service entity. These two attributes are subsequently validated by the model layer, which attempts to retrieve all entities with the inserted IDs and then evaluates which of these IDs do not exist. Such validations are performed even when the entity's change set is empty. These prepared validations are present in almost every entity in the monitored application. In extreme cases, the monitored system contains 20 validation processes that are executed with each instance of an entity being saved.

10 Proposals for Measures

To address the above-mentioned issues, the following actions have been proposed:
Low Performance and Low Throughput are primarily caused by the volume of processed data, entity metadata overhead from the framework, and caching. As part of optimizing this problem, it is necessary to limit the usage of the ORM cache mechanism. Additionally, intelligent data retrieval from the relational database should be implemented, and data segmentation and processing in smaller portions or changing the ORM hydration mode should be considered.

The issue of Entity Joins is mainly based on inappropriate implementation of join tables. To optimize this problem, the reduction of such joins should be proposed, along with a suitable approach for migrating to join tables that can utilize database indexes. Furthermore, a design for optimizing the change in the data layer should be considered.

To ensure better data consistency and integrity, similar measures should be incorporated as those proposed for addressing data joining changes. These measures will enable the utilization of standard database mechanisms and thus automatically ensure commonly available consistency and integrity checks.

11 Conclusion

From the initial case studies, it is evident that the basic implementation of ORM frameworks is not an ideal solution. In further stages of investigation, it is expected that more precise vulnerabilities of ORM frameworks when working with the data layer will be identified, along with proposals for their resolution. The article indicates that due to the inconsistent use of database tools for maintaining data consistency, an excessive number of unnecessary database queries arises in the data layer. These queries often serve only as substitutes for foreign keys or unique indexes and evaluate very simple constraints. These simple constraints often involve checking for duplicate records within operators. For a comprehensive view of the object paradigm issues at the data layer, it is necessary to include an overall analysis of the object approach that takes place in interaction with schematic and non-schematic databases at different sizes of processed data. The main inputs are the case studies under investigation and the actual analyses that will enable the comparison of the object-oriented paradigm. The main outputs are then the fabrication of several prototypes usable in software development leading to concrete solutions to the problem domains. Other outputs will be sample simulations with existing and proposed design patterns or anti-design patterns so as to achieve more efficient development and data layer work.

References

1. Buraga, S.C., Amariei, D., Dospinescu, O.: An OWL-based specification of database management systems. Comput. MAteriuals Continua **70**(3), 5537–5550 (2022)
2. Čerešňák, R., Kvet, M.: Comparison of query performance in relational a non-relation databases. Transp. Res. Procedia **40**, 170–177 (2019)
3. Chawla, G., Aman, N., Komondoor, R., Bokil, A., Kharat, N.: Verification of ORM-based controllers by summary inference. In: Proceedings of the 44th International Conference on Software Engineering, pp. 2340–2351. (2022)
4. Chen, T.H., Shang, W., Jiang, Z.M., Hassan, A.E., Nasser, M., Flora, P.: Finding and evaluating the performance impact of redundant data access for applications that are developed using object-relational mapping frameworks. IEEE Trans. Softw. Eng. **42**(12), 1148–1161 (2016)
5. Chen, T.H.: Improving the quality of large-scale database-centric software systems by analyzing database access code. In: 2015 31st IEEE International Conference on Data Engineering Workshops, pp. 245–249. IEEE (2015)
6. Choina, M., Skublewska-Paszkowska, M.: Performance analysis of relational databases MySQL, PostgreSQL and Oracle using Doctrine libraries. J. Comput. Sci. Inst. **24**, 250–257 (2022)
7. Dospinescu, O., Chiuchiu, S.: Physical integration of heterogeneous web based data. Informatica Economica **23**(4), 17–25 (2019)
8. Gorodnichev, M., Moseva, M., Poly, K., Dzhabrailov, K., Gematudinov, R.: Exploring object-relational mapping (ORM) systems and how to effectively program a data access model. PalArch's J. Archaeol. Egyptol. Egyptol. **17**(3), 615–627 (2020)
9. Huang, Z., Shao, Z., Fan, G., Yu, H., Yang, K., Zhou, Z.: Hbsniff: A static analysis tool for java hibernate object-relational mapping code smell detection. Sci. Comput. Program. **217**, 102778 (2022)
10. Lorenz, M., Hesse, G., Rudolph, J.P.: Object-relational mapping revised-a guideline review and consolidation. In: ICSOFT-EA, pp. 157–168 (2016)
11. Keith, M., Stafford, R.: Exposing the ORM cache: familiarity with ORM caching issues can help prevent performance problems and bugs. Queue **6**(3), 38–47 (2008)
12. Kotiranta, P., Junkkari, M., Nummenmaa, J.: Performance of graph and relational databases in complex queries. Appl. Sci. **12**(13), 6490 (2022)

13. Nazário, M.F.C., Guerra, E., Bonifácio, R., Pinto, G.: Detecting and reporting object-relational mapping problems: an industrial report. In: 2019 ACM/IEEE International Symposium on Empirical Software Engineering and Measurement (ESEM), pp. 1–6. IEEE (2019)
14. Perri, D., Simonetti, M., Gervasi, O.: Deploying efficiently modern applications on cloud. Electronics **11**(3), 450 (2022)
15. Węgrzynowicz, P.: Performance antipatterns of one to many association in hibernate. In: 2013 Federated Conference on Computer Science and Information Systems, pp. 1475–1481. IEEE (2013)
16. Zmaranda, D., Pop-Fele, L.L., Gyorödi, C., Gyorödi, R., Pecherle, G.: Performance comparison of crud methods using net object relational mappers: a case study. Int. J. Adv. Comput. Sci. Appl. **11**(1) (2020)

System for Preparing and Executing Math Exams Online – A Case Study

Dawid Bugajewski[1]([⊠]) and Monika Bugajewska[2]

[1] Cybernetics Faculty, Military University of Technology, Warsaw, Poland
dawid.bugajewski@wat.edu.pl
[2] NASK – National Research Institute, Warsaw, Poland
monika.bugajewska@nask.pl

Abstract. When teaching remotely, it is much more difficult to supervise students' independent task solving during tests. Students have almost unlimited opportunities to communicate both among themselves and with third parties. From the experience of one of the authors of the paper as a mathematics teacher there are often cases of exchange of solutions between students. Such cheating attempts often feature omitting key elements of the solution and nevertheless receiving correct results or duplicating unusual errors. During the COVID pandemic when the system has prepared the scale of such behaviors was noticeably bigger. Remote learning makes it ever more challenging to effectively teach and verify progress. When remotely administering tests, it is easy to identify some of the problems that affect both students and teachers. Some of them are cheating and sharing solutions, problems with timely delivery of assignments and increased time it takes to grade submitted solutions compared to ones received on paper. System described in this paper proposes a novel approach to increasing the number of groups at the test. The assumption was that increasing the number of groups along with automated preparation of different data in the tasks for each student can make it much more difficult to exchange solutions between students. Automatic assignment variant generation and support for grading of mathematics tests could reduce the teacher's time to prepare and grade the tests as well as increase the confidence in students working individually. These assumptions were verified by a survey among science teachers before the development of the system and as part of its testing. A similar thesis was proposed and partially confirmed in for tests in computer science in higher education.

Keywords: e-learning systems · web applications · symbolic mathematics

1 Introduction

When remotely administering tests, it is easy to identify some of the problems that affect both students and teachers. Some of them are cheating and sharing solutions, problems with timely delivery of assignments and increased time it takes to grade submitted solutions compared to ones received on paper. In Poland this was observed by government organizations as evidenced by changes in requirements during the eighth grade and high

© The Author(s), under exclusive license to Springer Nature Switzerland AG 2024
K. S. Soliman (Ed.): IBIMA-AI 2023, CCIS 2101, pp. 318–329, 2024.
https://doi.org/10.1007/978-3-031-62843-6_30

school exams [1]. As some of the existing solutions to the above-described problem are greater control during tests [2], abandoning tests in favor of oral answers [3] and increasing the number of groups [4].

Cheating when completing assignments or competing over internet is common [5], it can be seen in online games, online quizzes, as well as in the remote exams. Cheating can often be detected similarly to the tests implemented in the classroom, that is, based on repeated unusual answers. When the test has repeating questions or low variance of the tasks cheating can also be detected based on the short time spent to complete the exam, as shown in [5], but this is only possible if assignments are submitted through some kind of system that helps measure such metrics. Studies show that preparing individual sets of tasks prevents the exchange of solutions and makes it difficult to get help from other students in the same class [4].

When exams are executed using instant messaging like Microsoft Teams, or Zoom, and email, problems often arise when sharing tests with students, as well as receiving solutions from them. Sometimes students report that they did not receive the test, or that they have problems with the connection or cannot see the tasks on the shared screen. When the test is completed, the teacher does not have context about the duration of the task solution (during in-class tests, students are eager to leave after the test is over), and often messages with submitted solutions are incomplete, damaged, or poorly formatted.

Using systems dedicated to executing tests helps to avoid those problems. It also ensures that all students get access to the assignments by a certain date, the time for answering each question will be recorded, and the answers be immediately available to the teacher in a unified format.

When the exam requires students to submit handwritten solutions to some of the tasks it greatly increases difficulty of grading them. Due to the solutions to the tasks being on many photos, and the photos themselves being often in a mixed order or rotated checking such solutions requires printing or combining photos to be able to annotate the entire test. These problems add to the time required to check solutions compared to classic tests. Allowing the student to enter answers to individual tasks could allow the system to automatically verify them and propose a grade for the test [6].

In case of the need to check the complete solution, the support for the teacher could be the handling of the process of uploading written solutions by the system and allowing the student or the teacher to mark the solutions of subsequent tasks and download the resulting file.

This paper was divided into three sections. First section describes existing solutions. Second section describes solution architecture, applications being part of the system as well the supported use cases. Third section describes the implementation of the key use cases that allow for automated test variants generation. Finally, the results have been summarized and future work directions have been described.

2 Existing Solutions

There are many systems on the market that support the preparation or execution of tests. Few of them allow the implementation of both functionalities at the same time. Solutions of this type are usually included in Learning Management System (LMS) class of systems that support preparing educational content, interaction with students, assessments and reporting of learning progress and student activity [7].

Research of existing systems was focused on solutions that address the issues presented in the introduction and that would support automatic generation of task variants and conducting tests. Two systems that support this were identified Learnosity Math and Moodle with relevant add-ons.

Learnosity Math is one of the products developed by Learnosity Ltd. It is commercial and information about the cost of obtaining a license cannot be found on the website. It is part of a group of online learning support solutions and is used to test knowledge in science subjects. It allows you to enter mathematical expressions and compare answers with a template. The functionality of the math question generator allows automatic generation of tasks according to a specific pattern by specifying a list of parameters with their sets of values, a scheme for calculating the solution and the form of the expected result.

Moodle is one of the most popular LMS platforms. It is widely used for e-learning all over the world, including Poland [8]. Platform can be customized according to users' preferences using a wide range of extensions. STACK and Formulas Question Type extensions are particularly noteworthy. The former allows comparison of mathematical equations in simplified form [9] and is widely used within STEM education worldwide [10]. The second allows the generation of variants of mathematical tasks to increase the variety of task variants.

Another notable mention is testportal.net an online test preparation platform, while unlike the previously described platforms, it does not allow automatic generation of task sets or operations on equations, it has interesting security features and is recommended by Polish eTwinning ambassadors [11]. The eTwinning progame aims to promote support for the use of information technology to support teaching in Europe [12]. In addition to intuitive test preparation, the application allows monitoring student activity and supervise whether they leave the test tab.

Those systems presented in this chapter were compared using the following criteria the ability to generate task variants, ability to evaluate the correctness of the equations, ease of configuration, deployment model, security measures, license. Results are presented in Table 1.

Table 1. Comparison of some of the existing systems supporting remote exam execution

	Learnosity Math	Moodle	Moodle + STACK + Formulas Question Type	Testportal.net
Task variants generation	Yes	No	Yes	No
Equations evaluation	Yes	No	Yes	No
Deployment model	SaaS	On-premise	On-premise	SaaS
Security measures	No	No	No	Detection of leaving the tab
License	Commercial, per seat basis	Open source	Open source	Commercial. Free of charge for public education teachers

3 System Overview

Before building the system, a feasibility study was conducted on a test group of 126 teachers through Google Forms platform. The survey consisted of following questions:

1. Do you think that remote teaching makes it more difficult to conduct tests?
2. In your opinion if test is conducted online are students more likely to exchange answers among themselves?
3. Are classic tests conducted online sufficient to reliably assess students' knowledge?
4. Can the introduction of individualized tests help in assessing students' knowledge?
5. Would you use a platform that generates individualized tests for students?

In the end 100 teachers submitted the answers, and their answers are presented on Fig. 1.

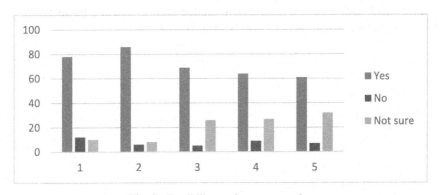

Fig. 1. Feasibility study survey results.

The feasibility study confirmed that according to the control group teaching makes it more difficult to conduct tests, and students are more likely to exchange answers among themselves. Most of the surveyed teachers agreed that classic tests do not allow to reliably test students' knowledge, and individualization of tasks can allow to assess their knowledge more effectively. It can also be seen that 93% of the respondents are willing to use or would consider using a platform that generates individualized tests, these people were invited to test the system.

3.1 Solution Architecture

Figure 2 shows high level architecture of the system. Both teacher and student web clients connect to the backend services using HTTPS communication with a REST API. REST was selected instead of GraphQL due to performance, scalability as well as reliability considerations [13].

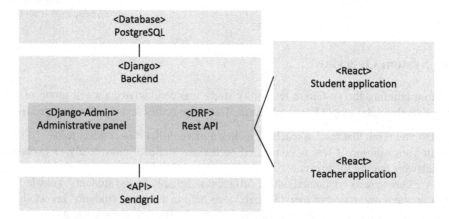

Fig. 2. High level architecture of the solution.

System consists of three major elements that are the backend services and administrative panel, and two client applications one for teachers and one for students. They have been presented in more detail on Fig. 3 and Fig. 4.

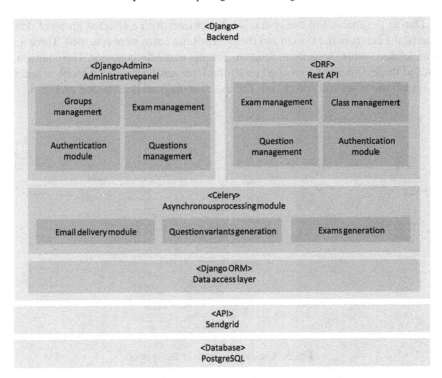

Fig. 3. Backend services architecture

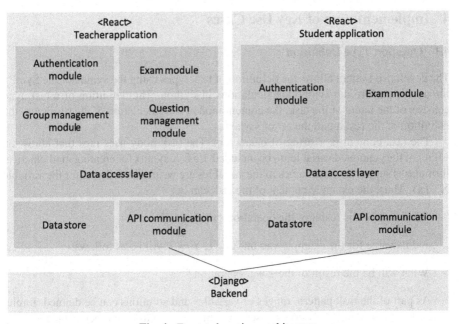

Fig. 4. Frontend services architecture

During the analysis of the system's requirements with a selected group of domain experts, the actors in the system and the system's use cases were specified. Three actors were defined within the system: Student, Teacher and Administrator. The common use cases of these actors were grouped under the User actor. During the problem analysis, 15 system use cases were proposed. The use case diagram is presented on Fig. 5.

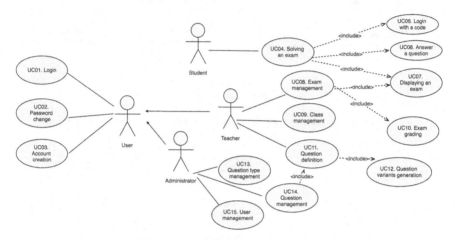

Fig. 5. Use case diagram of the system.

4 Implementation of Key Use Cases

4.1 Question Type Definition

The developed system allows the definition of task types using the syntax of the SymPy library for performing symbolic calculations in Python. The definition of a task type consists of the name of the task, the content model, the calculation of the result and the definition of the result and the set of variables.

The task content is a string of characters. The task body uses tags that allow the values of the generated variables to be included. LaTeX syntax for creating mathematical formulas is supported. The names of the variables are written as follows: for the variable X - {x}. Thus, the example content of the task can be:

"What will be the result of the operation $\{x\} + \{y\}$?"

and its value for the example variant $X = 1$, $Y = 2$ will be as follows:

"What will be the result of the $1 + 2$ operation?"

As part of the task pattern, ranges of variables and solutions can be defined. Implemented system supports following sets of numbers: natural numbers, integers, real numbers with a given precision, and the set of numbers F defined as:

$$F = \left\{-8, -7, -6, -5, -4, -3, -\sqrt{5}, -2, -\sqrt{3}, -\sqrt{2}, -1, 0, 1, \sqrt{2}, \sqrt{3}, 2, 3, \sqrt{5}, 4, 5, 6, 7, 8\right\}$$

At the same time, each set of variables can be constrained using comparison to real numbers by constraints of type: greater than, greater equal to, different, lesser than, or lesser equal to.

4.2 Generation of Question Variants

The generation of solution variants is performed by reviewing all permutations of the input variables therefore it is important that this set is finite. Another important element is the use of the SymPy library so that calculations are performed using symbolic variables. The algorithm for calculating the question variants is presented on Fig. 6 and its implementation is presented on the Listing 1.

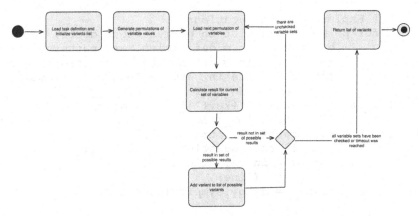

Fig. 6. Algorithm of question variants generation.

Listing 1. Implementation of question variant generation.

```
def build_variants(definition: QuestionType):
    rs = definition.result_set.values
    rs_set = []
    # Prepare set of possible results
    for r in rs.split(','):
        rs_set.append(eval(r))
    # Prepare variables
    variables    =    {a.name:    [eval(x)    for    x    in
a.values_set.values.split(',')]         for         a         in
zad.variables.all()}
    keys, values = zip(*variables.items())
    # Calculate all permutations of variations
    permutations_dicts = [dict(zip(keys, v)) for v in
itertools.product(*values)]
    questions = []

    # Explore all permutations
    for permutations_dict in permutations_dicts:
        question_text = definition.text_pattern
        question_calc = definition.calculation_logic
        for key, value in permutations_dict.items():
            question_text                              =
question_text.replace("{"+key+"}", str(value))
            question_calc                              =
question_calc.replace(key, str(value))
        calc_lines = question_calc.split()
        for line in calc_lines[:-1]:
            eval(line)
        result = sympy.sympify(question_calc[-1])

        # Check if results is in set of possible
results
        if result in rs_set:
            questions.append(Question(
                question_type=definition,
                question=question_text,
                answer=result,

    variables_list=str(permutations_dict))
                )

    return questions
```

Example question type definition along with its variants and example of one of the variants shown in the exam portal are presented the Fig. 7.

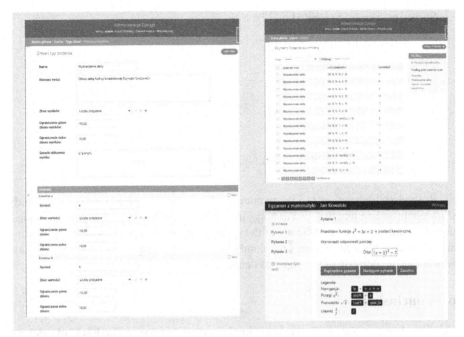

Fig. 7. Example question definition along with generated variants and view from the student perspective

5 System Validation

The system during the test deployment was shared with teachers who declared their willingness to participate in the tests in the feasibility study. After test deployment another survey was executed that consisted of following questions:

1. Do you think the tested system makes it easier to conduct tests when teaching remotely?
2. Did students exchange answers with each other when exams were executed using the system?
3. Do the tests conducted online using the system allow you to assess students' knowledge more reliably than classic tests conducted online?
4. Did the individualized tests help assess students' knowledge?
5. Would you like to continue using the tested platform if possible?
6. Did the platform shorten the preparation time of the tests?
7. Did the platform reduce the time for grading the tests?
8. Has the use of the platform reduced the number of students' suspicions of cheating?

Survey results are presented on Fig. 8.

Fig. 8. Results of survey after system testing.

Responses to question 1–5 when compared to questions asked on feasibility study show confirmation that the system helps in the identified problems. Responses to questions 6, 7 and 8 confirm that the use of the system reduces the teacher's time in preparing and evaluating tests and reduces the number of students' suspicions of unselfish work, which was the purpose of the paper to demonstrate.

6 Conclusion

Developed system was verified in a test implementation involving high school teachers. The results of the test implementation show that, with the current level of development, the system had a positive impact on the conduct of tests and exhibited the characteristics specified in the purpose of the work. The conducted surveys confirm the statement system allowing automatic variants and supporting the grading of mathematics tests does reduce the teacher's time spent for preparing and grading the tests and reduced the suspicions of cheating. The system can be further developed by implementing new supported task patterns, expanding supported input ranges and solutions. Consideration could also be given to allowing the input of more than one answer and the definition of closed questions. Input of answers in mathematical form on mobile devices is something that could be further improved as well. The system could be also used to prepare practice questions and exercise books as it allows to easily define and generate multiple variants of tasks along with answers.

References

1. Ordinance of the Polish Minister of Education and Science of December 16, 2020 amending the Ordinance on special arrangements during the period of temporary restriction of the operation of units of the educational system (2020)
2. Lee, J., Kim, R.J., Park, S.-Y., Henning, M.A.: Using technologies to prevent cheating in remote assessments during the COVID-19 pandemic. J. Dent. Educ. (2020)
3. Giordano, A.N., Christopher, C.R.: Repurposing best teaching practices for remote learning environments: chemistry in the news and oral examinations during COVID-19. J. Chem. Educ. **97**(9), 2815–2818 (2020)
4. Rusak, G., Yan, L.: Unique Exams: designing assessments for integrity and fairness. In: Proceedings of the 52nd ACM Technical Symposium on Computer Science Education, pp. 1170–1176 (2021). https://doi.org/10.1145/3408877.3432556

5. Bilen, E., Matros, A.: Online cheating amid COVID-19. J. Econ. Behav. Organ. **182**, 196–211 (2021). https://doi.org/10.1016/j.jebo.2020.12.004
6. Sangwin, C.: Computer Aided Assessment of Mathematics. OUP, Oxford (2013)
7. Kasim, N.N.M., Khalid, F.: Choosing the right learning management system (LMS) for the higher education institution context: a systematic review. Int. J. Emerg. Technol. Learn. **11**(6) (2016)
8. Smyrnova-Trybulska, E., Stach, S., Burnus, A., Szczurek, A.: Wykorzystanie LCMS Moodle jako systemu wspomagania nauczania na odległość. Katowice Wydaw. Uniw. Śląskiego Stud. (2012)
9. Sangwin, C.: Computer aided assessment of mathematics using STACK BT. In: Cho, S. (ed.) Selected Regular Lectures from the 12th International Congress on Mathematical Education, pp. 695–713. Springer, Cham (2015). https://doi.org/10.1007/978-3-319-17187-6_39
10. Sangwin, C.J.: Who uses STACK? A report on the use of the STACK CAA system. University of Brimingham (2010)
11. Mojsiejonek, M.: TestPortal - prosty sposób na ocenę postępów uczniów. eTwinning Polska (2020). https://etwinning.pl/testportal-prosty-sposob-na-ocene-postepow-uczniow/. Accessed 23 May 2021
12. Papadakis, S.: Creativity and innovation in European education. Ten years eTwinning. Past, present and the future. Int. J. Technol. (2016)
13. Fielding, R.T.: Architectural Styles and the Design of Network-Based Software Architectures, vol. 7. University of California, Irvine (2000)

Security and Privacy

Watermarking Scheme for Physical Documents

Michał Glet[1]([✉]), Kamil Kaczyński[1], and Paweł Zielski[2]

[1] Faculty of Cybernetics, Institute of Mathematics and Cryptology, Military University of Technology, Warsaw, Poland
{michal.glet,kamil.kaczynski}@wat.edu.pl
[2] TiMSI sp. z o. o., Warsaw, Poland
pawel.zielski@timsi.pl

Abstract. The use of watermarks for protecting digital documents is well-established, but the application of watermarks to physical documents has received comparatively little attention. In this paper, we propose an invisible watermarking scheme for physical documents, which may be considered an effective solution for protecting physical documents from disclosure and allowing effective tracking of leakage. Overall, our findings suggest that watermarking physical documents can provide valuable security and traceability benefits, but that careful consideration must be given to the specific context and requirements of each application.

Keywords: Watermarking · Security · Document Tracking

1 Introduction

Watermarks have been divided into two basic categories - visible and invisible. A visible watermark is a pattern that is located within the document. Its design may resemble a visible watermark found on banknotes. Such watermarks are widely used to protect graphics by portals engaged in their distribution. This type of watermark should allow for familiarity with the work, but its removal should cause significant distortion, which is meant to protect against further use of the work with the removed watermark.

Compared to steganography, watermarking provides higher resistance to attacks. The existence of a watermark is apparent, whereas its removal should be impossible for an attacker without possessing the key. The resistance of watermarks arises from the smaller amount of data it uses, which allows for increased redundancy compared to steganography. Watermarking should be considered a complementary technique to steganography, possessing different conditions of use and basic properties.

Invisible watermarks store information about the owner of a given document in a way that is closely related to its content, making it difficult to remove. The watermark is placed in such a way as not to disturb the way information is presented in the document. Attempts to remove an invisible watermark should result in significant modification of the marked document, making it difficult to execute in practice.

In this paper, we propose a mechanism for embedding watermarks in printed documents, which was successfully implemented in one of the commercial solutions available on the market.

K. S. Soliman (Ed.): IBIMA-AI 2023, CCIS 2101, pp. 333–337, 2024.
https://doi.org/10.1007/978-3-031-62843-6_31

2   Watermarking Algorithm

The process of placing an invisible watermark on a printed document takes a form similar to that of electronic document watermarking. Analysis of invisible watermarking can only be performed using a digitized copy of the document, using its reproduced features. This adds a problem of synchronization of document features to the analysis. The process of invisible watermarking is carried out using visual cryptography algorithms. This method of watermarking allows for document marking without the need to introduce any changes to its structure, using only the properties of the document's graphic layer. The process requires the creation of two shares – a main (master share) and a secret share. The hidden watermark is reconstructed based on the combination of the two shares. The main share is reconstructed from the analyzed image, while the secret share is kept by the document owner, and its content is verified by a trusted third party – the document circulation system.

Due to the possible loss of synchronization after the digitization process, the system must provide the ability to restore it. Therefore, the system should store information about the location of three characteristic points that allow for the restoration of the document plane. All the data necessary for the analysis process will be placed in an image fragment of a specified, constant size. The algorithm also requires the image to be reduced to the initial colour palette - for implementation reasons, 256 shades of grey or a binary image can be assumed.

The watermarking mechanism takes place in the digital domain, and after the synchronization stage, it proceeds like an algorithm for an electronic document. The algorithm for determining the master share is as follows:

1) We calculate the average pixel value of the image.
2) We choose m pixels from the image pseudorandomly, where $m = x * y$, and x and y are the dimensions of the placed watermark.
3) We generate a new image - the master share - if the pixel value is greater than the average, template 1 is inserted, if it is smaller, template 2 is inserted. The dimensions of the resulting image are $2x * 2y$ (Figs. 1, 2 and 3).

Fig. 1. Template 1

Fig. 2. Template 2

Fig. 3. Generated master share image

The algorithm for determining the owner share is as follows:

1) Calculate the average pixel value of the image.
2) Choose m pixels from the image pseudorandomly, where m = x * y and x and y are the dimensions of the located watermark.
3) Generate a new image - owner share - if the pixel value is greater than the average and we hide a bit 0 - we use template 1, hide 1 - use template 2, if the pixel value is less than the average and we hide 0 - use template 2, hide 1 - template 1 is used.
4) The resulting owner share image has dimensions of 2x * 2y (Fig. 4).

Fig. 4. Generated owner share image

The algorithm for determining the hidden watermark is as follows:

1) We retrieve the master share from the analyzed image.
2) We perform an XOR operation on the master share the image with the owner share image.

3) The resulting image has the same dimensions as the master/owner share, but it can be normalized to the original size (four times smaller) (Fig. 5).

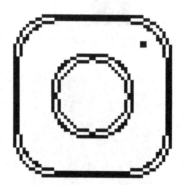

Fig. 5. Retrieved watermark

The algorithm for synchronizing verification data for a printed document is as follows:

1) Choose three characteristic points - areas that bound the text.
2) Based on the selected points, determine a parallelogram containing a section of the document.
3) Geometrically transform the parallelogram into a rectangle.
4) Adjust the rectangle to the size of the pattern stored in the system. After performing the above steps, an image is obtained that allows for the reconstruction of the master share and consequently the recovery of the hidden watermark. The algorithm is very resistant to introduced geometric distortions and noise, hence recovering the invisible watermark from a digitised version of a printed document is not a problem.

3   Conclusions and Future Work

We proposed the watermarking algorithm, which provides a reliable and robust method for embedding and extracting watermarks in printed documents. The algorithm uses a combination of template matching, and geometric transformations to ensure that the watermark is resistant to various types of attacks and distortions.

Future work could involve further testing and validation of the algorithm's performance under different scenarios and conditions, including a more extensive analysis of its resistance to attacks such as document cropping and the addition of noise. Additionally, the exploration of new techniques for embedding and extracting watermarks, such as deep learning-based approaches, could be investigated to further improve the algorithm's efficiency and effectiveness.

Acknowledgement. This work was partially funded by the European Regional Development Fund, "Regionalny Program Operacyjny Województwa Mazowieckiego na lata 2014–2020", Poland. The project number was RPMA.01.02.00-14-9407/17.

References

1. Huang, S., Wu, J.K.: Optical watermarking for printed document authentication. IEEE Trans. Inf. Forensics Secur. **2**(2), 164–173 (2007)
2. Rashid, A.: Digital watermarking applications and techniques: a brief review. Int. J. Comput. Appl. Technol. Res. **5**(3), 147–150 (2016)
3. Sun, Q.B., Feng, P.R., Deng, R.: An optical watermarking solution for authenticating printed documents. In: Proceedings International Conference on Information Technology: Coding and Computing, pp. 65–70. IEEE (2001)
4. Naor, M., Shamir, A.: Visual cryptography. In: De Santis, A. (ed.) EUROCRYPT 1994. LNCS, vol. 950, pp. 1–12. Springer, Heidelberg (1995). https://doi.org/10.1007/BFb0053419

Extended Differential Privacy Model: Additional Performance and Security Considerations

Olga Dziegielewska[⊠] and Boleslaw Szafranski

Military University of Technology, Warsaw, Poland
{olga.dziegielewska,boleslaw.szafranski}@wat.edu.pl

Abstract. The differential privacy model until today was extended and implemented by many researchers. One of the recent extensions proposed two metrics that are designed to allow for better calibration of the security and accuracy based on the risk of the statistical query. The quality of this extension shows that the method as defined can be considered a better candidate than the original version in certain conditions. This paper further improves the extended differential privacy model with selected aspects of the implementation of the mechanism that may contribute to improving the performance and security of the solution at a system level.

Keywords: differential privacy model · VIOLAS Framework · retrofitting of security mechanisms · statistical databases security

1 Introduction

The differential privacy model [1] is a perturbative statistical disclosure control mechanism that involves adding appropriate random noise to the statistical queries to provide a countermeasure against inference attacks directed at statistical answers. The differential privacy model allows a data solicitor to collect data and infer meaningful information from the data without individual record attribution, i.e., the mechanism allows a solicitor to collect sensitive data, but the data cannot be attributed to any party [2].

Until today, the differential privacy model is still quite an unexplored statistical disclosure control mechanism, however, some researchers attempted to extend it and improve it in various ways (e.g. [3–5]). One of the extended versions of this model, introduced in [6] proposes two metrics – risk-accuracy and information score – to adjust the noise that is added over the calculations to improve the security of the retrieved statistics without losing the accuracy aspect of the data:

- Risk-Accuracy Metric – an adjustable metric that allows manipulating the statistical noise in such a way that the result would provide a selected level of a tradeoff between the accuracy and the security, which could be easily adapted for the real-life usages of statistical databases, e.g., the different tradeoffs for data processed only internally by an entity and sent to external entities or providing role-based tradeoffs at the database level.

K. S. Soliman (Ed.): IBIMA-AI 2023, CCIS 2101, pp. 338–348, 2024.
https://doi.org/10.1007/978-3-031-62843-6_32

- Information Score Metric – an incremental metric that by design automatically changes the noise of the same or similar query retrieved multiple times. This metric intends to mitigate the risk of statistical disclosure in case of dynamic inference attacks while the results remain statistically integral. This factor potentially can be expanded to provide a multi-source inference control mechanism, i.e., in attack scenarios where more than one database is used.

The efficiency of the extended differential privacy method was determined by the statistical security criteria defined in the VIOLAS Framework [7] and threat modeling showed that the method as defined can be considered a better candidate than the original version in certain conditions [8], e.g., when the data can be correlated with multiple external sources to retrieve sensitive statistics (Fig. 1).

```
INFORMATION SCORE METRIC DERIVATION
        Prerequisites:
p1      AR_DB
p2      HIST_DB
        Input:
i1      P (a set of parameters of the submitted query)
i2      C (asked statistical characteristic)
i3      S (optional, default=1)
        Algorithm:
a1      if (query was asked before)
a2              return ism=ism_hist
a3      else
a4              while (AR_DB has next)
a5                      if (P and C in AR_DB_i)
a6                              add {P,C,ism=1·S} into HIST_DB
a7                              return ism=1·S
a8                      else
a9                              while (HIST_DB has next)
a10                                     if (P_hist_i,C_hist_i,P in AR_DB_i)
a11                                             add {P_hist_i,C_hist_i,P,C,ism=1·S
                                to HIST_DB
a12                                             return ism=1·S
a13                                     else
a14                                             add {P,C,ism=0} into HIST_DB
a15                                             return ism=0
```

Fig. 1. The original algorithm for Information Score Metric Derivation [6]

This paper further improves the extended differential privacy model with selected aspects of the implementation of the mechanism that may contribute to improving the performance and security of the solution.

2   Statistical Disclosure Control Mechanisms Implementation Considerations

In real-life implementations, the decision on the differential privacy variant's application is based on the system's business requirements and key performance indicators which the system needs to comply with, which vary from one system to another. The ultimate responsibility for the overall security and the performance of the system belongs to the system's owner, meaning that if the components of the system underperform significantly, the system's owner has the authority to approve correcting actions to address the issues. In the case of statistical disclosure controls, it would also be a system's owner's decision to make a final call on the parameters and features required from the business perspective, however, the technical team needs to design and propose appropriate solutions, e.g., differential privacy mechanism, to meet the desired effect.

On top of the business functional requirements implementation of the statistical disclosure control method, non-functional requirements, including security, need to be taken care of. In the case of the security requirements, preventive, detective, and corrective controls at each stage of the SDLC and DBLC are defined and the whole development lifecycle must adhere to them.

Currently, with modern shift-left approach, the security requirements and mechanisms are added much before the implementation stage, what mitigates major security risks by preventing them at early stages of the system's lifecycle (Fig. 2).

```
RISK-ACCURACY METRIC DERIVATION
                Prerequisites:
p1      r_preset(preset of the risk component of the database)
p2      a_preset(preset of the accuracy component of the database)
                Input:
i1      P (a set of parameters of the submitted query)
i2      C (asked statistical characteristic)
                Algorithm:
a1      calculate ism for {P,C}
a2      risk=r_preset*ism
a3      if risk=0
a4              ram=a_preset-1
a5      else
a6              ram=a_preset*risk+risk
```

Fig. 2. The original algorithm for Information Score Metric Derivation [6]

The latest trends can be easily adapted to the newly developed systems, but the transformation for the already existing systems remains a challenge.

Since the IT environments evolve over time, retrofitting is a process that will occur for most of the IT systems to adapt to new functional and non-functional requirements. The extended differential privacy method could be used in both cases – newly developed and already existing solutions, thanks to its post-processing interfaced nature, i.e., the data are derived from the raw data sets, and the algorithm itself can be implemented as an additional end-user interface, without affecting the existing system's implementation. It must be noted however, that in the case of the systems that collect data that are already affected by some perturbative method at the data collection time, the method will not be as effective in terms of accuracy, as additional noise will be added to existing distorted data.

2.1 Implementing the Extended Differential Privacy Model

There are two ways in which perturbative statistical disclosure control methods can be applied: at the time of data collection, where the raw data is modified and the database stores already noisy data, or as a part of the statistical derivation interface of the database, where the raw data is stored in the database without any added noise before the derivations. The advantage of the second case is that neither the data collection method nor the data model of the database must satisfy any statistical security-by-design measures and the extended differential privacy model is an example of such a statistical disclosure control mechanism.

Adopting the post-processing approach makes the method applicable in a broader context, as it can be easily implemented not only for future databases, but more crucially, it can be integrated as an additional end-user interface for existing databases. The demand for retrofitting applications has grown, underscoring the significance of developing a statistical disclosure control method that is compatible with already established and functional systems. This approach would have a greater business impact on the current IT landscape than designing an infallible method that is only applicable to future databases [6].

As with any perturbative statistical disclosure control method used as an external, non-customized interface, there is an increase in processing time for the executed database queries. However, this cost is necessary to ensure the privacy of the statistical output.

The initial considerations regarding the implementation prerequisites were included in the original paper [6] and assume that:

- The data in the statistical database is stored in non-perturbed manner.
- The database has different statistical access roles, that have different sensitivity levels assigned to them.
- The association database and historical database are preprocessed (Fig. 3).

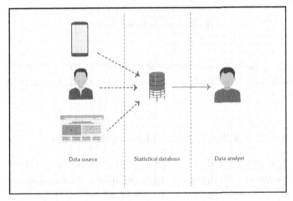

Data source   Statistical database   Data analyst

Fig. 3. The scheme depicts the place of applying the extended differential privacy (marked with a solid arrow).

The process itself starts with the verification of the required presets (the sensitivity level, risk level accuracy level) for a database access role of a user who submitted a query. The preset values are valid throughout the validity of a user session.

Each query is verified first in the historical database and the associations are verified to determine the risk profile of the query and the ism (information score metric output) is either calculated from scratch or gathered from the historical data. Later, the *ism* is used by the risk-accuracy metric and the output of the calculations is passed to the noise generation function as one of the inputs. After the error rate has been determined and the noise generation function has been applied to the raw data, the perturbed output is returned to the user [6] (Fig. 4).

The user should not receive any result from the database until the statistical disclosure control process is not terminated. In case of an error occurred before the output retrieval,

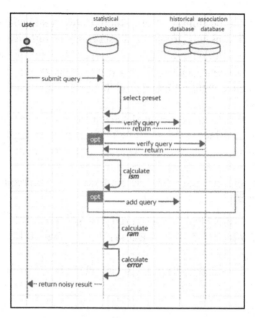

Fig. 4. Transaction scheme [6]

all the transactions made into the supporting databases that could affect future results must be rolled back, i.e., any data that has been added to the historical database must be deleted [6].

2.2 Implementation-Specific Performance Improvements

The original *Enhancing Distribution* algorithm [6] is designed in such a way that it follows the fundamental differential privacy premise, i.e., the noise is added to all the results, regardless of its risk profile or the risk profile of the database.

However, in case the risk profile of the database (*r_preset*) or the risk profile of the retrieved query (*ism*) is within a negligible margin, then some steps may be skipped, to improve the performance. This could however affect the classification of the method as a differential privacy mechanism; therefore, it was not proposed in the original design.

The algorithm below shows an improved noise distribution enhancement algorithm, that improves the performance of non-critical systems or queries (Fig. 5).

The changes include breaking the execution and returning non-perturbed results if the risk profile of the database (line a1) or the asked query (line a5) is equal to 0. If the risk profile of the query is equal to 0, which renders no potential inference attacks discovered for the query, then the algorithm returns an unmodified result. If the risk profile of the query is not equal to 0, then the randomized generator receives values greater than 0, which reflects that the risk factor is taken into account by the generator, and the noise must be modified accordingly, therefore the error rate must be increased.

```
ENHANCING DISTRIBUITION
                    Prerequisites:
p1        D(d_q)
                    Input:
i1        q
                    Algorithm:
a1        calculate ram for q
a2        if ram≤0
a3                  use D(d_q-normalize(ram)¹)
a4        else
a5                  use D(d_q+normalize(ram)¹)
```

Fig. 5. The original algorithm for Information Score Metric Derivation (paper) 1) In the original paper, the normalization step is defined as a multiplication function, however, it was altered in this paper for better clarity.

```
ENHANCING DISTRIBUITION - IMPLEMENTATION-IMPROVED VERSION
                Prerequisites:
p1    D(d_q)
p2    r_preset
                Input:
i1    q
                Algorithm:
a1    if r_preset = 0
a2              return non-perturbed result
a3    else
a4              calculate ram for q
a5              if ram=0
a6                      return non-perturbed result
a7              else
a8                      D(d_q+normalize(ram))
```

Additionally, a change in the risk-accuracy metric derivation algorithm needs to be done to adapt to the new conditions – in case *ism = 0*, then the *ram = 0*, i.e. if the risk profile of the query is equal to 0, what renders no potential inference attacks discovered for the query, then the returned value is 0. If the risk profile of the query is not equal to 0, then the randomized generator receives values greater than 0, which reflects that the risk factor is taken into account by the generator, and the noise must be modified accordingly.

```
RISK-ACCURACY METRIC DERIVATION - - IMPLEMENTATION-IMPROVED VERSION
                Prerequisites:
p1    r_preset(preset of the risk component of the database)
p2    a_preset(preset of the accuracy component of the database)
                Input:
i1    P (a set of parameters of the submitted query)
i2    C (asked statistical characteristic)
                Algorithm:
a1    calculate ism for {P,C}
a2    risk=r_preset*ism
a3    if risk=0
a4              ram=0
a5    else
a6              ram=a_preset*risk+risk
```

It must be noted however, that without covering all the results with the noise distribution function, the security can be affected, e.g., in case a risk of a particular query is wrongly categorized as negligible risk, due to the insufficient quality of the *AR_DB* or *HIST_DB*, then the retrieved results remain unprotected from the inference attacks. Therefore, the performance-enhancing solution needs to be adopted carefully over the system. Obviously, the proposed performance enhancements may be further adapted, e.g., only *r_preset* verification can be added in the *Enhancing distribution algorithm*, leaving the noise addition method in all the rest cases.

Apart from the algorithmic improvements, database-level improvements can be considered. Typically, statistical databases themselves are relational databases, however, to improve the lookup time the *AR_DB* and *HIST_DB* databases could be implemented as non-relational databases. Nonetheless, the decision on the actual database type should not only consider the performance, but also the technological stack of the organization that the solution is implemented.

3 Additional Security Considerations

As was already mentioned, the extended differential privacy model was evaluated using VIOLAS Framework [7] designed for statistical disclosure control methods and additional threat modeling to ensure a better quality of the outputs [8]. The evaluations confirmed that the model of the method itself is secure under the statistical disclosure control mechanism conditions, i.e., satisfies statistical confidentiality, statistical integrity, statistical accuracy, and statistical transparency [7].

The statistical disclosure control methods typically focus on the data layer of the system, as the statistical inference attacks are classified as business logic abuse rather than environment or implementation-related attacks. The attacks leverage the vulnerable data model design as in the inference attack scenarios it is assumed that the access to the dataset is granted by default to a certain group of system users, and the users abuse the legitimate data-level access.

However, since the security of the working environment also plays a major part in the overall security of the system, other factors must also be considered while assessing the risk of the system in scope. For IT systems, the security requirements can be split into two categories: procedural and technical.

3.1 Procedural Security Assumptions

The procedural security requirements embed security aspects into the business processes that are supported by an IT system. Typically, such requirements include but are not limited to regulatory compliance, service continuity, system, and data governance, third-party risk management, and access model definition.

In the case of the extended differential privacy model, there are several procedural aspects that must be properly defined and implemented, as they directly influence the effectiveness of the elaborated method, are:

- Regulatory compliance
- Access model definition
- System and data governance

Other aspects, despite being important from a high-level system perspective, do not immediately influence the elaborated method, therefore will not be commented.

The *regulatory compliance* should be treated with the highest priority as a lack of compliance with local or global legislations or formal requirements may result in legal actions and regulatory fines which may have a direct impact on an entity that intends to implement the proposed mechanism. The personal data privacy is especially sensitive in some geographic areas (e.g., EU, South Korea, Russia) or fields (medical data), therefore before considering the proposed solution, regulatory validation should be performed. When it comes to the compliance of the model against reidentification of the individual records, it is proven by the research, that the model can suffice this sort of requirement. However, there may exist regulations that would prevent from using the extended model, e.g., if a legislator bans abusing integrity of the statistics in any way, then both base and extended differential privacy models cannot be implemented.

The *access model* requirements should be carefully defined at different layers. First of all, the database's statistical and non-statistical access must be considered, however, apart from the database, other system components should be also addressed. As the immediate risk for the effectiveness of the proposed method originates from the implementation and configuration of the algorithms, the access model for the system code base pipeline, the algorithm's configuration, and the system's configuration must also be established following the least-privilege principle. Regular users should not have permission to modify algorithms setup (S, a_preset, r_preset, $D(d\_q)$) or to modify the system's configurations to prevent overwriting the security setup of the system. Additionally, the system's developers should not have a direct possibility to effectively push and render changes in the production environments, to prevent introducing uncontrolled modifications in the algorithm. The code development pipeline should be configured following secure software development standards (e.g., OWASP SAMM [9], BSIMM [10], ISO series: 9000 [11], ISO/IEC 12207 [12], ISO/IEC 15288 [13], ISO/IEC 24748 [14]).

The *system and data governance* aspect that is important for the quality of the results returned by the extended differential privacy model is the assignment of the variable values S, a_preset, r_preset. An appropriate strategy is needed to define those values for the IT system to fully leverage the functionalities of the extended differential privacy model. Obviously, the values of the variables are the key to a successful implementation of the model, however, it must be noted that the variables can be set at a different level for a different types of users. This way, the results can not only be calibrated at a system layer but also at an individual level per each user or group of users, which makes the proposed model even more adaptive.

3.2   Technical Components Security Assumptions

The technical components of security are a separate area that is not covered in the scope of the extended differential privacy model but still states a significant part of the overall security of the implementation. Two aspects are critical in terms of satisfying the security of the statistical disclosure control methods at the technical level: the environment and the implementation security. The best practice for defining specific security requirements in those two areas is to follow one of the commonly used and globally approved standards for IT system development.

One of them is OWASP Application Security Verification Standard [15], which thoroughly covers all the phases of the Software Development Lifecycle with controls to apply in certain aspects of the developed solution. OWASP ASVS v. 4.0.2 covers 70 specific validation points divided into 14 categories. It must be stressed, that for the overall security of the system, it is important to cover all the requirements, however, from the perspective of the extended differential privacy model, the key categories that should be considered mandatory are:

- V1: Architecture, Design and Threat Modeling Requirements
- V4: Access Control Verification Requirements
- V7: Error Handling and Logging Verification Requirements
- V8: Data Protection Verification Requirements
- V9: Communications Verification Requirements
- V11: Business Logic Verification Requirements
- V14: Configuration Verification Requirements

It must be assumed that the environment is secured accordingly and follows best security practices, to prevent any side-channel data leakage, which would lead to releasing sensitive data, thus rendering the model ineffective, in particular:

- the statistical database, historical database, and association database are properly secured at the access level, including external connectivity if it is necessary from the business perspective;
- the sensitive properties: variables (S, a_preset, r_preset) and functions ($D(d\_q)$) are considered critical and secured with the mechanism preventing or limiting from direct access and modification;
- the communication between the database users and the database is properly secured with the latest communication in-transit recommendations (e.g., the highest available TLS version with secure cipher suites); this is especially important during the data acquisition process;
- the sensitive actions over the systems' components, especially databases, are logged to detect any suspicious alterations or unauthorized access.

Apart from the environmental perspective, it is crucial that all the technical security requirements are properly reflected through the implementation of the solution; in particular, it must be assumed that:

- the implementation of the proposed model is free from errors that would affect the security of the solution, e.g. business logic errors that would affect the processing of the data;
- the system is free from backdoors that would intend to bypass the security mechanisms;
- the system hardening and security configuration (e.g., defined access model implementation) is effectively implemented and free from errors;
- the fail-safe rule is effectively implemented, especially error handling does not reveal any excessive information, sensitive properties are never revealed through the error condition;

- other application-level errors and vulnerabilities are detected at the early stages of the SDLC lifecycle and properly addressed.

4 Final Remarks

Ensuring the quality of any proposed statistical disclosure control models must always go beyond the design. Even if the mathematical model is assessed and tested there may be still a way of improving the solution at implementation level. Although achieved measurable and impactful performance improvements beyond algorithmic definition may be hard to achieve, the overall security of any statistical disclosure control model depends on the robust security of the system that applies this model. The paper summarized the fundamental aspects of the implementation-level improvement for the performance and security which can be applied to the extended differential privacy model. Additionally, what is worth noting is that through this paper we can determine that the quality of any statistical disclosure control mechanism should consider ease for implementation and retrofitting which is not covered in the statistical disclosure control evaluation framework [7], thus the framework itself should be extended by the additional implementation characteristics.

References

1. Dwork, C.: Differential privacy. In: Bugliesi, M., Preneel, B., Sassone, V., Wegener, I. (eds.) ICALP 2006. LNCS, vol. 4052, pp. 1–12. Springer, Heidelberg (2006). https://doi.org/10.1007/11787006_1
2. Dzięgielewska, O.: Anonymization, tokenization, encryption. How to recover unrecoverable data. Comput. Sci. Math. Modell. **6**, 9–13 (2017)
3. Dwork, C., Kenthapadi, K., McSherry, F., Mironov, I., Naor, M.: Our data, ourselves: privacy via distributed noise generation. In: Vaudenay, S. (ed.) EUROCRYPT 2006. LNCS, vol. 4004, pp. 486–503. Springer, Heidelberg (2006). https://doi.org/10.1007/11761679_29
4. Hall, R., Rinaldo, A., Wasserman, L.: Random differential privacy. arXiv:1112.2680 (2011)
5. Chatzikokolakis, K., Andrés, M.E., Bordenabe, N.E., Palamidessi, C.: Broadening the scope of differential privacy using metrics. In: De Cristofaro, E., Wright, M. (eds.) PETS 2013. LNCS, vol. 7981, pp. 82–102. Springer, Heidelberg (2013). https://doi.org/10.1007/978-3-642-39077-7_5
6. Dzięgielewska, O.: Defeating inference threat with scoring metrics. In: 36th IBIMA Conference on 4–5 November 2020 Granada, Spain: Conference Proceedings, USA (2020). ISBN 978-0-9998551-5-7
7. Dzięgielewska, O.: Evaluating quality of statistical disclosure control methods – VIOLAS framework. In: Domingo-Ferrer, J., Muralidhar, K. (eds.) PSD 2020. LNCS, vol. 12276, pp. 299–308. Springer, Cham (2020). https://doi.org/10.1007/978-3-030-57521-2_21
8. Dziegielewska, O.: Evaluating adaptive differential privacy model. Comput. Sci. Math. Modell. **13–14**, 5–16 (2022)
9. OWASP Software Assurance Maturity Model. https://owasp.org/www-project-samm/ BSIMM. BSIMM Framework. https://www.bsimm.com/framework.html
10. ISO 9000 FAMILY QUALITY MANAGEMENT. https://www.iso.org/iso-9001-quality-management.html
11. ISO/IEC 12207:2008 Systems and software engineering—Software life cycle processes. https://www.iso.org/standard/63712.html

12. ISO/IEC 15288:2008 Systems and software engineering—System life cycle processes. https://www.iso.org/standard/63711.html
13. Systems and software engineering—Life cycle management—Part 1: Guidelines for life cycle management. https://www.iso.org/standard/72896.html
14. OWASP Application Security Verification Standard. https://owasp.org/www-project-application-security-verification-standard/

Hiding Data in Printed Documents

Michał Glet[1], Kamil Kaczyński[1(✉)], and Paweł Zielski[2]

[1] Faculty of Cybernetics, Institute of Mathematics and Cryptology, Military University of Technology, Warsaw, Poland
{michal.glet,kamil.kaczynski}@wat.edu.pl
[2] TiMSI Sp. z o. o., Warsaw, Poland
pawel.zielski@timsi.pl

Abstract. The security of the data in printed documents is one of the most underestimated security areas. Mainly researchers only consider the electronic version of the documents. However, printed documents are still widely used, especially in many strategic areas, such as governments, justice, military, etc. In this paper, we present the basic ideas and examples of how our mechanism works to hide data in printed documents. Using this mechanism, an organization can build a printed document security solution that meets its needs.

Keywords: printed document · hiding data · security

1 Introduction

Securing printed data is a very tough task. The are many market solutions that are trying to deal with this problem. Some of them are trying to secure the whole process of the creation of printed data e.g. by monitoring printing queues, printing authorizations, etc. [1–3]. Another solution is adding visible watermarks to printed data [4]. Our approach is quite different. Along with more standard ways to secure printed data, like e.g. visible watermarks, we have developed a solution that allows hiding data in printed documents. Data are hidden by e.g. introducing some lines, words and letters shifting. The main purpose is to make those changes hardly unseen by the end user. Because of this user is not aware that printed documents carry some hidden data. Our mechanism allows the building of custom security solutions. For example, every printed document can be marked with the user identifier. Then, after the leakage system administrator can recover this identifier from a scanned version of this document and identify the user who is responsible for the leakage.

In this paper, we present algorithm basics that were developed during the first phases of the project and were used in the first phases of the implementation process. This process was carried out together with the testing phase in an iterative manner. Because of that, we were able to make a lot of changes and improvements that led us to develop a fully functional proof-of-concept.

K. S. Soliman (Ed.): IBIMA-AI 2023, CCIS 2101, pp. 349–355, 2024.
https://doi.org/10.1007/978-3-031-62843-6_33

2 Algorithm Basics

This section describes the basics and principles that were used during the first phases of the implementation process.

Steganographic algorithms used in paper documents must allow for reading from a copy made using digitization techniques such as scanning. Based on the obtained image, it is possible to analyze the document for the presence of hidden data necessary in the process of verifying the source of the document. The designed system assumes the use of algorithms that operate on the line and word shifting. Each method's steganographic capacity will be increased using syndrome coding mechanisms.

The line-shift coding algorithm uses manipulation of vertical spacing between lines of text in a document. The algorithm requires the identification of control lines, which serve as a reference point for elevated and lowered lines. Information coding uses the following relationship:

- 0 - lowered line - decreased spacing
- 1 - elevated line - increased spacing

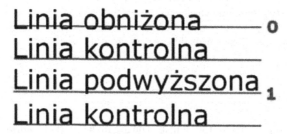

Fig. 1. Changes created by a line-shift coding algorithm

Line shifting is implemented using a distance of 1/300 of an inch, which guarantees imperceptibility of marking using human vision while maintaining resistance to distortions up to the 10th copy. An average A4 page contains about 40–50 lines of text, and each hidden message must be preceded by a control line that allows for the reading of the introduced information. This means that each page will have a maximum of 20 lines for carrying hidden information. Due to the lack of benefit from using syndrome coding (a limited set of lines), data stored using line shifting should be an identifier stored in a database and linked with other characteristics of the document.

The data-hiding algorithm is as follows:

1. Retrieve a binary sequence of n bits, which will be the document identifier.
2. Retrieve a seed k for the permutation algorithm.
3. Select a set of n lines that can be shifted.
4. Perform permutation on the set of lines using seed k.
5. Perform the line shift operation for each line according to the pattern shown in Fig. 1.
6. If the document has more than one page, each subsequent page takes the seed value of $k + 1$ to avoid repeat shifts on document pages. Data is embedded on each page of the document.

The data extraction algorithm is as follows:

1. Retrieve seed k for the permutation algorithm.
2. Retrieve information about the location of lines in the document.
3. Based on the location information, assign values of 0, 1, or none (control line) to the lines and assign them to the n-bit sequence.
4. Perform reverse permutation on the recovered sequence.

The second algorithm used is the word-shift algorithm. Data is transferred through the spacing between a given word and its preceding word. Even spacing represents a hidden bit of 0, odd spacing represents a hidden bit of 1. The selection of words carrying the content is performed using a pseudo-random algorithm operating on a given key. All hidden data is compressed using syndrome coding of Hamming code error correction (Fig. 2).

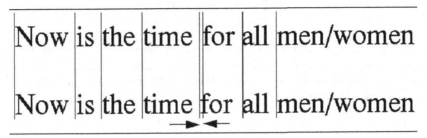

Fig. 2. Changes created by a word-shift algorithm

The information input algorithm proceeds as follows:

1. Retrieve a binary sequence of n bits that will serve as the document identifier.
2. Retrieve the key k for the pseudorandom algorithm.
3. Select a set of words that can carry hidden information based on the results of the pseudorandom generator.
4. From the set in step 3, retrieve the next 7 words that can be shifted.
5. Retrieve the next 3 bits of the message - the document identifier.
6. Calculate the syndrome for the 7 carrier bits. For example, if the 7 carrier bits have a value of 1001001 and the hidden message is 101, calculate the syndrome:

$$s = \begin{bmatrix} 1\,0\,1\,0\,1\,0\,1 \\ 0\,1\,1\,0\,0\,1\,1 \\ 0\,0\,0\,1\,1\,1\,1 \end{bmatrix} \begin{bmatrix} 1 \\ 0 \\ 0 \\ 1 \\ 0 \\ 0 \\ 1 \end{bmatrix} = \begin{bmatrix} 0 \\ 1 \\ 0 \end{bmatrix}$$

7. If the calculated syndrome matches the hidden message, proceed to step 4. Otherwise, determine the bit that will be changed according to the following pattern:

$$\begin{cases} x_1 + x_3 + x_5 + x_7 = s_1 \\ x_2 + x_3 + x_6 + x_7 = s_2 \\ x_4 + x_5 + x_6 + x_7 = s_3 \end{cases}$$

8. For the presented example, the bit that should be changed is x7. 8. We introduce the modification to the carrier bits according to the determined change. For the above example, the codeword has a value of 1001000. Its correctness can be checked by calculating the syndrome.

$$s = \begin{bmatrix} 1\,0\,1\,0\,1\,0\,1 \\ 0\,1\,1\,0\,0\,1\,1 \\ 0\,0\,0\,1\,1\,1\,1 \end{bmatrix} \begin{bmatrix} 1 \\ 0 \\ 0 \\ 1 \\ 0 \\ 0 \\ 0 \end{bmatrix} = \begin{bmatrix} 1 \\ 0 \\ 1 \end{bmatrix}$$

9. Make changes to the spacings (even/odd) according to the change determined in step 8.
10. If not all message bits have been hidden, repeat steps 4–9.
11. Repeat steps 4–10 on the next pages of the document.

To ensure greater resilience of the embedded information, it is possible to repeat the embedding process within a single page. The algorithm offers much greater capacity compared to the line shift algorithm, allowing for multiple hiding of the document identifier. The process of retrieving embedded data can be carried out according to the following steps:

1. Obtain the key k for the pseudorandom algorithm.
2. Select a set of words that can carry the hidden information, based on the results of the pseudorandom generator.
3. From the set in step 2, extract the next 7 words that may have been shifted.

4. Calculate the syndrome for the 7 carrier bits from step 3. For example, if the 7 carrier bits have a value of 1001001, the hidden message is equal to the calculated syndrome.

$$
s = \begin{bmatrix} 1 & 0 & 1 & 0 & 1 & 0 & 1 \\ 0 & 1 & 1 & 0 & 0 & 1 & 1 \\ 0 & 0 & 0 & 1 & 1 & 1 & 1 \end{bmatrix} \begin{bmatrix} 1 \\ 0 \\ 0 \\ 1 \\ 0 \\ 0 \\ 1 \end{bmatrix} = \begin{bmatrix} 0 \\ 1 \\ 0 \end{bmatrix}
$$

5. If not all message bits have been read, repeat steps 3 to 4.
6. Repeat steps 2 to 5 on the next pages of the document.

3 Implementation and Examples

During implementation phase we have conducted a lot of tests and made a lot of changes and improvements in the describe above basics. As a result we have created a system, that can successfully hide data in the printd documents. Data can be hidden, for example, regardless of the text alignment used in the document. The general rule is that the more text in the document, the more data can be hidden in it. Below we present scans of documents in which the value 0x80FF01 has been hidden (Fig. 3).

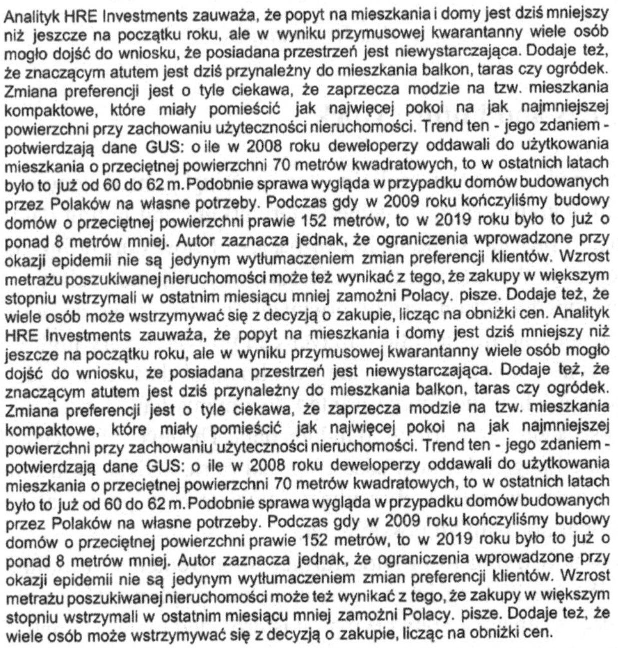

Analityk HRE Investments zauważa, że popyt na mieszkania i domy jest dziś mniejszy niż jeszcze na początku roku, ale w wyniku przymusowej kwarantanny wiele osób mogło dojść do wniosku, że posiadana przestrzeń jest niewystarczająca. Dodaje też, że znaczącym atutem jest dziś przynależny do mieszkania balkon, taras czy ogródek. Zmiana preferencji jest o tyle ciekawa, że zaprzecza modzie na tzw. mieszkania kompaktowe, które miały pomieścić jak najwięcej pokoi na jak najmniejszej powierzchni przy zachowaniu użyteczności nieruchomości. Trend ten - jego zdaniem - potwierdzają dane GUS: o ile w 2008 roku deweloperzy oddawali do użytkowania mieszkania o przeciętnej powierzchni 70 metrów kwadratowych, to w ostatnich latach było to już od 60 do 62 m. Podobnie sprawa wygląda w przypadku domów budowanych przez Polaków na własne potrzeby. Podczas gdy w 2009 roku kończyliśmy budowy domów o przeciętnej powierzchni prawie 152 metrów, to w 2019 roku było to już o ponad 8 metrów mniej. Autor zaznacza jednak, że ograniczenia wprowadzone przy okazji epidemii nie są jedynym wytłumaczeniem zmian preferencji klientów. Wzrost metrażu poszukiwanej nieruchomości może też wynikać z tego, że zakupy w większym stopniu wstrzymali w ostatnim miesiącu mniej zamożni Polacy. pisze. Dodaje też, że wiele osób może wstrzymywać się z decyzją o zakupie, licząc na obniżki cen. Analityk HRE Investments zauważa, że popyt na mieszkania i domy jest dziś mniejszy niż jeszcze na początku roku, ale w wyniku przymusowej kwarantanny wiele osób mogło dojść do wniosku, że posiadana przestrzeń jest niewystarczająca. Dodaje też, że znaczącym atutem jest dziś przynależny do mieszkania balkon, taras czy ogródek. Zmiana preferencji jest o tyle ciekawa, że zaprzecza modzie na tzw. mieszkania kompaktowe, które miały pomieścić jak najwięcej pokoi na jak najmniejszej powierzchni przy zachowaniu użyteczności nieruchomości. Trend ten - jego zdaniem - potwierdzają dane GUS: o ile w 2008 roku deweloperzy oddawali do użytkowania mieszkania o przeciętnej powierzchni 70 metrów kwadratowych, to w ostatnich latach było to już od 60 do 62 m. Podobnie sprawa wygląda w przypadku domów budowanych przez Polaków na własne potrzeby. Podczas gdy w 2009 roku kończyliśmy budowy domów o przeciętnej powierzchni prawie 152 metrów, to w 2019 roku było to już o ponad 8 metrów mniej. Autor zaznacza jednak, że ograniczenia wprowadzone przy okazji epidemii nie są jedynym wytłumaczeniem zmian preferencji klientów. Wzrost metrażu poszukiwanej nieruchomości może też wynikać z tego, że zakupy w większym stopniu wstrzymali w ostatnim miesiącu mniej zamożni Polacy. pisze. Dodaje też, że wiele osób może wstrzymywać się z decyzją o zakupie, licząc na obniżki cen.

Fig. 3. Scan of a document with a hidden value: 0x80FF01

Scenariusz pierwszy zakłada stopniowe znoszenie restrykcji gospodarczych, które rozpoczyna się w maju i trwa do końca czerwca. Od lipca uruchomione są niemal wszystkie sektory gospodarki, lecz nadal utrzymywany jest rygor sanitarny. Scenariusz drugi - od bazowego odróżnia się przede wszystkim skutkami drugiej fali zachorowań - w tym wariancie analitycy PIE zakładają, że mimo rygoru sanitarnego druga fala będzie podobna lub większa niż pierwsza, w związku z czym jesienią konieczne będzie ponowne zamknięcie niektórych sektorów gospodarki na 1-2 miesiące. W prognozie PIE uwzględnił spadek konsumpcji krajowej rzędu 15-30 proc. w miesiącach objętych restrykcjami (rozłożony nierównomiernie między sektory) oraz wyraźny spadek popytu zewnętrznego. W tym drugim przypadku PIE posługuje się prognozą Międzynarodowego Funduszu Walutowego.

"W pierwszym scenariuszu PKB Polski w 2020 r. zmniejszy się o 4,0 proc. (w porównaniu z 2019 r.). Oznaczałoby to, że w relacji do prognoz sprzed kilku miesięcy, epidemia obniża wzrost gospodarczy w Polsce o 7,5 pkt. proc. Z tego około 40 proc. jest wynikiem spadku konsumpcji krajowej, a około 60 proc. - spadku popytu zewnętrznego oraz zakłóceń po stronie podażowej związanych z przerwaniem międzynarodowych łańcuchów dostaw" - napisano. "W drugim scenariuszu PKB Polski w 2020 r. zmniejszy się o 7,1proc. W tym wariancie wpływ epidemii przekracza 10 pkt. proc. a podział źródeł spadku na popyt krajowy i sytuację zewnętrzną rozkłada się niemal po połowie" - dodano. Wreszcie Niemcy, naszego głównego partnera handlowego - choć nieco słabiej niż w pozostałe państwa Europy Zachodniej. Popyt zewnętrzny był najważniejszym czynnikiem wzrostu naszej gospodarki w ostatnich kilkunastu latach, a teraz jest znacząco osłabiony wyjaśniono jedną z głównych przyczyn gwałtownego kurczenia się polskiej gospodarki.

"W pierwszym scenariuszu PKB Polski w 2020 r. zmniejszy się o 4,0 proc. (w porównaniu z 2019 r.). Oznaczałoby to, że w relacji do prognoz sprzed kilku miesięcy, epidemia obniża wzrost gospodarczy w Polsce o 7,5 pkt. proc. Z tego około 40 proc. jest wynikiem spadku konsumpcji krajowej, a około 60 proc. - spadku popytu zewnętrznego oraz zakłóceń po stronie podażowej związanych z przerwaniem międzynarodowych łańcuchów dostaw" - napisano. "W drugim scenariuszu PKB Polski w 2020 r. zmniejszy się o 7,1 proc. W tym wariancie wpływ epidemii przekracza 10 pkt. proc. a podział źródeł spadku na popyt krajowy i sytuację zewnętrzną rozkłada się niemal po połowie" - dodano. Wreszcie Niemcy, naszego głównego partnera handlowego - choć nieco słabiej niż w pozostałe państwa Europy Zachodniej. Popyt zewnętrzny był najważniejszym czynnikiem wzrostu naszej gospodarki w ostatnich kilkunastu latach, a teraz jest znacząco osłabiony wyjaśniono jedną z głównych przyczyn gwałtownego kurczenia się polskiej gospodarki.

Fig. 3. (*continued*)

4 Conclusions and Future Work

We have developed a complete solution for securing printed documents. It consists of e.g. classical watermarking, invisible watermarking and hiding data. In this paper, we were trying to provide some technical basics of how our hiding data mechanism works. We are aware that there is no 100% sure way to secure printed documents, but by using a developed solution wisely, organizations can create an additional layer of security. In our opinion, this additional layer can provide a very high level of security and should prevent stealing and revealing confidential data. Every identified leakage could be examined when the source printed documents have been found. Our system can process those scans and retrieve all hidden data. The level of success depends on the number of scanned pages. In most cases, we can retrieve data from only one scanned page. In cases where the retrieved results are unclear (e.g. poor scan quality), we are presenting the operator with all possible data.

Now we are still trying to provide further improvements in hiding and detection success rates. We are making improvements in our implementation and algorithmics theory. The feedback that we are working on is provided by testers and clients. What is more, we will try to provide some cloud solutions that will allow securing documents with an "on-demand" business model.

Acknowledgement. This work was partially funded by the European Regional Development Fund, "Regionalny Program Operacyjny Województwa Mazowieckiego na lata 2014–2020", Poland. The project number was RPMA.01.02.00-14-9407/17.

References

1. https://www.epapersign.com/data-leak-prevention-printers. Accessed March 2023
2. http://support.ricoh.com/bb_v1oi/pub_e/oi_view/0001080/0001080399/view/security/int/pri nted.htm. Accessed March 2023
3. https://itwatch.info/Products/PrintWatch. Accessed March 2023
4. https://www.papercut.com/help/manuals/pocket-hive/features-in-detail/make-printing-sec ure/watermarking-and-digital-signatures/. Accessed March 2023

Computer Modeling of Evacuation Patterns Comparison and Crowd Dynamics: A Use of NetLogo

Livia D. Iancu[1]([✉]), Paul A. Dragoi[2], and Camelia Delcea[1]

[1] Bucharest University of Economic Studies, Bucharest, Romania
livia.diana.iancu@gmail.com, camelia.delcea@csie.ase.ro
[2] Politehnica University of Bucharest, Bucharest, Romania
paul_adrian.dragoi@stud.acs.upb.ro

Abstract. Evacuating people during emergencies is crucial for their safety and well-being. Whether it's a natural disaster like an earthquake, or a man-made accident, a prompt evacuation leads to saving more lives. Evacuating people during emergencies is an essential measure to minimize the risks and protect the health and safety of those affected by the crisis. This paper explores the topic of emergency evacuations through the lens of a model developed using NetLogo 6.3.0. The model is designed to simulate the evacuation of a medium-sized event hall in the event of an emergency, such as a fire or an earthquake. The paper examines the key factors that influence the success of an evacuation, including the layout of the building, the number of occupants, and the behavior of individuals during the evacuation. The model is used to test different scenarios and strategies for improving evacuation procedures. Overall, the paper contributes to the ongoing efforts to improve emergency preparedness and response, and demonstrates the potential of modeling tools like NetLogo to support this important work.

Keywords: Evacuation Patterns · Crowd Dynamics · Agent-Based Modelling · Public Spaces Evacuation

1 Introduction

Emergency evacuations are critical to protecting human life in the event of natural disasters, terrorist attacks, fires, and other emergencies. The success of an evacuation largely depends on a variety of factors, including the number of occupants, the layout of the building, and the behavior of individuals during the evacuation process. Modeling tools such as NetLogo ("NetLogo Home Page," n.d.) can help researchers better understand the dynamics of emergency evacuations, as well as identify strategies to improve evacuation procedures.

Several studies have used modeling approaches to examine various aspects of emergency evacuations. For instance, [8] developed a model to simulate pedestrian flows during evacuations, while [17] developed a model to study the impact of human factors in emergency evacuations. Other studies have examined the impact of room information on evacuation times [12], or taken into account people with locomotor disabilities [16].

This paper builds on this body of research by using NetLogo to model emergency evacuations from a generic medium-sized event hall. The model is used to explore and compare two different algorithms that conduct how the simulated agents react and move during the evacuation simulations and determine ways of improving evacuation procedures.

The naïve algorithm, where agents simply choose the nearest available exit, is a straightforward approach to crowd dynamics in emergency evacuations. However, this algorithm does not take into account factors such as congestion or obstacles, which can result in inefficiencies and potentially dangerous situations during an evacuation. By contrast, the inverted ant colony optimization algorithm considers the congestion rate of each exit and guides agents towards the least congested exit, resulting in a self-organizing process that minimizes congestion and maximizes efficiency. This algorithm simulates the behavior of individuals in a more realistic way, taking into account the complexity of real-life evacuation scenarios.

The paper is structured as follows: Sect. 2 provides theoretical background related to the evacuation simulations field; in Sect. 3, we describe the NetLogo model and its key components; next, in Sect. 4, we present the results of the simulations, including a comparison between the two crowd-dynamics algorithms used, naïve and inverted ant colony optimization; and finally, in Sect. 5, we discuss the implications of these findings for emergency preparedness and response.

2 Theoretical Background

Emergency evacuation simulations have been a popular topic of research for many years, and several methods have been developed to model and analyze evacuation scenarios. Cellular automata, agent-based modeling, and social force models are some of the most widely used techniques in this field. Cellular automata models, such as those proposed by [10], divide a space into a grid of cells and simulate the movement of individuals based on simple rules. Agent-based models, as proposed by [7], represent individuals as autonomous agents and simulate their interactions with the environment and other agents. Social force models, first introduced by [9], simulate the movement of individuals based on the interactions between them and their environment. Each of these methods has its own strengths and weaknesses, and researchers have attempted to combine and refine them over the years to create more accurate and effective simulations.

Nowadays, the agent-based modelling has gained an increased attention from the research community in the evacuation models as it provides a simple mean for incorporating the characteristics of the agent, rules of behavior and interactions, both among evacuees and among them and the environment [1]. Additionally, as most of the agent-based modelling platforms offer a graphical user interface, the agent-based modelling has started to be used in the evacuation simulations as it offers the possibility to easily discover the occurrence of various elements that might be behind a prolonged evacuation process (e.g. the occurrence of a bottleneck, the dimensions of an exit, the preference of the evacuees towards a certain exit, etc.). As a result, even in the case of the present paper, the simulation environment has been built through the use of an agent-based modeling platform.

3 The Model and Its Key Components

The NetLogo model used in this paper simulates the evacuation of people from a medium-sized indoor event hall. The model is designed to simulate different emergency scenarios, such as fires or earthquakes, and to test the effectiveness of different evacuation strategies. The model features several key components, including the layout of the room, the number and behavior of occupants, and the presence of obstacles or hazards. The model is agent-based, meaning that it simulates the behavior of individual agents and their interactions with each other and their environment [2].

This allows for a detailed analysis of the factors that influence evacuation success, including the impact of crowd behavior, the availability of exit routes, and the effectiveness of different evacuation strategies.

The environment under consideration has been partitioned into small pieces of ground with a square surface measuring 0.5 × 0.5 m, in order to construct the agent-based model [1, 4, 5]. The remaining components of the agent-based model (objects, doors, stage, people, etc.) are scaled to meet multipliers of these values as a result of this segmentation of the surface into small areas.

The model's graphical user interface (GUI) is displayed in Fig. 1. The interface allows the configuration of a number of items. The variables needed to build the environment of the agent-based model were inspired by measurements taken from actual concert halls, and the variables related to population structure were taken from statistics relating to the typical attendance at indoor events. The variables that refer to the characteristics of the evacuation population have been extracted from the scientific literature (e.g., speed).

In terms of population, one can set up the number of people attending an event, the structure of the population (children, adults, seniors, and people with locomotion

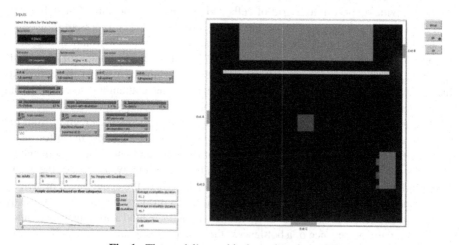

Fig. 1. The model's graphical user interface (GUI)

impairment), the presence or absence of staff members, the location of the people serving as staff at the event.

The agent-based model, as provided in the following sub-sections, was constructed based on a number of assumptions. Two different kinds of agents have been employed: the event hall has been divided into squares by patches, which are small pieces of ground with characteristics that help the turtle agents better understand their surroundings and direct them to the available exits. The second type of agents used, the turtles, are agents that resemble humans in terms of assessing their surroundings and making necessary evacuation decisions.

3.1 Location

The medium-sized indoor event hall chosen as the location for the simulated evacuations provides a realistic and practical setting for the study of emergency evacuation scenarios. The hall's design, including its size, layout, and exit locations, reflects many indoor event spaces commonly found in urban areas. The hall is equipped with multiple exits that aid the evacuation process. Additionally, the hall's capacity is large enough to accommodate a significant number of agents, allowing for a comprehensive evaluation of the evacuation process under varying conditions. The use of this setting provides valuable insights into

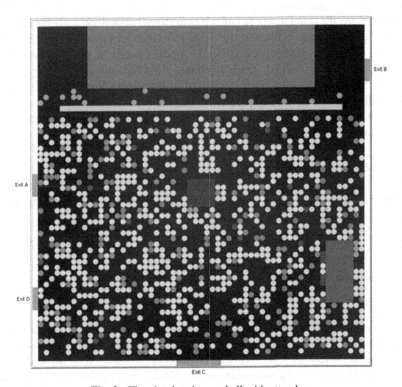

Fig. 2. The simulated event hall with attendees

the challenges and opportunities of evacuating people from indoor event spaces and can inform the development of effective emergency evacuation plans for such scenarios.

The location used in this study is a standard medium-sized indoor event hall (30 × 30 m) with a capacity of maximum 1000 people, excluding the staff members and artists. The room has four exits, three of which the same size of 2 m in width, and one larger one, double in size, that facilitate the evacuation of the public. It is equipped with a stage, delimited with a fence, a technical desk placed in front of the stage and a bar with stools. These objects are considered by the simulated population as obstacles and they must be bypassed in order to reach one of the exits (Fig. 2).

3.2 Population and Assumptions

The simulated population in the emergency evacuation simulation is a critical component of the study, as it represents the people who may need to evacuate during an emergency. The population is diverse, consisting of agents of different ages and physical abilities, reflecting the real-world variability of populations in indoor event spaces. Each agent is programmed with unique characteristics, such as movement speed, based on the available data on human behavior during emergency situations. Understanding the behavior and response of the simulated population to different scenarios is essential to identify the most effective emergency evacuation strategies and improve the safety of individuals during emergency situations.

Furthermore, the simulated population is considered rational and, once the evacuation starts, the agents will move towards the exits. The number of attendees can be selected by the user through the dedicated slider in the model's interface. The distribution of the population in terms of age and physical abilities is also customizable, making possible for the interested parties to adjust the model to better suit the desired simulated event.

The information provided by [11] has been used to determine the movement speed of the agents representing the "standard occupants" involved in an evacuation process, as shown in Table 1.

Table 1. Average movement speeds based on the category of the participants

Population category	Average movement speed (m/s)	Speed range (m/s)
Child	0.90	0.90 ± 0.30
Adult	1.25	1.25 ± 0.30
Senior	0.80	0.80 ± 0.30
Person with locomotor disability	0.79	0.79 ± 0.30

We have taken into consideration the uniform probability distribution for the speed as given by [11] Table 1, because not all individuals involved in an evacuation process have the same movement speed. This assumption is consistent with the finding made by [15] who noted that walking speeds can be calculated using distributions in order to account for the variety of people's abilities. The typical movement and speed range for those with locomotor impairment have been extracted from [6] research.

3.3 Algorithms Used for Crowd Dynamics

Two algorithms for crowd dynamics have been used for this study and compared in the following section: the naïve algorithm (where people choose the nearest exit) and the inverted ant colony optimization algorithm (where evacuees take into consideration traffic and choose the less congested exit). In the model's interface there is a chooser button that lets the user opt for any of the two algorithms (Naïve or IACO).

The naïve algorithm for crowd dynamics in emergency evacuations is a simple and intuitive approach. In this algorithm, individuals exit through the nearest exit from their current location. This algorithm assumes that individuals will make rational decisions based solely on their proximity to the exit, without taking into account any other factors such as congestion or obstacles in the environment. While this approach is easy to implement, it may not accurately reflect the behavior of individuals in a real-life emergency evacuation scenario. For example, individuals may not be able to reach the nearest exit due to obstacles or congestion, resulting in inefficient and potentially dangerous evacuations.

The inverted ant colony optimization algorithm, on the other hand, takes into account traffic and congestion to guide individuals towards the least congested exit. This algorithm is based on the behavior of ants [3], who follow pheromone trails left by other ants to find the shortest path to a food source. In the inverted ant colony optimization algorithm, individuals simulate the behavior of ants by leaving virtual pheromone trails as they move towards an exit. Other individuals can then detect and avoid these trails, resulting in a self-organizing evacuation process that minimizes congestion and improves overall efficiency. This algorithm is more complex to implement than the naive algorithm but can provide more accurate results and better reflect the behavior of individuals in a real-life emergency evacuation scenario.

4 The Results of the Simulations

The results of the emergency evacuation simulations based on an agent-based model provide valuable insights into the effectiveness of different evacuation strategies and the impact of various factors on the evacuation process. This chapter presents an analysis of the simulation results, including the performance of the two algorithms used for the turtle agents. The findings of this study are purely theoretical and might lead to the development of more effective emergency evacuation strategies and improve the safety of individuals during emergency situations.

As mentioned before, two different algorithms that dictate the behavior of the evacuees have been implemented, and, through the model's interface, one can choose the type of the algorithm with the help of a selection button. For this study, the population will not vary (number of evacuees and the population distribution will remain constant throughout all the simulation scenarios). Only the availability of the exits and the route-choice algorithm will be changed according to the scenarios described later on. The population is a constant of 1000 people (attendees) and an additional 21 staff members that have a predefined area where they can be spawned (near the stage and bar). The staff is colored in cyan, while the general population varies from yellow (adults), green (children), gray (seniors) to red (people with disabilities). The objects that appear in the simulated space must be bypassed by the agents (stage – pink, fence – gray, front of house – magenta, bar & stools – blue). The exits that are available are colored in green, and the ones that are closed in red. For an easier comparison between the two algorithms, the distribution of the population is kept constant throughout the simulations (13% children, 10% seniors, 1.3% persons with disabilities and the rest adults). For other research purposes, the percentages previously described can be modified according to the type of event that is simulated.

In Fig. 3 one can see a snapshot of the evacuation process while using the naïve algorithm. The agents in this case will chose the nearest available exit from their starting position, regardless of the number of people surrounding it. This leads to heavier congestion near some of the exits, depending on the number of agents spawned near it. On the left side of the figure, a real time chart of the evacuees can be monitored, alongside a couple of key indicators: number of agents still evacuating at the given moment of time (separated according to population categories), the average evacuation duration in seconds for an agent, the average evacuation distance in meters and the total evacuation time for all agents in seconds.

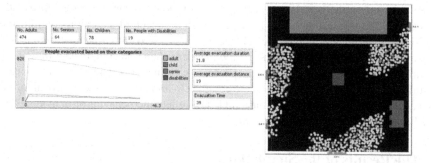

Fig. 3. Simulation results using the naïve algorithm (Color figure online)

A snapshot of an evacuation using the Inverted Ant Colony Optimization can be seen in Fig. 4. As in the previous figure, on the right side of the image a real-time chart and statistics of the evacuees can be observed. On the right side we can see the simulated area and its evacuees. In comparison to the naïve algorithm, here agents will leave a green trail that increases in its color intensity according to how much traffic there is in the respective area. The brighter the color, the more congested that space is and evacuees will avoid it and reconsider their path towards the exit. This way, the agents will not necessarily choose the closest available exit, but will take into con-sideration the level of congestion and opt for another path (or even another exit) that has less traffic.

Through a series of sliders in the interface, one can modify three parameters, in order to accurately reflect the population behavior. We can control the decongestion rate (the rate at which the pheromone trail left by the agents evaporates over time; a high decay rate means that the pheromone trail dissipates quickly, while a low decay rate means that the pheromone trail re-mains visible for a longer period of time), the congestion value (it determines how strong the pheromone left by the agent will be; a higher value will mean that other agents will avoid this particular spot, while a lower one means that the zone is free) and the diffusion rate (this determines much of the congestion value pheromone will also spread to the surrounding area).

For this research, we have used a diffusion rate of 50, a decongestion rate of 10 and a congestion value of 1. These values remain constant throughout all simulations and are in line with the original model that inspired this one ("NetLogo Models Library: Ants," n.d.).

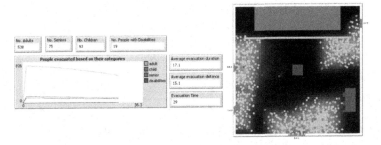

Fig. 4. Simulation results using the Inverted ACO algorithm

The simulations are based on 4 different scenarios that are described in Table 2. The variable that differentiates the scenarios is the availability of the 4 possible exits.

In Scenario 1, where all exits are open, we can expect the evacuation process to be relatively smooth and efficient, assuming that people are able to find and use the nearest exit. However, even with all exits available, it is important to consider factors such as the capacity of each exit and the behavior of people during an emergency, as these can impact the overall safety and success of the evacuation.

In Scenario 2, where only exit C is open, the evacuation process may be more challenging as people may need to navigate unfamiliar routes to reach the available exit. This could result in delays and potentially cause congestion at the exit, especially if the capacity of the exit is not sufficient to accommodate the number of people trying to use it. In this scenario, it may be important to provide clear signage and guidance to help people find the exit and reduce confusion and panic.

In Scenario 3, where only exits A and D are open, people may need to traverse longer distances to reach an available exit, which could also result in delays and potential congestion. However, if people are able to quickly and efficiently move towards the available exits, this scenario may still result in a successful evacuation. It may be important to consider the overall lay-out of the event hall and the location of the exits to optimize the evacuation process in this scenario.

In Scenario 4, where only exits A and B are open, people may once again need to navigate unfamiliar routes to reach an available exit. This could cause confusion and delays, potentially leading to congestion at the available exits. However, if clear signage and guidance are provided, and people are able to quickly and efficiently move towards the exits, this scenario may also result in a successful evacuation.

Overall, by simulating these different scenarios, one can gain insights into the potential challenges and opportunities of different exit configurations during an emergency evacuation. This information can help inform emergency planning and preparedness efforts, and identify strategies to improve the safety and efficiency of emergency response.

Table 2. Scenarios used in the simulations

Scenario	Exit availability*			
	A	B	C	D
S1	✓	✓	✓	✓
S2	✗	✗	✓	✗
S3	✓	✗	✗	✓
S4	✓	✓	✗	✗

* where ✓ means the exit is opened and ✗ means the exit is closed

The results of the simulations using the scenarios described earlier can be seen in Table 3. In order to highlight the differences between the two path-finding algorithms used, we have calculated the difference in percentage between the measurements recorded using the inverted ant colony optimization algorithm and the naïve one.

Table 3. Results of the simulations using the scenarios in Table 2

Scenario	Algorithm	Overall evacuation time		Average evacuation time		Average distance travelled	
		Measured (s)	IACO vs Naïve (%)	Measured (s)	IACO vs Naïve (%)	Measured (m)	IACO vs Naïve (%)
S1	Naïve	211	31.3	64.5	20.6	51.8	11.8
	Inverted ACO	145		51.2		45.7	
S2	Naïve	279	13.3	122.9	4.72	91.5	-4.8
	Inverted ACO	242		117.1		95.9	
S3	Naïve	224	4.5	102.8	0.3	80.9	-4.9
	Inverted ACO	214		102.5		84.9	
S4	Naïve	392	36.2	153	21.1	107.3	6.9
	Inverted ACO	250		120.7		99.9	

In Scenario 1, where all exits are open, the inverted ant colony optimization algorithm out-performed the naive algorithm, resulting in a shorter overall evacuation time, shorter average evacuation time, and less distance travelled by evacuees. This suggests that using more advanced optimization algorithms can significantly improve the efficiency of an evacuation, even in scenarios where all exits are open and the evacuation process is relatively straightforward.

In Scenario 2, where only exit C is open, both algorithms resulted in longer overall evacuation times and average evacuation times, as well as longer distances travelled by evacuees. This suggests that having only one exit available can significantly impact the efficiency of an evacuation, even when using advanced optimization algorithms. However, the inverted ant colony optimization algorithm did result in slightly shorter overall and average evacuation times, suggesting that it may still be helpful in minimizing delays and improving safety.

In Scenario 3, where only exits A and D are open, both algorithms resulted in relatively short overall evacuation times and average evacuation times, with only slightly longer distances travelled by evacuees when using the inverted ant colony optimization algorithm. This suggests that having fewer available exits may not necessarily have a significant impact on evacuation efficiency, especially when using optimization algorithms to help guide evacuees towards the available exits.

In Scenario 4, where only exits A and B are open, the inverted ant colony optimization algorithm significantly outperformed the naive algorithm, resulting in a much shorter overall evacuation time, shorter average evacuation time, and less distance travelled by evacuees. This suggests that even in scenarios where only a few exits are available, using advanced optimization algorithms can still be highly effective in improving the efficiency and safety of an evacuation.

An interesting fact that can be seen from the simulation results is that the inverted ant colony optimization algorithm better outperforms the naïve one when the available exits are further away from each other, as seen in the results from Scenario 3. When the available exits are near one another, the difference between the two algorithms is not as significant because the agents cannot opt for an entirely different evacuation path and are forced to remain in the same congested evacuation area.

Overall, the results of the simulations demonstrate the importance of considering both the number and location of available exits, as well as the algorithms used to guide evacuees towards these exits, in optimizing the efficiency and safety of emergency evacuations.

5   Conclusions

As it has been demonstrated, the agent-based model in NetLogo has proven to be a powerful tool for simulating and analyzing emergency evacuations. Through our experiments, we have gained valuable insights into the behavior and interactions of individuals during emergency situations. Our analysis of the two algorithms for crowd dynamics, the naive algorithm and the invert-ed ant colony optimization algorithm, has shown that the choice of algorithm can have a significant impact on the efficiency and safety of the evacuation process.

The naive algorithm, while simple and easy to implement, has several limitations. In particular, it assumes that individuals will always choose the nearest exit, without considering factors such as congestion or obstacles. This can result in inefficient and potentially dangerous evacuations, particularly in large or complex environments. By contrast, the inverted ant colony optimization algorithm takes into account the density of individuals at each exit and guides them to-wards the least congested exit. This results in a self-organizing process that maximizes efficiency and minimizes congestion.

In conclusion, our experiments have shown that the inverted ant colony optimization algorithm is superior to the naive algorithm for crowd dynamics in emergency evacuations. By taking into account the density of individuals at each exit and guiding them towards the least congested exit, the inverted ant colony optimization algorithm is able to minimize congestion and improve overall efficiency. We hope that our findings will be useful for researchers, emergency planners, and others who are interested in improving the safety and effectiveness of emergency evacuations.

Acknowledgment. This paper was co-financed by The Bucharest University of Economic Studies during the PhD program.

References

1. Cotfas, L.-A., Delcea, C., Iancu, L.-D., Ioanas, C., Ponsiglione, C.: Large event halls evacuation using an agent-based modeling approach. IEEE Access **10**, 49359–49384 (2022). https://doi.org/10.1109/ACCESS.2022.3172285
2. Cotfas, L.-A., Delcea, C., Mancini, S., Ponsiglione, C., Vitiello, L.: An agent-based model for cruise ship evacuation considering the presence of smart technologies on board. Expert Syst. Appl. **214**, 119124 (2023). https://doi.org/10.1016/j.eswa.2022.119124
3. Dorigo, M., Birattari, M., Stutzle, T.: Ant colony optimization. IEEE Comput. Intell. Mag. **1**, 28–39 (2006). https://doi.org/10.1109/MCI.2006.329691
4. Edrisi, A., Lahoorpoor, B., Lovreglio, R.: Simulating metro station evacuation using three agent-based exit choice models. Case Stud. Transp. Policy **9**, 1261–1272 (2021). https://doi.org/10.1016/j.cstp.2021.06.011
5. Fu, L., Luo, J., Deng, M., Kong, L., Kuang, H.: Simulation of evacuation processes in a large classroom using an improved cellular automaton model for pedestrian dynamics. Procedia Eng. **31**, 1066–1071 (2012). https://doi.org/10.1016/j.proeng.2012.01.1143
6. Hashemi, M.: Emergency evacuation of people with disabilities: a survey of drills, simulations, and accessibility. Cogent Eng. **5**, 1506304 (2018). https://doi.org/10.1080/23311916.2018.1506304
7. Helbing, D., Farkas, I., Vicsek, T.: Simulating dynamical features of escape panic. Nature **407**, 487–490 (2000). https://doi.org/10.1038/35035023
8. Helbing, D., Johansson, A.: Pedestrian, crowd and evacuation dynamics. In: Meyers, R.A. (ed.), Encyclopedia of Complexity and Systems Science, LNCS. Springer, New York, New York, NY, pp. 6476–6495 (2009). https://doi.org/10.1007/978-0-387-30440-3_382
9. Helbing, D., Molnár, P.: Social force model for pedestrian dynamics. Phys. Rev. E **51**, 4282–4286 (1995). https://doi.org/10.1103/PhysRevE.51.4282
10. Kirchner, A., Schadschneider, A.: Simulation of evacuation processes using a bionics-inspired cellular automaton model for pedestrian dynamics. Phys. Stat. Mech. Appl. **312**, 260–276 (2002). https://doi.org/10.1016/S0378-4371(02)00857-9

11. Korhonen, T., Hostikka, S., n.d.: Fire Dynamics Simulator with Evacuation: FDS+Evac. Technical Reference and User's Guide
12. Liu, S., Yang, L., Fang, T., Li, J.: Evacuation from a classroom considering the occupant density around exits. Phys. Stat. Mech. Appl. **388**, 1921–1928 (2009). https://doi.org/10. 1016/j.physa.2009.01.008
13. NetLogo Home Page [WWW Document], n.d. URL http://ccl.northwestern.edu/netlogo/. Accessed 23 Mar 2023
14. NetLogo Models Library: Ants [WWW Document], n.d. http://ccl.northwestern.edu/netlogo/ models/Ants. Accessed 23 Mar 2023
15. Ronchi, E., Uriz, F.N., Criel, X., Reilly, P.: Modelling large-scale evacuation of music festivals. Case Stud. Fire Saf. **5**, 11–19 (2016). https://doi.org/10.1016/j.csfs.2015.12.002
16. Sørensen, J.G., Dederichs, A.S.: Evacuation characteristics of visually impaired people - a qualitative and quantitative study: evacuation characteristics of visually impaired people. Fire Mater. **39**, 385–395 (2015). https://doi.org/10.1002/fam.2200
17. Wang, Y., Kyriakidis, M., Dang, V.N.: Incorporating human factors in emergency evacuation – an overview of behavioral factors and models. Int. J. Disaster Risk Reduct. **60**, 102254 (2021). https://doi.org/10.1016/j.ijdrr.2021.102254

Concurrent Programs, Finalizers and Cleaners in Java - Security Problems

Jerzy Krawiec[1], Piotr Gorny[2], and Maciej Kiedrowicz[2(✉)]

[1] Warsaw University of Technology, Warsaw, Poland
jerzy.krawiec@pw.edu.pl
[2] Military University of Technology, Warsaw, Poland
{piotr.gorny,maciej.kiedrowicz}@wat.edu.pl

Abstract. The article presents the mechanisms of safe programming in Java applications. We indicate some mechanisms of protection against known vulnerabilities of Java applications considering concurrent programs, finalizers, and cleaners. We give source code examples that may threaten the operation of the applications. The paper considers the security mechanisms in the context of possibly performing dangerous operations by malicious code.

Keywords: Java code · security mechanisms · concurrent programs · finalizers · cleaners

1 Introduction

Since the inception of Java technology, there has been a steadily growing interest in the security of this platform. There are new security issues related to the implementation of Java technology.

From the technology vendor's point of view, there are two aspects to Java security. First, make the Java platform secure on which applications designed in Java can be safely run. Second, provide security tools and services implemented in Java programming that enable a wider range of security-sensitive applications (Security Developer's Guide, 14, 2020).

The Java platform (JDK) was designed with a strong emphasis on security. Security tools and services implemented in the Java programming language provides a wider range of security-sensitive applications. Java is type-safe and provides automatic garbage collection, increasing the reliability of the application code. The Java security architecture includes a large set of APIs, tools and implementations of commonly used security algorithms, mechanisms, and protocols (Security Developer's Guide, 15, 2020).

One of the significant issues is removing the need to lock out garbage collection when Java objects are used with native code. Native code can block garbage collection for several minutes, which can deviate from native code, adversely affecting throughput. In many applications, the GC design must improve its throughput and recovery timeliness, requiring much larger heap sizes to compensate. In rare cases, the use of native code

© The Author(s), under exclusive license to Springer Nature Switzerland AG 2024
K. S. Soliman (Ed.): IBIMA-AI 2023, CCIS 2101, pp. 368–378, 2024.
https://doi.org/10.1007/978-3-031-62843-6_35

improves the performance of the application, but we may find that we introduce security risks to such an application.

The are many threats in programming in Java. The research question of this article is to identify the threats in coding in Java and how to avoid such situations or implement security mechanisms to protect applications built in Java.

The article presents the mechanisms of safe programming. We indicate some mechanisms of protection against known vulnerabilities of Java applications considering concurrent programs, finalizers, and cleaners. We give source code examples that may threaten the operation of the applications. The paper considers the security mechanisms in the context of possibly performing dangerous operations by malicious code.

2 Literature Review

Security in Java starts at the level of language features. It allows us to write secure code and use many hidden security features. Java is a statically typed language (*Static Data Typing*), which reduces the ability to detect type errors at run time. Java allows using various access modifiers, such as public and private, to control access to fields, methods, and classes. In addition, using automatic memory management based on eliminating garbage elements frees developers from manual management. Java is a compiled language that converts code to platform-independent bytecode, and the runtime verifies each bytecode loaded for execution [3].

Java's nature fundamentally causes the need to encapsulate the runtime as an open programming environment. Java 16 and Java 17 provide a foundation of enhanced encapsulation that will provide a safer and simpler future for both application developers and JDK internal programmers alike [4].

Java Design Program extends traditional design patterns with new functional programming features, such as: functional interfaces, lambda expressions and security mechanisms. The result is a new approach to design patterns that can increase their usefulness using best practice [11].

The use of serialization, i.e., converting an object into a stream of bytes, involves risks related not only to performance and correctness but also to the security and maintainability of the program code. The fundamental problem with serialization is the scope of the attack, which is too large to be effectively protected. Object graphs are deserialized (recreating an object from byte form) by calling the *readObject()* method for an object of the *ObjectInputStream* class. In practice, this method is a constructor that creates objects of any type, provided that the *Serializable* interface is implemented. In byte-stream deserialization, the method executes code, and the potential attack scope is code of all these types. The scope of such an attack includes classes from standard Java libraries, external libraries, and classes of this application. Java programming languages provide a native way to implement the serialization or deserialization mechanism. Developing a code that writes and reads any objects is often a laborious task. The main advantage of this approach is the universality of the program code [9].

For validating the deserialized data, the records are deserialized with a constructor, which allows invariants to be added to the constructor. It is impossible with standard classes as there is always some risk of deserializing unsafe data. Since the data may come from external sources, this must be considered. Using the compact record builder, we do not need to specify parameters or set record fields explicitly. When deserializing previously serialized records, every instance should have a valid state. Otherwise, it is generated by the record builder. It can be verified by modifying the serialized data of only one record so that the data no longer follows the validation logic [8].

Performing dangerous operations with malicious code provides unauthorized access to system resources. It concerns limitations in methods, encapsulation problems, general types and methods, defensive copying, and cloning aspects. The method can leave the object in an invalid state, which may result in an error in that part of the program. Incorrectly applied inheritance can result in error-prone program code. Thus, the safe use of inheritance is to use it within the same package, implementing the base and child classes in the same package. The security of types and generic methods can be increased by automatically parameterizing types that allow the creation of classes, interfaces, and methods. We can use defensive copying before validating parameters and checking itself on copies of objects [10].

Writing concurrent programs takes work. Software written for concurrency must leverage the power of today's modern multicore CPU architectures. Moreover, most computers now have access to graphics processing units (GPUs) that allow developers to solve parallel problems at unprecedented speed quickly. However, native coding for GPUs is also problematic. Developers build software, which has changed. More and more systems are event-driven or reactive, but most programming languages and algorithms do not model well in this new paradigm. These challenges come when developers are expected to be more productive and to produce reliable, performant, scalable software. We can use *Concurnas*, a new programming language targeting the JVM. *Concurnas* was designed to build modern, reliable, scalable, high-performance, concurrent, distributed, and parallel systems [13].

Garbage Collector (GC) is an essential HotSpot JVM (Java Virtual Machine) component in ensuring Java security. The GC manages the entire lifecycle of application heap objects. The core functions of the GC are primarily garbage collection in the JVM. We have many ways to meet these requirements, but no one-size-fits-all algorithm exists. For this reason, the JDK provides several garbage collection algorithms. Each of these algorithms is optimized for different use cases. Their implementation determines the behavior of one or more of the three key performance and security metrics [12].

3   Methodology

3.1   Concurrent Programs

The use of multithreads allows you to perform various activities in one program. Concurrency is a natural way to get high performance on multi-core processors. In this aspect, ensuring synchronization of access to jointly modified data is essential. The synchronization mechanism consists not only of mutual exclusion or protection of an object from reading an inconsistent state of one thread while another thread is modifying it. The thread is created in a consistent state and is blocked by methods that access it. These methods allow you to read the state and can cause a transition between states, leading to the transfer of an object from one consistent state to another. Thus, synchronization prevents reading a value from an object that is in an unstable state. However, without synchronization, changes from one thread may not be visible to other threads. Thus, synchronization not only protects against reading an unstable state of an object but also ensures the visibility of previous modifications. Java language mechanisms provide atomicity of reading and writing a variable. It means that the returned value will equal the value written by another thread, even when multiple threads modify this variable simultaneously without a synchronization mechanism. This rule does not apply to *long* or *double* variables. However, atomism does not guarantee another thread's visibility of written data. Thus, both synchronization and exclusion are necessary for reliable communication between threads. It is due to the technical solutions of the Java language, i.e., the memory model. We should note that lack of ensuring synchronization of access to a shared variable can lead to severe consequences, even when the variable is read and written in an atomic form.

Actions in synchronized methods can be atomic even without synchronization. The synchronization of these methods is used only to ensure communication. The purpose would be to introduce the volatile modifier, which guarantees another thread's visiblility of the saved value. However, the use of the volatile modifier poses some risks. Here is a fragment of the program that generates the counter:

```
private static volatile int next_counter = 0;
public static int generate_counter() {
    return next_counter++;
}
```

This program fragment uses the *generate_counter()* method to generate a *counter* value. The generator state has only one field, written as an atomic operation (*next_counter*). All field values are allowed. However, this method requires synchronization. Several parallel threads can read, modify, write, and return the same counter value because read operations are performed simultaneously. Consequently, this violates the security principle, as the program needs to generate correct results.

Therefore, we need to add the *synchronized* modifier in the method declaration to remove this security violation. It will ensure that parallel invokings do not overlap and that each invoking will show the results of the previous invoking. Then we can remove the volatile modifier. For additional security of this method, we should change the type of the field to *long* or throw an exception when the value of the *next_counter* field has a maximum value.

However, in this case, a better solution is to use the *AtomicLong* class, which is included in the *java.util.concurrent.atomic* package. This package contains mechanisms for creating thread-safe code and does not use locks on single variables. In addition, the package provides atomicity, although variables with the volatile modifier indicate synchronization. This solution offers better performance than the synchronized version:

```
private static final AtomicLong next_counter = new AtomicLong();
public static long generate_counter() {
    return next_counter.getAndIncrement();
}
```

Modifying object data has been accepted for some time. Only then should the object be made available to other threads using synchronization when sharing references to the object. Other threads can read the object until it is synchronized again. This transfer of object references ensures safe publishing.

Other ways to safely publish an object reference include storing the reference in a *static* field at class initialization, placing it in a *volatile, final,* or shared field using standard locking, and placing it in a concurrent collection.

Regarding the ability to modify a class, we have two ways to ensure concurrency. The first way is to ensure synchronization from the outside by having clients block entire objects. The second way is to provide thread safety by achieving higher concurrency through internal synchronization. Using the latter method, and we can use the *java.util.concurrent* collection. We can use synchronization techniques to achieve high concurrency control, such as lock splitting, lock lifting, and lockless concurrency control. If a method modifies a static field, internal synchronization of access to such a field must be ensured. The field is treated as a global variable, even if the field is private. Such a field can be read and written by unrelated clients.

Creating concurrent programs has become more manageable, but writing programs that improve performance and are valid is already challenging. An integral part of concurrent programming (parallelized streams of streams) is lifetime and security violations. Parallelizing a stream of streams does not improve program performance if its source is *stream.iterate()* or an indirect operation is *limit()*. An increase in program performance by parallelizing the streams of streams can be achieved using classes *ArrayList, HashMap, HashSet, ConcurrentHashMap,* arrays, and simple types (*int* and *long*) [1].

Parallelism of stream of streams can also lead to security violations as the stream uses mappings, filters, and other functional objects that do not conform to the Stream specification. Stream defines the requirements for such objects quite accurately, e.g., aggregation or link functions passed to *reduce()* should be concatenated, independent, and stateless. The link function is the *BinaryOperator <V>* interface, where *V* is the type of the mapping value. The cost of improper stream parallelization may be a bug in the program (security breach) or, at best, limiting the program's performance [2].

A natural way to perform operations on multi-core processors is concurrency. Concurrent programs require that an object be secured against reading an inconsistent state by a thread being modified by another thread. This operation is known as synchronizing access to mutually modified data. When creating an object in a consistent state, the object is blocked by methods that allow reading the state of the object and can move the object from one consistent state to another [5]. The correct application of synchronization ensures that the method cannot read a value from an object that is in an inconsistent state. Both synchronization and mutual exclusion are required to ensure reliable communication between threads. It is due to Java's use of a memory model that governs when and how threads should be visible. Both read and write operations must be synchronized. By using timing synchronization of the object reference, we can modify the object's data for a specified time and only then make it available to other threads. Thus, the reader and writer thread must benefit from locking when several threads are used from the modified data. Failure to synchronize access to data may cause errors in the security system and reduce program stability.

Using a multi-threaded class requires a documented level of thread safety. Thread-safe is mutable objects where the methods contain an internal synchronization, meaning the objects can be used in parallel. Examples of such classes are *AtomicLong* and *ConcurrentHashMap*. Conditionally thread-safe are classes that contain methods that require external synchronization. Examples are the *Collections.synchronized* shield classes where iterators require external synchronization. Classes determined to be non-thread-compatible can create mutable objects to be safely used in parallel, provided that the method calls are closed in an externally synchronized block. Examples are the *ArrayList* or *HashMap* classes, which make up general-purpose collections. Threads cannot use classes identified as dangerous to threads in parallel. It also applies to situations where method calls are synchronized externally. A description of class safety for threads is included in the doc comments. Holding a publicly available blockade for a more extended period (intentionally or accidentally) creates the conditions for a DOS (Denial of Service) attack. In this case, a *private alpha* object should be used instead of synchronized methods, e.g.

```
private final Object alpha = new Object();
public void delta() {
    synchronized (alpha) {
    ...
    }
}
```

A private *alpha* object is not available for class members. It means that it does not affect the synchronization of this object. Therefore, it must encapsulate the lock object in the synchronized object. Note that the *alpha* field is declared final, which prevents accidental change of value, which can lead to unsynchronized access to the object. Therefore, the *alpha* field should always be declared final. A private *alpha* object should only be used in unconditionally thread-safe classes. Using an internal blocking object is of particular importance for base classes, as a child class may inadvertently interfere with the base class's own locking operation.

Thread poses some risks. Once the work queue is used, the client can execute a method that requests the background thread to exit safely after all jobs in the queue have finished. However, such code is vulnerable to performance issues and threats if the code is not correctly executed. In this case, we would use the *java.util.concurrent* package. It includes the *Executor Framework*, which provides a flexible interface-based execution mechanism. This mechanism can be written:

ExecutorService exec = Executors.newSingleThreadExecutot();

Sending an object of the *Runnable* class is as follows:

exec.execute(runnable);

Whereas the safe termination of the object operation is done in the following way:

exec.sutdown( );

Using such a mechanism, we can wait for the safe termination of the task using the *awaitTermination( )* method. When several threads are used, thread pools with a fixed or variable number of threads can be created using a static factory method, for example, with the *java.util.concurrent.Executors* class. For custom operations, we can use the *ThreadPoolExecutor* class directly. It allows direct control of every aspect of the thread pool operation.

In most practical multi-threaded applications, two or more threads must share access to the same data. What if two threads access the same object, and each invoke a method that modifies the state of the object? Depending on the order in which the data is accessed, objects can be corrupted, referred to as a race condition. Access must be properly synchronized to avoid corruption of shared data by multiple threads [6].

There are two mechanisms to protect a code block from concurrent access: the *synchronized* keyword and the *ReentrantLock* class. *Synchronized* provides the lock automatically, which is convenient in most cases that require explicit locking. In contrast, the *java.util.concurrent* framework provides separate classes for these core mechanisms. It is important that the unlock operation is contained in the *final* clause because if the code in the critical section throws an exception, the lock must be unlocked. Otherwise, other threads will be blocked forever. If we use locks, we cannot use the *try-with-resources* statement. First off, the unlock method is not called *close*. However, even if it is renamed, the *try-with-resources* statement would not work because its header expects the declaration of a new variable. However, when we use a lock, we want to keep using the same variable shared among threads. Thus it will not work. If we want to protect blocks of code that update or inspect a shared object, we can be assured that these operations run to completion before another thread can use the same object. Ensure that the code in a critical section is not bypassed by throwing an exception. If an exception is thrown before the end of the section, the *final* clause will relinquish the lock, but the object may be left in a damaged state.

Paying the cost of synchronization to read or write the instance fields seems excessive. However, with modern processors and compilers, there is plenty of room for errors. Computers with multiple processors can temporarily hold memory values in registers or local memory caches [7]. Consequently, threads running in different processors may see different values for the exact memory location. Compilers can reorder instructions for maximum throughput. Compilers will not choose an ordering that changes the meaning of the code, but they assume that memory values are changed only when there are explicit instructions in the code. However, a memory value can be changed by another thread. We will not have these problems if we use locks to protect code accessed by multiple threads. Compilers must respect locks by flushing local caches as necessary and not inappropriately reordering instructions.

Writing concurrent programs takes work. Software written for concurrency must leverage the power of today's modern multicore CPU architectures. Moreover, most computers now have access to graphics processing units (GPUs) that allow developers to solve parallel problems at unprecedented speed quickly. However, native coding for GPUs is also problematic [13].

3.2 Finalizers

A finalizer is a method called when an object is disposed of by garbage collection. Unlike the destructor, it is known precisely when the program will run this way. Finalizers open the class to finalization attacks [1]. The malicious subclass finalizer can run on a partially constructed object that should be deleted during its creation. The finalizer can write a reference to the object in the statistic field, which means the object cannot be deleted. Then we deal with a damaged object (the object should not exist) on which any methods can be called. In such a situation, the exception thrown from the constructor level should prevent the creation of the object. However, the operation of the finalizer results in such an object being created. Therefore, protection against a finalization attack relies on introducing an empty *finalize()* method.

For classes that use resource release mechanisms (files, threads), the *AutoCloseable* interface should be implemented instead of finalizers. In the case of thread cleanup, the try-with-resources construct would have to be used, ie, the implicit call to the *close()* method. When the object's owner does not call the *close()* method, finalizers are used as so-called "Safety nets". Some Java library classes implement such finalizers. These classes include *FileInputStream, FileOutputStream, ThreadPoolExecutor*, and *java.sql.Connection*. The second use of finalizers is with objects with external parents. Such objects reference the operating system directly through core methods. In such a situation, it is impossible to carry out the process of removing the external object while removing the main object. Then the finalizer will run, provided the parent is not blocking critical resources. The class should also include a *close()* method for an external object that uses resources that should be released quickly.

3.3 Cleaners

Cleaners are trickier to use but do not clutter the public class API like finalizers. We assume that the *Alpha* class needs to be cleaned before reuse, then the class implementing the *AutoCloseable* interface uses the cleaner as a safety mechanism:

```
public class Alpha implements AutoCloseable {
    private static final Cleaner gamma = Cleaner.create();
    private static class Beta implements Runnable {
    long number_piles;
    Beta(int number_piles) {
        this.number_piles = number_piles;
    }
     @Override public void run() {
        System.out.println ("Cleaning");
        number_piles = 0;
     }
   }

    private final Beta status;
    private final Cleaner.Cleanable kappa;
    public Alpha(int number_piles) {
        status = new Beta(number_piles);
        kappa – cleaner.register(this, status);
    }
    @Override public void close() {
        kappa.clean();
   }
 }
```

The nested, static *Beta* class holds the resources required by the *cleaner* object. The *number_piles* field means disorder. The *Beta* class implements the *Runnable* interface. After registering the *Beta* instance in the *cleaner* inside the *Alpha* constructor code, we get the *kappa* object. This object only invokes the *run()* method once. The invoking of this method can be caused by the *close()* method from the *Alpha* class, which invokes the *clean()* method from *Cleanable*. The cleaner will invoke the *run()* method from *Beta*. If the *close()* method is not invoked before the *Alpha* instance is passed for garbage collection, the *cleaner* will invoke the *run()* method from the *Beta* class.

There must be no reference in the *Beta* instance to the class *Alpha* object. Creating such a reference would cause a loop of references, making it impossible to indicate the *Alpha* instance for automatic garbage collection, i.e., automatic cleaning. Therefore, the *Beta* class must be a static nested class.

In this case, the *Alpha* class *cleaner* serves as a safety mechanism. If we wrap *Alpha* object in *try with resources* code, then automatic cleaning is not needed, which can be written as:

```
public class Test1 {
    public static void main(String[] jekr) {
        try (Alpha omega = new Alpha(5)) {
            System.out.println("Goodbye");
        }
    }
}
```

Test1 program displays "Goodbye" and then "Cleaning". However, in the absence of an automatic cleaning mechanism in the program (Test2):

```
public class Test2 {
    public static void main(String[] jekr) {
        new Alpha(99));
            System.out.println("Bye");
    }
}
```

The text "Cleaning" will not be displayed as the program will terminate. The reaction of cleaner when invoking *System.exit* depends on its implementation. In this situation, there is no guarantee that the cleanup action will be performed.

4   Results and Discussions

Using a multi-threaded class requires a documented level of thread safety. Thread-safe is mutable objects where the methods contain an internal synchronization, meaning the objects can be used in parallel. In order to reduce the risk related to cybersecurity, it is necessary to use a class that ensures encapsulation of the runtime environment.

Unsynchronized access to data can lead to vulnerabilities in the program code and reduce its stability. Such anomalies may be conditioned by timing dependencies, Virtual Machine implementation details, and the type of computer the program is running on. In order to ensure proper communication between threads, an advanced technique, which is the *volatile* modifier, should be used as an alternative to synchronization.

In order to avoid threats such as deadlocks and data corruption, the number of operations in a synchronized block should be limited, i.e., not invoking a foreign method from a synchronized block. When designing a modifiable class, we should consider its synchronization. However, synchronization should be used only in justified cases. The use of multi-core processors should enforce the principle of not abusing synchronization.

Developers build software, which has changed. More and more systems are event-driven or reactive, but most programming languages and algorithms do not model well in this new paradigm. These challenges come when developers are expected to be more productive and to produce reliable, performant, scalable software.

Malicious subclass finalizers can run on the partially constructed object. Because finalizers can write a reference to an object in the statistic field, which means the object cannot be dropped. Then the exception thrown from the constructor level should prevent the creation of such an object.

Besides using security mechanisms or releasing operating system resources, cleaners and finalizers (up to Java 8) should not be used. However, be aware of the unpredictability and impact on program performance.

Acknowledgments. This work was financed/co-financed by Military University of Technology under research project UGB 22-810.

References

1. Bloch, J.: Effective Java, 3rd edn. Pearson Education, Inc., London (2018)
2. Bruno, E.J.: Streaming analytics with Java and Apache Flink, Java Magazine, 6 July 2020
3. Chandrakant, K.: The Basics of Java Security, 3 July 2022. https://www.baeldung.com/java-security-overview
4. Evans, B.: A peek into Java 17: continuing the drive to encapsulate the Java runtime internals, Java Magazine, 30 April 2021
5. Gosling, J., Joy, B., Steele, G., Bracha, G., Buckley, A., Smith, D.: The Java® Language Specification, Java SE, 13 Edition, Oracle America, Inc. (2019)
6. Horstmann, C.: Synchronization in Java, Part 1: race conditions, locks, and conditions, Java Magazine, 4 February 2022
7. Horstmann, C.: Synchronization in Java, Part 3: atomic operations and deadlocks, Java Magazine, 2 March 2022
8. Kivy, F.: Diving into Java records: serialization, marshaling, and bean state validation, Java Magazine, 6 November 2020
9. Krawiec, J., Gorny, P., Kiedrowicz, M.: Vulnerability of object-oriented applications – problems with deserialization. In: 37th International Business Information Management Association Conference (IBIMA), 2021, 30–05–2021–31–05–2021, Online (2021)
10. Krawiec, J., Gorny, P., Kiedrowicz, M., Gepner, P., Wybraniak-Kujawa, M.: Proceedings of the 39th International Business Information Management Association Computer (IBIMA), 30–31 May 2022, Granada, Spain. Theory and Practice in Modern Computing: Vision 2025 in the Era of Pandemic/Soliman Khalid S. (red.), Proceedings of the International Business Information Management Association (IBIMA) (2022). IBIMA Publishing, ISBN 978-0-9998551-9-5
11. Sciore, E.: Java Program Design: Principles, Polymorphism, and Patterns, Apress, New York (2019)
12. Schatzl, T.: Java garbage collection: the 10-release evolution from JDK 8 to JDK 18, Java Magazine, 16 June 2022
13. Tatton, J.: Concurrent programming with concurnas. Java Magazine, 22 June 2020
14. Java SE Platform Security Architecture, Security Developer's Guide. https://docs.oracle.com/en/java/javase/14/security/java-se-platform-security-architecture.html
15. Java Security Overview, Security Developer's Guide. https://docs.oracle.com/en/java/javase/14/security/java-security-overview1.html

Examining Telework Adoption Through Cybersecurity and Industry 5.0

Arturo Bedon[1]([✉]), Francisco A. Pujol[2], and Tamai Ramirez[2]

[1] Universidad Central del Ecuador, Quito, Ecuador
`cbedon@uce.edu.ec`
[2] Universidad de Alicante, Alicante, Spain
`{fpujol,tamai.ramirez}@ua.es`

Abstract. Teleworking has gained significant importance in recent years, especially with the arrival of Industry 5.0, where automation, digitalization and connectivity play a fundamental role in the transformation of industries. The COVID-19 pandemic has accelerated the adoption of teleworking, without people and organizations being prepared to do so. This has led to an increase in the number of successful cyberattacks attributed to executing activities remotely. For this reason, it is essential to examine the adoption of teleworking and its implications for cybersecurity in the context of Industry 5.0. Although there are investigations that have addressed these issues, we consider it pertinent to investigate the relationship between the adoption of teleworking, cybersecurity practices and the specific challenges that teleworking poses in the context of Industry 5.0. The objective of this research is to propose effective strategies that guarantee secure teleworking environments within the framework of Industry 5.0, based on the best cybersecurity practices in the industry. The research highlights the importance of implementing a series of measures to protect teleworking environments effectively. This includes secure network architectures, strong endpoint protection, multi-factor authentication, security awareness training, and proper incident response planning. Finally, we discuss the implications of blockchain for the security of remote work environments, including authentication, data integrity, fraud detection, and integration with machine learning.

Keywords: Teleworking · Cybersecurity · Industry 5.0 · Blockchain

1 Introduction

Telework, also known as remote work or telecommuting, has become increasingly prevalent in recent years, especially with the global shift brought about by the COVID-19 pandemic. Organizations have rapidly adopted telework to ensure business continuity and employee safety. However, this shift to remote work has brought forth a range of cybersecurity challenges. This work aims to highlight the key cybersecurity challenges associated with telework adoption and provide insights into addressing these challenges effectively.

K. S. Soliman (Ed.): IBIMA-AI 2023, CCIS 2101, pp. 379–388, 2024.
https://doi.org/10.1007/978-3-031-62843-6_36

As a result, technology and industry experts warned organizations and workers of the growing threat of cyber-attacks around the world, which according to the FBI the number of successful attacks had skyrocketed in the US, reaching an estimated 600% and worldwide by 300, since the COVID-19 pandemic began, estimated at 600% and worldwide at 300%, since the COVID-19 pandemic began, with this increase in successful attacks attributed to the number of people moving to working remotely.

In addition, teleworkers had little or no training in information security and cybersecurity, making them the weakest link in the chain and therefore the preferred attack vector for cybercriminals to breach information security, with 90% of unauthorized access incidents attributed to the human factor.

The convergence of telework and Industry 5.0 brings both opportunities and challenges. This paper aims to investigate the relationship between telework adoption, cybersecurity challenges, and the context of Industry 5.0. The main goals of this paper are to analyze the impact of telework adoption on cybersecurity practices, explore the unique challenges posed by telework in the context of Industry 5.0, and propose strategies to ensure secure telework environments within the framework of Industry 5.0.

2   Industry 5.0: Digitization, Automation, and Connectivity

The emergence of Industry 5.0 represents a transformative phase in industrial evolution, characterized by the integration of physical and digital systems, advanced automation, and enhanced connectivity [8]. This section explores the key principles and technologies of Industry 5.0 and highlights the role of telework in achieving its objectives. These key principles are, among others:

- *Integration of Physical and Digital Systems:* Industry 5.0 emphasizes the seamless integration of physical and digital systems, enabling a high degree of interoperability and real-time data exchange. Cyber-physical systems (CPS) play a vital role in this integration, enabling physical objects to be connected and controlled digitally. Through telework, employees can remotely access and interact with these connected systems, facilitating the convergence of physical and digital work environments. This integration enables remote workers to collaborate, monitor, and control industrial processes from any location, leading to increased flexibility and productivity [10].
- *Advanced Automation:* Automation is a fundamental aspect of Industry 5.0, where intelligent machines and systems work alongside humans to optimize operations and enhance efficiency. Telework enables the remote operation and monitoring of automated systems, allowing employees to leverage advanced automation technologies such as robotics, artificial intelligence (AI), and machine learning (ML) from remote locations. By remotely controlling robotic systems or utilizing AI algorithms for decision-making, teleworking employees can contribute to the automation efforts in Industry 5.0, leading to increased productivity and cost savings [4].
- *Enhanced Connectivity:* Connectivity forms the backbone of Industry 5.0, facilitating seamless communication and data transfer between various components within the industrial ecosystem. Telework leverages advanced communication technologies and high-speed internet connectivity to enable remote workers to collaborate with

colleagues, access real-time data, and control industrial systems. This enhanced connectivity enables teleworkers to participate in virtual meetings, share information, and contribute to collaborative projects, irrespective of their physical location. By embracing telework, organizations can tap into a geographically dispersed talent pool and foster global collaboration [4].

- *Cybersecurity Considerations:* As Industry 5.0 relies heavily on the integration of digital systems and connectivity, cybersecurity becomes paramount. Telework introduces additional cybersecurity challenges as employees access critical systems and sensitive data remotely. Organizations must ensure that robust cybersecurity measures are in place to protect industrial systems and data from cyber threats. This includes implementing secure network architectures, robust endpoint protection, multi-factor authentication, and security awareness training for teleworking employees. By addressing these cybersecurity challenges, organizations can leverage the benefits of telework while maintaining a secure Industry 5.0 environment [3].
- *Human-Machine Collaboration:* Industry 5.0 emphasizes human-machine collaboration, where humans and intelligent machines work together synergistically. Telework enables this collaboration by providing remote workers with the tools and connectivity to interact with intelligent machines and systems. Through telework, employees can remotely control robotic systems, monitor their performance, and collaborate with AI algorithms for decision-making processes. This collaboration enhances productivity, efficiency, and innovation, as humans and machines bring their unique strengths and capabilities together [1]. Table 1 shows the main principles of Industry 5.0 and how cybersecurity supports them.

Industry 5.0 is a transformative phase in industrial evolution, marked by the integration of physical and digital systems, advanced automation, and enhanced connectivity. Telework plays a crucial role in realizing the objectives of Industry 5.0 by enabling remote access, control, and collaboration with digital systems and intelligent machines [2]. However, organizations must also address the cybersecurity challenges associated with telework in this context. By embracing the principles of Industry 5.0 and implementing robust cybersecurity measures, organizations can leverage telework to unlock the benefits of integration, automation, and connectivity, leading to enhanced productivity, agility, and innovation [9].

Table 1. How does Cybersecurity technology support the implementation of Industry 5.0 principles?

Principle	Implementation Strategy
Interoperability	Implementing cyber security measures in systems and devices from different vendors that interconnect to share data and information from the production process

(continued)

Table 1. (*continued*)

Principle	Implementation Strategy
Virtualization	Creating test and simulation environments to assess the security of systems and applications, and to train security teams in cyber threat management
Decentralization	Implementing appropriate cyber security measures to protect information assets considering that decentralization can also make it difficult to enforce security policies across the network
Real-Time Capability	Implementing intelligent tools that can predict attacks and repel them in real time
Service Orientation	Implementing adequate cyber security measures to protect the virtual services that are offered to both customers and suppliers
Modularity	Implementing intelligent and modular tools that can increase or decrease capabilities to predict and repel attacks in real time

3   Cybersecurity Challenges in Telework Adoption

The increased reliance on telework introduces various cybersecurity challenges that must be addressed to protect organizational assets and ensure data privacy. This section discusses the vulnerabilities associated with remote work, including network security risks, endpoint security concerns, and the human factor in cybersecurity [9].

- *Network Security Risks:* Telework introduces new vulnerabilities to network security. Remote workers connect to organizational networks through various devices and networks, such as home Wi-Fi networks and public hotspots. These networks may lack proper security configurations and expose sensitive data to potential threats. Additionally, the increased reliance on cloud-based services and file-sharing platforms further expands the attack surface. Organizations must implement secure virtual private networks (VPNs), firewalls, and encryption protocols to protect data in transit and establish secure connections between remote workers and organizational resources.
- *Endpoint Security Concerns:* The use of personal devices, such as laptops, smartphones, and tablets, for telework can lead to endpoint security challenges. These devices may lack adequate security measures, making them vulnerable to malware, ransomware, and phishing attacks. Organizations should enforce strict security policies, including the use of strong passwords, regular software updates, and the installation of endpoint protection software. Endpoint security solutions can help detect and prevent unauthorized access, data breaches, and malware infections on remote devices [6].
- *Data Privacy and Protection:* Telework raises concerns regarding the privacy and protection of sensitive data. Remote workers handle confidential information outside the controlled office environment, increasing the risk of data breaches. Organizations must implement robust data protection measures, such as encryption, access controls, and data classification, to safeguard sensitive data [5]. Clear policies and guidelines should be established to define the handling, storage, and disposal of data

in remote work settings. Employee awareness and training programs on data privacy and protection are also essential to ensure responsible telework practices.

- *Authentication and Authorization:* The authentication and authorization mechanisms used in traditional office settings may not be sufficient for telework scenarios. Remote workers often access organizational resources from different locations and devices, necessitating stronger authentication methods. Multi-factor authentication (MFA), biometrics, and token-based authentication can enhance security by adding an additional layer of verification. Organizations should implement MFA protocols to ensure that only authorized individuals can access critical systems and data [7].
- *Human Factor in Cybersecurity:* The human factor remains a significant cybersecurity challenge in telework adoption. Remote workers may be more susceptible to social engineering attacks, phishing attempts, and the inadvertent sharing of sensitive information. Organizations must prioritize cybersecurity awareness training to educate employees about potential threats, safe online practices, and the importance of reporting suspicious activities. Regular training sessions simulated phishing exercises, and clear communication channels can empower remote workers to become active participants in maintaining cybersecurity [9].

As telework becomes an integral part of modern work environments, organizations must address the cybersecurity challenges it presents. By understanding and addressing the network security risks, endpoint security concerns, data privacy and protection issues, authentication and authorization challenges, and the human factor in cybersecurity, organizations can create a secure telework environment. Implementing robust security measures, promoting awareness, and training programs, and staying updated with evolving threats are essential for successful telework adoption with minimal cybersecurity risks. Proactive measures in addressing these challenges will not only protect organizations' assets but also contribute to the growth and resilience of telework in the future.

4   Securing Telework in the Industry 5.0 Era

The adoption of telework in the context of Industry 5.0 introduces unique cybersecurity challenges that organizations must address to ensure the protection of their digital assets. This section explores strategies and measures to secure telework in the Industry 5.0 era, taking into consideration the integration of physical and digital systems, automation, and human-machine collaboration [11].

- *Secure Network Architectures:* Organizations should implement secure network architectures to establish a robust foundation for telework security in the Industry 5.0 era. This includes segmenting networks to isolate sensitive systems and data, implementing firewalls and intrusion detection/prevention systems, and deploying network access controls. Virtual private networks (VPNs) can provide secure connections for remote workers accessing organizational resources. Network monitoring tools should be employed to detect and respond to any potential security incidents promptly.
- *Robust Endpoint Protection:* Endpoint security is crucial in securing telework in the Industry 5.0 era. Organizations should enforce policies that mandate the use of endpoint protection software on all remote devices. This software should include

features such as anti-malware, firewall protection, and vulnerability scanning. Regular updates and patches should be applied to address emerging threats and vulnerabilities. Additionally, organizations can implement remote device management solutions to enforce security configurations and remotely wipe data in case of loss or theft.

- *Multi-factor Authentication (MFA):* Traditional username and password authentication may no longer be sufficient in the Industry 5.0 era. Implementing multi-factor authentication (MFA) adds an extra layer of security by requiring additional verification, such as a unique code sent to a mobile device or a biometric identifier. MFA significantly reduces the risk of unauthorized access to organizational resources and strengthens the overall security posture of telework environments.

- *Security Awareness Training:* The human factor remains a critical component in telework security, particularly in the Industry 5.0 era where human-machine collaboration is emphasized (Yang et al. 2022). Organizations should provide comprehensive security awareness training programs for remote workers, educating them about potential threats, safe online practices, and the importance of adhering to security policies. Training sessions should cover topics such as identifying phishing attempts, recognizing social engineering techniques, and securely handling sensitive information.

- *Incident Response Planning:* Having a well-defined incident response plan is crucial for effective telework security in the Industry 5.0 era. Organizations should establish clear protocols and procedures to identify, respond to, and mitigate security incidents. This includes establishing communication channels, defining roles and responsibilities, and conducting regular drills to test the efficacy of the plan. Incident response plans should also incorporate remote work-specific scenarios and address the unique challenges associated with telework in the Industry 5.0 context.

- *Continuous Monitoring and Adaptation:* Telework security in the Industry 5.0 era requires continuous monitoring and adaptation to evolving threats and technologies. Organizations should implement security monitoring tools that provide real-time visibility into network traffic, user activity, and system logs. By actively monitoring telework environments, organizations can detect and respond to security incidents promptly. Regular security assessments and penetration testing can help identify vulnerabilities and ensure that security measures remain effective in the dynamic Industry 5.0 landscape.

Securing telework in the Industry 5.0 era necessitates a comprehensive approach that addresses network security, endpoint protection, authentication mechanisms, security awareness, incident response planning, and continuous monitoring. By implementing these strategies and measures, organizations can create a secure telework environment that aligns with the principles of Industry 5.0. The integration of secure network architectures, robust endpoint protection, multi-factor authentication, security awareness training, and incident response planning will enable organizations to adapt to the evolving telework landscape and safeguard their digital assets effectively.

One of the emerging technologies to secure telework is Blockchain [7]. Blockchain is a Distributed Ledger Technology (DLT) where records are not controlled by a central authority, eliminating the need for intermediaries to verify transactions and ensuring ownership while addressing the issue of double spending. Security is a significant challenge in telework, requiring all the workers involved to detect and trust each other. Blockchain technology offers unique characteristics that make it an emerging technology to watch and exploit in the coming years. Blockchain networks are peer-to-peer, and all nodes must be able to write data or transactions to the chain, going through a process of authentication and authorization before integration. The technology provides confidentiality, data integrity, authenticity of entities, and data origin.

Blockchain can secure communications within the network and offer solutions to potential security threats in teleworking. The consensus algorithms and other features ensure that participants have the same perception and data. Blockchain can facilitate decision-making in a company by introducing transactions and allowing pre-established situations to be voted upon by members. It also supports advanced collaborative models such as multi-signature, where multiple network members sign a transaction to ensure the security of decisions. Blockchain, originally developed for digital assets, can also serve as an API and has the potential to enhance the use of telework in Industry 5.0. Sensing-as-a-Service, a business model growing in IoT and related fields like the Internet of Robotic Things (IoRT), can be applied to Industry 5.0, providing agents with information from all teleworkers, improving their performance.

5 Proposal

Our proposal is a decentralized application, that is, an app that do not depend on a central system, but on the community of users that use it. This application would consist of an online clock in/clock out system for workers with Blockchain technology to ensure that the times results cannot be modified. To implement this, the system should include different elements that are shown in Fig. 1.

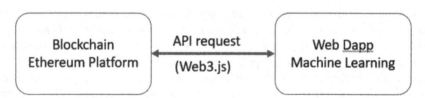

Fig. 1. Decentralized application elements for telework security system.

First, we have the Blockchain technology. It is proposed to use Ethereum Platform to make the contract and create the node and logic of the Blockchain. Ethereum Platform is a Blockchain which is programmable, so developers can use it to build new applications. It has its own language called Solidity, which is influenced by C++, Python and JavaScript. Like other Blockchain, Ethereum has a native cryptocurrency called Ether (ETH). To interact with some of Ethereum applications, the user needs a wallet, which is an application that make it easy to hold and send ether.

Then we need to create a Web application, where teleworkers are already registered (linking their Ethereum wallet), complete the clock in/clock out process, and share it with their supervisor(s). To connect the Blockchain Platform and the Web Application, it is necessary to use an API to make requests. Ethereum web provides some APIs with Javascript. In this case, the application could be implemented by using Web3.js, which is a collection of libraries which allow us to interact with a local or remote Ethereum node, using a HTTP or IPC connection.

Finally, Machine learning can play a crucial role in optimizing and improving clock-in and clock-out systems for telework scenarios that utilize blockchain technology. Here are some ways machine learning can enhance these systems:

- *User Authentication:* Machine learning algorithms can be used to analyse user behavior patterns, such as keystrokes or mouse movements, to authenticate teleworkers. By creating user-specific models, the system can verify the identity of remote workers and detect any anomalies that may indicate unauthorized access.
- *Activity Monitoring:* Machine learning algorithms can monitor and analyse teleworkers' activities during their work hours. By capturing data on application usage, websites visited, and files accessed, the system can identify unusual patterns or potential security breaches. This can help organizations detect insider threats or unauthorized access to sensitive information.
- *Productivity Analysis*: Machine learning models can analyse the work patterns and productivity of teleworkers. By considering factors such as task completion times, application usage, and collaboration patterns, the system can provide insights into individual and team productivity. This information can help organizations optimize resource allocation and identify areas for improvement.
- *Anomaly Detection:* Machine learning algorithms can detect anomalies in teleworkers' behaviour that may indicate potential security threats or policy violations. By continuously monitoring and analysing data, the system can identify deviations from normal patterns and trigger alerts for further investigation. This helps organizations respond promptly to security incidents and enforce telework policies effectively.

In view of all elements that need to be implemented, the different programming languages to be used according to the application to be developed could be HTML5, CSS3 and JavaScript for the frontend, and JavaScript, Python and Solidity for the backend.

It is important to note that the application of machine learning in clock-in and clock-out systems for telework using blockchain technology requires careful consideration of data privacy and security. Implementing robust encryption mechanisms and adhering to privacy regulations is crucial to protect sensitive information and ensure trust in the system.

6   Conclusions

In conclusion, our paper emphasizes that while telework offers numerous benefits, it also introduces significant cybersecurity risks that organizations must address to ensure the protection of their digital assets. The integration of physical and digital systems, advanced automation, and enhanced connectivity in the Industry 5.0 era further intensifies these challenges. The paper underscores the importance of implementing secure network architectures, robust endpoint protection, multi-factor authentication, security awareness training, and incident response planning to secure telework environments effectively. It also emphasizes the need for continuous monitoring and adaptation to evolving threats and technologies. By addressing these cybersecurity challenges and leveraging the principles of Industry 5.0, organizations can create a secure telework environment that maximizes productivity, innovation, and flexibility while minimizing potential risks. The findings of this study provide valuable insights for organizations seeking to navigate the telework landscape in the context of cybersecurity and Industry 5.0.

This work has served to confirm that the expectations and concerns that workers have when adopting teleworking are valid but it is necessary that companies execute some actions to close the gaps that cause the adoption of teleworking such as the lack of a methodology of evaluation by objectives and the lack of a culture in cybersecurity both companies and workers, with which the implementation of teleworking could serve to take advantage of the benefits offered by teleworking, especially with productivity and the reduction of travel that as already raised by other researchers can solve problems of vehicular congestion and environmental pollution.

In light of the research conducted in this paper several lines for future work emerge. First, further investigation can be undertaken to explore the evolving landscape of telework and its impact on cybersecurity in specific industries or sectors. This could involve case studies and empirical research to understand the unique challenges and best practices in telework adoption within different organizational contexts. Second, exploring emerging technologies and their implications for telework security in the Industry 5.0 era would be beneficial. The integration of technologies such as the Internet of Things (IoT), edge computing, and artificial intelligence (AI) can introduce new dimensions to telework and cybersecurity, warranting further analysis. Additionally, conducting longitudinal studies to assess the long-term effects of telework adoption on cybersecurity posture and organizational resilience would provide valuable insights. Lastly, exploring the socio-economic implications of telework, including its impact on job markets, work-life balance, and employee well-being, could provide a holistic understanding of telework adoption and cybersecurity considerations. By focusing on these areas of future work, researchers can continue to enhance our understanding of telework adoption, cybersecurity challenges, and their intersection with the evolving Industry 5.0 landscape.

References

1. Adel, A.: Future of industry 5.0 in society: human-centric solutions, challenges and prospective research areas. Adel J. Cloud Comput. **11**, 40 (2022). https://doi.org/10.1186/s13677-022-00314-5. Accessed 26 Apr 2023
2. Akundi, A., Euresti, D., Luna, S., Ankobiah, W., Lopes, A., Edinbarough, I.: State of industry 5.0—analysis and identification of current research trends. Appl. Syst. Innovation **5**(1), 27 (2022). https://doi.org/10.3390/asi5010027
3. Alexa, L., Pislaru, M., Avasilcăi, S.: From industry 4.0 to industry 5.0—an overview of European Union enterprises. Sustain. Innovation Manuf. Enterprises: Ind. Models Assess. Ind. 5.0, 221–231 (2022)
4. Fatima, Z., et al.: Production plant and warehouse automation with IoT and industry 5.0. Appl. Sci. **12**(4), 2053 (2022)

5. Kasinathan, P., et al.: Realization of sustainable development goals with disruptive technologies by integrating industry 5.0, society 5.0, smart cities and villages. Sustainability **14**(22), 15258 (2022). https://www.mdpi.com/2071-1050/14/22/15258

6. Leng, J., et al.: Industry 5.0: prospect and retrospect. J. Manuf. Syst. **65**, 279–295 (2022). https://www.sciencedirect.com/science/article/pii/S0278612522001662

7. Leng, J., et al.: Secure blockchain middleware for decentralized IIoT towards industry 5.0: a review of architecture, enablers, challenges, and directions. Machines 10(10) (2022). https://www.mdpi.com/2075-1702/10/10/858

8. Maddikunta, P.K.R., et al: Industry 5.0: a survey on enabling technologies and potential applications. J. Ind. Inf. Integr. **26**, 100257 (2022). https://www.sciencedirect.com/science/article/pii/S2452414X21000558

9. Paschek, D., Luminosu, C.-T., Ocakci, E.: Industry 5.0 challenges and perspectives for manufacturing systems in the society 5.0. Sustain. Innovation Manuf. Enterprises: Indic. Models Assess. Ind. 5.0, 17–63 (2022)

10. Wang, W., et al.: BIM information integration based VR modeling in digital twins in industry 5.0. J. Ind. Inf. Integr. **28**, 100351 (2022). https://www.sciencedirect.com/science/article/pii/S2452414X2200022X

11. Xian, W., Yu, K., Han, F., Fang, L., He, D., Han, Q.-L.: Advanced manufacturing in industry 5.0: a survey of key enabling technologies and future trends. IEEE Trans. Ind. Informatics, 1–15 (2023). https://doi.org/10.1109/TII.2023.3274224

12. Yang, J., Liu, T., Liu, Y., Morgan, P.: DETC2022–89711 Review of Human-Machine Interaction Towards Industry 5.0: Human-Centric Smart Manufacturing (2022)

Damages Caused by Ransomware and Selected Preventive Countermeasures

Lukas Vaclavik[✉]

Faculty of Business and Management, Brno University of Technology, Brno, Czech Republic
xvacla21@vutbr.cz

Abstract. Protecting the data of organizations against a wide range of cyber threats is undoubtedly one of the current topics in which there is considerable interest worldwide. This contribution discusses the principle of ransomware, the payment methods used, and an overview of the actual damage caused in the form of the ransom and the subsequent affected costs of the organization. The presented data was obtained based on an extensive analysis of relevant publicly available sources and reports. Cybercriminals are always one step ahead in their efforts to exploit identified and undetected vulnerabilities, putting significant pressure on cyber security professionals in organizations. Finally, the study also provides an overview of selected security measures to ensure protection against this kind of cyber threats, which can contribute to increasing awareness in this area and the general organizations security.

Keywords: ransomware · economics of ransomware · cryptocurrencies · cyberthreat · bitcoin

1 Introduction

The growing organizations dependence on computing resources can be described as undeniable. Nowadays cyber attackers are aware of this fact and are exploiting vulnerabilities in systems and processes to their advantage in the form of cyber-attacks. One such attack is through ransomware, which encrypts the victim's data and demands payment of a ransom in return for decryption and re-access. This type of attack technique is nowadays a thriving business in which the amount of money demanded by the attackers is astronomical.

Cybersecurity Ventures, one of the world's leading cybersecurity researchers and contributors, predicts the total cost of cybercrime to be $8 trillion by 2023. Compared to 2021, when it was $6 trillion, we can undoubtedly speak of a noticeable increase in these costs. In 2021, $20 billion of these costs were to be attributable to damage caused by ransomware, with attacks occurring every 11 s. By 2031, the cost of ransomware attacks is predicted to reach $265 billion. The boom and increase from previous years make this cyber threat the fastest growing form of cybercrime [11]. Victims are from large corporations, medium and small businesses, or individual users. In past years, small and medium-sized businesses were primarily off the cyber criminal's radar. However, in the last few years, we have seen a significant increase in attacks specifically targeting SMBs in various sectors [2].

© The Author(s), under exclusive license to Springer Nature Switzerland AG 2024
K. S. Soliman (Ed.): IBIMA-AI 2023, CCIS 2101, pp. 389–401, 2024.
https://doi.org/10.1007/978-3-031-62843-6_37

2 Definition of Ransomware

Ransomware is a malware which denies a victim access to a computer, data, or browser with an offer to regain access to these user resources upon payment of a ransom to the attacker [8]. Thus, the victim is usually presented with a message on the affected device about the conditions for unlocking it (the amount of the ransom), but it is also possible for the attacker to impersonate a law enforcement agency in this message or, for example, display images of illegal child abuse (child pornography) and blackmail the victim with possible prosecution for possessing this objectionable material on their device.

The original ransomware creator is Joseph Popp. In 1989, he created the first ransomware program called "AIDS" (PC Cyborg), which was deployed as a Trojan horse and distributed via computer floppy disks. Once the victim inserted the floppy disk into the computer, the software encrypted the hard drive and demanded a ransom payment of $189 to a PO Box in Panama. Overall, however, the use of AIDS ransomware failed from the attacker's perspective due to timing for several reasons (sparse number of victims, encrypted assets value, insufficient level of cryptography) [13]. There are two basic variants of ransomware, and these are according to (Bhardwaj et al., 2016):

- *Ransomware - Crypto:* performs file and data locking by preserving the operating system functionality when it hits the end-users' system but performs a silent search for user data and files, which are subsequently encrypted and prevented from using them. It then demands a ransom from the user to make them available again. The file extensions that this malware searches for are FLV, PDF, RTF, MP3, MP4, PPT, CPP, ASM, CHM, TXT, DOC, XLS, JPG, CGI, KEY, MDB and PGP.
- *Ransomware - Locker:* denies a user access to a system that is locked by malware. A lockout message is displayed on the screen prompting the user to enter a ransom amount. After entering it, the malware prompts the user to pay this amount to restore access. Since the user's files and system is untouched, it is easy to remove this malware compared to the previous variant.

However, advances in computer and network security have subsequently led to the development of stronger encryption algorithms or increased computing power, thereby improving the attacker's capabilities. Virtual currencies existence and anonymous networks has provided cyber criminal's platform for their profitable operations and the lucrative business sector creation. Their quest for continuous improvement and learning from past mistakes creates constant challenges for security analysts [8].

2.1 Ransomware Spreading Methods

Attack campaigns use a variety of distribution ransomware. Spam emails are a common method in untargeted campaigns. In the case of a targeted campaign, attackers typically use phishing[1] [4]. In practice, we can also see a phishing and social engineering combination which is targeting on inattentive users, usually from the ranks of employees [9]. A spam message may contain a malicious link or attachment that directly triggers ransomware. Likewise, it may be an email attachment that appears to be a legitimate file.

---

[1] A toolkit used by cybercriminals to attack vulnerabilities in systems.

However, this file contains malicious code that executes when file is opened. Another distribution method are exploiting kits[2], where attackers exploit software vulnerabilities to download and install malware. For example, attackers can use this technique to modify a web server by redirecting traffic to infected advertisements or malicious links that contain ransomware. Other forms include password cracking, SMS messages or third-party app stores [3]. Apart from those already mentioned, a very popular entry point for ransomware is the unsecured remote access, the so-called RDP, which is pre-installed in the Windows operating system[3] [10]. According to Coveware report, smaller organizations are susceptible to unsecured RDP. Due to reduced IT budgets, they often do not have email filtering software and have less trained employees in cybersecurity issues. Larger organizations are in turn inundated with more spam emails but face more pressure to manage vulnerabilities. In 2021, these organizations often faced attacks through VPN vulnerabilities and poorly secured corporate firewalls [15].

2.2 The Attack Course

Ransomware typically communicates with the attacker's C2[4] control server at some point in the attack process, depending on the attack type. In Fig. 1 we can see a typical attack. Depending on the ransomware family, the C2 server will signal a successful infection to the system for registration. The ransomware will then start encrypting the target user data and display a request to the user for payment of the ransom. Certain families of ransomware, such as WannaCry, come with a built-in RSA public key (K_p), which is then used to encrypt a host-generated symmetric key (K_{Secret}). In this case, the ransomware generates the K_{Secret} symmetric key based on robust encryption such as AES from the CryptoAPI function of the infected host's operating system. The files of the affected system are encrypted using this K_{Secret} symmetric key. The second attack structure generates the RSA public subkey pair K_s & K_p before generating the symmetric K_{Secret} key pair. The asymmetric private key from the subkey pair is encrypted with the implanted public key, while the AES K_{Secret} encrypts the corresponding public key after it successfully encrypts the user's target files. At this point, a notification of the requested ransom is displayed on the victim's screen. The victim needs the symmetric AES K_{Secret} key to decrypt the files. However, this has been encrypted with the RSA K_s public subkey. What the public RSA subkey encrypted K_p can only be decrypted by the corresponding private RSA subkey K_s. Then this private RSA subkey K_s was encrypted with the implanted RSA public passkey. What is encrypted by the RSA passkey can only be decrypted by the corresponding RSA private passkey, which is initially stored by the attacker on C2. The victim is thus asked to pay a certain amount, usually in Bitcoins, to gain access to this key.

The new versions of the ransomware scan the entire network to which the affected guest is connected and look for other vulnerable nodes. This means that online backups will also be encrypted. In addition, vulnerable hosts on neighboring networks on both private and public IP addresses are also searched for [23]. Data recovery outside of offline

---

[2] A fraudulent technique used to obtain sensitive victim data by posing as a trusted authority.

[3] Remote Desktop Protocol.

[4] Command and Control.

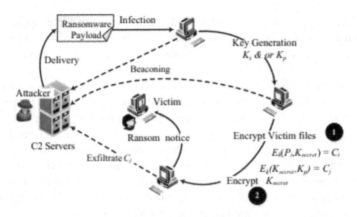

Fig. 1. Typical ransomware attack process. Source: (24 & Chishimba, 2019) [23].

backups is made impossible by removing shadow copies of volumes and overwriting the original files [24].

2.3 Payment Methods

Ransomware has been created to generate profit for its creators. Cyber criminals have therefore adopted many payment techniques over the years, with an emphasis on keeping them as anonymous as possible. From the use of SMS messages to premium rate numbers to various payment services such as Yandex Money (a Russian website similar to PayPal) or Western Union and PayPal. However, these services were not ideal for the ransomware creators as they were linked to bank accounts that could be traced and used to identify the perpetrators. Prepaid ransom services were a more suitable alternative as they used online payment systems and were not linked to a bank account. Cryptocurrencies, which allow users to exchange credits for goods and services, provided a perfectly suitable platform for criminals to pay ransoms [13].

Bitcoin has skyrocketed in popularity in this area, as it provides anonymity by sending and receiving addresses associated with pseudonyms rather than a traditional account [18]. Therefore, this cryptocurrency has become an integral part of the ransomware ecosystem in many campaigns that have required ransom payment specifically through Bitcoins. This allows criminals to obtain funds through instantaneous transfer as opposed to other forms of cybercrime such as selling stolen data with sensitive information or using this data for further attack [13]. Cybersecurity Ventures made an estimate that by 2021, more than 70% of all cryptocurrency transactions were from illicit activity, and by 2025, the global costs caused through cryptocurrencies will reach $30 billion [11].

3 Damages Caused by Ransomware

There are two types of ransomware costs according to [24]:

1. *Ransom* - ransom amounts range from a few hundred dollars to thousands of dollars,

2. *Loss of production and costs incurred for restoration* - these costs range from thousands to millions of dollars. These costs can also be incurred if a ransom is paid, for example, when the attacker fails to comply with the agreement and decrypts the data, or if the decryption of the data fails due to implementation errors or the eventual decryption inefficiency.

Other costs include damage to the name. According to a survey conducted by NinjaRMM in collaboration with Coveware [19] it was found that 51% of respondents expect to lose clients in the 48 h downtime due to a ransomware attack.

According to the UK company Sophos, as reported in its 2020 report, 73% of cyber criminals were successful in encrypting data, 24% of those affected were able to stop the encryption process and 3% of those affected were demanded to pay a ransom but the data was not encrypted. 94% of victims regained access to their data [21].

The following table (Table 1) shows Emsisoft's New Zealand data for 2020. The statistical data is based on available company data. The company itself states that more accurate data cannot be obtained due to the limitations of available datasets, limited information sharing between entities and the absence of security incident disclosure requirements. It is therefore an imprecise estimate of the true global cost of ransomware, which is derived from the amount of incidents submitted to the 'ID Ransomware' ransomware identification service by both private and public organizations and does not include data from private users. The second column represents the total number of logins to the service, the third the minimum range of costs caused by the ransomware and the last an estimate of the actual costs (Minimum Costs column multiplied by four). The main goal of this dataset was to alert law enforcement andlawmakers to the need to be more proactive in combating the biggest cyber threats [21].

Table 1. Total cost: ransom demand costs + downtime costs in 2020

Country	Total Submissions	Minimum Costs (USD)	Estimated Costs (USD)
United States	15,672	$4,893,699,209	$19,574,796,838
France	4,476	$1,387,058,087	$5,548,232,346
Spain	4,088	$1,272,238,829	$5,088,955,314
Italy	3,835	$1,198,933,932	$4,795,735,727
Germany	3,747	$1,159,985,450	$4,639,941,801
Canada	3,236	$1,011,008,551	$4,044,034,203
U.K	2,718	$838,750,742	$3,355,002,968
Australia	2,072	$648,093,574	$2,592,374,295
Austria	819	$256,822,720	$1,027,290,881
New Zealand	265	$82,569,552	$330,278,209

Source: (The cost of ransomware in 2021: A country-by-country analysis, 2021) [21]

Israeli software analytics company Cognyte conducted an extensive ransomware attacks analysis in 2020, based on data collected from the twenty-one attack groups websites that were focused on attacking organizations with this type of malware. Based on this data, it was found that 1,112 organizations from sixty-three countries in a total of eighteen industries were affected that year. In the following year, for comparison, in the first half of the year alone, there were 1,097 organizations affected from sixty-six countries originating from twenty-three ransomware groups. We can therefore undoubtedly observe a noticeable increase in attacks in this area, as well as an increase in the number of attack groups. The attacks detected included exfiltration and leakage of victim data, with 60% of these attacks coming from three main groups - Conti, Avaddon and Revil ("GLOBAL THREAT INTELLIGENCE REPORT", 2021).

The company's statistics has also shown that the most affected sectors of the economy were manufacturing, financial services, transport, and technology. The number of organizations affected by ransomware in each country in 2020 can be seen in Table 2. Again, the highest frequency of attacks was reported in the United States, followed by Canada, the United Kingdom and France [17].

Table 2. Most targeted countries by ransomware in 2020

Country	Victioms	Percentage
United States	615	56%
Canada	83	8%
United Kingdom	59	5%
France	57	5%
Germany	48	4%
Italy	31	3%
Australia	19	2%
Brazil	19	2%
Spain	16	1%
India	14	1%

Source: (RANSOMWARE ATTACK STATISTICS 2021 – GROWTH & ANALYSIS, 2021) [16]

US company Palo Alto Networks presents in 2021 report similar statistics for the countries most affected by ransomware, with a remarkably similar ranking. However, the total attacks numbers are increasing and within the United States alone the company records over 1,200 affected organizations in various sectors, and a similar trend applies to the other countries analyzed [1].

Table 3 shows a summary of the affected organizations including the sector with the attack date, the type of ransomware used, the attack vector, the ransom demanded including the estimated recovery cost from the attack. Although the attacks are older in date, of particular interest is the relationship between the ransom amount demanded and the estimated restoring cost for the organization's operations.

At first glance, it may seem that paying the ransom is economically more advantageous compared to the estimated restoration cost. However, according to findings by

Table 3. Financial losses due to recovery efforts and loss of production

Victim	Economic sector	Campaign	Infection vector	Ransom demand	Estimated recovery cost	Period
City of Atlanta	Government	SamSam	RDP	$50,000	$3 million	March 2018
Merck	Health	NotPetya	EC	$50,000	$310 million	June 2017
Colorado Transp. Dept	Government	SamSam	RDP	$51,000	$15 million	February 2018
Maersk	Transport	NotPetya	EC	$51,000	$300 million	June 2017
FedEx	Transport	NotPetya	EC	$51,000	$300 million	June 2017
Nuance Communications	Health, finance	NotPetya	EC	$50,000	$92 million	June 2017

Source: (Zimba & Chishimba, 2019) [23]

UK-based Sophos, paying the ransom doubles the total remediation cost compared to not paying or recovering data through backups. The average cost of remediation for 2020 was $1,448,458 if a ransom was paid, compared to $732,520 otherwise. The company argues that even if the affected organization pays the ransom, there will still be a cost to restore them [21]. This fact is reaffirmed by the company in its 2023 report, where the average restoration cost for 2022 is $1.82 million [22]. IBM, in its 2022 report, again cites an average ransomware attack cost of $4.54 million.

The average amount of the ransom demanded is following a steadily increasing trend. According to the data published in the 2021 US company Palo Alto Networks report, the average ransom increased by 44% compared to the previous year to USD 2.2 million [17].

So, the general advice is: "Don't pay the ransom". But if all else fails, some victims see paying the ransom as the most direct route to obtaining irreplaceable data [13]. Unfortunately, these individuals further motivate cybercriminals to continue their activities and provide them with the coveted financial resources to improve their technical sophistication.

4 Preventing Ransomware Attacks

Protecting against ransomware attacks requires more of a preventative approach. The thesis that "prevention is better than cure" applies here. Unlike other types of malwares, removing it from the affected system or network is not enough. The data still needs to be recovered once the encryption has been completed. Therefore, prevention and protection against this type of malware entering the internal network is more necessary than for other types of malicious code [23].

There are many steps that organizations can take to prevent ransomware, but their potential effectiveness varies both in general and, more importantly, in the context of the organization.

4.1 Employee Training

Raising ransomware awareness is an essential security measure. As it only takes the single employee mistake to affect an organization, they must be able and trained to identify a suspicious email, attachment, or link as a potential infection point for the organization [6]. Since training is not remarkably effective on employees at every potential step, efforts must also be made to increase security [7].

However, according to an IBM survey, only 38% of state and local government employees, for example, are trained to prevent ransomware, and only 29% of small businesses have experience with this type of malware [14].

4.2 Protective Systems and Policies

Since email spam is one of the most common ransomware distributing ways, the use of email filters can eliminate some unsolicited messages and reduce the risk of an inattentive employee clicking on a dangerous link or file [12]. Intrusion detection and prevention systems, anti-virus and anti-malware protection systems are another protection form. For remote access, it is advisable to implement policies regarding the devices acceptable for accessing the organization's network, called Bring-Your-Own-Device Restrictions. Unregulated use of unsecured devices poses an unnecessary risk to the organization's network. Other tools can include blocking suspicious websites, anomaly detection tools and many others [7].

Since ransomware attacks also use brute force attacks, it is necessary to implement the usual security measures and policies like strong passwords, multi-factor authentication or user permissions minimization, especially for accounts accessing the Internet [10].

4.3 Data Backup

Data backup is a preventive security solution for many critical situations and cyber-attacks. If an organization has regular and recoverable data backups, this data can be used to restore to the nearest backup point. As a result, the organization does not have to pay a ransom or communicate with the attacker in any way. Several tools are available. An organization can use a number of cloud-based solutions that allow data synchronization with a redundant copy in the cloud or even offer multiple older data versions [12]. However, these backups may not help in some cases of ransomware as new versions of ransomware can encrypt online backups as well. This risk can be eliminated by regular offline backups [7].

According to Sophos, 56% of ransomware hits in 2020 used backups to successfully recover data [21]. Without a backup system, the victim of an attack is completely reliant on the criminal to return (decrypt) the stolen data after paying the ransom [13].

4.4 Cyber Risk Insurance

According to AdvisorSmith, cyber risk insurance can help if an organization is affected by ransomware. This protection can help pay the ransom costs to recover encrypted data or systems. However, many companies that provide such insurance provide limited coverage for ransomware or cyber extortion attacks. The sub-limits of coverage for this risk are as high as $25,000, although the overall limit tends to be much higher. Depending on the provider, such insurance may cover such things as ransoms demanded by attackers, crisis management and investigation costs, hardware replacement, hiring negotiators, and other costs [5]. The cyber risk insurance use is expected to increase due to the growing number of large-scale cyber-attacks that force the organization's management to deal with the associated financial risks [11].

According to (Cimpan, 2020), cyber risk insurance claims in the first half of 2020 accounted for 41% of ransomware hits. This was based on data from Coalition, one of the largest cyber risk insurance providers in North America. In the second half of 2021, the company observed a 23% increase in reports of ransomware hits by its customers [2].

4.5 Measures in Terms of Time and Impact

There are a plethora of safeguards that an organization can implement. Their specific mix needs to be based on the specific organization in relation to their activities, priorities and, not least, budgetary possibilities. NinjaOne conducted a survey of Managed Security Service Providers (MSPs), internal IT professionals and consultants from North America, the UK, France, and Germany during 2020 [19] (Fig. 2).

Rating	1 least effective	2	3	4	5 most effective
Enforce MFA across the organization	2%	2%	19%	29%	48%
Invest in proper backup isolation configuration, and testing	0%	1%	5%	17%	76%
Deploy next-gen AV and/or endpoint detection and response (EDR) software	1%	4%	24%	38%	32%
Invest in system hardening, access controls, and network segmentation	1%	7%	21%	42%	30%
Invest in patch management	3%	7%	21%	35%	35%
Increase security training for all staff	3%	2%	14%	31%	50%
Enlist cybersecurity experts to secure the organization	7%	16%	32%	24%	21%

Fig. 2. What are the best immediate ways to protect organizations from ransomware? Source: (*The 2020 Ransomware Resiliency Report*, 2021) [19]

In a report produced by this company, it was found that from the perspective of the experts surveyed, in 76% of the responses, investing in proper isolation, configuration and testing of backups was the most effective of a list of protective measures, considering the speed of deployment of the measure. This option was followed by investing in employee security training and enforcing multi-factor authentication throughout the organization, with 50% and 48% of respondents respectively identifying these changes as the most effective. This was followed by investments in system hardening, the process of ensuring system security by eliminating potential risks, as well as access control and network segmentation (Fig. 3).

Rank (#1 = biggest impact)	1	2	3	4	5
Individual MSPs improving their security practices	55%	26%	8%	3%	8%
Individual MSPs outsourcing security functions to a MSSP / SOC service	6%	22%	44%	20%	6%
Vendors enforcing best practices and more restricitive controls	25%	36%	27%	9%	4%
Insurance providers increasing their requirements for (affordable) coverage	4%	10%	15%	56%	15%
Legislation that bans ransom payments	11%	6%	5%	13%	66%

Fig. 3. Which would have the most significant impact on reducing the threat of ransomware to MSPs and their clients? Source: (*The 2020 Ransomware Resiliency Report*, 2021) [19]

In terms of the impact on reducing the ransomware infection risk, 55% of respondents said that they perceived improving the Manager Service Providers (MSPs) security policies as potentially the most effective measure. They saw the best-practices enforcement by vendors with more restrictive controls or the security functions to a Managed Security Service Provider (MSSP) outsourcing or Security Operations Center (SOC) providing continuous resources monitoring for the eventual identification and early security incidents resolution that arise within the organization as another potentially effective approach.

Conversely, they identified the least effective measures as the potential legislative restriction creation that would prohibit organizations from paying ransoms or increasing the cyber risk insurance providers requirements to make cyber risk coverage more affordable.

5   Conclusion

The contemporary organizations dependence on data and all ICT resources providing a plethora of necessary functionalities is undeniable and inherently belongs to their essential existence means.

There is no doubt that an attack through ransomware fulfils the several offences facts described in most, if not all, criminal codes and can cause severe damage to any organization or individual. When affected by this malware type, data is rendered inaccessible and problems arise both in terms of reputation loss and customer confidence, for example, as well as in the potential threat to the organization's business continuity. This brings with it pressure to prevent and protect these assets from any damage or compromise by any cyber-attack.

Cyber criminals are always one step ahead in their efforts to exploit identified and undetected vulnerabilities in the ICT assets and systems they use to their advantage. The ransomware attacks area is becoming an attractive business for attackers with the potential for high profits. Since its inception, this cybercrime segment has been biding its time for decades due to the gradual powerful and robust encryption algorithms development with long encryption keys that are considered unbreakable by conventional computing capabilities and capacities. Cryptocurrencies are another and next important factor playing a useful role in this area. These provide criminals with the necessary anonymity to pass on ransoms by transferring the money equivalent through a number of existing cryptocurrencies, but most commonly Bitcoin. Cybersecurity Ventures predicts the global cybercrime cost conducted through cryptocurrencies to be nearly $30 billion by 2025 [11].

The paper provides an insight into the basic principle of ransomware, including the payment methods used by attackers. When attackers encrypt data and demand a ransom for its re-disclosure, the subject becomes their hostage facing the decision of whether to pay the ransom. In the case of paying the ransom, the victim must rely on an agreement with the attacker, which may not always be fulfilled. In the case of non-payment, it depends on the potential loss of data, or its relevance, or other individual factors. From the data, we can conclude that paying ransoms is unprofitable for the subjects, although at first glance the management of the organization may draw the opposite conclusion. Paying the required amount also represents an increase in future negative externalities for other potential victims in the form of better funded and more sophisticated attackers. Such a trend is evidenced by the data on the attacks number, other emerging groups engaged in these attacks, and the ever-increasing average ransom amount demanded.

This text also presents selected protective measures from the wide and varied possibilities range, including the relevant practical view of specialists working in this field. When choosing security measures, organizations make decisions based on their requirements, priorities, best-practices, and budgetary possibilities. However, insufficient budgetary options for cybersecurity can result in a threat to the organization both operationally and existentially.

References

1. 2022 Unit 42 Ransomware Threat Report: Understand trends and tactics to bolster defenses. Palo Alto Networks (2022). https://www.paloaltonetworks.com/content/dam/pan/en_US/assets/pdf/reports/2022-unit42-ransomware-threat-report-final.pdf. Accessed 14 May 2023
2. Cyber Claims Report: An in-depth analysis of cyber claims data from Coalition. Coalition Insurance Solutions (2022).https://info.coalitioninc.com/rs/566-KWJ-784/images/DLC-2022-03-Coalition-Claims-Report-2022.pdf. Accessed 16 May 2023
3. Herrera Silva, J., Barona López, L., Valdivieso Caraguay, Á., Hernández-Álvarez, M.: A survey on situational awareness of ransomware attacks—detection and prevention parameters. Remote Sens. 11(10), 1168 https://doi.org/10.3390/rs11101168 (2019)

4. Huber, M., Mulazzani, M., Weippl, E., Kitzler, G., Goluch, S.: Friend-in-the-middle attacks: exploiting social networking sites for spam. IEEE Internet Comput. **15**(3), 28–34 (2011). https://doi.org/10.1109/MIC.2011.24
5. Chen, P.: Ransomware Insurance. AdvisorSmith (2021).https://advisorsmith.com/business-insurance/cyber-liability-insurance/ransomware-insurance/. Accessed 14 May 2023
6. Chung, M.: Why employees matter in the fight against ransomware. Comput. Fraud Secur. **2019**(8), 8–11 (2019). https://doi.org/10.1016/S1361-3723(19)30084-3
7. Ingalls, S.: Ransomware protection: how to prevent ransomware attacks. eSecurity Planet: Internet Security for IT Professionals (2023). https://www.esecurityplanet.com/threats/ransomware-protection/. Accessed 14 May 2023
8. Kalaimannan, E., John, S., DuBose, T., Pinto, A.: Influences on ransomware's evolution and predictions for the future challenges. J. Cyber Secur. Technol. **1**(1), 23–31 (2016). https://doi.org/10.1080/23742917.2016.1252191
9. Krombholz, K., Hobel, H., Huber, M., Weippl, E.: Advanced social engineering attacks. J. Inf. Secur. Appl. **22**, 113–122 (2015). https://doi.org/10.1016/j.jisa.2014.09.005
10. Kurpjuhn, T.: The guide to ransomware: how businesses can manage the evolving threat. Comput. Fraud & Secur. **2019**(11), 14–16 (2019). https://doi.org/10.1016/S1361-3723(19)30117-4
11. Morgan, S.: Top 10 Cybersecurity Predictions And Statistics For 2023. Cybercrime Magazine (2022). https://cybersecurityventures.com/top-5-cybersecurity-facts-figures-predictions-and-statistics-for-2021-to-2025/. Accessed 14 May 2023
12. Nadir, I., Bakhshi, T.: Contemporary cybercrime. In: 2018 International Conference on Computing, Mathematics and Engineering Technologies (iCoMET), pp. 1–7 (2018).https://doi.org/10.1109/ICOMET.2018.8346329
13. O'Kane, P., Sezer, S., Carlin, D.: Evolution of ransomware. IET Netw. **7**(5), 321–327 (2018). https://doi.org/10.1049/iet-net.2017.0207
14. Public Sector Security Research: IBM-Harris Poll Survey 2020. IBM (2020).https://www.ibm.com/downloads/cas/74JKYWZQ. Accessed 14 May 2023
15. Q2 Ransom Payment Amounts Decline as Ransomware becomes a National Security Priority. Coveware: Ransomware Recovery First Responders (2021). https://www.coveware.com/blog/2021/7/23/q2-ransom-payment-amounts-decline-as-ransomware-becomes-a-national-security-priority. Accessed 22 Nov 2021
16. RANSOMWARE ATTACK STATISTICS 2021 – GROWTH & ANALYSIS. Cognyte | Actionable Intelligence for a Safer World (2021). https://www.cognyte.com/blog/ransomware_2021/. Accessed 22 Nov 2021
17. RANSOMWARE THREAT REPORT 2022. Palo Alto Networks (2022). https://www.paloaltonetworks.com/content/dam/pan/en_US/assets/pdf/reports/2022-unit42-ransomware-threat-report-final.pdf. Accessed 14 May 2023
18. Reid, F., Harrigan, M.: An analysis of anonymity in the bitcoin system. In: 2011 IEEE Third International Conference on Privacy, Security, Risk and Trust and 2011 IEEE Third International Conference on Social Computing, pp. 1318–1326 (2011). https://doi.org/10.1109/PASSAT/SocialCom.2011.79
19. The 2020 Ransomware Resiliency Report. NinjaOne (2021). https://www.ninjaone.com/blog/2020-ransomware-resiliency-report/. Accesssed 25 Nov 2021
20. The cost of ransomware in 2021: A country-by-country analysis. Emsisoft - Award-Winning Anti-Malware & Anti-Virus Software (2021).https://blog.emsisoft.com/en/38426/the-cost-of-ransomware-in-2021-a-country-by-country-analysis/. Accessed 22 Nov 2021
21. THE STATE OF RANSOMWARE 2020: Results of an independent study of 5,000 IT managers across 26 *countries*. *Sophos* | Fully Synchronized, Cloud-Native Data Security (2021). https://www.sophos.com/en-us/medialibrary/Gated-Assets/white-papers/sophos-the-state-of-ransomware-2020-wp.pdf. Accessed 25 Nov 2021

22. The State of Ransomware 2023. Sophos Group plc (2023). https://assets.sophos.com/X24 WTUEQ/at/c949g7693gsnjh9rb9gr8/sophos-state-of-ransomware-2023-wp.pdf.   Accessed 14 May 2023
23. Zimba, A., Chishimba, M.: On the economic impact of crypto-ransomware attacks: the state of the art on enterprise systems. Eur. J. Secur. Res. **4**(1), 3–31 (2019). https://doi.org/10.1007/s41125-019-00039-8
24. Zimba, A., Wang, Z., Simukonda, L.: Towards data resilience: the analytical case of crypto ransomware data recovery techniques. Int. J. Inf. Technol. Comput. Sci. **10**(1), 40–51 (2018). https://doi.org/10.5815/ijitcs.2018.01.05

Ransomware Attack on the QNAP Device: A Case Study

Jakub Bajera and Michał Glet[✉]

Faculty of Cybernetics, Military University of Technology, Warsaw, Poland
jakub.bajera@student.wat.edu.pl, michal.glet@wat.edu.pl

Abstract. In today's world, cloud services and NAS devices are gaining progressively more attention. Both private users and large organizations use NAS servers to create personal clouds. Because of this trend, cybercriminals are targeting many ransomware attacks on NAS devices. In many cases, successful attacks lead to permanent loss of valuable data. In this paper, we wanted to take a closer look at such kind of attack in order to establish the vulnerabilities used by cybercriminals in real-case scenarios. The topic of NAS devices being targeted by ransomware software is rarely touched upon, despite it becoming more and more of a problem nowadays. Analyzing a NAS device affected by ransomware could reveal a lot of valuable information. In this paper, we briefly describe the real attack on the QNAP device we have been working on. Carried-out studies allowed us to find a number of exemplary vulnerabilities present on the device in question. As a result, we were also able to provide some simple precautions that can allow users to avoid ransomware attacks in the future.

Keywords: QNAP · NAS · QLocker · ransomware · recovery

1 Introduction

The constant technological progress nowadays leads to more and more frequent use of cloud services – cloud disk storage in particular. Recent increases in the remote working field forced many companies to so-called cloud migration. Moving a company's digital assets into the cloud has many benefits. Extended access for the employees, lowered maintenance costs, easier scalability, less physical space needed and so forth. All this considered, we can be sure that cloud services will be increasingly more popular with time. However, the interest of cybercriminals and crime organizations in this field is growing as well. Ransomware is one of the most popular and dangerous cybersecurity threats these days. It's relatively easy to prepare, spread and use. The potential of high profit encourages crime organizations to develop new versions and types of ransomware programs. The ever-increasing cloud usage nowadays creates more opportunities for cybercriminals to use ransomware than ever before. In this paper, we will discuss the dangers of ransomware in this field by taking a closer look at some of the recent ransomware attacks targeted at NAS devices produced by QNAP. The main goal of this work is to thoroughly understand the nature of such attacks and to propose exemplary ways of counteracting them. Our results are based on the real attack on the QNAP device we have been working on.

K. S. Soliman (Ed.): IBIMA-AI 2023, CCIS 2101, pp. 402–406, 2024.
https://doi.org/10.1007/978-3-031-62843-6_38

2 NAS, QNAP and Ransomware

Network Attached Storage (NAS) [1] servers are, as the name suggests, devices used to store files and share them on a computer network. They resemble standalone computers and often have no keyboard or screen, as they are usually accessed through a web browser interface. Their primary task is to enable access to the stored data from various devices operating in the same local network. This solution allows for parallel access of many users and quick data exchange between different devices. NAS servers offer many more useful features, like creating additional backups and organizing our files. What's more, with proper configuration, those devices can be accessed remotely via the Internet. Recently, more and more often NAS servers are used to create "personal" cloud storage in both small private networks and large company networks. These devices are available at a variety of prices and complexities, matching the needs of all kinds of users.

QNAP (Quality Network Appliance Provider) [2] is one of the leading companies in the field of NAS devices. The company's products extended the basic functionality of NAS servers with several practical solutions. The greatest technological achievement of the organization is the constantly improved and updated operating system for NAS devices - QTS. It is used in most of the company's products and it offers access to numerous applications, an interactive user interface, several security features and all the basic functions for data management. Currently, QNAP is developing the Cloud NAS technology. It is a subscription-based service that gives access to a virtual cloud provided via the Internet. Yet again, we can see the growing popularity of cloud services.

Over the last few years, however, many vulnerabilities and oversights were found in the QNAP devices and software. Crime organizations that commit ransomware attacks usually start their work by scanning the network for visible and active devices. For this purpose, they use dedicated search engines and specific programs. The goal of attackers is to find devices without properly configured security or with outdated software. Some of the applications running on these devices have vulnerabilities that allow unauthorized access from the Internet. In the examined cases, these vulnerabilities were mostly related to the QTS operating system, QNAP firmware and optional applications for NAS devices. Cybercriminals were quick to use these oversights to launch their ransomware attacks against devices visible on the Internet. Let's take a look at some examples. In the year 2019, QNAP NAS devices were repeatedly targeted by Muhstik [3] ransomware. At that time, cybercriminals used a vulnerability present in the outdated phpMyAdmin application on NAS devices. In the year 2020, many users had their data encrypted by AgeLocker [4]. This time cybercriminals exploited an oversight in the Photo Station application, an optional program for storing and managing photos published by QNAP. Furthermore, vulnerabilities in the company's operating system, QTS, turned out to be another attack vector for criminals. Another ransomware targeting NAS devices, that appeared at a similar time, is eCh0irax. After some time, users started calling it "QNAPCrypt" because of how many QNAP devices were affected by it. The list goes on. Every day cybercriminals search the Internet for incorrectly configured devices, gain access to them and launch their ransomware programs to encrypt users' valuable data. A big part of the problem is users' disregard for the need to update the system and installed software.

During the years 2021 and 2022 ransomware attacks targeting QNAP devices were even more frequent and serious. The most notable and "successful" ransomware of this period are QLocker [5] and DeadBolt [6]. Both of these programs exploited similar weaknesses – outdated programs with critical vulnerabilities, like Photo Station and HBS (Hybrid Backup Sync), outdated QTS and other oversights. Crime organizations behind the attacks also claim to have found a few other zero-day vulnerabilities in QNAP software. Just like in previously described attacks, cybercriminals managed to gain unauthorized remote access to the devices and execute ransomware programs through the aforementioned weaknesses. Thousands of users lost access to their data. Many of them decided to pay the ransom, which further encouraged crime organizations to launch even more malware campaigns. It's worth noting that many of the described vulnerabilities were already patched at the time of the attacks. Despite that, lots of users simply haven't updated their devices regularly.

3   Case-Study

An important part of the carried-out research was a case study of a real ransomware attack that targeted a QNAP NAS server. The device in question was a TS-251 [7] NAS model and it was infected by QLocker ransomware in January 2022. Almost 400 GB of data has been encrypted. We had three main goals: to recover as much data as possible, to find out why the attack was successful and to find a way to minimize the possibility of future attacks.

3.1   Data Recovery

The analyzed QNAP device was attacked by the QLocker ransomware. During the attack, QLocker created new files with encrypted content and deleted the original ones. The encryption was done using the AES-256 [8] algorithm as a part of the 7z compression process [9]. Thanks to the first fact, we were able to scan the entire disk area and recover deleted data. Thanks to the second fact, we were able to match the content we found with files that were deleted by a QLocker – we recovered the names and hashes of the original files from the 7z files. Fortunately, most of the data on the attacked drives have not yet been overwritten and we were able to recover more than 95% of the encrypted data.

It is worth remembering that many other variants of ransomware directly modify files and affect various device functions, making it difficult to recover data without paying the ransom. Moreover, the process of recovering lost data can be lengthy and is not always successful - remember that prevention is better than cure. The case study gave us a better understanding of the ransomware infection process and helped us make important recommendations for protecting against ransomware attacks.

3.2   Reasons of the Attack's Success

After a thorough examination, many possible reasons for the attacker's success have been found. QTS operating system of the device in question was severely outdated. Based on the carried-out research, it has not been updated for almost six months. A similar issue with the antivirus was found – defensive software was just as outdated.

Furthermore, proper security configuration was lacking. The owner of the device did not configure any form of secure connection (for example, a VPN [10]). Many unused services were turned on by default, creating additional potential ways of interacting with the device. To make matters worse, the owner of the device did not perform regular backups.

3.3 Precautions

This and many of the aforementioned ransomware attacks could have been avoided by taking simple precautions.

First and foremost, we shouldn't set up remote access to our NAS devices at all if we don't plan to frequently use them remotely. If we decide to configure remote access, we should use a VPN (Virtual Private Network) connection, adding another layer of protection.

Furthermore, NAS devices should be systematically updated. The best way to keep our software up to date is to set up automatic updates. Installing a dedicated antivirus or scanner is also recommended. Regular automatic scans can help us detect new vulnerabilities or malware that already infected the device.

Another important part of the configuration – NAS devices offer many services, turned on by default, that we don't personally use at all. It is suggested to disable such unused services, making it harder for cybercriminals to detect and attack our NAS server.

Last but not least, we should remember about backing up our data regularly. This task can be easily automated and it provides us with a chance to get our data back even in case of a successful attack.

4 Conclusions

Based on the results of this research, it was possible to understand the behaviour of NAS ransomware software and learn about the most commonly used vulnerabilities. Furthermore, we were able to define exemplary security recommendations and good practices in the field of counteracting ransomware attacks dedicated to NAS devices. We learned that staying vigilant and cautious is very important these days. Many cyberattacks are successful due to the general lack of attention. We can't personally predict vulnerabilities within software or firmware, but the proper configuration of remote access and some other precautions go a long way. Many users neglect the basic rules of maintaining network security while performing just a few routine tasks can significantly reduce the chance of success of cyberattacks. Regular updates of installed software and creating systematic backups can significantly reduce the risk of success of a potential attack. Let us remember that just a few routine actions can protect our data from ransomware attacks.

References

1. https://en.wikipedia.org/wiki/Network-attached_storage. Accessed 04 2023
2. https://en.wikipedia.org/wiki/QNAP_Systems. Accessed 04 2023
3. https://www.qnap.com/en/security-advisory/nas-201910-02. Accessed 04 2023
4. https://www.bleepingcomputer.com/news/security/agelocker-ransomware-targets-qnap-nas-devices-steals-data/. Accessed 04 2023
5. https://www.bleepingcomputer.com/news/security/massive-qlocker-ransomware-attack-uses-7zip-to-encrypt-qnap-devices/. Accessed 04 2023
6. https://www.trendmicro.com/en_us/research/22/f/closing-the-door-deadbolt-ransomware-locks-out-vendors-with-mult.html. Accessed 04 2023
7. https://www.qnap.com/en-us/product/ts-251. Accessed 04 2023
8. https://en.wikipedia.org/wiki/Advanced_Encryption_Standard. Accessed 05 2023
9. https://en.wikipedia.org/wiki/7-Zip. Accessed 05 2023
10. https://en.wikipedia.org/wiki/Virtual_private_network. Accessed 05 2023

Author Index

A

Alaya, Bechir 107
Alghieth, Manal 135
Amuzang, Gilly Njoh 3, 30
Arman, Nabil 20
Augustyniak, Piotr 195, 224
Awad, Eman 20

B

Bajera, Jakub 402
Bedon, Arturo 379
Bier, Agnieszka 62
Bistroń, Marta 58
Blaszczuk, Karolina 86
Borkovcova, Monika 308
Bugajewska, Monika 318
Bugajewski, Dawid 78, 318

C

Cegielska, Katarzyna 43
Czuba, Przemysław 71

D

Delcea, Camelia 356
Dłużniewski, Artur 119
Dragoi, Paul A. 356
Dziegielewska, Olga 338

F

Fetahu, Paolo 159
Firth, Ryan 173

G

Gabrielczyk, Emilia 86
Gałązka, Marek 267
Glet, Michał 333, 349, 402
Gorny, Piotr 368

H

Hajlaoui, Rejab 107
Hernik, Jozef 43

I

Iancu, Livia D. 356
Itoe, Micheal Blake Somaah 3, 30

J

Jekateryńczuk, Gabriel 131
John, Łukasz 119

K

Kachel, Leszek 119
Kaczmarek, Paweł 296
Kaczyński, Kamil 333, 349
Kalinowski, Paweł 210
Karpiel, Grzegorz 250
Khamayseh, Faisal 20
Kiedrowicz, Maciej 368
Krawiec, Jerzy 368
Krol, Karol 43
Kukulska-Koziel, Anita 43

L

Linke, Hans Joachim 43

M

Mah, Pascal Muam 3, 30
Mahfoudhi, Sami 107
Majerik, Filip 308
Manka, Michał 250
Michalski, Marek 143, 151, 187

P

Pełech-Pilichowski, Tomasz 3
Piotrowski, Zbigniew 52, 58, 86, 131, 296
Prusak, Daniel 250
Pujol, Francisco A. 379

K. S. Soliman (Ed.): IBIMA-AI 2023, CCIS 2101, pp. 407–408, 2024.
https://doi.org/10.1007/978-3-031-62843-6

R
Ramirez, Tamai 379
Rogowicz, Olgierd 224

S
Salata, Tomasz 43
Sellami, Lamaa 107
Skalna, Iwona 3
Skóra, Jakub 195
Skrzypecki, Stanisław 237
Srivastava, Mukesh 159, 173
Sroczynski, Zdzislaw 62
Szafranski, Boleslaw 338
Szajewska, Anna 210
Szajewski, Krzysztof 210
Szczepaniak, Paweł 210
Szymański, Jerzy 267

T
Tah, Ning Frida 3, 30

V
Vaclavik, Lukas 389

W
Walczyna, Tomasz 52
Węgrzyn, Kamil 93
Worwa, Kazimierz 280

Z
Zielski, Paweł 333, 349
Zwierzykowski, Piotr 195, 224

Printed in the United States
by Baker & Taylor Publisher Services